2008

The Original

Pets Welcome!

**Including our Guide to Pet Friendly Pubs
and Holidays with Horses**

5

FHG
·P·E·R·A·R·D·

Taking your pet to France – all you need to know

Contents

© FHG Guides Ltd, 2007
ISBN 978-1-85055-406-6

Maps: ©MAPS IN MINUTES™ / Collins Bartholmew 2007

Typeset by FHG Guides Ltd, Paisley.
Printed and bound in Singapore by Imago.

Distribution. Book Trade: ORCA Book Services, Stanley House,
3 Fleets Lane, Poole, Dorset BH15 3AJ
(Tel: 01202 665432; Fax: 01202 666219)
e-mail: mail@orcabookservices.co.uk
Published by FHG Guides Ltd., Abbey Mill Business Centre,
Seedhill, Paisley PA1 ITJ (Tel: 0141-887 0428 Fax: 0141-889 7204).
e-mail: admin@fhguides.co.uk

Pets Welcome! is published by FHG Guides Ltd,
part of Kuperard Group.

Cover design: FHG Guides
Cover Pictures: With thanks to
WINALOT, for picture of *Holly*
and Mrs Dawson of Welshpool, for picture of *Saskia's* pups.

All the advertisers in **PETS WELCOME!** have an entry in the appropriate classified section and each classified entry may carry one or more of the following symbols:

🐕   This symbol indicates that pets are welcome free of charge.

£   The £ indicates that a charge is made for pets. We quote the amount where possible, either per night or per week.

pw!   This symbol shows that the establishment has some special provision for pets; perhaps an exercise facility or some special feeding or accommodation arrangements.

⌂   Indicates separate pets' accommodation.

PLEASE NOTE that all the advertisers in **PETS WELCOME!** extend a welcome to pets and their owners but they may attach conditions. The interests of other guests have to be considered and it is usually assumed that pets will be well trained, obedient and under the control of their owner.

Foreword

Everyone included, even the dog!

Over the years, the demand for holiday accommodation where pets are allowed has increased, and more and more proprietors are coming to realise that people just won't go off on holiday and leave their pets behind. This edition of **Pets Welcome!** contains a wide variety of accommodation where pets are warmly welcomed. With the choice ranging from hotels and B&Bs to self-catering and caravans, there is sure to be something to suit everyone. All our advertisers go out of their way to ensure that the whole family enjoy their holiday and some even make special provision for pets.

Owners should always act responsibly when on holiday with their pets by discouraging them from jumping up on furniture or people. Remember also that dogs should never be left unattended in a strange environment as they can easily become depressed and unhappy, and more likely to get into mischief.

Most of our entries are of long standing and are tried and tested favourites with animal lovers. However as publishers we do not inspect the accommodation advertised in Pets Welcome! and an entry does not imply our recommendation. Some proprietors offer fuller facilities for pets than others, and in the classified entry which we give each advertiser we try to indicate by symbols whether or not there are any special facilities and if additional charges are involved. However, we suggest that you raise any queries or particular requirements when you make enquiries and bookings.

If you have any problems or complaints, please raise them on the spot with the owner or his representative in the first place. We will follow up complaints if necessary, but we regret that we cannot act as intermediaries nor can we accept responsibility for details of accommodation and/or services described here. Happily, serious complaints are few. Finally, if you have to cancel or postpone a holiday booking, please give as much notice as possible. This courtesy will be appreciated and it could save later difficulties.

Boarding your Pet (Page 12), Preparing your Dogs and Cats for Travel Abroad (Page 14), Readers' Offer Vouchers (Page 371), Holidays with Horses (Page 355), and The Guide to Pet Friendly Pubs (Page 360) are now regular features, and on page 42 you will find some useful information on keeping your pet happy in warm weather. Our latest selection of Pets Pictures starts on page 45.

Those who like to venture further afield will find a selection of holiday properties in France – see pages 19-37, and we have included some practical advice about the Pets Travel Scheme to ensure that you are fully prepared.

We would be happy to receive readers' suggestions on any other useful features. Please also let us know if you have had any unusual or humorous experiences with your pet on holiday. This always makes interesting reading! And we hope that you will mention **Pets Welcome!** when you make your holiday inquiries or bookings.

Anne Cuthbertson, **Editor**

Before you go anywhere take a trip to Pets at Home

With a comprehensive range of quality food, treats, toys and bedding, we have everything a pet could ask for every day of the year. And when it's holiday time, there's even a fantastic choice of accessories for pets on the move, including pet carriers, portable travel bowls, toothbrushes, travel blankets and more.

Plus, if it's travel tips you're looking for, we can offer all the expert advice you need to ensure a smooth journey.

Wherever you're heading, head for Pets at Home first!

Visit the FHG website

www.holidayguides.com

for details of the wide choice of accommodation

featured in the full range of FHG titles

The finest lochside Location in the Southern Highlands.

HOTELS

BEST LOVED

INVESTOR IN PEOPLE

The Four Seasons Hotel
St Fillans, Perthshire PH6 2NF
Tel: 01764 685 333   e-mail: sham@thefourseasonshotel.co.uk

See Advertisement under Perthshire, St. Fillans

PET PRODUCTS

Give them an easy ride

For safe, comfortable travel for your four-legged friends, it's RAC to the rescue.

Car Seat Cover

Hard-wearing, machine washable covers simply slip over your seats – with a zipper section so you can still get to the seatbelts.

Travel food & water box

This handy feeding case opens out to form two full size bowls, and contains a water bottle too.

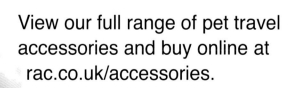

Dog Travel Harness

With adjustable collar and straps, this harness attaches to any car seatbelt. Available in five sizes, see below for details.

View our full range of pet travel accessories and buy online at rac.co.uk/accessories.

The Dog Travel Harness is available in Small 30-41cm (12-16"), Medium 41-58cm (16-23"), Large 51-76cm (20-30"), Extra Large 56-89cm (22-35") and Jumbo 66-107cm (26-42").

Provided by RAC Motoring Services, (Registered No. 01424399) Head Office: 8 Surrey Street, Norwich NR1 3NG.

Boarding Your Pet

by Kenn Oultram
Blue Grass Animal Hotel

THE remarkable growth of travel and tourism has provided satellite industries like Animal Boarding Establishments (ABE) with year-round financial benefits, though ABE owners will reveal they were never entirely dependent on the holiday-maker. For this is very much a service industry in its own right; greatly appreciated by, for example, pet owners who may be moving house...entering hospital...taking a work assignment abroad...having the builders in...throwing a fireworks party...coping with a bitch in season or, perhaps, a cat recuperating from surgery. As looking after pets is an awesome responsibility and a job for the professional, is it reasonable to expect a neighbour or pet-sitter to take this on?

Staff at an ABE must be alert for blood, constipation, diarrhoea, lethargy, coughing, fleas, incontinence, sneezing, worms and vomit! It is taken for granted that an ABE will accept the allergic, the arthritic, the diabetic, the epileptic, the hyper-active and the neurotic...and administer pills, drops and injections. Most of all they will be expected to guarantee the safe-keeping of your pet during your absence. Postmen may claim they face the risk of dog bites, but try opening the kennel door of an outsize hound with a 30 inch neck and two cute rows of flashing stained teeth.

Early advance booking at an ABE for your pet's boarding card is now essential as the equation of 5,000 kennels/catteries to cope with a potential 11 million UK dogs and cats simply doesn't balance and, at peak times, you'll discover there's no room at the inn.

All ABEs are inspected annually by an officer from the Environmental Health Department of the Local Authority which issues a licence to operate. It is illegal to run an ABE without a licence and this must be displayed for all to see (usually in the reception area).

Some general guidelines:

- A brochure indicates a professional approach. Ring round requesting these.

- Do NOT book if the ABE will not permit you to inspect the facilities. On arrival ask to see the exercise area for dogs (leaving dogs to their own devices all day in outside runs is NOT exercise). In catteries check that sneeze barriers are installed.

- If vaccinations are not necessary do NOT book; especially if dogs are not required to be vaccinated against kennel cough.

- Ask if the ABE's insurance covers your pet's stay; otherwise a nasty vet's bill could be awaiting your return.

- Many pet owners have more than one dog or cat. Look for family-sized units and check heating facilities (after all, our winters are twice the duration of our summers...and the ABE staff need to be kept warm too!)

- Check that your pet will not come into contact with another client's pet.

- On arrival – your ears, eyes and nose will tell all! You are looking for cleanliness, contented boarders and an experienced, caring staff. If apprehensive ask if you may send someone to visit your pet during its stay. You could also try your pet for a day (or a night) prior to the planned lengthy stay.

- If your pet is taken ill, ensure that the ABE is advised whether to call its own veterinarian or your own. Leave a contact number.

- If the ABE does not stock your pet's favourite food, offer to supply this, though there may not be any discount off your bill by doing so.

- Ask if a grooming service is offered. Some ABEs do. Others provide a collection and delivery service.

  Finally, the time has surely come for an exhaustive, independent survey of British kennels and catteries with a one-to-four star ratings assessment.
  Perhaps one of the major motoring organisations should attempt this....
  after all, 99% of ABE clients arrive on four wheels.

For free advice and addresses call the Animal Boarding Advisory Bureau on 01606 891303 or the Feline Advisory Bureau on 0870 742 2278 during office hours. You may even wish to recommend your own Animal Boarding Establishment.

Preparing your Dogs and Cats for travel abroad

How can my pet travel? Because of stringent requirements, dogs and cats travelling under the so-called pet passport scheme cannot make last minute reservations; in general, six-month advance planning is required. Veterinarians must implant a microchip in the animal, inoculate it against rabies, have a laboratory recognized by the Department for Environment, Food and Rural Affairs (DEFRA) confirm by blood sample that the vaccine is active, and issue a PETS certificate. Certificates are valid from six months after obtaining the blood sample results until the date of the animal's next rabies booster shot. (Dogs and cats resident in Britain whose blood sample was drawn before Feb 29, 2000 are exempt from this six month rule). Dogs and cats must also be treated against ticks and tapeworms no less than 24 nor more than 48 hours before check-in (when the animal enters carrier's custody). Animals travelling by air are placed in containers bearing an official seal (the number of which is also inscribed on the PETS certificate) to ensure animals are not exposed to disease en route. Sealing requirements do not apply to Cyprus or Malta. Owners must also sign a certificate attesting that the animal has not been outside participating territories in the last six months. Travellers are cautioned that Britain will enforce its rules rigorously.

Your pet must be injected with a harmless identification ISO (International Standards Organisation) approved microchip. This chip will be read by a handheld scanning device.

From and back to the UK

Ask your vet to implant an ISO (International Standards Organisation) approved microchip - then to vaccinate against rabies recording the batch number of the vaccine on a veterinary certificate together with the microchip number.

Approximately 30 days later your vet should take a blood sample and send it to one of the DEFRA approved laboratories to check that the vaccine has provided the correct level of protection.

Your vet will then issue you with a certificate confirming all the above – in the UK this is called The Pet Travel Scheme Re-Entry Certificate. It is valid for the life of the rabies vaccine, so keep your rabies vaccine up to date and a new certificate will be issued without the need for further blood tests.

Six months from the taking of a successful blood test you will be able to enter or re-enter the UK from Western Europe and 28 other countries including Australia, Japan and Singapore.

Pets must be treated for ticks and for the echinococcus parasite by a qualified vet who will record this on an official UK certificate not less than 24 hours and not more than 48 hours before entry into the UK. We are trying to secure changes in this very awkward timetable, which is being rigidly enforced.

On entering the UK you must therefore have two official certificates; one for the microchip, rabies vaccine and blood test; the second for treatment against ticks and parasites. You will also have to sign a residence declaration form - provided by the travel operator who is carrying out the checking. It simply confirms that the pet has not been outside the approved countries in the previous six months.

From Europe to the UK

As above, you must microchip your pet, vaccinate against rabies and approximately 30 days later your vet will take a blood test sending it to one of the laboratories from the list of those approved by MAFF. SIX MONTHS after a successful blood test your pet will be allowed to travel to the UK providing it has been treated against ticks and worms.

Costs:

- Microchip: Should be in the region of £25.00
- Vaccine: Varies according to vet but again approximately £30.00
- Blood test: We know that the blood testing laboratory at Weybridge (VLA)
                  charge £49.50 per test.

Therefore anything in addition is that levied by the vet. Providing the rabies vaccination is kept up to date the blood test will not have to be repeated. Should there be a break between rabies vaccines a further blood test would have to be taken and then a period of 6 months allowed before re-entry to the UK would be permitted.

Therefore: Microchip and blood-test are one-off costs but the rabies vaccination is
                  a yearly or 3 yearly cost depending on the vaccine used.

More information can be obtained from

Department of Environment, Food and Rural Affairs PETS
website: www.defra.gov.uk/animalh/quarantine/index.htm

Scottish Executive Environment and Rural Affairs Department
website: www.scotland.gov.uk/AHWP

PETS Helpline:
0870 241 1710 (Monday to Friday – 08.30 to 17.00 UK time)
E-mail:

pets.helpline@defra.gsi.gov.uk (enclose your postal address and daytime telephone number)

Current ports of entry are Dover (from Calais by ferry), Portsmouth (from Caen, Cherbourg, Le Havre or St Malo by ferry) and Folkestone (from Calais or Cheriton by Eurotunnel). London Heathrow is the authorised port-of-entry for : British Midland Airlines from Amsterdam-Schiphol, Brussels, Madrid, Palma Majorca, and Paris (Paris for guide dogs only); Finnair from Helsinki; and Lufthansa from Frankfurt.

The laboratories approved by MAFF for blood testing:

Veterinary Laboratory Agency
New Haw, Addlestone
Surrey KT15 3NB
UNITED KINGDOM

Tel: (+44) 01932 357 840
Fax:(+44) 01 932 357 239

Costs: £49.50

BioBest
Pentlands Science Park
Bush Loan
Penicuik
Midlothian EH26 0PZ
SCOTLAND

Tel: (+44) 0131 445 6101
Fax: (+44) 0131 445 6102

Costs: £32.50

Agence Francaise De Securite
Sanitaire des Aliments
Nancy
Domaine de Pixerecourt
BP9 F-54220 Maizeville
FRANCE

Tel: (+33) 3 83 298950
Fax:(+33) 3 83 298959

Costs: 425ff = approx £42

National Veterinary Institute
Commission of Diagnosites
Section of Diagnostic
Department of Virology
S -75189 Uppsala
SWEDEN

Tel: (+46) 1867 4000
Fax:(+46) 1867 4467

Costs: 500K=approx £40

Danish Veterinary Institute for
Virus Research
Lindholm
DK-4771 Kalvehave
DENMARK

Tel: (+45) 72 34 60 00
Fax:(+45) 72 34 79 01

Costs: 252K=approx £25

National Veterinary and Food
Research Institute
Mustialankatu 3
FI - 00790 Helsinki
FINLAND

Tel: (+35) 20 77 24 576
Fax:(+35) 20 77 24 363

Costs: 396.50 Fmark = approx £26.00

Institut fur Virologie
Frankfurter Strasse 107
D35392 Giessen

Tel: (+49) 641 99 38350
Fax: (+49) 641 99 38359

GERMANY	Costs: 72.60DM= approx £25
Dept. for Equine, Pets and	Tel: (+43) 2236 46 640 909
Vaccine Control Virology Unit	Fax:(+43) 2236 46 640 941
Federal Institute for the Control	
of Viral Infection in Animals	
Robert-Koch-Gasse 17	
A-2340 Modling	
AUSTRIA	Costs: 600 schillings= approx £30
Instituto Zooproftilattico	Tel: (+39) 4980 84 259
Sperimentale delle Venezie	Fax:(+39) 4988 30 530
Via Romea 14/A	
1-35020 Legnaro	
ITALY	Costs: price unknown
Laboratorio central	Tel: (+34) 958 44 03 75
de veterinaria de Santa Fe	Fax:(+34) 958 44 12 00
Camino del Jau s/n	
E-18320 Santa Fe (Granada)	
SPAIN	Costs: price unknown
Institute Pasteur of Brussels	Tel: (+32) 2 373 32 56
642, Rue-Engeland-Straat	Fax:(+32) 2 373 33 86
B 1180 Brussels	
BELGIUM	Costs: 1,500BF- approx £25
Institute of Veterinary Virology	Tel: (+41) 31 631 2378
Schweizerische Tollwutzentrale	Fax:(+41) 31 631 2534
Langgass-Strasse 122	
CH-3012 Bern	
SWITZERLAND	Costs: 96.75 SF= approx £40

What we musn't forget?

✔ *Medicine, if needed* ✔ *Toys* ✔ *Health certificates* ✔ *Food and drink dishes*

✔ *The dog's basket or blanket – it is extremely important that your dog has something to make him feel at home* ✔ *A thermometer* ✔ *A bell to hang around the dog's collar*

✔ *A can opener if you have canned food*

✔ *A deodorant for the hotel room* ✔ *Paper towels* ✔ *Brushes to brush your dog*

✔ *A towel to dry the dog in case of rain or when you get back to the hotel room*

Who benefits from your Will – the taxman, or the ones you love?

This year over £2 <u>billion</u> from Wills went to pay inheritance tax in the UK. Those Wills could easily have been made more tax efficient by leaving something to a charity such as the RSPCA.

Nobody does more for animals than the RSPCA and its branches.

And for every £10 we need to spend, £6 comes from people's Wills.

Our simple guide in plain English could help <u>your</u> Will be more tax efficient.

For a free copy, simply phone the number below, (quoting reference 06NL030054).

0870 754 0239
or e-mail jcurtis@rspca.org.uk

Registered charity no: 219099

Holidays in France

For you and your pets

Since the advent of the pet's passport scheme more and more owners are opting to take their 'best friend' on holiday to other countries.

With that in mind, we have included in this edition of **Pets Welcome!** a small selection of holiday properties in France.

You will find details of each property, plus some very useful practical information and a brief description of the regions.

Enjoy your stay!

AQUITAINE

This region of wide open spaces includes Europe's largest forest and offers a long list of outdoor activities. There are many quality golf courses which makes this France's leading region for golfers. For those interested in the past, there are a number of prehistoric sites and a fascinating variety of artefacts. Visitors should make a point of seeing the many cave paintings and engravings found in the Dordogne Valley. Enjoy the bustling towns, peaceful countryside and villages, and sample the fine wines of Bordeaux and the gastronomic specialties of the region, which include Foie Gras and truffles.

Le Manoir de St Marcel, Dordogne

PETS WELCOME

5 high quality, attractively restored and well equipped properties.
Sleep 2 to 12 (people).
Resident owners: committed to ensure that you have a wonderful stay.
Even if you are not bringing your dog or horse: Still come!
You will appreciate a warm welcome from fellow animal lovers.
Our vet speaks English and can help with formalities.
Telephone (from Britain) 020 7617 7115 • in France +33(0)5 53 61 06 17
www.LeManoir.org   **e-mail: reservations@LeManoir.org**

St Marcel du Perigord (Dordogne)

St Marcel is situated off the D32, 12 miles from Bergerac and 6 miles from St Alvere. There is a good restaurant and bar in the village. The nearest large town is Lalinde, 7 miles, which has one of the prettiest markets in the area. Market day is Thursday.

LE MANOIR DE ST MARCEL. 5 high quality, attractively restored and well equipped properties, sleep 2-12. Resident owners. You will appreciate a warm welcome from fellow animal lovers. Our vet speaks English and can help with formalities. Tel: 020 7617 7115 (UK), +33(0)5 53 61 06 17 (France).[🐾]
e-mail: reservations@LeManoir.org   website: www.LeManoir.org

Visit the FHG website
www.holidayguides.com
for details of the wide choice of accommodation
featured in the full range of FHG titles

Three period cottages with fenced pool in South Dordogne, set in 65 acre private estate with fishing lake.

- **Kiwi** sleeps 2/3. One double bedroom. Separate shower room.
- **Wren** sleeps 4/6 Two double bedrooms. Separate shower room.
- **Honeysuckle** sleeps 6. Two separate shower rooms.

Great countryside for walking. 10 minutes to the nearest shops/restaurants and convenient for Sarlat and Bergerac.

Local English-speaking vet to assist with formalities for pets' return to UK.

Please visit our website for details/photos - www.lessarrazinies.com - or telephone Mike/Lindy Crowcroft on 0033 (0) 553 03 23 20 (summer) • 020 8340 2027 (winter) e-mail: mikecrowcroft@onetel.com

Le Bugue (Dordogne)

The pretty town of Le Bugue provides an excellent range of shops, including supermarkets, banks, chemists, post office and English-speaking doctor. There is a colourful and busy market every Tuesday, offering a wide selection of local produce, poultry, meats, pates and cheeses. Further afield you can visit prehistoric caves, some with world-famous cave drawings.

SOUTH DORDOGNE. Three period cottages with fenced pool on 65-acre estate with fishing lake. Sleep 2/6. Great countryside for walking. Local English-speaking vet. Contact Mike/Lindy Crowcroft 0033 (0) 553 03 23 20 (summer); 020 8340 2027 (winter). [🐴]
e-mail: mikecrowcroft@onetel.com   website: www.lessarrazinies.com

Family outings in Dordogne

Bergerac Aquapark – four swimming pools with water chutes and other activities.

Prehisto Parc, Les Eyzies – cavemen, mammoths and everything prehistoric.

Jacqou Park, Le Bugue – three parks on one site, an animal park, and aqua park and an amusement park.

Le village du Bournat, Le Bugue – a reconstructed village showing life in 1900. With animals on a working organic farm, crafts, and a working windmill.

Airparc Perigord, St-Vincent-de-Cosse – a treetop adventure park on the river, one of the most exciting parks for children.

Please note

All the information in this book is given in good faith in the belief that it is correct.
However, the publishers cannot guarantee the facts given in these pages, neither are they responsible for changes in policy, ownership or terms that may take place after the date of going to press. Readers should always satisfy themselves that the facilities they require are available and that the terms, if quoted, still apply.

AUVERGNE

Lying in the heart of France only an hour from Lyon or three hours from Paris the Auvergne region has a volcanic terrain with a natural beauty and dramatic landscapes. The area is ideal for sporting activities, including skiing, golfing, hiking and hang-gliding, and for the watersports enthusiast, there are excellent opportunities for canoeing, fishing, swimming and sailing.

Gîtes du Château de Coisse ❖ Auvergne

Situated in a small hamlet in the heart of the Livradois Forez Regional Park, get away from the stress and grind of daily life in this tranquil, beautiful part of France.
★★ **2 person gîte** is on the ground floor of this recently converted 18th century barn.
★★★ **6 person gîte** forms the first and second floors and has its own south-facing terrace.
Both have been carefully restored to keep many original features but are also modern, fully equipped and child/pet friendly.

Fiona & Graham Sheldon, Gîtes du Château de Coisse, 63220 Arlanc, France • Tel: 04 73 95 00 45
e-mail: fiandgra@chateaudecoisse.com • www.chateaudecoisse.com

Coisse (Puy-de-Dôme)

Tiny village in the rolling hills of Monts du Livradois, an area of outstanding natural beauty. Town of Arlanc, 2km away, has all amenities.

FIONA & GRAHAM SHELDON, GITES DU CHATEAU DE COISSE, 63220 ARLANC (04 73 95 00 45) Two restored gîtes in this tranquil, beautiful part of France. 2 star/2 person gîte on ground floor of 18th century barn. 3 star/ 6 person gîte on first and second floors with its own south-facing terrace. Child/pet friendly.[🐕]
e-mail: fiandgra@chateaudecoisse.com   website: www.chateaudecoisse.com

Things to do and see in Puy-de-Dome

Parc Naturel Régional du Livradois-Forez - an area of outstanding beauty with a volcanic region to the north west and many mountains. A rambler's paradise.

Rock climbing and paragliding at Job – for the more adventurous.

The Plan D'Eau near Arlanc – for those who love being beside the water. There is also an open air swimming pool, and tennis courts. Nearby is the Jardin pour la Terre, which is a large map of the world planted with trees and flowers from their native countries.

Chantagrele, Auvergne

Two beautifully restored stone Gites, in a stunning location within the Livradois Forez National Park, with undisturbed valley views.

Light and spacious, these pretty stone cottages are bright, clean and comfortable, and tastefully decorated, with exposed beams , stone walls and wooden floors. Fully equipped, with three bedrooms, sleeping 4/5; log burners; central heating.

Secluded spacious garden with plunge pool, summer house and BBQ area.

Sauxillanges, 6km away, has all amenities, including convenience shopping and quality restaurants.

Mountain biking, walking, horse riding and fishing are all popular in the area, and skiing is available a short drive away. Open all year.

Contact:

Richard and Elaine Clements
Chantagrele
63490 Condat les Montboissier
Auvergne, France
Tel: 0033 (0) 4 73 72 18 95
e-mail: elaine-clements@hotmail.co.uk

Sauxillanges (Puy-de-Dôme)

Small village with all amenities, including convenience shopping, 2 highly acclaimed restaurants, 4 bars and a weekly market. Ambert and Issoire, two historic towns, and Clermont Ferrand are within easy reach.

RICHARD & ELAINE CLEMENTS, CHANTAGRELE 63490, CONDAT LES MONTBOISSIER, AUVERGNE (0033 (0) 4 73 72 18 95). Two beautifully restored stone Gites, in a stunning location within the Livardois Forez National Park, with undisturbed valley views. Light and spacious. Fully equipped. 3 bedrooms, sleep 4/5. Plunge pool, summer house and BBQ area. Mountain biking, walking, horse riding and fishing in the area, and skiing a short drive away. Open all year. [🐴]
e-mail: elaine-clements@hotmail.co.uk

Visit the FHG website
www.holidayguides.com
for details of the wide choice of accommodation
featured in the full range of FHG titles

Laquairie, (High Auvergne)

In a tiny hamlet perched high above Rhue Gorge, one hour from Clermont Ferrand. At the heart of Europe's largest national park, 5 minutes from bakers, butcher, café, supermarket and garage in Condat. A beautiful yet little known part of France.

Comfortable, spotlessly clean cottage at the edge of the tiny hamlet perched high above the Rhue Gorge. Large living room, huge fireplace, fully fitted kitchen (plus cheese cellar). Main bedroom en suite, small second bedroom. Exclusively for non-smokers. Contact DI SCOTT (00334 7178 6357). [Dogs 20 euros per week, to SPA].
e-mail: discott@auvergnehols.co.uk   website: www.auvergnehols.co.uk

Things to do and see in High Auvergne

Vulcania – a science oriented Theme Park dedicated to volcanoes.

Haras National d'Aurillac – one of the world's largest studs of heavy breed stallions.

Ecomusée de la Margeride near St Flour - several sites, telling the past and present story of the people of the area, includes houses, gardens, objects, sounds and smells.

Lioran Aventure at Le Lioran – an adventure playground claiming to be a cross between Tarzan and Indiana Jones.

Le Train Touristique running from Bort Les Orgues to Lugarde – a relaxing way to explore the countryside.

BRITTANY

This is a region steeped in tradition, and has maintained its Celtic traditions throughout the centuries. Mont Saint-Michel is reputed to be Brittany's best-known attraction. The beautiful bay of the Gulf of Morbihan is dotted with dozens of little islands, and you can visit fairy tale woods in the Ille aux Moines. Inland is the medieval forest of Merlin the Magician, where it is said that the Knights of the Round Table searched for the Holy Grail. The coast is a great attraction for tourists, who enjoy such activities as wind surfing, water skiing and underwater diving and, as you would expect, there is a wonderful variety of seafood available, including lobsters, oysters salmon and trout.

Baud (Morbihan)

Small town overlooking the picturesque Eivel Valley, located within easy reach of the major towns of Vannes amd Lorient. Well supplied with shopping facilities, including two supermarkets, four boulangeries and eight restaurants to suit all tastes.

JACKIE & DAVID GILES, LES CHEMINEES, BAUD 56150 (00 33 2 97 39 14 61). Beautiful 300 year old Farmhouse and Longeres set in 2 acres in a quiet location on the edge of Baud. Sleep 2-8. Morbihan beaches easily accessible; horse riding and golf tours. All linen provided. Swimming pool, BBQ, patio and games area.
e-mail: info@baud-gites.com   website: www.baud-gites.com

Collorec (Finistere)

The village lies within easy reach of the north and Atlantic coasts and beaches, theme parks, excellent horse riding facilities, and a zoo. There is a local market once a week, a good choice of restaurants, and a supermarket providing a wide range of produce for your daily needs. Huelgot, nearby, is a fascinating and beautiful area famous for its lake, forest walk and rock formations.

GUILLEC VIHAN, COLLOREC, NEAR HUELGOAT. Charmingly renovated 18th century cottage, on quiet and peaceful farm. Sleeps 6+cot. Ideal for those having difficulty with stairs. Pets welcome. For details contact: ROBBIE & FIONA RAINBIRD (00 33 2 98 73 93 60). [🐾]
e-mail: info@rainbird-gites.com   website: www.rainbird-gites.com

Pleine Fougeres (Rennes)

In a picturesque valley between the historical town of Dol-de-Bretagne in Brittany, and Pontorson in Normandy, and an excellent base for exploring the D-Day Beaches, the Bayeaux Tapestry, Chateaux and zoos. 15 minutes from the unique Bay of Mont-St-Michel. Good shopping, hypermarkets, golf and riding are virtually on the doorstep.

A cosy yet luxurious detached stone cottage in the beautiful Bay du Mont St Michel. Sleeps 2 adults and 2 children (+ baby), and we welcome pets by prior arrangement. Garden with BBQ, table and chairs. We can arrange appointments with a local vet for passport appointments. Contact the owners:JO AND STEVE SANDERS (0033 2 99 48 71 30) [🐾]
e-mail: joandsteve@free.fr   website: www.lepinholidays.com

dogswelcome.fr
Looking for a comfortable cottage for your holiday in Brittany?

We have several specially selected cottages sleeping two, four, six and eight people. Prices from £120 pw.

Tel: Nicola Harrington on 01342 322272
E-mail: nicola@frenchgites.com
www.harrington.fr

Malestroit (Morbihan)

This beautiful medieval town located on the river Oust has shops, restaurants, bars and banks. The Museum of the Resistance to the Second World War is located in nearby St Marcel.

FRENCH GITES. Looking for a comfortable cottage for your holiday in Brittany? We have several specially selected cottages sleeping two, four, six and eight people. Prices from £120 pw. Contact Nicola Harrington (01342 322272). [Pets £15 per week].
E-mail: nicola@frenchgites.com　　　　　　　　www.harrington.fr

Symbols

🐕　Indicates that pets are welcome free of charge.

£　Indicates that a charge is made for pets: nightly or weekly.

pw!　Shows some special provision for pets; exercise facility, feeding or accommodation arrangement.

⌂　Indicates separate pets accommodation.

Publisher's note

While every effort is made to ensure accuracy, we regret that FHG Guides cannot accept responsibility for errors, misrepresentations or omissions in our entries or any consequences thereof. Prices in particular should be checked.
We will follow up complaints but cannot act as arbiters or agents for either party.

St Georges de Reintembault (Ille-et-Villaine)

Quiet hamlet on the Brittany/Normandy border. It has a quaint market place, shops, post office and cinema. Small town of St James, with full shopping facilities and large supermarket is four miles away.

ST GEORGES DE REINTEMBAULT, BRITTANY. (+33 (0)2 99 97 04 91; Fax: +33 (0)2 99 97 04 92). Two ★★★★ gites with pool on Normandy/Brittany border, in idyllic rural countryside. Woodland and country walks. 2km from village. Fully furnished and fitted to high standard. La Grange: Sleeps 8. La Pommeraie: Sleeps 8. [🐾]
e-mail: info@kingswell.net

St Nicolas du Pelem/Rostrenen (Côtes D'Armor)

Small town with shops, Tourist Office, supermarket and garage. Many places to eat and drink. Just 15 minutes' drive from large lake offering all kinds of watersports.
Rostrenen is a traditional Breton market town with shops, post office, tourist office and a range of places to eat and drink.

Well furnished accommodation on two rural sites in Central Brittany. Fenced, heated swimming pool. Ideal for walking, watersports; coast 40 minutes. Small towns nearby. Local English-speaking vet. Contact CAROLYN JARMAN (00 33 29 63 65 961) or visit our website. [🐾]
e-mail: jarmankermarch@aol.com   website: www.holidaysinbrittanyfrance.co.uk

Readers are requested to mention this FHG
guidebook when seeking accommodation

LANGUEDOC-ROUSSILLON

The region has a widely varying landscape from mountains and plateaux, to moorlands and coastal plains. The coast is a blend of resorts such as Cap d'Agde and Port Camargue, and old villages and fishing ports. Good beaches offer a variety of watersports and there are many golf courses throughout the region. There are health spas and nature reserves as well as good fishing, cycling and riding, and the area is ideal for walkers. In winter there are good cross-country ski routes and excellent skiing. Markets can be found in towns and villages from early spring until late autumn, and festivals, fetes and concerts can all be enjoyed.

The area is noted for its seafood, including oysters and anchovies, and Sete, the largest Mediterranean fishing port on the coast of France has many excellent fish restaurants. Strong Mediterranean flavours dominate the local dishes, with rich game or beef stews, and, of course, the famed Cassoulet. Other regional specialities include olives, fruit, honey, full fruity red wines and delicious dessert wines.

Your Own Private Domaine — **Two lovely houses with large pool and tennis court**

In a beautiful elevated position overlooking the medieval village of Montagnac, Domaine de l'Hortevieille, a former wine-making property is set in 10 acres of fields, gardens and orchards with its own large, secure pool and tennis court. Two individually designed spacious houses are available for rental - each one well equipped with washing machine, dishwasher, microwave, fridge/freezer, television, DVD player and mini hi-fi. Each has its own private furnished terrace with barbecue facilities. Horse riding is available and mountain bikes are provided for you to explore the beautiful adjacent countryside.

The property is ideally suited for a tranquil summer holiday by the pool or on the beach or if you prefer a more active break in or out of season there are endless possibilities to get to know this rich and historic area. Whatever your interests - wine, good food, golf, fishing, antiques, history, the list is endless - the Domaine's English owners are on hand to help you enjoy your stay to the full.

Weekly rental rates from €500 or £370 to €1800 or £1350 inclusive of maid service, bed linen and towels and a welcome pack when you arrive. **For more information or to make a booking contact Malcolm or Alyson at hortevieille@wanadoo.fr or telephone 00 33 467 24 13 98.**

Montagnac (Herault)

Montagnac is within easy reach of Beziers and Montpellier and only a few kilometres from the A75 motorway. The nearest beach is about 10 minutes' drive away. The village centre has been recently renovated and there is a good selection of shops including bakers, general stores and butcher, as well as two bars – one of which serves snacks.

DOMAINE DE L'HORTEVIEILLE, MONTAGNAC. Two spacious houses, each well equipped, with private terrace and BBQ. Horse riding and mountain bikes available. English owners on hand to help you enjoy your stay to the full. Contact Malcolm or Alyson (00 33 467 24 13 98). e-mail: hortevieille@wanadoo.fr

Visit the FHG website
www.holidayguides.com
for details of the wide choice of accommodation
featured in the full range of FHG titles

LIMOUSIN

The Limousin region, situated in the centre of France, offers visitors a peaceful and traditional way of life. This is a charming and historic land of hills and valleys, forests and plains, rivers and picturesque ancient cities. The region takes its name from the Capital Limoges, which is renowned for its exquisite enamel and porcelain. This pleasant town has many parks and gardens, and the old quarter with its narrow medieval streets and houses

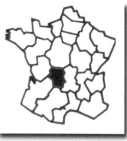

is worth a visit. There are many opportunities to enjoy swimming, sailing, canoeing and water skiing on the numerous rivers and lakes, and there are several golf courses throughout the region. There is good riding country in the south and many riding establishments catering for all standards of rider. Here you will find the National Stud and racecourse at Arnac-Pompadour. There are many fairs and markets in towns and villages on various days of the week, and you can enjoy pates and foie gras, and perhaps even sample the local speciality, an excellent potato pie made with smoked ham and herbs.

Argentat (Coreze)

This delightful market town is an ideal holiday destination offering peace and quiet, and beautiful scenery. Excellent food and wine can be enjoyed in attractive riverside restaurants and other good eating places. There is a wide variety of cultural and sporting activities to enjoy, and many shows and exhibitions take place during the summer.

UPPER DORDOGNE VALLEY. Character Cottage, sleeps two. On the edge of a picturesque village. One bedroom with en suite shower room. Kitchen/diner. Sitting room. Terrace and sun deck. Walk from cottage into amazing countryside. Contact JIM MALLOWS for details
e-mail: au-pont@wanadoo.fr   website: www.argentat.co.uk

FHG Guides

publish a large range of well-known accommodation guides.
We will be happy to send you details or you can use the order form
at the back of this book.

Estivals (Corréze)

The village is centrally located for visiting many places of interest including attractive prehistoric and medieval sites and interesting cave formations. Brive la Gaillarde, 16km north east offers a variety of supermarkets and shops, and the nearby village of Cressensac has a mini-market and bakery.

LE CHANT D'OISEAU, ESTIVALS. Four oak-timbered gites provide perfect relaxation in tranquil countryside. Fully equipped kitchen with microwave, dishwasher and washing machine. Bed linen. Pets welcome. Close to many attractions, with horse riding, cycling, canoeing, walking, golf and tennis easily available. Contact ROBIN OR LORAINE CORNISH (00 33 5 55 85 31 28) [🐴]
e-mail: robin.cornish@wanadoo.fr   website: www.lechantdoiseau.com

Things to do around Correze

The Splash Centre In Argentat – an aquatic park incorporating many outdoor activities.

Gouffre de Padirac – a series of underground lakes accessed via a hole deep into the earth – the underground boat ride is an experience not to be missed.

Plan d'eau du Coiroux , Aubazine - Supervised swimming, fishing, children's games. Windsurfing allowed. Other activities: 18-hole golf course, 9-hole pitch and putt, "Mayaventure" adventure park.

Les Aubarèdes, Beaulieu sur Dordogne – swimming and fishing. Canoeing and kayaking centre. Water sports centre. River trips on traditional flat-bottomed gabares.

Vol en Montgolfière, Arnac Pompadour - Ballooning flights from Pompadour and other sites subject to demand.

Eymoutiers (Haute Vienne)

On the banks of the River Vienne, approx 40 km from Limoges. Attractive upland town of tall, narrow stone houses crowding round a Romanesque church. Within easy reach of many beautiful places of interest.

CHRIS & LORI HILL, LA VARACHE, 87120 EYMOUTIERS (00 33 555 69 27 47) 2 tastefully converted self-catering gites situated in the heart of the lush and unspoilt Limousin countryside. Sleep up to 8/9 persons. Well equipped and furnished. Excellent base to explore surrounding countryside.
e-mail: enquiries@limousingite.com   website: www.lavarache.com

Things to do and see in Haute Vienne

Chateau de Chalus - Final resting place of Richard 1st (Richard the Lionheart) mortally wounded during the siege of the castle in 1199

Les Loupes de Chabrières, Gueret - A variety of wolf species (including the white wolf) being bred in a natural environment.

Parc du Reynou, near Limoges - Walk among the animals at this open Wildlife park with a difference.

Aquarium , Limoges - In the centre of Limoges this aquarium has 300 different species and and more than 2500 fish.

LOWER NORMANDY

The region of Normandy, with its lush countryside and a coastline warmed by the Gulf Stream, has long been a favourite destination with holidaymakers. There are many resorts and seaside towns and, inland, magnificent forests, tranquil streams and the many orchards which are indicative of this fruit producing region. There are many delights to discover such as the picturesque harbour of Honfleur, the Bayeux Tapestry and William the Conquerors birthplace. Normandy promises many gastronomic delights, from seafood and duck, to cream, cheeses and the famous Calvados. Why not explore the 'Cider Road' and the 'Cheese Road', or simply relax on a horse drawn carriage ride.

Set in 2 acres of beautiful grounds, **La Détourbe** is a stone longère, with a barn conversion providing two gites, which are fully equipped to a very high standard. All bedrooms have en suite facilities.

La Détourbe

Gite 1 • ground floor; lounge, corner kitchen, double bedroom (plus double bed-settee in lounge).

Gite 2 • ground floor; as gite 1, plus first floor with 2 double bedrooms, one with additional single bed.

Ideal location for enjoying the peace and tranquillity of the countryside within the Normandy regional park.

See our website for more information.

John and Chris Gibson • La Détourbe • Beauvain • 61600 La Ferté-Macé • Orne • France

Tel: 0033 (0) 2 33 30 12 68 • Fax: 0033 (0) 2 33 30 12 70

e-mail: johnandchrisg@orange.fr • www.normandy-gites.co.uk

La Ferté-Macé (Orne)

Small town with a range of shops and restaurants. Beach offers water sports, fishing and supervised swimming. 10km from the spa town of Bagnoles-de-l'Orne with good shopping, sports facilities, casino and golf.

JOHN AND CHRIS GIBSON, LA DETOURBE, BEAUVAIN, 61600 LA FERTE-MACE, ORNE. (0033 (0) 2 33 30 12 68; Fax: 0033 (0) 2 33 30 12 70). A stone longère set in two acres of beautiful grounds, with a barn conversion providing two gites. Ideal location for enjoying the peace and tranquillity within the Normandy regional park. [🐶]
e-mail: johnandchrisg@orange.fr   www.normandy-gites.co.uk

Visit the FHG website
www.holidayguides.com
for details of the wide choice of accommodation
featured in the full range of FHG titles

La Petite Maison à La Denillière

Gite finished to exceptional standard with beautiful artwork, lovely rugs and antiques. Sleeps up to 4. Separate fitted kitchen with cooker, microwave, fridge, dishwasher, washing machine and dining area. Comfortable lounge with 3-piece suite, tables and desk. Downstairs shower room and loo. Upstairs two double bedrooms, one with double bed, the other two singles. Hanging space. (There is also a small double sofa-bed in lounge).

Set amidst beautiful countryside just outside the small village of Le Gast, very near the stunning St Sever Forest, and mid way between Vire and Villedieu les Poeles.

We are central enough to tour to Normandy's historic sites including the WWII landing beaches, Bayeux, Mont St Michel and the Swiss Normand. There are local amenities such as swimming baths, golf and horse riding, plus of course wonderful walks in the forest. Miles of lovely sandy beaches are within an easy drive. Once outside the main towns, dogs are allowed on beaches all year round.

We welcome pets and responsible owners to our gite.

Please contact the owners on either **0871 717 4235** or **0033 2 31 66 94 59**
E-mail: info@french-holidaygite.co.uk
or visit our website at www.french-holidaygite.co.uk

Le Gast (Calvados)

Small hamlet in a peaceful setting. Easy driving distance to beach and close to many famous attractions. 10km from market town of Villedieu-les-Poeles with restaurants and bars and 35km from the resort town of Granville with Dior Museum.

LA PETITE MAISON A LA DENILLIERE. Gite finished to exceptional standard with beautiful artwork, lovely rugs and antiques. Amidst beautiful countryside just outside the small village of Le Gast. Central for touring Normandy's historic sites. Sleeps up to 4. Pets and responsible owners welcome. Contact owners on (0871 717 4235 or 0033 2 31 66 94 59).
e-mail: info@french-holidaygite.co.uk   website: www.french-holidaygite.co.uk

Please note

All the information in this book is given in good faith in the belief that it is correct. However, the publishers cannot guarantee the facts given in these pages, neither are they responsible for changes in policy, ownership or terms that may take place after the date of going to press. Readers should always satisfy themselves that the facilities they require are available and that the terms, if quoted, still apply.

MIDI-PYRENEES

The largest region in France, the Midi Pyrenees lies midway between the Mediterranean and the Atlantic and subsequently enjoys a particularly pleasant climate. The varied landscape and wide open spaces offer all kinds of holiday opportunities such as rafting, canoeing and skiing, as well as hiking, horse riding and cycling. There is also a choice of spas for the health and fitness enthusiast. The fascinating sites of Rocamadour and Padirac in Lot and the medieval village of Cordes-sur-Ciel in Tarn are certainly worth a visit, and don't overlook the must-see museum of Toulouse-Lautrec's work in Albi. On the other hand, whether religious or not, a visit to Lourdes can be inspiring.

Wherever you travel in the region you will be overwhelmed by the friendliness of the people. There is usually some sort of festival being held, and countless local markets will give you the opportunity to sample such culinary delights as Roquefort cheese, cassoulet and foie gras, or to enjoy the wines of Cahors and Armagnac.

La Brise
Superb riverside holiday cottage

A large, light and airy house divided into two separate areas. Standing in a quiet garden leading down to the edge of the river, with magnificent far reaching views, and 5 minutes' walk down the riverside to the medieval village of Puy L'Eveque, set deep in the heart of the Lot Valley.

Libelulle (sleeps 6)
Well equipped to a high standard. 3 bedrooms with en suite dressing and bathroom. Large lounge, French windows to balcony. Kitchen and dining room. Wood burner.

Papillon (sleeps 4)
Well equipped; 2 double bedrooms with French windows to balcony. Bathroom with separate WC. lounge with woodburner. Laundry room with separate washer and dryer.

Both accommodation areas have private BBQ and seating areas. Riverside seating. Pool overlooking the river; Swedish sauna. Use of canoe, dinghy and evening boat trip up the river.

The valley of the River Lot is one of France's most vibrant and beautiful areas, with limestone gorges, majestic chateaux and ancient villages perched precariously on the side of cliffs. Amazingly this area is still unspoilt and you can find total isolation as well as busy market towns. The climate is excellent and the warm season extends from early April to late October.
Welcome pack with wine offered on arrival.
Prices from £275 inclusive. No hidden extras.

Please contact:
Chris & Edwina Flannery, La Brise,
8, Rue des Balmes, Puy L'Eveque,
46700 Lot, France
Tel: 07801 909850 or 00 33 565 35 20 29
e-mail: chrsfln@aol.com
website: www.labrise.co.uk

Puy L'Eveque (Lot)

Beautiful medieval town on the edge of the River Lot, with ancient timber framed houses and narrow cobbled streets. Several restaurants and bars, bakers, bank and post office, and a small supermarket on the edge of the village. The town of Cahors is thirty minutes away. One and a quarter hour's drive from Bergerac airport.

CHRIS & EDWINA FLANNERY, LA BRISE, 8 RUE DES BALMES, PUY L'EVEQUE, 46700 LOT (07801 909850 OR 00 33 5 65 35 20 29. Superb riverside cottage in quiet garden, with two separate accommodation areas. Sleep 4 and 6, pool, sauna. Both well equipped to a high standard, kitchen, dining room, woodburner. Linen included.
e-mail: chrsfln@aol.com   website: www.labrise.co.uk

POITOU-CHARENTES

Poitou-Charentes is a very unspoilt region with pleasant countryside, bustling ports and harbours, long sandy beaches, islands and marinas. Enjoy 300 miles of Atlantic coast for sunbathing, sailing or windsurfing, take a cruise on the Charente River or discover the secrets of Cognac by visiting its cellars and distilleries. There are numerous vineyards, castles and Romanesque churches to visit, or experience the futuristic universe at Futuroscope Theme Park outside Poitiers. If walking or cycling is your thing the mainly flat agricultural land away from the coastline is ideal. The cuisine of this abundant region includes the famous Marennes Oleron oysters, melons, goat cheeses such as chabichou and Pineau, a mixture of grape juice and cognac.

Maison Renard & La Côte

Tastefully restored south-facing Charentaise house and cottage in a quiet hamlet, surrounded by lakes and beautiful countryside.

Maison Renard Sleeps 6. Large family room, sleeps 3, double room, en suite single room, family bathroom, lounge, living/dining room and kitchen, satellite TV, video, hi-fi.

La Côte Sleeps 3. One double and one single bedroom, bathroom and living areas, satellite TV.

Both have fully equipped kitchens including microwave, dishwasher, fridge freezer, modern cookers and use of washing machine. South-facing gardens and patios with garden furniture and BBQ. Indoor pool. PETS WELCOME.

Contact: John & Sally Fox,
Tel: 01724 720384
or 00 33 54 521 73 87
E-mail: foxjns@aol.com
or enquiries@maisonrenard.co.uk

Visit our website: www.maisonrenard.co.uk

La Rochefoucauld (Charente Lakes)

Quiet hamlet, surrounded by lakes and beautiful countryside, in the heart of the Charente. Restaurant bars and shops a few minutes away. Ideal for walking, cycling, birdwatching, golf, fishing and water sports in the Charente Lakes.

MAISON RENARD & LA CÔTE Tastefully restored Charentaise house and cottage in quiet hamlet. Sleeps 6 and 3. Fully equipped kitchens, BBQ, indoor pool. South-facing gardens. Contact: JOHN & SALLY FOX (01724 720384 or 00 33 54 521 73 87). [🐾]
e-mail: foxjns@aol.com or enquiries@maisonrenard.co.uk   website: www.maisonrenard.co.uk

WESTERN LOIRE

This region, with its pleasing warm climate, has long been a favourite holiday destination. The visitor is spoilt for choice as lush countryside, vineyards, long sandy beaches and salt marshes vie for attention with fascinating cities, sleepy villages, ancient buildings and castles with stunning artwork, and cultural festivals galore. The famous 24-hour race is held at Le Mans-Laval, and there are facilities throughout the region for a huge variety of sporting activities, both land and water based. The countryside is easily explored by bicycle or on foot, or you may prefer to spend a day cruising on the tranquil waterways. Explore the Loire Valley vineyards, and enjoy the delicious and famous wines of the area with fresh fruit and vegetables, game, wild mushrooms and generous platters of seafood from the region's rivers and the sea.

Les Augerelles
Vendée/Charentes Border

3 bed house (7/9) and 1 bed gite (2/4)
• Well equipped and recently refurbished • secure garden with sun and shade • part-covered barbeque area with furniture • 4.5m raised pool with removable steps • heating for off-season, thick stone walls • quiet hamlet but with market town nearby • 200 hectares of common land opposite, good walks • ideal location for Atlantic coast, Marais and Bocage • managed by family members resident in the region • available together for main holiday season or separately for longer lets and off-season by negotiation.

For more details contact:
Janet & John Nuthall • 01249 443458
e-mail: jnuthall2@toucansurf.com for brochure
or visit **www.vendee-gites.co.uk/lesaugerelles.htm** for much more information and pictures

Fonteney le Comte (Vendée)

A town of art and history with elegant squares and gardens. Nôtre Dame church and the Vendée museum are worth a visit. Numerous festivals and events take place throughout the year..

LES AUGERELLES, VENDEE/CHARENTES BORDER. 3 Bed house (sleeps 7/9) and 1 bed gite (sleeps 2/4). Well equipped and recently refurbished. Swimming pool. Heating for off season. Quiet hamlet with market town nearby. Managed by family members resident in the region. Contact: JANET & JOHN NUTHALL (01249 443458) [🐏]
e-mail: jnuthall2 @toucansurf.com   website: www.vendee-gites.co.uk/lesaugerelles.htm

🐏   Indicates that pets are welcome free of charge.

£   Indicates that a charge is made for pets: nightly or weekly.

pw!   Shows some special provision for pets; exercise facility, feeding or accommodation arrangement.

⌂   Indicates separate pets accommodation.

Symbols

DogsTrust
the new name for the *NCDL*

Dogs**Trust**: A Dog is For Life

Are you thinking of going on holiday in the UK with your dog?

If so, the Dogs Trust has a free factsheet which will be of particular interest.

"Safe travel and happy holidays with your hound in the UK"

For this and any other of our free Dogs Trust factsheets please contact us at:

Dogs Trust,
17 Wakley St. London EC1V 7RQ.
Tel: 020 7837 0006
Website: www.dogstrust.org.uk
or e-mail us, info@dogstrust.org.uk

Last year Dogs Trust cared for over 11,500 stray and abandoned dogs at our network of 15 Rehoming Centres.

So if you are looking for a companion for your dog or you have a friend who might like a dog, just contact your nearest Dogs Trust Rehoming Centre.

We care for around 1,600 dogs on any given day, so we are sure we will be able to find your perfect partner. The Dogs Trust never destroys a healthy dog. For details of our Sponsor-a-Dog scheme please call 020 7837 0006 or visit www.sponsoradog.org.uk

Dogs Trust Rehoming Centres

ENGLAND

Dogs Trust Canterbury
01227 792 505

Dogs Trust Darlington
01325 333 114

Dogs Trust Evesham
01386 830 613

Dogs Trust Ilfracombe
01271 812 709

Dogs Trust Kenilworth
01926 484 398

Dogs Trust Leeds
01132 613 194

Dogs Trust Merseyside
0151 480 0660

Dogs Trust Newbury
01488 658 391

Dogs Trust Roden
01952 770 225

Dogs Trust Salisbury
01980 629 634

Dogs Trust Shoreham
01273 452 576

Dogs Trust Snetterton
01953 498 377

WALES

Dogs Trust Bridgend
01656 725 219

SCOTLAND

Dogs Trust West Calder
01506 873 459

NORTHERN
IRELAND

Dogs Trust Ballymena
028 2565 2977

Registered Charity No. 227523

Donate £1 to your favourite Pets Charity

FHG has agreed to donate £1 from the price of this Pets Welcome! Guide to EITHER

The Royal Society For The Prevention of Cruelty to Animals,

Dogs Trust,

The Kennel Club,

or the Scottish Society for the Prevention of Cruelty to Animals

To allow the Charity of your choice to receive this donation simply complete the slip below and return to FHG at

FHG Guides Ltd, Abbey Mill Business Centre
Seedhill Paisley PA1 1TJ
Closing date 25th APRIL 2008

Note: Original forms only please, do not send photocopies.

Please donate £1 from the price of this Pets Welcome! guide to:

RSPCA ☐   DOGS TRUST ☐   KENNEL CLUB ☐   SSPCA ☐

Name...

Address ....

....

Postcode ....Date ....

FHG Guides may send readers details of discount offers for our holiday guides.

If you do not wish to receive this information please tick here ☐

Your details will not be passed on to any other organisation.

THE KENNEL CLUB
Making a difference for dogs

Dogs and the Kennel Club

Founded well over a hundred years ago, in 1873, the Kennel Club registers around 275,000 dogs a year. It is the governing body of dogs in the United Kingdom, and its main objective is to promote in every way, the general improvement of dogs, and encourage responsible dog ownership.

From running the largest dog show in the world, Crufts, to giving critical advice to owners, the media and politicians alike, as well as providing educational schemes, such as teaching safety around dogs. It covers both the fun and the serious side of dogs, and dog ownership, and is central to all dogs and dog owners.

The number of breeds recognised by the Kennel Club is ever increasing, with 208 breeds currently eligible for registration. The KC has three registers - the Breed, the Activity and the Companion Dog register – one for every kind of dog and activity, as both the Activity register and Companion Dog register are open for crossbreeds.

The small cost to register dogs ensures that money is being put back into dogs, enabling the Kennel Club to run its schemes, and also to be the voice for dogs in Government on behalf of all their owners. The variety of schemes run by the KC, reflect its diverse role with dogs and their place in society as a whole.

For those wanting to buy a pedigree dog there is access to, and information on, the best breeders through the Accredited Breeder Scheme and the Puppy Sales Register, all easily accessible on the Kennel Club website, as well as breed specific health research. And for those who want a pedigree dog but would prefer an adult dog, there are many breed specific rescue centres. They also offer the support of expert knowledge and advice on specific breeds.

The Kennel Club Charitable Trust raises and disburses funds to a variety of deserving causes, such as canine health research projects, specialist studies and canine charities. Every penny that is raised goes directly to the Trust, ensuring that our dog friends and people within the canine field enjoy the maximum benefit.

The Kennel Club has a role to play for lost dogs through Petlog, the UK's largest national pet identification scheme. The details on Petlog (**www.petlog.org.uk**) are available to local authorities, police and established welfare and rescue organisations. This ensures that lost or stray animals are speedily reunited with their owners when found and scanned for details on a previously inserted microchip, even when abroad.

Safety for children around dogs is another priority for the Kennel Club, which has led to the development of its fun and informative popular online game called 'Safe and Sound' (www.safeandsound.org.uk), which is free to play. Children's lives are enriched by living with dogs, as they learn responsibility and empathy while interaction with a dog can increase their self-esteem.

Ensuring dogs are well behaved means also teaching the owners how to achieve this, which is where the Good Citizen Dog Scheme (GCDS) comes into focus. It is the largest dog training programme in the UK and has four levels of assessment, from Puppy Foundation through to Gold. 190,000 dogs have successfully passed through the scheme, with more than 1,800 training clubs across the UK running the programme. Training your dog helps to create a better bond between a dog and its owner, and it is a responsible dog owner's job to ensure that you have a well behaved and lovable dog.

The Accredited Instructors scheme for dog training and canine behaviour is for anyone training dogs or teaching people to train dogs. It provides a network of instructors, trainers and advisors to help, and is a voluntary scheme, which aims to give a worthwhile qualification, in which scheme members and the public can have confidence.

The Young Kennel Club (YKC) is a vital part of the Kennel Club, ensuring that youngsters have an opening into the world of dogs. The Young Kennel Club is for young members from 6 – 24 years (www.ykc.org.uk)

Keep an eye open for the forthcoming 'Kennel Club – Dogs Welcome' sticker in locations from cafés to castles, to be reassured that your dog is welcome. To find out more visit the Kennel Club's website (www.thekennelclub.org.uk) or make an appointment to visit the Kennel Club's headquarters, which also holds Europe's definitive canine library and art gallery, located in Mayfair, London. The Press Office is available to provide comment on all dog issues and Kennel Club related subjects. If you require any further information, please do not hesitate to contact the team.

Kennel Club Press Office:
Telephone 020 7518 1008 • press.office@thekennelclub.org.uk
www.thekennelclub.org.uk

www.winalot-dog.co.uk

For many of us enjoying a country holiday also means taking our dogs on scenic walks, or for a journey in the car - often in warm weather, and at these times they may need a little extra care and attention. The following tips could make your pet's life on hot days considerably more comfortable:

WATER!

A normal 20kg dog will drink about one and a half pints of water a day. In the heat this can increase by 200 to 300%. Water should always be available. Make sure you take plenty for your pet, as well for yourself when out walking and in the car. Stabilising non-spill water bowls are great for travel, while handy inflatable bowls are ideal for stowing in your knapsack. You can even buy water bottles that your dog can carry.

SHADE

Encourage your dog to favour shady, cool spots when you stop for a rest - rather than sunbathe with the rest of the family!

CAR

NEVER leave your dog in the car unattended. Placing a dog in the back of any car even with an open rear window is undesirable and may be fatal. Remember - even a car parked in shade in the morning when it's cool could reach over 100 degrees very quickly as the sun moves. Heat stroke can occur within minutes.

EXERCISE

Plan your walk so you avoid strenuous exercise during the hottest part of the day. Some dogs like to paddle or swim - if there is no water around and your dog seems uncomfortably hot, seek a shady spot and provide water.

HEALTH

A dog's heat loss system is dependent on overall health. If your dog is fit, supple and active then walking will be a pleasurable experience, however, if there is any indication of heart or respiratory problems arising, controlled exercise in the cool is recommended. Veterinary advice should be sought if problems persist during heat stressful times.

HEAT STROKE

This is an emergency and potentially life threatening situation. If in doubt take the following action, then seek advice. A chilled dog is better than an overheated one.

- Cease any form of exercise.
- Move the dog into a cool place.
- Sponge the dog with cold water - all over, avoiding water round the mouth or nose.
- Do not offer food or fluids until evident recovery.
- Seek veterinary advice if in doubt.

NEW

Winalot Roasts - Mealtimes never tasted so good!

Tender pieces of meat, gently cooked to give that special roasted taste, then smothered in a thick meaty gravy to give your dog that extra taste sensation he deserves!

Available in Chicken, Beef and Lamb varieties.

Readers' Pets Pictures

Send us your favourite Pet Photo!

On the following pages are a selection of Pets photos sent in by readers of **Pets Welcome!**

If you would like to have a photo of your pet included in the next edition (published in April 2008), send it along with a brief note of the pet's name and any interesting anecdotes about them. Please remember to include your own name and address and let us know if you would like the pictures returned.

We will be happy to receive prints, transparencies or pictures on disk or by e-mail to editorial@fhguides.co.uk

All pictures should be forwarded by the end of January 2008.

Thanks to everyone who sent in pictures of their pets and regret that we were unable to include all of them, pictures not included in this edition will be considered for use in the future.

See the following pages for this year's selection.

Send your Pet photo to: FHG Guides, Abbey Mill Business Centre, Seedhill, Paisley PA1 1T

Catch me if you can
says ISLA.
Jean Williamson, Paisley

Smiling MEL.
Bryan Riley, Cambuslang

TROY in profile.
Mrs Thomson, Barrhead

SAMELY and TOTO –
'Wedded Bliss'
Mrs Sumery, Blackpool

What a strange fish I've caught says DAISY.
Mrs Currid, Lichfield

SOPHIE'S sandy vigil,
Miss Thomson, Enfield

BRADLEY can't decide what
to wear for Halloween.
Maureen from Shortroods

LOTTY Is 'Pretty as a Picture'.
Sue Lloyd, Malvern.

HANNAH
playing Hide and Seek.
Mrs M. Smith, Wolverhampton

SASSI guards the gardens.
Mrs MacDonald, Barrhead

PADDY and TIGGIE
strike a pose.
Judy Farnham, Skelmersdale

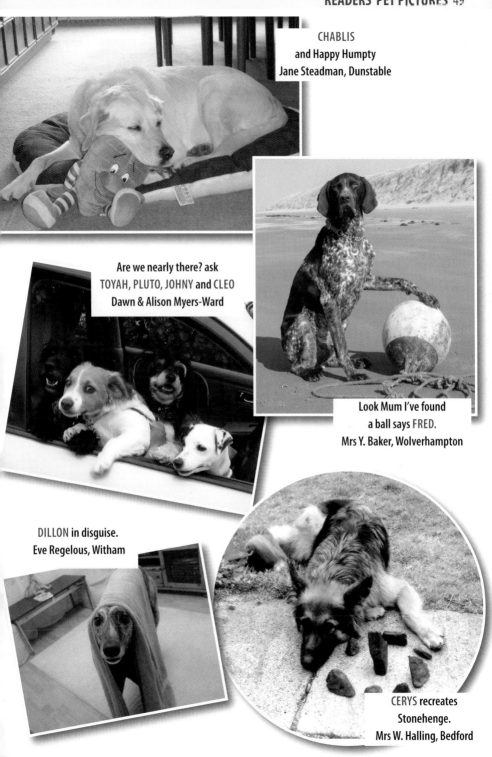

CHABLIS
and Happy Humpty
Jane Steadman, Dunstable

Are we nearly there? ask
TOYAH, PLUTO, JOHNY and CLEO
Dawn & Alison Myers-Ward

Look Mum I've found
a ball says FRED.
Mrs Y. Baker, Wolverhampton

DILLON in disguise.
Eve Regelous, Witham

CERYS recreates
Stonehenge.
Mrs W. Halling, Bedford

RIO, DEXTER, FRED and LADDIE
– the best of friends.
Mrs H. Willis, Braunton

Family Portrait
Mrs Dawson, Welshpool

These shoes are far too big
says TOBY.
Jackie Whitaker, Nottingham

CHARLIE'S raring to go,
R. Stevenson, Paisley

The sea air is so bracing
says PADDY.
Sharon Symons, Bude

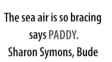

I'm sure there was a stick around here
somewhere says BESSIE.
Jennifer & Victor Gibbons, High Peak.

LOTTY and DALLY dressed up
to beat the Winter blues.
Sue Lloyd, Malvern

SAM the Mountain Goat.
Mrs Currid, Lichfield.

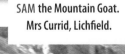

JAKE with his
favourite Teddy.
Lorraine Rodgers, Swindon

I do like to be beside the seaside says FRED.
Mrs Y Baker, Wolverhampton

I'll let you know if it's safe PADDY tells TIGGIE.
Mrs J. Farnham, Skelmersdale.

Baby BUSTER'S bed time.
Lorraine MacGowan,
Hunterhill

It's all fine and DANDY
Claire Mansfield-Smith

We only need 10 more for a footie team says DOODLE.
Claire Robinson, Weybridge

SUMMER and KACEE among the flowers.
Mrs Dawson, Welshpool

Anyone for seconds? asks OZY,
Lynn Abbott
& Ian Pearson, Somerset

TOBY & REXY like to share.
Lesley Blumberg, London

IVOR sitting pretty.
Jane McDonald, Rippingale.

IF YOU LOVE DOGS YOU'LL LOVE YOUR DOG

BRITAIN'S BEST-SELLING DOG MAGAZINE

your dog

September 2007 £3.25

YOUR PROBLEMS SOLVED

20 pages of

DOG ANSWERS
- Guest expert on cancer
- Older dogs special

page 58

Teach your dog to do the housework!
We show you how

Why dogs turn bad
The causes of aggression

Onwards and upwards
Tackling the Good Citizen Dog Scheme

A-Z of breeds
Schipperke
Swedish Vallhund

£9,000 puppy food giveaway

Quality control
Treating dogs with cancer

Come fly with me...
Have a go at flyball

DOG STUFF!
page 52
- New products • Tried & tested • Book reviews

OUT & ABOUT
page 86
- How to put your best foot forward • My favourite walk

MAGAZINE your dog
MAGAZINE

Your Dog is Britain's **best-selling dog magazine,** a monthly read that's packed with tips and advice on how to get the best out of life with your pet.

Every issue contains in-depth features on your dog's health, behaviour and training, and looks at subjects such as how to pick the perfect puppy for your lifestyle.

My favourite walk
Other owners share the walks they most enjoy with their dogs from a stroll in the wood to an energetic countryside ramble.

Dog Answers
Twenty pages of your problems solved by our panel of experts — everything from training, health, behaviour, feeding, breeds, grooming, legal and homoeopathy.

Dog stuff!
All the latest product news plus long and short-term testing of everything from tough dog toys to wellies.

And lots, lots more...

Your Dog Magazine is available from your newsagent; price £3.25. Alternatively, why not take out a subscription? To find out more, contact the subscriptions hotline on tel. 01858 438854 and quote ref PW03.

A dog-friendly walk in...
The Peak Distric

Britain's first national park, the Peak District, is at the heart of England and offers visitors a contrast of picturesque valleys and rolling farmland, impressive peaks and wild moorland.

Sheffield
Macclesfield Buxton • Chatsworth
• Bakewell
Leek Matlock

Derby

Ashford in the Water

Stride out through the marvellous limestone countryside starting from the pretty village of Ashford in the Water. Stop and stare at Monsal Head and Dale before exploring one of the Peak District's great wonders. **By Paul and Sandy Biggs.**

Monsal Viaduct crosses the river Wye in picturesque Monsal Dale.

Sheepwash Bridge over the River Wye at Ashford in the Water.

Distance: 6.4km (4 miles).
Time: About 3 hours.
Maps: Explorer OL 24, The Peak District, White Peak Area; Landranger 119.
Start/parking: Ashford in the Water; grid ref: SK195697.
Terrain: Hills and valleys.
Nearest town: Bakewell.
Refreshments: Little Longstone, Ashford in the Water and at Monsal Head.
Public toilets: Ashford in the Water and Monsal Head car parks.
Public transport: Contact Traveline East Midlands, tel. 0870 608 2608.
Stiles: 15.
Suitable for: All the family and dogs who can be lifted over stiles.

1 From the car park, walk back to the small village green and turn right towards Monsal Head. Go uphill along the road passing Highfield Farm to a public footpath signpost, right for Monsal Head. Cross a short field to a minor road then descend to the next field. Walk by a boundary wall then pass farm buildings to reach Longstone Lane.

2 Cross, continue over grassy fields going along the bottom of a hill. A grassy path leads past a wood and continues on to come to the Monsal Trail. Cross, keep to the trail left, then walk ahead over several more fields to reach Little Longstone.

3 Turn left, walk along the road passing the Packhorse Inn and after a quarter of a mile you'll reach Monsal Head Hotel. Go past the hotel and cafe, then turn right at a public footpath signpost that overlooks Monsal Dale. Go down the steps and continue down along a path into Monsal Dale. Turn left, cross the pretty bridge over the river, and turn left back towards Monsal Head. Take the path right, up on to Monsal Viaduct and cross the bridge again over the river. Just before the closed tunnel entrance turn left and follow the path back up to Monsal Head to a signpost for Ashford.

4 Continue along a path on the top of Monsal Dale. Walk uphill to reach a public signpost by two wooden viewpoint seats. Turn left towards Ashford and join a walled path. The way ahead is most obvious and it is a case of climbing stiles and following waymarks. The path turns into a stony track and, just past some farm buildings, turn right at a public signpost.

5 Walk over the field making for a stile to the right of some houses. A narrow path leads past the rear of some houses descending to a road. Turn right and return to Ashford in the Water village car park.

A dog-friendly walk in...
The South Down

Stop off at the South Downs, with its chalk hills that afford beautiful views of the coast and nearby beaches. Designated as an Area of Outstanding Natural Beauty, the South Downs extends through the counties of East Sussex, West Sussex and part of Hampshire.

The view over the downs from Chanctonbury.

Chanctonbury Ring

Take the opportunity to explore one of the most mysterious and magical sites on the South Downs. The ring is a fascinating place at any time of year and in any weather. Don't be deterred if the top is shrouded in low cloud as this only adds to the atmosphere. On a clear day the views are second to none and a camera can't do them justice. **By Sylvie Dobson.**

HAMPSHIRE
Winchester
WEST SUSSEX
THE SOUTH DOWNS
NATIONAL PARK
Burgess Hill
Southampton
EAST SUSSEX
Chichester
Brighton
Eastbourne
Portsmouth
Worthing
Littlehampton
Bognor Regis
Beachy
Head
Isle of Wight

Trees frame the view from Chanctonbury hill.

the right for a short while before turning and looking back. In the distance you will see Cissbury Ring and beyond that the sea. Ahead the imposing sight of the Chanctonbury Ring comes into view. Pass through a gate and on to access land where you can roam freely.

3 By all means explore the ring but then keep over to the right and aim for the trig point from where you can get an all-round view of the surrounding area. On a clear day you can see the Isle of Wight away to the south-west and far away to the north beyond the Weald you should be able to make out the North Downs. Return to the main track, spending a few minutes by the nearby dew pond, and continue the walk. You may be tempted to use an alternative route through the adjoining access land but be aware that there are likely to be sheep grazing. The track is a safer proposition and just as enjoyable.

4 Keep right at a fork and start a steady descent. You will

1 Leave the car park and continue ahead along the rough ascending track. Soon you will be in the shelter of the trees covering the flanks of the hill. Bear left at an apparent fork and then just keep climbing on the main track. From the bottom the climb looks daunting but once you get started you will quickly get into a rhythm and before long will emerge from the trees to join a wide crossing track. This is the renowned South Downs Way.

2 From here the views are limited, so walk along to

pass another gate leading on to the access land and over to your left you will see a short, grassy runway used for the occasional light aircraft. You should look for the track that leads to this airstrip; immediately beyond this take the narrow path on the right following it down the hillside to a stile and on to a road.

5 Turn right and just beyond the turning to St Mary's Church you will see a stile on the right. Pass over the stile and then a short footbridge before climbing some strategically placed steps up the hillside. Continue through open pasture where sheep may be grazing. Keep walking with the hedge to your left but be alert for a finger post that may at times be partly hidden by foliage. You are directed diagonally right across open fields and on to a gate at the foot of Chanctonbury Hill — you don't have to climb it again! Turn left along a wide track which contours the lower slopes of the Scarp before eventually joining the path you followed from the car park.

Your Dog Magazine is available from all good newsagents. For more information, contact the editorial department on tel. 01780 766199.

Fact file

Distance: 2.5km to 3km (4½ miles).
Time: 2 – 3 hours.
Map: OS Explorer 121 Arundel and Pulborough.
Start/parking: Chanctonbury Ring car park and picnic area signed from the A283 between Washington and Steyning. Grid ref: 146123.
Terrain: An initial climb on to the ridge of the downs followed by a less noticeable descent. Paths are well used and clearly defined.
Nearest towns: Worthing.
Refreshments: The Frankland Arms in Washington village.
Public toilets: None.
Public transport: Full details from Traveline, contact tel. 0870 608 2608. Compass Travel operates a local service that passes the track to the car park, contact tel. 01903 690025.
Stiles: Six.
Suitable for: Dogs and owners used to exercise. Lots of off lead opportunities.

A283

A24

Washington

Frankland Arms

5

1

3

Trig point
Dew Pond

Chanctonbury Ring

4

2

A dog-friendly walk in...
The Cairngorms

The Cairngorms National Park is the largest in Britain. Visitors can enjoy some of the most beautiful and dramatic views in the country, ranging from tranquil lochs to spectacular mountain peaks.

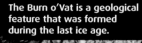
The Burn o'Vat is a geological feature that was formed during the last ice age.

Muir of Dinnet

Take a stroll through the Muir of Dinnet National Nature Reserve consisting of extensive birch wood, wetlands and heather moor. There are two large lochs, Davan and Kinord, in the centre and the chance to discover the Burn o'Vat, a wonderful geological feature. **By Andrew Macdonald.**

Elgin
Inverness
Aviemore
Braemar
Aberdeen
CAIRNGORMS NATIONAL PARK
Dundee
Perth

Loch Kinord has a couple of islands including Castle Island which was turned into a medieval fortress.

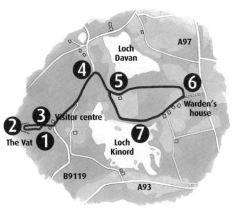

1 From the car park, head left past the visitor centre and continue past the public toilets, following the path around the left-hand side of the building. Continue on this path and cross the burn via the small wooden bridge.

2 The route continues up the small glen, passing another wooden footbridge on the right, until you come to a dead end at what appears to be an impenetrable rock barrier. There is a burn running through a gap in the huge boulders; this is the route into the Vat. Use the larger stones in the burn as stepping-stones to avoid getting your feet wet. Once inside the Vat, you will find a huge bowl-like cavern. It is possible to climb out the other side of the Vat, over the rocks to the left of the burn, but this is only recommended for those with a reasonable level of fitness.

3 Exit the Vat by the same route you entered and follow the burn back to the footbridge now on the left-hand side. Cross the bridge and climb the steps ahead. Follow the well-worn track and emerge from the woods back at the public toilets and the car park. Leave the car park and turn left on to the B9119. Walk about half a mile.

4 Further along the path pass a tall memorial stone on the right. Continue along the road until you reach an opening and gate on the right; there is also an information board and map here.

5 Follow the track into the woods. Loch Davan can be seen through the trees on the left. Where the track forks, go left. Pass some ruined buildings on the right. This is all that remains of the Old Kinord Farm.

6 Continue along the route but look closely for another track that leads off to the right. This path leads to an Iron Age settlement. Leave the settlement and continue on the track as before until it reaches the road from Dinnet. Turn right past the warden's house and out into the open ground above Loch Kinord.

7 There is a rough track on the right down to the loch; you have to look carefully for it in places as it is hidden. Near the loch side is a Pictish symbol stone (fenced in). Not far from the stone the track turns away from the loch heading along a field on the right. The track goes back past the old farm ruins and links up with the path that leads back up to the B9119. At the road, turn left, and head back to the car park where the walk began.

Fact file

Distance: The loop around the Vat is 1.5km (1 mile). The loop between Lochs Davan and Kinord is 4km (2½ miles).
Time: 3 hours for both parts of the walk.
Map: OS Explorer 395 Glen Esk & Glen Tanar.
Starting: Car park at the Burn o'Vat visitor centre on the B9119.
Terrain: Flat and solid underfoot. Sturdy boots advisable if viewing the Vat.
Nearest Town: Aboyne, Ballater.
Refreshments: No refreshments at the site, but many places in either towns.
Public toilets: At the Vat visitor centre.
Public transport: Full details from Traveline Scotland, contact tel. 0870 608 2608 or visit www.traveline.org Stagecoach Bluebird operates a service from Aberdeen (route 201) to Braemar, stops at Dinnet Village Hall, contact tel. 01343 544222.
Suitable for: All the family and well-behaved dogs.

A dog-friendly walk in...
The Norfolk Broa

The Norfolk Broads National Park has rich history and unique wildlife. Restored windmills, medieval churches, charming villages and peaceful waterways are just a few of the delights that visitors discover when they explore the Broads.

Horsey Windpump

Recognized as an internationally important wildlife site, the Horsey Estate is also a superb destination for anyone who enjoys birdwatching. This route allows visitors to enjoy the peace and tranquillity of the area along with the chance to walk by the sea.
By Anita Delf.

The 'big Norfolk skies' at Horsey beach.

The Broads offers visitors a peaceful and tranquil holiday destination.

Pic: The Broads Authority.

windpump ahead and the end of the path. Turn right, climb the stile and walk on the field edge to the houses ahead. Climb the stile at the end of the path to reach a lane. If you wish to take the shorter walk turn right by the footpath sign and follow the lane round to the church and main road. The Nelson Head public house is then directly opposite on the main road or you can turn right to return to the car park. Otherwise at the lane turn left and walk to the main road. Turn right along this road walking with care as it can be busy.

3 At the sharp bend turn left down the gravel track taking you back into the Horsey Estate, to reach a small car parking area. There is a choice of route here, you can turn right going through the kissing gate and along the path by the dunes or, if you prefer, you can continue ahead through Horsey Gap to reach the sea and turn right to walk along the beach.

Horsey Mill is owned by The National Trust.

4 Turn right at the next concrete gap on to a wide fenced track. If you choose the beach walk then you will need to turn right away from the beach, climbing the short sand hill. The track is then directly ahead of you. Continue on this track to arrive at the Nelson Head pub. From the Nelson Head turn right to the road, then turn left along it, following it back to the car park. This road is busy and must be walked with care, using the grass verge as much as possible.

Fact file

Distance: 8 km (5 miles) or 4.8 km (3 miles).
Time: Allow 2½ hours.
Map: Explorer OL 40, The Broads.
Start/parking: The National Trust car park at Horsey Windpump on the B1159. It costs 30p per hour; grid ref: TQ457224.
Terrain: Good paths; flat except for the climb through the sand dunes to beach.
Nearest town: Great Yarmouth.
Refreshments: Nelson Head pub — dogs welcome inside on a lead. Seasonal shop/tea room at Horsey mill, open Wednesday to Sunday, 10am – 4.30pm, with outside tables.
Public toilets: Horsey Mill car park — seasonal only.
Public transport: None.
Stiles: Two low wooden stiles — dogs may need to be lifted over.
Suitable for: All the family.

1 From the car park at the Horsey Windpump walk to the steps and footpath sign and then turn right along the towpath. Follow the path and boardwalk until it reaches a gate. To the left are wonderful views of Horsey Mere. From here on dogs will need to be kept on a lead as sometimes there is livestock in the fields. Go through the gate and cross the field diagonally left to a further gate. Pass through this and continue along the path and boardwalk to reach the cut.

2 Continue alongside the water's edge to the ruined

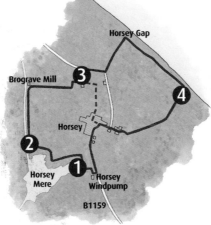

Horsey Gap

Brograve Mill

3

4

Horsey

2

1

Horsey Mere

Horsey Windpump

B1159

A dog-friendly walk in...
The Yorkshire Da

We pay a visit to the Yorkshire Dales National Park which includes some of the finest scenery in the country for you and your dog to explore and enjoy.

The limestone scar above Askrigg.

Askrigg circuit

This is a delightful walk through the Yorkshire Dales. It visits three lovely villages, passes by the site of a Roman fort and traverses tracks, paths and paved trods. The route also goes past several waterfalls and is a joy to walk from beginning to end. **By Mary Welsh.**

Penrith

DURHAM

CUMBRIA   Richmond

Askrigg
Kendal   Yorkshire
Dales   NORTH
YORKSHIRE
Barrow-in-
Furness   Leeds
LANCASHIRE   WEST
YORKSHIRE

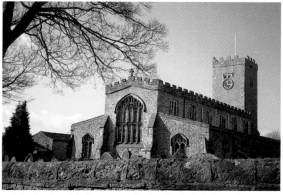

Askrigg's church is known as the 'Cathedral of the Dales'.

abutments of a former railway bridge.

2 Continue on the signed paved path. When the flags cease, carry on in the same general direction to take a gate tucked into the far left corner, which gives access to the road. Stroll left to cross Yore Bridge over the River Ure and go into the attractive village of Bainbridge. Head on over several greens and follow the A-road as it winds east over Bain Bridge. Stride on to pass, on the other side of the road, Brough Hill.

3 Take the right turn signposted Semerwater and then go over the gated stile through the wall on your left. Climb on up to a stile at the top of Brough Scar, with the signpost seen clearly above. Then head left along the scar passing through deciduous woodland with more freedom for the dog. Ignore the first signpost and then after three quarters of a mile from the start of the scar you reach the second. Take the right branch out of the trees, signposted Cubeck.

4 Walk uphill to a gate on the left and go on the gated way. An arrow by a telegraph pole directs you to the far-right corner. Pass to the right of the farmhouse and go on ahead to a narrow lane. Turn left and descend the pleasing way to the village of Worton. Cross the A-road with care and go through the quiet hamlet, still descending to a road bridge across the River Ure.

5 Beyond, take the flagged path heading for Askrigg Church visible on the skyline. When the flags cease, go along the distinct path to climb steps to a stile. Bear left and go through a kissing gate. Walk left along the bed of the old railway line, then leave it by the steps to climb a good path up a slope to pass through a gate. Carry on to pass through a small gate beside a farm gate. Then wind left to walk a narrow road, lined with charming cottages. This brings you to the centre of the village and the cobbled parking area.

1 Leave the cobbled parking area and walk left, with the church wall to your left. As you near the end of the dwellings on the left, turn left into a passage to join a paved way over two pastures. Go through a gap stile to join the B-road. Turn right, passing Low Mill Outdoor Centre and the next dwelling. Cross the road to a signposted opening and turn right to walk along the side of the former Wensleydale Railway, where the dog can have some freedom. Go past the former station building, with its platform still intact. Continue on until you reach the

Fact file

Distance: 6.5km (4 miles).
Time: 2 to 3 hours.
Map: Explorer OL30.
Start/parking: Park in the cobbled area outside Askrigg Church; grid ref: 948910. There is a box in the church wall for a donation.
Terrain: Generally easy walking except for the steepish climb up on to the Brough Scar.
Nearest town: Hawes.
Refreshments: Good choice in Askrigg and Bainbridge — pubs and cafes.
Public toilets: At the bottom of the High Street in Askrigg; beside the middle green at Bainbridge.
Public transport: Contact Dales and District, tel. 01677 425203; Traveline, tel. 0870 608 2608, will have all the details.
Stiles: Several gap stiles, wide enough for most dogs.
Suitable for: All the family with lots of freedom for the dog.

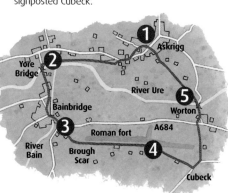

A dog-friendly walk in...
The Brecon Bea

The Brecon Beacons, stretch from Llandeilo in the west to Hay-on-Wye in the east, and is one of three national parks in Wales. This stunning area is a popular destination for visitors who enjoy the freedom and remoteness of the Welsh countryside.

Enjoy the views at Blaen Llia.

Blaen Llia & Sarn Helen

The main sandstone mass of the Brecon Beacons meets a narrow strip of limestone just north of Ystradfellte, on the southern edge of Fforest Fawr (the Great Forest). This open-country walk cuts across these contrasting landscapes on moorland tracks, past a small Iron Age hill fort, and finally along a section of Roman road. **By Evelyne Sansot.**

Along the Roman road with Fan Llia in the background.

Horsey Mill is owned by The National Trust.

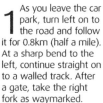

1 As you leave the car park, turn left on to the road and follow it for 0.8km (half a mile). At a sharp bend to the left, continue straight on to a walled track. After a gate, take the right fork as waymarked.

2 After the next gate take the left fork across the pasture, heading for the right of a limestone crag. Pass a derelict limekiln just below the crag and continue along the same path as it makes a curve to the left between the limestone escarpments of Carnau Gwynion. About 200m into the next field, keep along this main track, ignoring another one shooting off to the right.

3 Make an elbow turn to the right in front of the gate in the bottom corner (at an angle between the wall and the track you have just followed). The path is not clearly defined at this point as it cuts across the rough pasture. Keep heading towards some scraggy hawthorn trees in the distance then, as you reach the brink of the field, aim for a small circular wire fence enclosure around a swallow-hole, cross a track and continue straight up the slope to a gate in the wall.

4 Bear left past the remains of an Iron Age hill fort on the crest on your right, suddenly emerging above the valley of Nedd Fechan, with views to the north over some of Fforest Fawr's sandstone summits (from right to left, Fan Nedd and Fan Gyhirych). Go through a gate and walk down several fields along the clearly waymarked footpath to the bottom of the valley.

5 Turn right on to the narrow road and enter Blaen-nedd-Isaf Farm.

Walk past the farmhouse then turn immediately left across the farmyard to walk round the left-hand side of the barn. Cross the river over a footbridge and walk straight up a small wooded area then a pasture.

6 Turn right at the top, on to Sarn Helen, the Roman road, thereby joining the Beacons Way. Cross the river again over a footbridge and continue straight up the other bank, later to pass the Maen Madoc standing stone.

7 Turn right on to the road to rejoin the car park on your left.

Fact file

Distance: 8km (5 miles).
Time: Allow 3 hours.
Map: Explorer OL12 Brecon Beacons National Park, West and Central.
Start/parking: Blaen Llia car park; grid ref: SN927166.
Terrain: Mainly good tracks and footpaths across pastures with gentle ascents and descents.
Nearest towns: Glyn-Neath, Merthyr Tydfil, Brecon.
Refreshments: None.
Public toilets: None.
Public transport: None.
Stiles: None.
Suitable for: All.

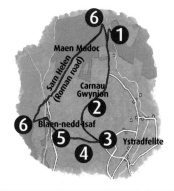

A dog-friendly walk in...
Dartmoor

Dartmoor has wild, dramatic vistas and colourful history steeped in folklore. Famed for its wide open spaces, impressive tors, wooded valleys and wildlife, Dartmoor is a popular destination for visitors.

Okehampton DEVON
Exeter
Tavistock Dartmoor
CORNWALL Torquay
Plymouth

Haytor Rocks

This classic open moorland walk combines terrific views with industrial archaeology. Haytor Rocks form one of Dartmoor's most dramatic granite tors. Granite from the Haytor Quarries was pulled by horse and wagon along Devon's first railway — with its rails hand cut from the rock. Some of the ground is uneven and both a map and a compass are essential. **By Robert Hesketh.**

A rusty winch stands guard of Haytor Quarry.

Haytor Rocks provide excellent walking and wonderful scenery.

The granite tramway — the rails were cut from local granite to serve the quarries.

1 From the car park, follow the broad path up to the summit of Haytor Rocks, an unmistakable serrated granite profile that looks like the toes of a half-buried giant's foot. Walk to the back of this rocky outcrop into a col — a dip between it and the next rocky summit.

2 Take a west north-west bearing and head roughly in the direction of Holwell Tor but somewhat to the west of it. Pick up a rough path that leads downhill through the gorse and heather to a disused quarry, distinguished by its piles of worked and part-worked rock. At the far end of the quarry, turn right on to the granite tramway.

3 Follow the tramway for 1.2km, to a point where it is joined by a spur line on the right. This junction shows the mason's craft to great effect. Follow this spur over a rock embankment and around to the left. Reaching a rocky gully, turn right and follow the rough path on the left of the gully uphill to a small wooden gate.

Continue ahead to visit Haytor Quarries — where your dog can swim in the water-filled pits and a rusty hand crane stands guard.

4 Retrace your steps around the tramline spur and back to the junction. Continue ahead along the tramway for 750m. Bear right on to a minor path through the furze to join the Bovey/Widecombe road by a red phone kiosk. Turn right and follow the verge back to the car park.

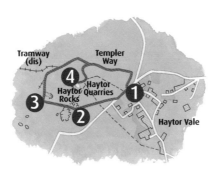

Fact file

Distance: 4.75km (3 miles).
Time: Allow 2 hours.
Maps: Landranger 191, Explorer OL 28 or Harvey's Dartmoor.
Start/parking: Haytor lower car park; grid ref: SX765772.
Terrain: Open moorland, with one steep ascent to start.
Nearest town: Bovey Tracey.
Refreshments: The Rugglestone and the Old Inn at Widecombe both welcome dogs.
Public toilets: At the start.
Public transport: Bus 193 from Newton Abbot, Wednesdays and Fridays only; limited service.
Stiles: None.
Suitable for: Dogs and all the family.

ISBN 13: 9781857334203
Sept 2007   £12.95
(Prev 9789814155014)

ISBN 13: 9781857334128
New   £12.95

ISBN 13: 9781857334173
NEW   £12.95

ISBN 13: 9781857334197
Sept 2007   £12.95

ISBN 13: 9781857334180
Sept 2007   £12.95

ISBN 13: 9781857334
Jan 2008   £1

The chic series are the definitive guides to the world's most luxurious and alluring hotels. The properties featured—whether a city hotel, a beachside resort or a rustic hacienda—have been chosen for their individuality and chic appeal.

Insights into the essence of each property help readers decide on the one that best suits their nee and preferences. A fact-packed panel summarises each hotel's facilities and nearby attractions.

thechicseries

Extraordinary destinations. Incomparable accommodations. Exceptional advice Join discerning travellers who have found everything they desire in the chic serie travel guides: hot properties, stunning photography and brilliant tips on where to g and how to do it in some of the worlds chicest locations.

ISBN 13: 9781857334159   ISBN 13: 9781857334104   ISBN 13: 9781857334081   ISBN 13: 9781857334067   ISBN 13: 9781857334

ISBN 13: 9781857334111   ISBN 13: 9781857334050   ISBN 13: 9781857334098   ISBN 13: 9781857334166   ISBN 13: 978185733

Order any chic guide via the Kuperard website and receive free postage on any quantity of guides. Visit www.kuperard.co.uk to see the full range in the series and type in the following promotional code chic2.
Or call us on 0208 446 2440 and quote the same code.

All titles are paperback priced £12.95

CULTURE SMART ! a quick guide to customs and etiquette

THE SMARTER WAY TO TRAVEL

In China it's rude to be late. In France it's rude to be on time. Never be unpleasant in Thailand, but in Russia, smiling at strangers may be seen as a sign of stupidity. Culture Smart! guides create steps towards understanding the people and instantly enriches your experience abroad.

Books are priced £6.95 and published by Kuperard. Order any Culture Smart! guide via the Kuperard website and receive free postage on any quantity of guides. Visit www.kuperard.co.uk and type in the following promotional code: CSG1, or call us on 0208 446 2440 and quote the same code.

    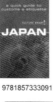 

England and Wales · Counties

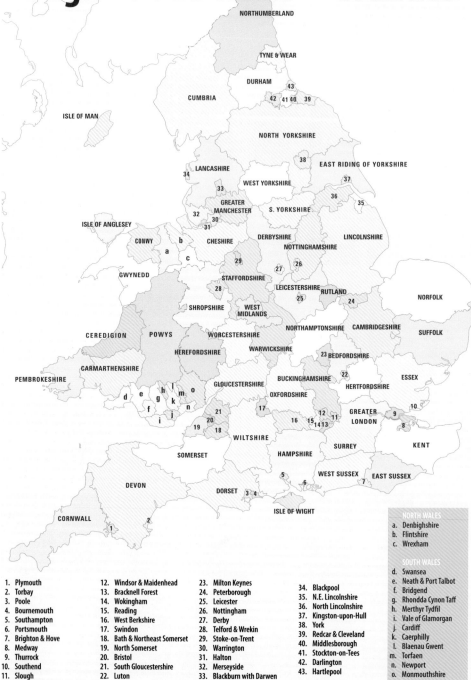

NORTHUMBERLAND

TYNE & WEAR

DURHAM

43

42 41 40 39

CUMBRIA

ISLE OF MAN

NORTH YORKSHIRE

38

LANCASHIRE

34

EAST RIDING OF YORKSHIRE

37

WEST YORKSHIRE

33

36

35

GREATER
MANCHESTER

32

30

S. YORKSHIRE

31

ISLE OF ANGLESEY

CONWY   b

CHESHIRE

DERBYSHIRE

LINCOLNSHIRE

a

c

NOTTINGHAMSHIRE

GWYNEDD

29

STAFFORDSHIRE

27   26

28

LEICESTERSHIRE

RUTLAND

25

24

NORFOLK

SHROPSHIRE

WEST
MIDLANDS

CEREDIGION

POWYS

WORCESTERSHIRE

NORTHAMPTONSHIRE

CAMBRIDGESHIRE

SUFFOLK

HEREFORDSHIRE

WARWICKSHIRE

CARMARTHENSHIRE

23 BEDFORDSHIRE

PEMBROKESHIRE

GLOUCESTERSHIRE

BUCKINGHAMSHIRE

22

ESSEX

d   e   h   l   m   o

HERTFORDSHIRE

g   k

OXFORDSHIRE

f   i   l   n

17

10

j

12   11

GREATER

9

16   15   14 13

LONDON

8

21

20

19   18

WILTSHIRE

SURREY

KENT

SOMERSET

HAMPSHIRE

DEVON

DORSET   3   4

WEST SUSSEX   EAST SUSSEX

5

6

7

ISLE OF WIGHT

CORNWALL

1

2

1. Plymouth	12. Windsor & Maidenhead	23. Milton Keynes	34. Blackpool
2. Torbay	13. Bracknell Forest	24. Peterborough	35. N.E. Lincolnshire
3. Poole	14. Wokingham	25. Leicester	36. North Lincolnshire
4. Bournemouth	15. Reading	26. Nottingham	37. Kingston-upon-Hull
5. Southampton	16. West Berkshire	27. Derby	38. York
6. Portsmouth	17. Swindon	28. Telford & Wrekin	39. Redcar & Cleveland
7. Brighton & Hove	18. Bath & Northeast Somerset	29. Stoke-on-Trent	40. Middlesborough
8. Medway	19. North Somerset	30. Warrington	41. Stockton-on-Tees
9. Thurrock	20. Bristol	31. Halton	42. Darlington
10. Southend	21. South Gloucestershire	32. Merseyside	43. Hartlepool
11. Slough	22. Luton	33. Blackburn with Darwen	

NORTH WALES
a. Denbighshire
b. Flintshire
c. Wrexham

SOUTH WALES
d. Swansea
e. Neath & Port Talbot
f. Bridgend
g. Rhondda Cynon Taff
h. Merthyr Tydfil
i. Vale of Glamorgan
j. Cardiff
k. Caerphilly
l. Blaenau Gwent
m. Torfaen
n. Newport
o. Monmouthshire

England

Ratings & Awards

For the first time ever the AA, VisitBritain, VisitScotland, and the Wales Tourist Board will use a single method of assessing and rating serviced accommodation. Irrespective of which organisation inspects an establishment the rating awarded will be the same, using a common set of standards, giving a clear guide of what to expect. The RAC is no longer operating an Hotel inspection and accreditation business.

Accommodation Standards: Star Grading Scheme

Using a scale of 1-5 stars the objective quality ratings give a clear indication of accommodation standard, cleanliness, ambience, hospitality, service and food, This shows the full range of standards suitable for every budget and preference, and allows visitors to distinguish between the quality of accommodation and facilities on offer in different establishments. All types of board and self-catering accommodation are covered, including hotels,
B&Bs, holiday parks, campus accommodation, hostels, caravans and camping, and boats.

The more stars, the higher level of quality

★★★★★
exceptional quality, with a degree of luxury

★★★★
excellent standard throughout

★★★
very good level of quality and comfort

★★
good quality, well presented and well run

★
acceptable quality; simple, practical, no frills

VisitBritain and the regional tourist boards, enjoyEngland.com, VisitScotland and VisitWales, and the AA have full details of the grading system on their websites

National Accessible Scheme

If you have particular mobility, visual or hearing needs, look out for the National Accessible Scheme. You can be confident of finding accommodation or attractions that meet your needs by looking for the following symbols.

 Typically suitable for a person with sufficient mobility to climb a flight of steps but would benefit from fixtures and fittings to aid balance

 Typically suitable for a person with restricted walking ability and for those that may need to use a wheelchair some of the time and can negotiate a maximum of three steps

 Typically suitable for a person who depends on the use of a wheelchair and transfers unaided to and from the wheelchair in a seated position. This person may be an independent traveller

 Typically suitable for a person who depends on the use of a wheelchair in a seated position. This person also requires personal or mechanical assistance (eg carer, hoist).

Visit the FHG website
www.holidayguides.com
for details of the wide choice of accommodation
featured in the full range of FHG titles

COTTAGE IN THE COUNTRY COTTAGE HOLIDAYS (01608 646833; Fax: 01608 646844). Lovely locations with superb walks in some of England's most picturesque countryside. We'll do our best to find the right place for you to call 'home'!
e-mail: enquiries@cottageinthecountry.co.uk   website: www.cottageinthecountry.co.uk

HOSEASONS. Tailwagging holidays at over 200 locations where your pet is as welcome as you are. Pine lodges surrounded by picturesque countryside. Or seaside holiday parks with miles of coastline to explore. Mid-week and weekend short breaks available. Many open all year round. Call for your free brochure on 0870 900 9011 Quote H0031 or book on-line.
website: www.hoseasons.co.uk

CAMPING & CARAVANNING CLUB (0845 130 7632). Visit one of our award-winning UK Club Sites. Our sites have dog walking areas for you and your dog to explore. A friendly welcome will be given to you and your pet on our sites, joining is great value for money. QUOTE REF NO 0716
website: www.campingandcaravanningclub.co.uk

THE INDEPENDENT TRAVELLER, FORD COTTAGE, THORVERTON, EXETER EX5 5NT (01392 860807 Fax: 01392 860552). For a wide choice of cottages and apartments throughout England, Scotland & the Isles. Pets welcome in many properties. Quality Cottages in coastal, country and mountain location. Property finding service.
e-mail: help@gowithit.co.uk   website: www.gowithit.co.uk

Go BLUE RIBAND for quality inexpensive self-catering holidays where your dog is welcome – choice of locations all in the borough of Great Yarmouth. Detached 3 bedroom bungalows, seafront bungalows, detached Sea-Dell chalets and modern sea front caravans. Free colour brochure: DON WITHERIDGE, BLUE RIBAND HOUSE, PARKLANDS, HEMSBY, GREAT YARMOUTH NR29 4HA (01493 730445). [pw! First pet free when booking through Pets Welcome!, 2nd pet £10 per week].
website: www.BlueRibandHolidays.co.uk

MR P.W. REES, "QUALITY COTTAGES', CERBID, SOLVA, HAVERFORDWEST, PEMBROKESHIRE SA62 6YE (01348 837871). Cottages set in all coastal areas, unashamed luxury, highest residential standards. Dishwashers, microwaves, washing machines. Log fires. Linen supplied. Pets welcome. [pw! 🐕]
website: www.qualitycottages.co.uk

DALES HOLIDAY COTTAGES. Over 500 personally inspected cottages in sublime locations anywhere from the Yorkshire Dales to the Highlands of Scotland. For couples, groups and families. Full of character, near great walks and country pubs, just right for pets. Call 0870 909 9500 or visit our website.
website: www.dalesholcot.com

THE FOUR SEASONS HOTEL, ST FILLANS PH6 2NF (01764 685333). Ideal holiday venue for pets and their owners. Spectacular Highland scenery, walking, fishing, watersports. Wonderful food. Full details on request. STB ★★★ Hotel, AA ★★★ and 2 Red Rosettes, Which? Hotel Guide, Johansens, Best Loved Hotels. [🐕]
e-mail: sham@thefourseasonshotel.co.uk   website: www.thefourseasonshotel.co.uk

THE WHITE POST FARM PET & REPTILE CENTRE, FARNSFIELD NG22 8HL (01623 882977). Everything you will need to keep your pet happy and healthy. Plus – The Pet & Reptile Hotel – providing peace of mind and the best care for your pet. Call 01623 883312. Open from 10am daily
website: www.whitepostfarmcentre.co.uk

Please note

All the information in this book is given in good faith in the belief that it is correct. However, the publishers cannot guarantee the facts given in these pages, neither are they responsible for changes in policy, ownership or terms that may take place after the date of going to press. Readers should always satisfy themselves that the facilities they require are available and that the terms, if quoted, still apply.

Cornwall

Cornwall receives most of its visitors over the summer months, exploring the beautiful beaches and indulging in the exceptional clotted cream teas - but the county has much to offer besides the Cornish pastie and the traditional bucket and spade holiday. The "shoulder" and winter months offer opportunities for the discerning visitor which may go unnoticed in the annual stampede to the beaches. There are villages boasting curious and ancient names - Come To Good, Ting Tang, London Apprentice and Indian Queens, often sporting parish churches, ancient graveyards and distinctive crosses which reveal their early Christian history. Wayside crosses, holy wells and Celtic stone circles are reminders that the Cornish are true Celts - it was they who embossed the headlands with cliff forts to repel marauders. To discover more about life in the Iron Age there are numerous settlements to visit, for example Castle an Dinas, one of the largest preserved hill forts in Cornwall. Alternatively Chysauster Ancient Village is a deserted Roman village comprising eight well-preserved houses around an open court. More up-to-date is St Michael's Mount with its 14th century castle, or Prideaux Place, a stunning Elizabethan House, and Lanhydrock, the National Trust's most visited property in Cornwall, which was once the residence of a local family whose wealth came from tin mining.

Bude, Crackington Haven

Falmouth

FHG Guides

publish a large range of well-known accommodation guides.
We will be happy to send you details or you can use the order form
at the back of this book.

Visit the FHG website
www.holidayguides.com
for details of the wide choice of accommodation
featured in
the full range of FHG titles

Fowey, Helston, Launceston, Liskeard

Liskeard, The Lizard

Looe

Looe, Manaccan, Mevagissey, Mousehole

POLPERRO

Affectionately let for 30 years for good old-fashioned family holidays, as well as for friends and couples to enjoy, where pets and children are most welcome.

VIEW FROM THE PROPERTIES

Comfortable holiday cottages, built around 250 years ago, full of character and charm, sleeping from 2 -14, with sunny terraced gardens, giving a Mediterranean-type setting.

Definitely located in one of the best positions in the village, directly overlooking picturesque harbour, of 16th century origins with smuggling connections, now a conservation area. 14 miles breathtaking panoramic sea views, stretching to Eddystone Lighthouse, with naval shipping, ocean-going yachts, local fishing boats and pleasure craft often forming part of the seascape.

The cottages are only 2 minutes from shops, excellent selection of quality restaurants, tearooms, olde-worlde pubs and the availability of Cornish pasties, ice cream and fish and chips. Close by, there is a small, sandy beach with rock pools, quay, pier and rock fishing and the beginning of miles of unspoilt National Trust cliff walks along stunning coastal paths of outstanding natural beauty, leading to outlying hamlets, with rocky inlets, beaches, coves and 13th century churches. Between Looe and Fowey, on South Cornish coast, 25 miles city of Plymouth, 12 miles A38 and 15 miles Eden Project.

Prices from £175-£575 per cottage, per week.

• PETS COME FREE • PRIVATE PARKING FREE
For brochure, please telephone **GRAHAM WRIGHTS OFFICES** **01579 344080**

Near Perranporth

Greenmeadow Cottages

Highly praised luxury cottages. Sleep 6. Superbly clean, comfortable and spacious. Open all year. Short Breaks out of season. Pets welcome in two of the cottages. Non-smoking available. Ample off-road parking.
For brochure and bookings

Tel: 01872 540483

Visit the FHG website
www.holidayguides.com
for details of the wide choice of accommodation

featured in

the full range of FHG titles

Port Isaac, Portreath, Portscatho, Portwrinkle

Portwrinkle, St Agnes

Please note

All the information in this book is given in good faith in the belief that it is correct. However, the publishers cannot guarantee the facts given in these pages, neither are they responsible for changes in policy, ownership or terms that may take place after the date of going to press. Readers should always satisfy themselves that the facilities they require are available and that the terms, if quoted, still apply.

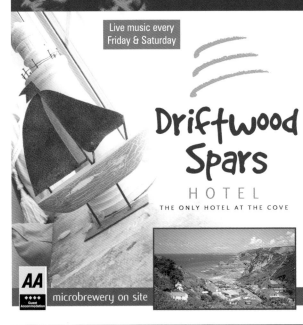

St Ives, St Mawes. St Tudy

Pet-Friendly
Pubs, Inns & Hotels
on pages 360-369

Please note that these establishments may not feature in the main section of this book

FHG Guides

publish a large range of well-known accommodation guides.

We will be happy to send you details or you can use the order form

at the back of this book.

Dalswinton

A Victorian stone-built house standing in 10 acres of gardens and meadowland in the glorious Vale of Lanherne, midway between Padstow and Newquay. Overlooking the village of St Mawgan, with views to the sea at Mawgan Porth, Dalswinton offers a warm welcome, friendly atmosphere, and great food prepared with fresh local produce.

We are totally non-smoking, and are not suitable for children under 16.

- Dogs free of charge and allowed everywhere except the restaurant
- 8 acres of private meadowland for dog exercise
- Dog-friendly beach 1.5 miles
- Bed & Breakfast from £39.00 per person per night
- Weekly rates available. Special offers Oct/Mar/Apr.
- Heated outdoor pool (in season). Car parking
- All rooms en suite, with tea/coffee making facilities, colour TV and radio
- Residents' bar, and restaurant serving breakfast and 3-course dinner
- Self-catering Garden Lodge (sleeps 3 adults)
- Easy access to Newquay Airport, Padstow and the Eden Project

Proprietors: Stuart and Sal Hope
Dalswinton House, St Mawgan-in-Pydar, Cornwall TR8 4EZ

Tel: 01637 860385

Visit us at www.dalswinton.com   e-mail: dalswintonhouse@tiscali.co.uk

Publisher's note

While every effort is made to ensure accuracy, we regret that FHG Guides cannot accept responsibility for errors, misrepresentations or omissions in our entries or any consequences thereof. Prices in particular should be checked.

We will follow up complaints but cannot act as arbiters or agents for either party.

CLASSY COTTAGES – Spectacular cottages feet from beach. Isolated residence on coast, isolated garden cottage. Open log fires. Dog-friendly beaches. Access to indoor swimming pool, gym and tennis courts. Local pubs serving good food, and allowing dogs. Contact FIONA & MARTIN NICOLLE (07000 423000). [pw! Pets £12 per week]
e-mail: nicolle@classycottages.co.uk   website: www.classycottages.co.uk

TOAD HALL COTTAGES (01548 853089 24 hrs). 300 outstanding waterside and rural properties in truly beautiful locations in Devon, Cornwall and Exmoor. Call for our highly acclaimed brochure. Pets welcome.
e-mail: thc@toadhallcottages.co.uk   website: www.toadhallcottages.co.uk

A fine selection of Self-catering and similar Cottages on both coasts of Cornwall and on Scilly. Pets welcome in many cottages. Free colour brochure from: CORNISH TRADITIONAL COTTAGES, BLISLAND, BODMIN PL30 4HS (01208 821666; Fax: 01208 821766). [Pets £16 per week]
website: www.corncott.com

WEST CORNWALL COTTAGE HOLIDAYS, 4 ALBERT STREET, PENZANCE TR18 2LR (01736 368575). Coastal and country cottages, town houses and apartments. Pets with well behaved owners welcome in many of our properties. [Charge for pets.]
website: www.westcornwallcottageholidays.com

CORNISH SEAVIEW COTTAGES (01428 723819). Ideal for walking coastal paths and accessing beaches. Pets welcome at most. Furnished and equipped to high standard; all have central heating, dishwashers etc and enclosed gardens. Visit our website for photos and virtual tours. [Pets £20 per week].
e-mail: enquiries@cornishseaviewcottages.co.uk   website: www.cornishseaviewcottages.co.uk

TRENCREEK FARM COUNTRY HOLIDAY PARK, HEWAS WATER, ST AUSTELL (01726 882540). Pet-friendly holidays in Cornwall. Luxury lodge, caravan and bungalow accommodation. Motorhome, tourer and tent pitches. Fishing lakes, farm animals, swimming pool and hot tubs. Call for your FREE brochure. ETC ★★★, David Bellamy Silver Award.[pw! Pets from £1 per night touring; £2 per night accommodation]
website: www.surfbayholidays.co.uk

Bodmin

Quaint county town of Cornwall, standing steeply on the edge of Bodmin Moor. Pretty market town and touring centre. Plymouth 31 miles, Newquay 20, Wadebridge 7.

PENROSE BURDEN, ST BREWARD, BODMIN PL30 4LZ (01208 850277 & 850617; Fax: 01208 850915). Holiday Care Award Winning Cottages featured on TV. Open all year. Outstanding views over wooded valley. Free Salmon and Trout fishing. Daily meal service. Superb walking area. Dogs welcome, wheelchair accessible. [Pets £15 per week]
website: www.penroseburden.co.uk

COOMBE MILL, ST BREWARD, BODMIN PL30 4LZ (01208 850344). An idyllic Cornish hamlet of quiet riverside cottages set amidst a glorious 30 acre estate. Gardens, friendly farm animals, tractor rides, play areas, wildlife, fishing lakes and river fishing. Four-posters, log burners, BBQs, home cooking and groceries delivered. Well behaved dogs welcome [pw! Pets £20 per week).
e-mail: mail@coombemill.com   website: www.coombemill.com

Bodmin Moor

Superb walking area attaining a height of 1375 feet at Brown Willy, the highest point in Cornwall.

HENWOOD BARNS HOLIDAY COTTAGES, HENWOOD, LISKEARD PL14 5BP (01579 363576/07956 864263). Three stone barns set around original courtyard on the edge of Bodmin Moor, with stunning views. Tranquil, village location, horse riding two minutes' walk. Woodburning stoves; sleep 2/5; within easy reach of North Cornwall and Devon. [Pets £15 per week]
e-mail: henwoodbarns@tiscali.co.uk   website: www.henwoodbarns.co.uk

Bude

Popular seaside resort overlooking a wide bay of golden sand and flanked by spectacular cliffs. Ideal for surfing; sea water swimming pool for safe bathing.

IVYLEAF BARTON HOLIDAY COTTAGES, NEAR BUDE EX23 9LD. Five cottages sleeping 2-8 in converted stone barns, some with spectacular coastal views. Comfortable, well-equipped with all modern conveniences. Laundry. Tennis court. Certain cottages welcome pets. Contact: ROBERT B BARRETT (01288 321237 or 07771 908108; Fax: 01288 321937). [Pets £16 per week].
e-mail: info@ivyleafbarton.co.uk   website: www.ivyleafbarton.co.uk

LESLEY SHARRATT, SUNRISE, 6 BURN VIEW, BUDE EX23 8BY (01288 353214; Fax: 01288 359911). Beautifully refurbished Victorian house providing stylish and comfortable accommodation, moments' walk from dog friendly beach and downs. Excellent breakfast menu, including vegetarian. B&B from £27. [🐾]
e-mail: sunriseguest@btconnect.com   website: www.sunrise-bude.co.uk

WILLOW VALLEY HOLIDAY PARK, BUSH, BUDE EX23 9LB (01288 353104). Two bedroom lodges equipped to high standard. Colour TV, bathroom, fully equipped kitchen. Two miles from beach and town. Brochure on request. [Pets £15 per week]
e-mail: willowvalley@talk21.com   website: www.willowvalley.co.uk

HEDLEY WOOD CARAVAN & CAMPING PARK, BRIDGERULE, (NR BUDE), HOLSWORTHY EX22 7ED (01288 381404). 16 acre woodland family-run site; children's adventure areas, bar, clubroom, shop, laundry, meals & all amenities. Static caravans for hire, Caravan Storage available. Dog walk nature trail. See main advertisement under Bude. [pw! 🐾]
website: www.hedleywood.co.uk

🐾   Indicates that pets are welcome free of charge.

£   Indicates that a charge is made for pets: nightly or weekly.

pw!   Shows some special provision for pets; exercise facility, feeding or accommodation arrangement.

⌂   Indicates separate pets accommodation.

Symbols

Crackington Haven

Small coastal village in North Cornwall set amidst fine cliff scenery. Small sandy beach, Launceston 18 miles, Bude 10, Camelford 10.

MINESHOP, CRACKINGTON HAVEN, BUDE EX23 0NR. Cornish Character Cottages, sleep 1 to 8, in tranquil location. Footpath leads through fields/woods to beach/pub. Excellent walking, breathtaking scenery. Open all year. Proud to be inspected and featured in The Good Holiday Cottage Guide. For more details phone CHARLIE or JANE (01840 230338). [£15 per pet per week.]
e-mail: tippett@mineshop.freeserve.co.uk   website: www.mineshop.co.uk

Five 18th century converted barns, beamed ceilings, log fires and secluded rural setting. Ideal touring base. Five miles to coast at Crackington Haven. Sleep 2/6. Pets welcome. Open all year. From £80 short breaks, £145 per week. ETC ★★★. APPLY: LORRAINE HARRISON, TRENANNICK COTTAGES, WARBSTOW, LAUNCESTON PL15 8RP (01566 781443). [pw! Pets £10 per stay]
e-mail: trenannick–1@tiscali.co.uk   website: www.trenannickcottages.co.uk

Crafthole

Village near sea at Portwrinkle. Fine views over Whitsand Bay and River Lynner. Golf course nearby. Torpoint 6 miles..

THE LISCAWN INN, CRAFTHOLE, NEAR TORPOINT PL11 3BD (01503 230863). Charming, family-run 14th Century Hotel. Close to Coastal Path in the forgotten corner of Cornwall. En suite accommodation; bar meals available. Open all year. Self-catering suites available. [🐾]
e-mail: enquiries@liscawn.co.uk   website: www.liscawn.co.uk

Crantock

Village near the coast 2miles/3 km SW of Newquay across the River Gannel

CRANTOCK BAY HOTEL, WEST PENTIRE, CRANTOCK TR8 5SE (01637 830229; Fax: 01637 831111). Superbly located for a holiday with your dogs; beach 10 minutes' walk. Comfortable bedrooms, quality restaurant, indoor pool, tennis etc. AA ★★★ [Pets £5 per night]
e-mail: stay@crantockbayhotel.co.uk   website: www.crantockbayhotel.co.uk

Cusgarne (near Truro)

Located four miles east of Redruth.

CUSGARNE (NEAR TRURO), JOYCE & GEORGE CLENCH, SAFFRON MEADOW, CUSGARNE, TRURO TR4 8RW (01872 863171). A cosy, single storey, clean, detached dwelling within grounds of Saffron Meadow. Own enclosed garden, secluded and surrounded by wooded pastureland, five miles west of Truro. [Pets £10 per week]

Falmouth

Well-known port and resort on Fal estuary, ideal for boating, sailing and fishing; safe bathing from sandy beaches. Of interest is Pendennis Castle (18th century). Newquay 26, Penzance 26, Truro 11.

SELF-CATERING BUNGALOW. Sleeps 6. Walking distance of harbour and town. Dogs welcome. For prices and availability contact MRS J.A. SIMMONS (01277 654425) or see our website. ETC ★★★. [Pets £10 per week]
website: www.parklandsbungalow.co.uk

PENMORVAH MANOR HOTEL & COURTYARD COTTAGES, BUDOCK WATER, NEAR FALMOUTH TR11 5ED (01326 250277; Fax: 01326 250509). Situated in 6 acres of mature gardens and woodland. Ideal for visiting Cornwall's superb gardens.Close to Falmouth and Coastal Paths. Well behaved dogs welcome. AA ★★★ Hotel, ETC ★★★★ Self-catering. [Pets £7.50 per night.]
e-mail: reception@penmorvah.co.uk   website: www.penmorvah.co.uk

PETER WATSON, CREEKSIDE HOLIDAY HOUSES, RESTRONGUET, FALMOUTH TR11 5ST (01326 372722). Spacious houses sleep 2/4/6/8. Peaceful, picturesque water's edge hamlet. Boating facilities. Use of boat. Own quay, beach. Secluded gardens. Near Pandora Inn. Friday bookings. Dogs welcome. [Pets £15 per week]
website: www.creeksideholidayhouses.co.uk

CREEKSIDE COTTAGES offer a fine selection of individual water's edge, village and rural cottages, sleeping from 2-10. All offer peaceful, comfortable and fully equipped accommodation. Just come and relax. For a colour brochure phone 01326 375972. [Pets £20 per week]
website: www.creeksidecottages.co.uk

Fowey

Historic town, now a busy harbour, Regatta and Carnival Week in August.

OLD FERRY INN, BODINNICK-BY-FOWEY PL23 1LX (01726 870237; Fax: 01726 870116). Family-run Inn, ideal for many varied walks. Excellent à la carte restaurant; bar meals available. Comfortable bedrooms with colour TV and tea/coffee. Rate £70-£95 per night for two people sharing. ETC ★★★ [Pets £3 per night per pet]
e-mail: royce972@aol.com   website: www.oldferryinn.com

Helston

Ancient Stannary town and excellent touring centre, noted for the annual "Furry Dance". Nearby is Looe Pool, separated from the sea by a bar. Truro 17 miles, St Ives 15, Redruth 11, Falmouth & Penzance 12.

BOSCREGE CARAVAN & CAMPING PARK, ASHTON, HELSTON TR13 9TG (01736 762231) Award-winning, quiet, family park close to beaches and attractions. No bar or clubs. Laundry. Static vans available. Pets welcome. AA Three Pennants. [🐾]
e-mail: enquiries@caravanparkcornwall.com   website: www.caravanparkcornwall.com

Launceston

On A30 about 1 mile from Cornwall/Devon border. The "Ancient Capital" and acknowledged as "The Gateway to Cornwall".

SWALLOWS & MEADOW COTTAGE. Well equipped cottages with field to the rear. Riverside walks. TV lounge and kitchen. Centrally located for visiting NT houses and gardens, Dartmoor, Bodmin Moor, beaches and harbours. Pets welcome by arrangement. ETC ★★★. Contact: LOWER DUTSON FARM, LAUNCESTON PL15 9SP (01566 776456).
e-mail: holidays@farm-cottage.co.uk   website: www.farm-cottage.co.uk

Liskeard

Pleasant market town and good centre for exploring East Cornwall. Bodmin Moor and the quaint fishing villages of Looe and Polperro are near at hand. Plymouth 19 miles, St Austell 19 miles, Launceston 16, Fowey (via ferry) 15, Bodmin 13, Looe 9.

LINDA & NEIL HOSKEN, HOPSLAND HOLIDAYS, HOPSLAND COMMONMOOR, LISKEARD, CORNWALL PL14 6EJ (Tel & Fax: 01579 344480). Hi, I'm Ki, an adorable border collie. Come and stay with your pets at my converted barn cottages. Fully equipped, all with DVD. Own field to exercise in or 150 yards from open moorland. ETC ★★★★ [pw! 🐾]
e-mail: hopslandholidays@aol.com   website: www.hopslandholidays.co.uk

BUTTERDON MILL HOLIDAY HOMES, MERRYMEET, LISKEARD PL14 3LS (01579 342636) Two-bedroom detached bungalows on idyllic rural site. Sleep up to six. Games barn; children's play areas. Ideal for touring coasts & moors. Discounts for Senior Citizens/couples Sept to June. Brochure available. [🐾]
e-mail: butterdonmill@btconnect.com

MICHELE & STEVE HORE, HAYLOFT COURTYARD COTTAGES, MENHENIOT, LISKEARD (01503 240879). Family-run cottages with many home-from-home comforts including jacuzzi bathrooms in most cottages. Excellent touring base. Restaurant on-site and meal delivery service. Children's play area. ETC ★★★★ [Pets £20 per week].
e-mail: courtyardcottage@btconnect.com   website: www.hayloftcourtyardcottages.com

CUTKIVE WOOD HOLIDAY LODGES, ST IVE, LISKEARD PL14 3ND (01579 362216). Six well-equipped cedar-clad lodges on country estate with wonderful views. Great for children, dogs welcome. Ideal for coasts, beaches, moors etc. Short breaks. Open all year. [pw! Pets £10 per week]
e-mail: holidays@cutkivewood.co.uk   website: www.cutkivewood.co.uk

CELIA HUTCHINSON, CARADON COUNTRY COTTAGES, EAST TAPHOUSE, NEAR LISKEARD PL14 4NH (Tel & Fax: 01579 320355). Luxury cottages in the heart of the Cornish countryside. Ideal centre for exploring Devon and Cornwall, coast and moor and Eden Project. Meadow and paddock (enclosed). Central heating and log burners for cosy off-season breaks. [pw! Pets £10 per week.]
e-mail: celia@caradoncottages.co.uk   website: www.caradoncottages.co.uk

Lizard

The most southerly point in England, with fine coastal scenery and secluded coves. Sandy beach at Housel Bay. Truro 28 miles, Helston 11.

MULLION COVE HOTEL, MULLION COVE, THE LIZARD TR12 7EP (01326 240328). Located on the Cornish Coastal Path in a spectacular position on the Lizard Peninsula. Stunning country and coastal walks. Dog-friendly lounge, comfortable bedrooms, excellent food. [Pets £5 per night]
e-mail: enquiries@mullion-cove.co.uk   website: www.mullion-cove.co.uk

MULLION HOLIDAY PARK, WESTSTAR HOLIDAYS (0870 444 0080). Award-winning holiday park near Helston in an Area of Outstanding Natural Beauty, close to safe sandy beaches. Dogs welcome! Quote WP. ETC ★★★★ [pw! Pets £35 per week]
website: www.weststarholidays.co.uk/pw

Longrock

Hamlet to the east of Penzance. Submerged forest to the east.

MRS DOREEN CAPPER, MOUNT VIEW HOTEL, LONGROCK, PENZANCE TR20 8JJ (01736 710416) A family-run pub with comfortable accommodation, situated 100 yards from Mount's Bay in Longrock village. Three en suite rooms and two with shared bathroom. Breakfast in dining room, lunch and dinner available. Dogs welcome by arrangement. Prices from £20 pppn. [🐾]

Looe

Twin towns linked by a bridge over the River Looe. Capital of the shark fishing industry; nearby Monkey Sanctuary is well worth a visit.

TREMAINE GREEN COUNTRY COTTAGES, PELYNT, NEAR LOOE PL13 2LT (01503 220333). A beautiful hamlet of 11 award-winning traditional cosy craftsmen's cottages. Clean, comfortable and well equipped. Set in award-winning grounds with country/coastal walks and The Eden Project nearby. [pw! Pets £18 per week]
e-mail: stay@tremainegreen.co.uk   website: www.tremainegreen.co.uk

LOOE BAY HOLIDAY PARK, WESTSTAR HOLIDAYS (0870 444 0080). Award-winning holiday park near Looe in an Area of Outstanding Natural Beauty, close to safe sandy beaches. Dogs welcome! Quote WP ETC ★★★★ David Bellamy Conservation Award. [pw! Pets £35 per week].
website: www.weststarholidays.co.uk/pw

COLDRINNICK COTTAGES, DULOE, NEAR LOOE. Attractively converted barns set in large secluded gardens. Excellent locality for walking and relaxing. Sleeps 2/6 people. Ideal place for families and dogs alike. ETC ★★★★. For a brochure contact BILL AND KAYE CHAPMAN, COLDRINNICK FARM, DULOE, LISKEARD PL14 4QF (01503 220251). [Pets £15 per week, pw!].
website: www.cornishcottage.net

FOX VALLEY COTTAGES, LANLAWREN, TRENEWAN, LOOE PL13 2PZ (01726 870115). Set in beautiful countryside, just three miles from Polperro. Indoor heated pool and spa. Open all year round. Field for dogs to run around. Contact ANDY & LINDA for details. [pw! Pets £20 per week]
e-mail: lanlawrenfarm@lycos.com   website: www.foxvalleycottages.co.uk

NEAR LOOE. In the picturesque Cornish fishing village of Polperro, comfortable, charming holiday cottages, sleeping 2-14, with terraced gardens and private parking, affectionately let for 30 years for family holidays, as well as for friends and couples to enjoy. Definitely located in one of the best positions in the village, directly overlooking 16th century harbour, with 14 miles breathtaking panoramic sea views. 2 minutes shops, excellent selection quality restaurants, tearooms, olde worlde pubs. Close by sandy beaches, quay, pier and rock fishing, miles of unspoilt National Trust cliff walks, along stunning coastal paths. Located between Looe and Fowey, on the South Cornish coast, 25 miles city of Plymouth, 12 miles main A38 and about 15 miles Eden Project and Lost Gardens of Heligan. Prices from £175-£575 per cottage, per week. Pets come free. For brochure, please telephone Graham Wrights offices (01579 344080). [🐕]

VALLEYBROOK, PEAKSWATER, LANSALLOS, LOOE PL13 2QE. Peaceful nine acre site with six superb villas and two delightful cottages, all dog friendly. Individual fenced gardens, dog walks, dog friendly beaches nearby. Short breaks. Open all year. 2 dogs max. ETC ★★★/★★★★. Contact DENISE, KEITH or BRIAN HOLDER (01503 220493). [pw! Pets £2 per night] website: www.valleybrookholidays.com

MARTIN AND WENDY WELCH, PENQUITE COUNTRY COTTAGES, DULOE, NEAR LISKEARD PL14 4QG (01503 220260). Four spacious one-bedroom barn conversions within easy reach of coast and moors. Well behaved dogs most welcome. No children.[Pets £15 per week] e-mail:stay@penquitecountrycottages.co.uk   website: www.penquitecountrycottages.co.uk

Idyllic 18th century country cottages for romantics and animal lovers. Looe three miles. Wonderful walks from your gate. Cottages warm and cosy in winter. Personal attention and colour brochure from: B. WRIGHT, TREWORGEY COTTAGES, DULOE, LISKEARD PL14 4PP (01503 262730). VisitBritain ★★★★★ Quality Assurance Scheme. [Pets £20.50 per week.] website: www.cornishdreamcottages.co.uk

WRINGWORTHY COTTAGES, LOOE (01503 240685). 8 traditional stone cottages set in 4 peaceful acres offer you and your pet space for the perfect break. A friendly welcome awaits in our fully equipped, centrally heated cottages, sleeping 2-8. Linen included, walks from our door and more! ETC ★★★★, Green Acorn Award. [First pet free, additional pets £18 per week] e-mail: pets@wringworthy.co.uk   website: www.wringworthy.co.uk

NEIL AND THERESA DENNETT, TALEHAY HOLIDAY COTTAGES, PELYNT, NEAR LOOE PL13 2LT (Tel & Fax: 01503 220252). Cosy, traditional cottages set in four acres of unspoilt countryside offering peace and tranquillity. Breathtaking coastal and country walks. An ideal location for dogs and their owners. Non-smoking. Close to the Eden Project. ETC ★★★ [Pets £3 per night, £15 per week] e-mail: infobookings@talehay.co.uk   website: www.talehay.co.uk

O. SLAUGHTER, TREFANNY HILL, DULOE, NEAR LISKEARD PL14 4QF (01503 220622). Nestling on a south-facing hillside, near coast. Delicious food. Heated pool, tennis, badminton, lake, shire horses. Enchanting 70 acre estate with bluebell wood, walking and wildlife. e-mail: enq@trefanny.co.uk   website: www.trefanny.co.uk

MRS BARBIE HIGGINS, TREWITH HOLIDAY COTTAGES, TREWITH, DULOE PL14 4PR (01503 262184; mobile: 07968 262184). Four refurbished cottages in peaceful location with panoramic views near Looe. Fully equipped, 1-3 bedrooms, tastefully furnished. Full central heating. Well behaved dogs welcome. [Pets from £15 per week] e-mail: holiday-cottages@trewith.freeserve.co.uk   website: www.trewith.freeserve.co.uk

BADHAM FARM, ST KEYNE, LISKEARD PL14 4RW (01579 343572). Farmhouse and farm buildings converted to a high standard. Sleep 2-10. All well furnished/equipped; prices include electricity, bed linen and towels. Well behaved dogs welcome (not in high season). Prices from £120 per week. ETC ★★★★ [Pets £4 per night, £20 per week]. e-mail: badhamfarm@yahoo.co.uk   website: www.badhamfarm.co.uk

www.holidayguides.com

Manaccan

Village 7 miles east of Helston.

Enchanting creekside cottages in a timeless and tranquil hamlet. Stunning coastal and riverside walks, country inns, local food, warm and comfortable with cosy log fires. Boat hire, moorings. Short breaks. Open all year. ST ANTHONY HOLIDAYS, MANACCAN, HELSTON TR12 6JW (01326 231 357). [Pets £3 per night, £21 per week].
e-mail: info@stanthony.co.uk   website: www.StAnthony.co.uk

Mevagissey

Central for touring and walking. Eden project nearby.

MRS M.R. BULLED, MENAGWINS, GORRAN PL26 6HP (MEVAGISSEY 01726 843517). Traditional cottage, sleeps two to five. Linen, towels, electricity supplied. Beach one mile. Large garden. Central for touring/walking. Near Eden Project and Heligan Gardens. Pets welcome. [🐶]

Mousehole

Picturesque fishing village with sand and shingle beach. Penzance 3 miles.

POLVELLAN HOLIDAY FLAT. In Mousehole, a quaint and unspoilt fishing village, a fully equipped self-catering flat with full sea views. Sleeps two. Microwave, cooker, fridge, TV, all bedding and towels provided. Open all year. Apply: MR A.G. WRIGHT, 164 PORTLAND ROAD, SELSTON, NOTTINGHAM NG16 6AN (01773 775347) [🐶]
e-mail: alang23@hotmail.com

Newquay

Popular family holiday resort surrounded by miles of golden beaches. Semi-tropical gardens, zoo and museum. Ideal for exploring all of Cornwall.

MRS DEWOLFREYS, DEWOLF GUEST HOUSE, 100 HENVER ROAD, NEWQUAY TR7 3BL (01637 874746). Single, double or family rooms, two chalets in rear garden. All rooms non-smoking with en suite facilities, colour TV and tea/coffee making facilities. Ideal for pets. AA ★★★★[🐶]
e-mail: holidays@dewolfguesthouse.com   website: www.dewolfguesthouse.com

RETORRICK MILL, ST MAWGAN, NEWQUAY TR8 4BH (01637 860460). Set in 11 acres, self-catering Retorrick Mill has two cottages and six chalets, all very well equipped. Pets including horses very welcome. For a brochure or further assistance contact Chris Williams.
website: www.retorrickmill.co.uk

TRETHIGGEY TOURING PARK, QUINTRELL DOWNS, NEWQUAY TR8 4QR (01637 877672). Friendly, family-run park minutes from surfing beaches. Touring caravans, tent and campervans welcome. Luxury holiday homes for hire. Shop, off-licence, free showers, electric hook-ups, laundry, children's play area, TV/games room, fishing, cafe and take-away food in summer. ETC ★★★★
e-mail: enquiries@trethiggey.co.uk   website: www.Trethiggey.co.uk

QUARRYFIELD CARAVAN & CAMPING PARK, CRANTOCK, NEWQUAY. Fully equipped modern caravans overlooking beautiful Crantock Bay. Separate camping field. Bar, pool, children's play area. Contact: MRS WINN, TRETHERRAS, NEWQUAY TR7 2RE (Tel & Fax: 01637 872792). [Pets £1.50 per night (camping only); £10 per week camping, £20 per week in caravan]

Padstow

Bright little resort with pretty harbour on Camel estuary. Extensive sands. Nearby is Elizabethan Prideaux Place. Newquay 15 miles, Wadebridge 8.

place descriptionRAINTREE HOUSE HOLIDAYS, WHISTLERS, TREYARNON BAY, PADSTOW PL28 8JR (01841 520228). We have a varied selection of accommodation. Small or large, houses and apartments, some by the sea. All in easy reach of our lovely beaches. Please write or phone for brochure.   [🐶]
e-mail: gill@raintreehouse.co.uk   website: www.raintreehouse.co.uk

Penzance

Well-known resort and port for Scilly Isles, with sand and shingle beaches. Truro 27 miles, Helston 13, Land's End 10, St Ives 8.

THE ABBEY HOTEL, ABBEY STREET, PENZANCE TR18 4AR (01736 366906). Situated in the heart of Penzance, with walled garden, courtyard and many period features providing characterful accommodation. Quiet and relaxed atmosphere. [🐎]
e-mail: hotel@theabbeyonline.com   website: www.theabbeyonline.co.uk

TORWOOD HOUSE HOTEL, ALEXANDRA ROAD, PENZANCE TR18 4LZ. Torwood is a small, family-run hotel, situated in a beautiful tree-lined avenue 500 metres from the seafront. All rooms en suite, with TV/DVD, tea/coffee makers and radios. Dinner available on request. For further details telephone LYNDA SOWERBY on 01736 360063.
e-mail: Lyndasowerby@aol.com   website: www.torwoodhousehotel.co.uk

Perranporth

North coast resort 6 miles south-west of Newquay.

GREENMEADOW COTTAGES, NEAR PERRANPORTH. Spacious, clean luxury cottages. Sleep six. Open all year. Short breaks out of season. Non-smoking available. Ample off road parking. Pets welcome in two of the cottages. For brochure and bookings tel: 01872 540483.

Polperro

Picturesque and quaint little fishing village and harbour. Of interest is the "House of the Props". Fowey 9 miles, Looe 5..

POLPERRO. In the picturesque Cornish fishing village of Polperro, comfortable, charming holiday cottages, sleeping 2-14, with terraced gardens and private parking, affectionately let for 30 years for family holidays, as well as for friends and couples to enjoy. Definitely located in one of the best positions in the village, directly overlooking 16th century harbour, with 14 miles breathtaking panoramic sea views. 2 minutes shops, excellent selection quality restaurants, tearooms, olde worlde pubs. Close by sandy beaches, quay, pier and rock fishing, miles of unspoilt National Trust cliff walks, along stunning coastal paths. Located between Looe and Fowey, on the South Cornish coast, 25 miles city of Plymouth, 12 miles main A38 and about 15 miles Eden Project and Lost Gardens of Heligan. Prices from £175-£575 per cottage, per week. Pets come free. For brochure, please telephone Graham Wrights offices (01579 344080). [🐎]

Visit the FHG website
www.holidayguides.com
for details of the wide choice of accommodation
featured in the full range of FHG titles

FHG Guides
publish a large range of well-known accommodation guides.
We will be happy to send you details or you can use the order form
at the back of this book.

Port Gaverne

Hamlet on east side of Port Isaac, near Camel Estuary.

GREEN DOOR COTTAGES. PORT GAVERNE. A delightful collection of 18C Cornish buildings built around a sunny enclosed courtyard, and 2 lovely apartments with stunning sea views. Situated in a picturesque, tranquil cove ideal for children. Dogs allowed on the beach year round. Half a mile from Port Isaac, on the Cornish Coastal Path. Traditional pub directly opposite. ETC ★★★/★★★★
For brochure: (01208 880293) [🐕]
e-mail: enquiries@gFages.co.uk   website: www.greendoorcottages.co.uk

Homes from home around our peaceful courtyard garden 100 yards from sea in bygone fishing hamlet. Each sleeps six and has full CH, fridge/freezer, washer/dryer, dishwasher, microwave, DVD, video, computer and broadband. £200 (February), £760 (August) weekly. Resident owner. APPLY:- MALCOLM LEE, GULLROCK, PORT GAVERNE, PORT ISAAC PL29 3SQ (01208 880106). [🐕]
e-mail: gullrock@ukonline.co.uk

Porthleven

Small town with surprisingly big harbour. Grand woodland walks. 2 miles SW of Helston.

PORTHLEVEN, KERNOW COTTAGES. Fishermen's cottages. Harbour, bay or country views. 3 minutes to beach, coast path, harbourside eating places. Open fires. Pets welcome. Please contact: MRS KERNO (01209 860410). [Pets £20 per week]

Port Isaac

Attractive fishing village with harbour. Much of the attractive coastline is protected by the National Trust. Camelford 9 miles. Wadebridge 9.

LONG CROSS HOTEL & VICTORIAN GARDENS, TRELIGHTS, PORT ISAAC PL29 3TF (01208 880243). Lovely Victorian country house hotel with four acres of restored gardenst. Close to the area's best beaches, golf courses and other attractions. Newly refurbished en suite bedrooms and suites. [Pets £5.00 per night.]
website: www.portisaac.com

PORT GAVERNE HOTEL NEAR PORT ISAAC PL29 3SQ (01208 880244; Fax: 01208 880151). Renowned 17th century inn in an unspoilt fishing cove on the rugged North Coast of Cornwall. Beach just 50 yards away. Pets welcome. Self-catering accommodation available. [Pets £3.50 per night].

Portreath

Coastal village 4 miles north west of Redruth.

Charming, elegantly furnished, self-catering cottages between Newquay and St Ives. Sleep 2 to 6. Fully equipped including linen. Beautiful beaches. Laundry and games room. Ample parking. Colour brochure – FRIESIAN VALLEY COTTAGES, MAWLA, CORNWALL TR16 5DW (01209 890901) [🐕

Portscatho

Tiny cliff-top resort on Roseland Peninsula overlooking beach or rocks and sand. Harbour and splendid views. Falmouth 5 miles.

THE ROSEVINE HOTEL, PORTHCURNICK BEACH, PORTSCATHO, NEAR ST MAWES TR2 5EW (01872 580206; Fax: 01872 580230). Luxury hotel in Cornwall. De luxe bedrooms and suites. Award-winning cuisine. Beautiful sub-tropical gardens facing safe sandy beach fronting the National Trust coastline. Warm heated indoor pool & jacuzzi. AA ★★★ 80% Britain's Best Hotels.[🐕]
e-mail: info@rosevine.co.uk   website: www.rosevine.co.uk

FREE or REDUCED RATE entry to Holiday Visits and Attractions – see our **READERS' OFFER VOUCHERS** on pages 371-390

Portwrinkle

Village on Whitsand Bay, 6 miles west of Torpoint.

WHITSAND BAY SELF-CATERING (01579 345688). Twelve cottages sleeping 4-10, all with sea views and situated by an 18-hole clifftop golf course. Children and pet-friendly.
website: www.whitsandbayselfcatering.co.uk

WHITSAND BAY HOTEL LEISURE & GOLF, PORTWRINKLE PL11 3BU (01503 230276). Character 32-bedroom hotel with stunning sea views and own 18-hole clifftop golf course. Innovative cuisine. Health & Fitness facilities. Indoor heated pool. Well behaved dogs most welcome. [Pets £10 per night].
e-mail: whitsandbayhotel@btconnect.com   website: www.whitsandbayhotel.co.uk

St Agnes

Patchwork of fields dotted with remains of local mining industry. Watch for grey seals swimming off St Agnes Head.

CHIVERTON PARK, BLACKWATER, TRURO TR4 8HS (01872 560667). Caravan and touring holidays only a short drive from magnificent beaches. Quiet, spacious; exclusive gym, sauna, steamroom; laundry, shop, play area and games room. All amenities. No club, bar or disco. [Dogs £15 per week]
e-mail: info@chivertonpark.co.uk   website: www.chivertonpark.co.uk

THE DRIFTWOOD SPARS HOTEL, TREVAUNANCE COVE, ST AGNES TR5 0RT (01872 552428/553323). Take a deep breath of Cornish fresh air at this comfortable Hotel ideally situated for a perfect seaside holiday. Dogs allowed on beach. Miles of footpaths for 'walkies'. Children and pets welcome.
AA ◆◆◆◆ [Pets £3 per night]
website: www.driftwoodspars.com

St Austell

Old Cornish town and china clay centre with small port at Charlestown (1½ miles). Excellent touring centre. Newquay 16 miles, Truro 14, Bodmin 12, Fowey 9, Mevagissey 6.

BOSINVER HOLIDAY COTTAGES, ST MEWAN, ST AUSTELL PL26 7DT (01726 72128). Award-winning individual cottages in peaceful garden surroundings. Close to major holiday attractions. Short walk to shop and pub. Phone for brochure. No pets during Summer School holidays. ETC
★★★★ [pw!, Pets £30 per week].
e-mail: reception@bosinver.co.uk   website: www.bosinver.co.uk

St Breward

North Cornwall Village 4 miles south of Camelford, edge Bodmin Moor, 12 miles from coast.

Warm and lovely cottage sleeps four/five in great comfort and utter peace. Log fires, large garden with stream, glorious moorland and coastal walking. Available all year. £200-£490 per week depending on season. Contact MRS PADDY POWELL (01208 850186). [Dogs £10 per week].
website: www.vacation-cornwall.co.uk

St Ives

Picturesque resort, popular with artists, with cobbled streets and intriguing little shops. Wide stretches of sand.

SPACIOUS COTTAGE. Sleeps 7/9. Near beaches, harbour, shops, Tate Gallery. Terms £350 to £735 per week. Dogs welcome. Available all year. Telephone: Carol Holland (01736 793015). [Pets £10 per week]

SANDBANK HOLIDAYS, ST IVES BAY, HAYLE (01736 752594). High quality Apartments and Bungalows for 2-6 persons. Heated, Colour TV, Microwave etc. Dogs welcome. [Pets £14 to £21 per week]
website: www.sandbank-holidays.co.uk

BOB AND JACKY PONTEFRACT, THE LINKS HOLIDAY FLATS, LELANT, ST IVES TR26 3HY (Tel & Fax: 01736 753326). Magnificent location overlooking golf course and beach. Wonderful spot for walking. Five minutes from beach where dogs allowed all year. Two well-equipped flats open all year. [🐕]

St Mawes

Village with harbour and two good beaches, excellent for swimming.

SEA PINK, NEAR ST MAWES, SOUTH CORNWALL. In a picturesque setting overlooking the coast, Sea Pink is ideally located for exploring the coast and attractions. Spacious lounge, dining area opening on to sun terrace and lawned garden, three bedrooms (one en suite). Contact JUDY JUNIPER (01872 863553). [Pets £10 per week, pw!]
e-mail: cottageinfo@btconnect.com   website: www.luxury-holiday-cottages.com

St Mawgan

Delightful village in wooded river valley. Ancient church has fine carvings.

DALSWINTON HOUSE, ST MAWGAN, CORNWALL TR8 4EZ (01637 860385). Old Cornish house standing in ten acres of secluded grounds. All rooms en suite, colour TV, tea/coffee facilities. Solar heated outdoor swimming pool. Restaurant and bar. Out-of-season breaks. No children under 16. ETC ★★★★ [🐾 pw!]
e-mail: dalswintonhouse@tiscali.co.uk   website: www.dalswinton.com

St Tudy

Village 5 miles north east of Wadebridge.

Comfortable end of terrace cottage in picturesque and friendly village. Enclosed garden and parking. Ideal location for exploring all Cornwall. Short Breaks and brochure available. Contact: MRS R REEVES, POLSTRAUL, TREWALDER, DELABOLE PL33 9ET (Tel & Fax: 01840 213120). [🐾]
e-mail: ruth.reeves@hotmail.co.uk   website: www.maymear.co.uk

Tintagel

Attractively situated amidst fine cliff scenery; small rocky beach. Famous for associations with King Arthur, whose ruined castle on Tintagel Head is of interest. Bude 19 miles, Camelford 6.

SANDY AND DAVE WILSON, SALUTATIONS, ATLANTIC ROAD, TINTAGEL PL34 0DE (01840 770287). Comfortable, well-equipped, centrally heated cottages sleeping two. Ideal for touring, walking and relaxing. Close to Coastal Path and village amenities. Private parking. Ring for brochure. Pets Free. [🐾]
e-mail: sandyanddave@tinyworld.co.uk   website: www.salutationstintagel.co.uk

Visit the FHG website
www.holidayguides.com
for details of the wide choice of accommodation
featured in the full range of FHG titles

Truro

Bustling Cathedral City with something for everyone. Museum and Art Gallery with interesting shop and cafe is well worth a visit.

HIGHER TREWITHEN, STITHIANS, TRURO TR3 7DR (01209 860863) The ideal centre for your pet and your family. We are surrounded by public footpaths and have 3½ acres of fields. [🐾]
e-mail: trewithen@talk21.com   website: www.trewithen.com

KING HARRY FERRY COTTAGES, FEOCK, TRURO TR3 6QJ (01326 319417). Two comfortable well equipped cottages in own charming gardens. Pets welcome. Beautiful woodland walks. Perfect for fishing and bird watching. [🐾]
e-mail: jean@kingharry.net   website: www.kingharry-info.co.uk

THE VALLEY (01872 862194). A secluded hamlet of contemporary cottages in a tranquil country valley. Beautiful gardens and woodland walks, ideal for dogs. Relax in luxury, with leisure facilities, and experience exquisite cuisine in the stylish Cafe Azur. ETC ★★★★★[Pets £20 per visit]
website: www.the-valley.co.uk

Wadebridge

Town on River Camel, 6 miles north-west of Bodmin

Three barn converted luxury cottage-style self catering homes near Wadebridge. Found along a leafy drive, with wonderful views, beside the lazy twisting Camel River with its "Trail" for walking and cycling. CORNWALL TOURISM AWARDS 2002 - Self Catering Establishment of the Year - "Highly Commended". Sleep 2-7 plus cot. Two dogs per cottage welcome. GARY NEWMAN, COLESENT COTTAGES, ST TUDY, WADEBRIDGE, CORNWALL PL30 4QX (Tel & Fax: 01208 850112). [pw! 🐾]
e-mail: pets@colesent.co.uk   website: www.colesent.co.uk

ISLES OF SCILLY

St Mary's

Largest of group of granite islands and islets off Cornish Coast. Terminus for air and sea services from mainland. Main income from flower-growing. Seabirds, dolphins and seals abound.

MRS PAMELA MUMFORD, SALLAKEE FARM, ST MARY'S TR21 0NZ (01720 422391). Self-catering farm cottage, available all year round. Sleeps 5. Woodburner. Near beach and coastal paths. Pets welcome. Write or phone for details. ETC ★★★

Please note

All the information in this book is given in good faith in the belief that it is correct. However, the publishers cannot guarantee the facts given in these pages, neither are they responsible for changes in policy, ownership or terms that may take place after the date of going to press. Readers should always satisfy themselves that the facilities they require are available and that the terms, if quoted, still apply.

Looking for holiday accommodation?
for details of hundreds of properties
throughout the UK visit:

www.holidayguides.com

Devon

Devon is unique, with two different coastlines: bare rugged cliffs, white pebble beaches, stretches of golden sands, and the Jurassic Coast, England's first natural World Heritage Site. Glorious countryside: green rolling hills, bustling market towns and villages, thatched, white-washed cottages and traditional Devon longhouses. Wild and wonderful moorland: Dartmoor, in the south, embraces wild landscapes and picture-postcard villages; Exmoor in the north combines breathtaking, rugged coastline with wild heather moorland. Step back in time and discover historic cities, myths and legends, seafaring characters like Drake and Raleigh, and settings for novels by Agatha Christie and Conan Doyle.

Devon is home to an amazing and diverse range of birds. Enjoy special organised birdwatching trips, perhaps on board a RSPB Avocet Cruise or a vintage tram. Devon is the walking county of the South West – imagine drifts of bluebells lit by dappled sunlight, the smell of new mown hay, the sound of the sea, crisp country walks followed by a roaring fire and hot 'toddies'! If pedal power is your choice, you will discover exciting off-road cycling, leisurely afternoon rides, and challenging long distance routes such as the Granite Way along Dartmoor, the Grand Western Canal and the coastal Exmouth to Budleigh Circuit.

ETC ★★★ - ★★★★

Mrs Angela Bell
Wooder Manor, Widecombe in the Moor,
Near Ashburton TQ13 7TR
Tel & Fax: (01364) 621391
www.woodermanor.com
e-mail: angela@woodermanor.com

Cottages and converted coach house on 170-acre working family farm nestled in the picturesque valley of Widecombe, surrounded by unspoilt woodland moors and granite tors. Half-a-mile from village with post office, general stores, two good pubs (dogs welcome) and National Trust Information Centre. Excellent centre for touring Devon with a variety of places to visit and exploring Dartmoor by foot or on horseback. Accommodation is clean and well-equipped with colour TV, central heating, laundry room. Children welcome. Large gardens and courtyard for easy parking. Open all year, so take advantage of off-season reduced rates. Short Breaks available. Two properties suitable for disabled visitors. Colour Brochure.

Parkers Farm Cottages

Come and stay on a real 400-acre farm in South Devon
FARM COTTAGES • STATIC CARAVANS
Friendly, family-run self-catering complex with cottages and static caravans surrounded by beautiful countryside. 12 miles from the sea and close to Dartmoor National Park. Perfect for children and pets, with farm animals and plenty of space to roam. Large area to walk your dogs. Laundry, bar and restaurant. Good discounts for couples. A warm welcome awaits you.
How to find us from Exeter: Take A38 to Plymouth. When you see the sign "26 miles Plymouth", take the second left at Alston Cross signposted Woodland - Denbury. Continue past Parkers Farm Holiday Park, cottages on right hand side part way up hill
British Farm Tourist Award • ETC ★★★★

PETS WELCOME

THE ROCKERY, CATON, ASHBURTON, DEVON TQ13 7LH • Tel: 01364 653008 • Fax: 01364 652915
e-mail: parkerscottages@btconnect.com • www.parkersfarm.co.uk

---

Parkers Farm Holiday Park

STATIC CARAVANS • TOURING SITE
Friendly, family-run touring site and static caravans situated in unspoilt countryside. Genuine farm. Spectacular views to Dartmoor. Two modern shower blocks; electric hook-ups. Bar and restaurant with area for dogs. Large dog-walking fields. Shop, launderette and indoor/outdoor play areas. 12 miles to coast. Short Breaks available.

PETS WELCOME

HIGHER MEAD FARM, ASHBURTON, DEVON TQ13 7IJ
Tel: 01364 654869 • Fax: 01364 654004
e-mail: parkersfarm@btconnect.com
www.parkersfarm.co.uk

2007
TOP 100 FAMILY PARKS
Practical **Caravan**
HOLIDAY PARK

Six secluded comfortable cottages, quiet countryside, parkland, woodland on 150-acre estate, with 3 mile all-weather footpaths, four wildlife ponds. The properties are surrounded by gardens and lawns, with views over lake to Dartmoor. All-weather tennis court; adults' snooker room, children's games room. Wood fires, central heating, dishwashers, washing machines, microwaves, colour TVs, DVD. Large summer house with barbecue, free fishing. Bed linen and towels supplied. Open all year. Credit cards accepted. Brochure available.

Braddon Cottages & Forest
Ashwater • Devon • UK

Ashwater, Beaworthy EX21 5EP • Tel & Fax: 01409 211350
e-mail: holidays@braddoncottages.co.uk • www.braddoncottages.co.uk

---

Readers are requested to mention this FHG
guidebook when seeking accommodation

Ashwater, North Devon EX21 5DF
Tel: 01409 211224 • Fax: 01409 211634

BLAGDON MANOR
HOTEL & RESTAURANT

 AA ★★

Liz and Steve, along with our two Chocolate Labradors, Nutmeg and Cassia, look forward to welcoming you to Blagdon Manor.

Restaurant: Enjoy excellent cuisine using locally sourced produce. Dinner available every night for residents.
Accommodation: 7 en suite bedrooms
Panoramic views of the Devon countryside and Dartmoor. Beautifully restored Grade II Listed building. Enjoy a peaceful location halfway between Dartmoor and Exmoor and only 20 minutes from the North Cornish coast at Bude.

3 acres of gardens and 17 acres of fields.
Children over the age of 12 and dogs are welcome.
Double/twin rooms £125.00 per night, based on two sharing. Single occupancy £85.00. Dogs £5.00 per night.

e-mail: stay@blagdon.com
www.blagdon.com

Lea Hill **MEMBURY, AXMINSTER EX13 7AQ**

Tranquil location • Wonderful scenery • Close to World Heritage Coast • Eight acres of grounds and gardens • Hot tub and barbecue • Comfortable, well equipped self-catering cottages with own gardens • B&B available out of season in well appointed rooms.
e-mail: reception@leahill.co.uk • www.leahill.co.uk • 01404 881881

Smallridge, Axminster. Detached cottage, carefully renovated, retaining the **Lilac Cottage** inglenook fireplace, oak beams, floors and doors. Oil-fired central heating, colour TV, fully-equipped all-electric kitchen. Furnished to a high standard, sleeps six plus cot. Children and pets are welcome. Walled garden and garage. The villages and surrounding countryside are beautiful on the borders of Devon, Dorset, and Somerset. Many seaside towns within 10 miles – Lyme Regis, Charmouth and Seaton. Contact: **Mrs J.M. Stuart, 2 Sandford House, Kingsclere RG20 4PA • Tel & Fax: 01635 291942 • e-mail: joanna.sb@free.fr**

Visit the FHG website
www.holidayguides.com
for details of the wide choice of accommodation
featured in the full range of FHG titles

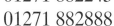

Looking for holiday accommodation?

for details of hundreds of properties
throughout the UK visit:

www.holidayguides.com

Brixham

Broadwoodwidger, Chulmleigh, Chudleigh, Combe Martin, Cullompton

FREE or REDUCED RATE entry to Holiday Visits and Attractions – see our
READERS' OFFER VOUCHERS on pages 371-390

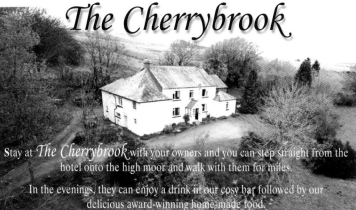

Dartmouth, Doddiscombsleigh, Dunsford, Exeter

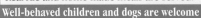

Readers are requested to mention this FHG
guidebook when seeking accommodation

Ilfracombe

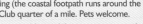

Kingsbridge, King's Nympton

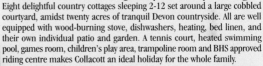

Lynton/Lynmouth

Paignton, Plymouth

www.holidayguides.com

Please note

All the information in this book is given in good faith in the belief that it is correct. However, the
publishers cannot guarantee the facts given in these pages, neither are they responsible for
changes in policy, ownership or terms that may take place after the date of going to press. Readers
should always satisfy themselves that the facilities they require are available
and that the terms, if quoted, still apply.

Seaton, Sidmouth

Totnes, Woolacombe

Eggworthy Farm Sampford Spiney, Yelverton, Devon PL20 6LJ **Holiday on Dartmoor!**
Moorland and valley walking within yards or just relax in the garden. Many local attractions. Comfortable rooms, one double en suite, one family suite with private bathroom; both with colour TV, tea /coffee facilities, and fridge. Non-smoking. Pets welcome. Open all year except Christmas. Brochure available. Terms from £23-£30. We look forward to seeing you. ETC ★★★
Tel/Fax 01822 852142 • e-mail: eggworthyfarm@aol.com • www.eggworthyfarm.co.uk

TOAD HALL COTTAGES (01548 853089 24 hrs). 300 outstanding waterside and rural properties in truly beautiful locations in Devon, Cornwall and Exmoor. Call for our highly acclaimed brochure. Pets welcome.
e-mail: thc@toadhallcottages.co.uk   website: www.toadhallcottages.co.uk

HELPFUL HOLIDAYS (01647 433535). Wonderful variety of cottages all over the West Country. Ideal for countryside rambles. Many welcome pets.
website: www.helpfulholidays.co.uk

FARM & COTTAGE HOLIDAYS (01237 479698). Over 850 of the finest selection of holiday cottages throughout Devon, Cornwall, Dorset and Somerset in superb rural and coastal locations.
website: www.holidaycottages.co.uk

NORTH DEVON HOLIDAY HOMES, 19 CROSS STREET, BARNSTAPLE EX31 1BD (01271 376322; Fax: 01271 346544). Free colour guide to the best value pet friendly cottages around Exmoor and Devon's National Trust Coast. [Pets £12 per week.]
e-mail: info@northdevonholidays.co.uk   website: www.northdevonholidays.co.uk

MARSDENS COTTAGE HOLIDAYS, 2 THE SQUARE, BRAUNTON EX33 2JB (01271 813777; Fax: 01271 813664). Over 300 Visit Britain inspected holiday cottages on North Devon's National Trust coastline and Exmoor. Pets welcome at over half our cottages at £15 per week. Online availability and booking.
e-mail: holidays@marsdens.co.uk   website: www.marsdens.co.uk

PORT LIGHT, BOLBERRY DOWN, MALBOROUGH, NEAR SALCOMBE TQ7 3DY (01548 561384 or 07970 859992). A totally unique location set amidst acres of National Trust coastline. Luxury en suite rooms. Superb home-cooked fare, specialising in local seafood. Licensed bar. Pets welcome throughout the hotel. Short Breaks throughout the year. Self-catering cottages also available.
Contact: Sean and Hazel Hassall. [🐾]
e-mail: info@portlight.co.uk   website: www.portlight.co.uk

HOLIDAY HOMES & COTTAGES S.W, 28 TORWOOD STREET, TORQUAY TQ1 1EB (01803 299677; Fax: 01803 664037). Hundreds of Self-Catering Holiday Cottages, Houses, Bungalows, Apartments, Chalets and Caravans in Devon and Cornwall. Please write or phone for free colour brochure.
e-mail: holcotts@aol.com   website: www.swcottages.co.uk

RECOMMENDED COTTAGE HOLIDAYS. 1st choice for dream cottages at very competitive prices in all holiday regions of beautiful Britain. Pets welcome. All properties inspected. Free brochure - call 01751 475547. [🐾]
website: www.recommended-cottages.co.uk

Ashburton

Delightful little town on southern fringe of Dartmoor. Centrally placed for touring and the Torbay resorts. Plymouth 24 miles, Exeter 20, Kingsbridge 20, Tavistock 20, Teignmouth 14, Torquay 14, Totnes 8, Newton Abbot 7.

PARKERS FARM COTTAGES, THE ROCKERY, CATON, ASHBURTON, NEWTON ABBOT TQ13 7LH (Tel: 01364 653008; Fax: 01364 652915). Farm Cottages and Static Caravans to let surrounded by beautiful countryside. Perfect for children and pets. Central for touring; 12 miles Torquay. ETC ★★★★ [pw! Pets £17 per week]
e-mail: parkerscottages@btconnect.com   website: www.parkersfarm.co.uk

MRS A. BELL, WOODER MANOR, WIDECOMBE IN THE MOOR, NEAR ASHBURTON TQ13 7TR (Tel & Fax: 01364 621391). Cottages nestled in picturesque valley. Surrounded by unspoilt woodland and moors. Clean and well equipped, colour TV, central heating, laundry room. Two properties suitable for disabled visitors. Colour brochure available. ETC ★★★ to ★★★★ [pw! £15 per week for first dog]
e-mail: angela@woodermanor.com   website: www.woodermanor.com

PARKERS FARM HOLIDAY PARK, HIGHER MEAD FARM, ASHBURTON TQ13 7LJ (01364 654869; Fax: 01364 654004). Static caravans to let, also level touring site with two toilet/shower blocks and electric hook-ups. Central for touring; 12 miles Torquay. ETC ★★★★, AA Four Pennants. [pw! Pets £1.20 per night touring, £17 per week static caravans]
e-mail: parkersfarm@btconnect.com   website: www.parkersfarm.co.uk

Ashwater

Village 6 miles south-east of Holsworthy.

BRADDON COTTAGES AND FOREST, ASHWATER, BEAWORTHY EX21 5EP (Tel & Fax: 01409 211350). Six secluded, comfortable cottages in quiet countryside. Surrounded by gardens and lawns. Bed linen and towels supplied. Pleasant walks, barbecue; free fishing. Open all year. Credit cards accepted.   Brochure.
e-mail: holidays@braddoncottages.co.uk   www.braddoncottages.co.uk

BLAGDON MANOR HOTEL AND RESTAURANT, ASHWATER, NORTH DEVON EX21 5DF (01409 211224 Fax: 01409 211634) Beautifully restored Grade II Listed building in peaceful location 20 minutes from Bude. 7 en suite bedrooms, three-acre gardens. No children under 12 years. AA ★★, 2 Rosettes. [pw! Dogs £5 per night]
email: stay@blagdon.com   website: www.blagdon.com

Axminster

Small friendly market town, full of old world charm, set in the beautiful Axe Valley. Excellent centre for touring Devon, Somerset and Dorset. 5 miles from coast.

LEA HILL, MEMBURY, AXMINSTER EX13 7AQ (01404 881881). Tranquil location. Wonderful scenery. Close to World Heritage Coast. Eight acres of grounds and gardens. Hot tub and barbecue. Comfortable, well equipped self-catering cottages with own garden. B&B available out of season. [pw! Pets £10.00 per week]
e-mail: reception@leahill.co.uk   website: www.leahill.co.uk

LILAC COTTAGE. Detached cottage, furnished to a high standard, sleeps six plus cot. Children and pets are welcome. Walled garden and garage. On borders of Devon, Dorset, and Somerset; many seaside towns within 10 miles. Contact: MRS J.M. STUART, 2 SANDFORD HOUSE, KINGSCLERE RG20 4PA (Tel & Fax: 01635 291942)
e-mail: joanna.sb@free.fr

🐾   Indicates that pets are welcome free of charge.

£   Indicates that a charge is made for pets: nightly or weekly.

pw!   Shows some special provision for pets; exercise facility, feeding or accommodation arrangement.

⌂   Indicates separate pets accommodation.

Symbols

Barnstaple

Market town at head of River Taw estuary, 34 miles north west of Exeter.

"VALLEY VIEW", GUINEAFORD, MARWOOD, BARNSTAPLE EX31 4EA (01271 343458). Set in 320 acres of farmland near Barnstaple, home to Helenbrie Miniature Shetland ponies. Two bedrooms each contain a double and single bed. Bed and Breakfast from £20. Children welcome. Pets by arrangement. Open all year.
website: www.helenbriestud.co.uk

MARTINHOE CLEAVE COTTAGES, MARTINHOE, PARRACOMBE, BARNSTAPLE EX31 4PZ (01598 763313). Perfect rural tranquillity overlooking the beautiful Heddon valley and close to the Exmoor National Park. Delightful cottages, equipped to a very high standard throughout. Open all year. Sleep 1-2. [🐾].
e-mail: info@exmoorhideaway.co.uk   website:www.exmoorhideaway.co.uk

NORTH HILL COTTAGES, NORTH HILL, SHIRWELL, BARNSTAPLE EX31 4LG (01271 850611 OR 07005 850413; mobile: 07834 806434; Fax: 07005 850423). Sleep 2-6. 17th century farm buildings, sympathetically converted into cottages. Indoor heated swimming pool, sauna, all weather tennis court and games room. [Pets £20 per week]
website: www.north-hill.co.uk

LOWER YELLAND FARM GUEST HOUSE, FREMINGTON, BARNSTAPLE EX31 3EN (01271 860101). Delightfully modernised farmhouse accommodation on working farm. Central for North Devon attractions. All rooms en suite, with TV and tea/coffee making. Breakfast includes free-range eggs and home-made bread etc. [Pets £2.50 per night, £15 per week]
e-mail: peterday@loweryellandfarm.co.uk   website: www.loweryellandfarm.co.uk

LOWER HEARSON FARM, SWIMBRIDGE, BARNSTAPLE EX32 0QH (01271 830702). Five holiday cottages on former dairy farm, five miles from Barnstaple. Ideal base for exploring North Devon. Outdoor pool, children's play area. Well behaved dogs welcome. [Pets £15 per week].
website: www.hearsoncottagesdevon.co.uk

Berrynarbor

This peaceful village overlooking the beautiful Sterridge valley has a 17th century pub and even older church, and is half-a-mile from the coast road between Combe Martin and Ilfracombe.

SANDY COVE HOTEL, BERRYNARBOR EX34 9SR (01271 882243 or 882888). Hotel set amidst acres of gardens and woods. Heated swimming pool. Children and pets welcome. A la carte restaurant. All rooms en suite with colour TV, tea-making. Free colour brochure on application. ETC ★★★ [🐾 one dog]
website: www.sandycove-hotel.co.uk

Bideford

Neat port village overlooking the beautiful Sterridge Valley has a 17th century pub and even older church, and is half-a-mile from the coast road between Combe Martin and Ilfracombe.

ROBERT & LISA IRETON, MEAD BARN COTTAGES, WELCOMBE, NEAR BIDEFORD EX39 3/4 Star Graded quality, self-catering cottages sleeping 2-26 people. Set in one and a half acres. Games room, tennis court, play area, swings, trampoline and gardens with barbecue area. [Pets £20 per week]
ETC ★★★/★★★★
e-mail: holidays@meadbarns.com   website: www.meadbarns.com

THE PINES AT EASTLEIGH, NEAR BIDEFORD EX39 4PA (01271 860561). Luxury B&B and cottages. Log-fires, king-size beds, garden room bar with library, maps and a warm welcome await our guests. B&B from £45; Cottages from £350 for 4 persons. No smoking. AA ★★★★ [pw! 🐾]
e-mail: pirrie@thepinesateastleigh.co.uk   website: www.thepinesateastleigh.co.uk

A useful index of towns/counties appears at the back of this book

Bigbury-on-Sea

A scattered village overlooking superb coastal scenery and wide expanses of sand.

MR SCARTERFIELD, HENLEY HOTEL, FOLLY HILL, BIGBURY-ON-SEA TQ7 4AR (01548 810240). Edwardian cottage-style hotel, spectacular sea views. Overlooking beach, dog walking. En suite rooms with telephone, tea making, TV etc. Home cooking. No smoking establishment. Licensed. ETC ★★ HOTEL and SILVER AWARD. AA ★★, GOOD HOTEL GUIDE, CESAR AWARD WINNER 2003, "WHICH?" GUIDE, COASTAL CORKER 2003. [Pets £4.00 per night.]

MRS J. TUCKER, MOUNT FOLLY FARM, BIGBURY-ON-SEA, KINGSBRIDGE TQ7 4AR (01548 810267). Cliff top position, with outstanding views of Bigbury Bay. Spacious, self-catering wing of farmhouse, attractively furnished. Farm adjoins golf course and River Avon. Lovely coastal walks, ideal centre for South Hams and Dartmoor. No smoking. Always a warm welcome, pets too! ETC ★★★ [pw! Pets £15 per week]
e-mail: chris.cathy@goosemoose.com   website: www.bigburyholidays.co.uk

Bradworthy

Village to the north of Holsworthy. Well placed for North Devon and North Cornish coasts.

PETER & LESLEY LEWIN, LAKE HOUSE COTTAGES AND B&B, LAKE VILLA, BRADWORTHY DEVON EX22 7SQ (01409 241962). Four well equipped cottages sleeping two to five/six. Quiet rural position; one acre gardens and tennis court. Half-a-mile from village shops and pub. Dog-friendly beaches eight miles. Also two lovely en suite B&B rooms with balcony, all facilities, from £28. [🐾]
e-mail: info@lakevilla.co.uk   website: www.lakevilla.co.uk

Braunton

5 miles north west of Barnstaple. To the south west are Braunton Burrows nature reserve, a lunar landscape of sand dunes noted for rare plants, and the 3 mile stretch of Saunton Sands.

LITTLE COMFORT FARM, BRAUNTON, NORTH DEVON EX33 2NJ (01271 812 414). Five spacious self-catering cottages sleeping 2-10 on organic family farm, just minutes from golden sandy beaches where dogs are allowed. Well stocked coarse fishing lake. Private 1½km farm trail. Wood fires for cosy winter breaks. PETS VERY WELCOME [pw! Pets £20 per week].
e-mail: info@littlecomfortfarm.co.uk   website: www.littlecomfortfarm.co.uk

Brixham

Lively resort and fishing port, with quaint houses and narrow winding streets. Ample opportunities for fishing and boat trips.

DEVONCOURT HOLIDAY FLATS, BERRYHEAD ROAD, BRIXHAM TQ5 9AB (01803 853748 or 07050 853748 after office hours). 24 self-contained flats with private balcony, colour television, heating, private car park, all-electric kitchenette, separate bathroom and toilet. Open all year. Pets welcome.
website: www.devoncourt.info

BRIXHAM HOLIDAY PARK, FISHCOMBE COVE, BRIXHAM TQ5 8RB (01803 853324). Situated on coastal path. Choice of one and two-bedroomed chalets. Indoor heated pool, free club membership, comfortable bar offering meals and takeaway service, launderette. 150 yards from beach with lovely walks through woods beyond. ETC ★★★★. [Pets £30 per week]
e-mail: enquiries@brixhamholpk.fsnet.co.uk   website: www.brixhamholidaypark.co.uk

Broadwoodwidger

Village 6 miles north east of Launceston.

MRS L. BANBURY, FRANKABOROUGH FARM, BROADWOODWIDGER, LIFTON PL16 0JS (01409 211308/07971 525550). Relax and enjoy a different pace of life. Set in 260 acres, the traditional working beef, sheep, dairy and arable farm offers a relaxing and revitalising break. Ideally situated near the A30 for discovering Devon and Cornwall. Four luxury barn conversions. Beauty therapy on site in luxury room. ETC ★★★★.[🐾]

WEST BANBURY FARM COTTAGES, BROADWOODWIDGER (01566 784946). 10 charming cottages, set around two courtyards. Sleep 2-8 (dogs welcome in all). Large indoor pool, sauna, games room etc. Ideal for exploring Devon and Cornwall. Contact AMANDA for details. [Pets £20 per week].
website: www.westbanbury.co.uk

Chudleigh

Small town 5 miles north of Newton Abbot.

S & G HARRISON CRAWFORD, LINDEN LEA, PARADE, CHUDLEIGH TQ13 0JG (01626 852172). Bungalow set well back from main road into town. One double en suite bedroom, use of large comfortable lounge. Good base for seeing Devon, plenty of places to walk dogs. B&B from £25 pppn. [🐾]

Chulmleigh

Mid-Devon village set in lovely countryside, just off A377 Exeter to Barnstaple road. Exeter 23 miles, Tiverton 19, Barnstaple 18.

SANDRA GAY, NORTHCOTT BARTON FARM COTTAGE, NORTHCOTT BARTON, ASHREIGNEY, CHULMLEIGH EX18 7PR (Tel & Fax: 01769 520259). Three bedroom character cottage, large enclosed garden, log fire. Special rates low season, couples and short breaks. Near golf, riding, Tarka Trail and RHS Rosemoor. ETC ★★★★ [🐾]
e-mail: sandra@northcottbarton.co.uk   website: www.northcottbarton.co.uk

Combe Martin

Coastal village with harbour set in sandy bay. Good cliff and rock scenery. Of interest is the Church and "Pack of Cards" Inn. Barnstaple 14 miles, Lynton 12, Ilfracombe 6.

WATERMOUTH COVE COTTAGES, WATERMOUTH, NEAR COMBE MARTIN EX34 9SJ (0870 241 3168). 8 beautiful cottages, most with four-poster and log fire, set beside grounds of Watermouth Castle, 200 yards from harbour/coastal path. Pets welcome all year. ETC ★★★ [Pets £20 per week]
e-mail: watermouthcove@googlemail.com   website: www.watermouth-cove-cottages.co.uk

Cullompton

Small market town off the main A38 Taunton - Exeter road. Good touring centre. Noted for apple orchards which supply the local cider industry. Taunton 19 miles, Exeter 13, Honiton 11, Tiverton 9.

FOREST GLADE HOLIDAY PARK (PW), KENTISBEARE, CULLOMPTON EX15 2DT (01404 841381; Fax: 01404 841593). Country estate with deluxe 2/4/6 berth caravans. All superbly equipped. Many amenities on site. Mother and Baby Room. Campers and tourers welcome. SAE for colour brochure. ETC ★★★★, AA Four Pennants De Luxe, David Bellamy Gold Award. [Pets £1 per night, pw!]
e-mail: enquiries@forest-glade.co.uk   website: www.forest-glade.co.uk

Dartmoor

365 square miles of National Park with spectacular unspoiled scenery, fringed by picturesque villages.

DEVONSHIRE INN, STICKLEPATH, OKEHAMPTON EX20 2NW (01837 840626). A real country pub! Out the back door past the water wheels, cross the river by ford or footbridge and up through the woods onto the north edge of Dartmoor proper. Dogs and horses always welcome, fed and watered. 1994 Winner National Beta Petfood Golden Bowl Competition for most dog-friendly pub!

THE CHERRYBROOK, TWO BRIDGES PL20 6SP (01822 880260). In the middle of Dartmoor National Park with seven comfortable en suite bedrooms. Award-winning, excellent quality, home-made food. See our website for details, tariff and sample menu. [🐾]
e-mail: info@cherrybrookhotel.co.uk   website: www.cherrybrookhotel.co.uk

DARTMOOR COUNTRY HOLIDAYS, MAGPIE LEISURE PARK, DEPT PW, BEDFORD BRIDGE, HORRABRIDGE, YELVERTON PL20 7RY (01822 852651). Purpose-built pine lodges in peaceful woodland setting. Sleep 2-7. Furnished to very high standard (microwave, dishwasher etc). Easy walk to village and shops. Launderette. Dogs permitted. [🐾]

THE ROSEMONT, GREENBANK TERRACE, YELVERTON PL20 6DR (01822 852175). Large Victorian house overlooking the green at Yelverton, just yards from lovely open moorland. All rooms en suite, all with TV and tea/coffee making facilities. Non-smoking throughout. B&B from £28 ETC/AA ★★★★[🐾]
e-mail: office@therosemont.co.uk   website: www.therosemont.co.uk

THE EAST DART HOTEL, POSTBRIDGE, YELVERTON PL20 6TJ (01822 880213; Fax: 01822 880313). Family-run former coaching Inn, with real fires, home cooked food using local produce and real ales. 11 en suite bedrooms. Riding, falconry and fishing. Well-behaved dogs welcome by prior arrangement.

PRINCE HALL HOTEL, DARTMOOR PL20 6SA (01822 890403). Small, friendly, relaxed country house hotel with glorious views onto open moorland. Walks in all directions. Nine en suite bedrooms. Log fires. Gourmet cooking. Excellent wine list. Fishing, riding, golf nearby. Three-Day Break from £100pppn. AA/VisitBritain ★★, AA Rosette for food. [🐾]
e-mail: bosun@princehall.co.uk　　　　　　　　website: www.princehall.co.uk

TWO BRIDGES HOTEL, TWO BRIDGES, DARTMOOR PL20 6SW (01822 890581; Fax: 01822 892306). Famous Olde World riverside Inn. Centre Dartmoor. Log fires, very comfortable, friendly, excellent food. Ideal walking, touring, fishing, riding, golf. Warning – Addictive. ETC/AA ★★[🐾]
e-mail: enquiries@warm-welcome-hotels.co.uk　　　website: www.warm-welcome-hotels.co.uk

Dartmouth

Historic port and resort on the estuary of the River Dart, with sandy coves and pleasure boat trips up the river. Car ferry to Kingswear.

PAM & GRAHAM SPITTLE, WATERMILL COTTAGES, HANSEL, DARTMOUTH TQ6 0LN (01803 Comfortable, well equipped old stone cottages in peaceful riverside setting. Wonderful walks in and around our idyllic valley near dog-friendly Slapton Sands and coastal path. Sleep 3-6. Enclosed gardens. Wood fires. Winter breaks. Brochure. [Pets £15 per week]
e-mail: graham@hanselpg.freeserve.co.uk　　　　website: www.watermillcottages.co.uk

DARTSIDE HOLIDAYS, RIVERSIDE COURT, SOUTH EMBANKMENT, DARTMOUTH TQ6 9BH (01803 832093; Fax: 01803 835135). Comfortable holiday apartments with private balconies and superb river and harbour views. Available all year with colour TV, linen and parking. Free Colour Brochure on request. [Pets £30 per week.]
website: www.dartsideholidays.com

BOAT HOUSE COTTAGE, TORCROSS APARTMENTS (01548 580206). 7 miles from Kingsbridge and Dartmouth, directly on the beach at Slapton Sands. Two bedrooms, one en suite. Washing machine, tumble dryer etc. Sleeps up to 7. Brochure available.
e-mail: enquiries@torcross.com　　　　　　　website: www.torcross.com

MRS S.R. RIDALLS, THE OLD BAKEHOUSE, 7 BROADSTONE, DARTMOUTH TQ6 9NR (Tel & Fax: 01803 834585). Four cottages (one with four-poster bed). Sleep 2–6. Near river, shops, restaurants. Blackpool Sands 15 minutes' drive. TV, video, linen free. Open all year. Free parking. Non-smoking. Green Tourism Bronze Award. ETC ★★★ [🐾]
e-mail: ridallsleisure@aol.com　　　　　　website: www.oldbakehousedartmouth.co.uk

Doddiscombsleigh

Village 6 miles south west of Exeter.

STATION LODGE, DODDISCOMBSLEIGH, EXETER (Tel & Fax: 01647 253104). Comfortably furnished apartment for two people in beautiful Teign River valley. Excellent location for exploring Dartmoor. From £180 per week. For further details contact: IAN WEST, STATION HOUSE, DODDISCOMBSLEIGH, EXETER EX6 7PW. [pw! 🐾]
e-mail: enquiries@station-lodge.co.uk　　　　website: www.station-lodge.co.uk

Dunsford

Attractive village in upper Teign valley with Dartmoor to the west. Plymouth 35 miles, Okehampton 16, Newton Abbot 13, Crediton 9, Exeter 8.

ROYAL OAK INN, DUNSFORD, NEAR EXETER EX6 7DA (01647 252256). Welcome to our Victorian country inn with real ales and home-made food. All en suite rooms are in a 300-year-old converted barn. Well behaved children and dogs welcome. [🐾]

Exeter

Chief city of the South-West with a cathedral and university. Ample shopping, sports and leisure facilities.

MRS SALLY GLANVILL, RYDON FARM, WOODBURY, EXETER EX5 1LB (01395 232341). 16th Century Devon Longhouse on working dairy farm. Open all year. Highly recommended. From £30 to £50pppn. ETC/AA ★★★★ [🐕]
website: www.rydonfarmwoodbury.co.uk

BEST WESTERN LORD HALDON HOTEL, DUNCHIDEOCK, NEAR EXETER EX6 7YF (01392 832483, Fax: 01392 833765). Extensive gardens amid miles of rolling Devon countryside. ETC ★★★, AA ★★★ and 2 Rosettes. [Pets £5 per night.]
e-mail: enquiries@lordhaldonhotel.co.uk   website: www.lordhaldonhotel.co.uk

LUCY & ANDY HINES, BUSSELLS FARM COTTAGES, BUSSELLS FARM, HUXHAM, EXETER EX5 4EN (01392 841238). Seven luxury barn conversion cottages, sleep 6/7. Coarse fishing lakes (securely fenced). Outdoor heated swimming pool (May to September), adventure playground and indoor games room. Open all year. ETC ★★★★ [🐕]
e-mail bussellsfarm@aol.com   website: www.bussellsfarm.co.uk

Exmoor

265 square miles of unspoiled heather moorland with deep wooded valleys and rivers, ideal for a walking, pony trekking or fishing holiday

THE STAGHUNTERS INN/HOTEL, BRENDON, EXMOOR EX35 6PS (01598 741222; Fax: 01598 741352). Family-run village inn set in four acres of garden and paddock. 12 en suite rooms with CH, TV and tea/coffee. Open all year. Shooting, fishing and riding. [🐕]
e-mail: stay@staghunters.com   website: www.staghunters.com

JAYE JONES AND HELEN ASHER, TWITCHEN FARM, CHALLACOMBE, BARNSTAPLE EX31 4TT (01598 763568). Comfort for country lovers in Exmoor National Park. High quality en suite rooms with TV. Meals prepared with fresh local and organic produce. Stabling £50 per week. B&B £26–£36, DB&B £46–£56. ETC ★★★★ [One dog free, two dogs £5]
e-mail: holidays@twitchen.co.uk   website: www.twitchen.co.uk

Hartland

Village 4 miles west of Clovelly.

WELCOMBE-IN, WELCOMBE CROSS (A39), HARTLAND EX39 6HD (01288 331130; mobile: 07714 664547). Comfortable ground floor guest rooms. Pet-friendly, non-smoking. Great breakfasts, local produce, packed lunches, evening meals. Stunning coastal North Devon. Plenty to entertain everyone. Small charge for pets.
website: www.welcombe-in.co.uk

Hexworthy (Dartmoor)

Hamlet on Dartmoor 7 miles west of Ashburton.

THE FOREST INN, HEXWORTHY, DARTMOOR PL20 6SD (01364 631211; Fax: 01364 631515). A haven for walkers, riders, fishermen, canoeists or anyone just looking for an opportunity to enjoy the natural beauty of Dartmoor. Restaurant using local produce wherever possible; extensive range of snacks; Devon beers and ciders. ETC ★★★ [🐕]
e-mail: info@theforestinn.co.uk

Hope Cove

Attractive fishing village, flat sandy beach and safe bathing. Fine views towards Rame Head; cliffs, Kingsbridge 6 miles.

HOPE BARTON BARNS, HOPE COVE, NEAR SALCOMBE TQ7 3HT (01548 561393). 17 stone barns in two courtyards and three luxury apartments in farmhouse. Farmhouse meals. Free range children and well behaved dogs welcome. For full colour brochure please contact: Mr & Mrs M. Pope. [pw! Pets £20 per week]
website: www.hopebarton.co.uk

Ilfracombe

This popular seaside resort clusters round a busy harbour. The surrounding area is ideal for coastal walks.

ST BRANNOCKS HOUSE, ST BRANNOCKS ROAD, ILFRACOMBE EX34 8EQ (Tel & Fax: 01271 863873). Lovely relaxing home with level walk to shops and harbour. Brilliant walks, Exmoor and beaches nearby. Great food, cosy bar, comfy lounge. Children and dogs welcome. Open all year. EnjoyEngland.com ★★ [🐕]
e-mail: barbara@stbrannockshotel.co.uk   website: www.stbrannockshotel.co.uk

VARLEY HOUSE, CHAMBERCOMBE PARK, ILFRACOMBE EX34 9QW (01271 863927; Fax: 01271 879299). Relax with your dog, fabulous walks nearby. Fully en suite non-smoking rooms with lots of thoughtful extras. Superb food, beautiful surroundings. Bar. Car park. Children over five years welcome. ETC/AA ★★★★ [🐕] WE WANT YOU TO WANT TO RETURN.
e-mail: info@varleyhouse.co.uk   website: www.varleyhouse.co.uk

WIDMOUTH FARM, NEAR ILFRACOMBE EX34 9RX (01271 863743). Comfortable, well equipped cottages in 35 acres of gardens, pasture, woodland and private beach. Wonderful scenery. Ideal for birdwatching, painting, sea fishing & golf. Dogs welcome. ETC ★★★. [pw! Pets £20 per week].
e-mail: holiday@widmouthfarmcottages.co.uk   website: www.widmouthfarmcottages.co.uk

THE FOXHUNTERS INN, WEST DOWN, NEAR ILFRACOMBE EX34 8NU (01271 863757; Fax: 01271 879313). 300 year-old coaching Inn conveniently situated for beaches and country walks. En suite accommodation. Pets welcome by prior arrangement.
website: www.foxhuntersinn.co.uk

Instow

On estuaries of Taw and Torridge, very popular with boating enthusiasts. Barnstaple 6 miles, Bideford 3.

BEACH HAVEN COTTAGE, INSTOW. Two seafront cottages with extensive beach and sea views. Sleep 5. Enclosed garden, own parking. Central heating, colour TV, coastal walks. Dog welcome. For colour brochure send SAE to MRS P. I. BARNES, 140 BAY VIEW ROAD, NORTHAM, BIDEFORD EX39 1BJ (01237 473801). [Dog £10 per week]
website: www.seabirdcottages.co.uk

Kingsbridge

Pleasant town at head of picturesque Kingsbridge estuary. Centre for South Hams district with its lush scenery and quiet coves.

MOUNTS FARM TOURING PARK, THE MOUNTS, NEAR EAST ALLINGTON, KINGSBRIDGE TQ9 7QJ (01548 521591). Family-run site in the heart of South Devon. We welcome tents, touring caravans and motor caravans. Children and pets welcome. Many safe, sandy beaches nearby.
website: www.mountsfarm.co.uk

BEACHDOWN, CHALLABOROUGH BAY, KINGSBRIDGE TQ7 4JB (01548 810089). Comfortable, fully-equipped chalets on private, level and secluded site in beautiful South Hams. 150 yards from beach and South West Coastal Path. [pw! Pets £15.00 per week].
e-mail: petswelcome@beachdown.co.uk   website: www.beachdown.co.uk

DITTISCOMBE HOLIDAY COTTAGES, SLAPTON, NEAR KINGSBRIDGE, SOUTH DEVON TQ7 2QF (01548 521272). Nature trail and 20 acres of open space. Perfect holiday location for dogs and owners. All cottages have gardens and views of surrounding valley. ETC ★★★★. [Pets £16 per week]
e-mail: info@dittiscombe.co.uk   website: www.dittiscombe.co.uk

MRS B. KELLY, BLACKWELL PARK, LODDISWELL, KINGSBRIDGE TQ7 4EA (01548 821230). 17th century Farmhouse, five miles from Kingsbridge. Ideal centre for Dartmoor, Plymouth, Torbay, Dartmouth and many beaches. Some bedrooms en suite. Bed and Breakfast. Evening meal optional. Dogsitting. Pets welcome free of charge. [🐕]

www.holidayguides.com

King's Nympton

3 miles north of Chulmleigh. Winner of CPRE Award for Devon Village of the year 1999.

COLLACOTT FARM, KING'S NYMPTON, UMBERLEIGH, NORTH DEVON EX37 9TP (01769 572491). Eight Country Cottages sleeping from 2 to 12 in rural area; lovely views, private patios and gardens. Well furnished and equipped. Heated pool, tennis court, BHS approved riding school. Laundry room. Open all year. [pw!, Pets £3 per night, £20 per week]
e-mail: info@collacott.co.uk   website: www.collacott.co.uk

Lynton/Lynmouth

Picturesque twin villages joined by a unique cliff railway (vertical height 500 ft). Lynmouth has a quaint harbour and Lynton enjoys superb views over the rugged coastline.

DOONE VALLEY HOLIDAYS. Comfortable self catering cottages sleeping up to 8. Perfect touring base to explore Exmoor. Camping facilities on-site. Riverside location, shop, off-licence, tearoom and gardens. Horse riding holidays with grazing and stabling. Contact: COLIN & JILL HARMAN, CLOUD FARM, OARE, LYNTON EX35 6NU (01598 741234; Fax: 01598 741154). VisitBritain ★★★★ [Pets £12 per week].
e-mail: doonevalleyholidays@hotmail.com   website: www.doonevalleyholidays.co.uk
                                                          www.doonevalleytrekking.co.uk

EXMOOR SANDPIPER INN, COUNTISBURY, LYNMOUTH EX35 6NE (01598 741263). Romantic coaching inn on Exmoor. 16 en suite bedrooms, extensive menus with daily specials, good wines. Horse riding, walking. No charge for dogs. [🐾]
website:www.exmoorsandpiper.com or www.exmoorsandpiper.co.uk

THE NORTH CLIFF HOTEL, NORTH WALK, LYNTON EX35 6HJ (01598 752357). On the South West Coastal Path, the North Cliff is an ideal base for discovering Exmoor and the North Devon Coast. Delicious home cooking. We welcome pets, children and groups. Self-catering flat, sleeps 6, also available. [Pets £3 per night].
e-mail: holidays@northcliffhotel.co.uk   website: www.northcliffhotel.co.uk

MOORLANDS. Where countryside and comfort combine. Two self-contained apartments within a family-run guesthouse, within the Exmoor National Park. Hotel amenities available for guests' use. Contact: MR I. CORDEROY, MOORLANDS, WOODY BAY, PARRACOMBE, NEAR LYNTON, DEVON EX31 4RA (01598 763224). ETC ◆◆◆◆ [🐾]
website: www.moorlandshotel.co.uk

COUNTISBURY LODGE HOTEL, COUNTISBURY HILL, LYNMOUTH EX35 6NB (01598 752388). Former Victorian vicarage, peacefully secluded yet only 5 minutes to Lynmouth village. En suite rooms, central heating. Ideal for birdwatching and moors. Parking. Short Breaks. Also available S/C cottage and apartment. AA ◆◆◆◆ [🐾]
website: www.countisburylodge.co.uk

JIM AND SUSAN BINGHAM, NEW MILL FARM, BARBROOK, LYNTON EX35 6JR (01598 753341). Exmoor Valley. Two delightful genuine modernised XVII century cottages by stream on 100-acre farm with A.B.R.S. Approved riding stables. Free fishing. ETC ★★★★. [pw! Pets £15 per week.]
e-mail: info@outovercott.co.uk   website: www.outovercott.co.uk

MRS W. PRYOR, STATION HOUSE, LYNTON EX35 6LB (01598 752275/752381; Fax: 01598 752475). Holiday accommodation situated in the former narrow gauge railway station closed in 1935, overlooking the West Lyn Valley. Centrally placed for Doone Valley and Exmoor. Parking available. £150 - £220 per week. [🐾]
e-mail: billthemovie@hotmail.com

Readers are requested to mention this FHG
guidebook when seeking accommodation

Mortehoe

Adjoining Woolacombe with cliffs and wide sands. Interesting rock scenery beyond Morte Point. Barnstaple 15 miles.

THE SMUGGLERS REST INN, NORTH MORTE ROAD, MORTEHOE EX34 7DR (Tel & Fax: 01271 870891). In the pretty village of Mortehoe. The Smugglers offers luxury accommodation from twin rooms to family suites. En suite rooms, satellite TV, full English breakfast, licensed bar, beer garden, home-cooked meals. Well trained pets welcome. [Pets £5 per week].
e-mail: info@smugglersmortehoe.co.uk   website: www.smugglersmortehoe.co.uk

Noss Mayo

Village 3 miles south west of Yealmpton, on south side of creek running into River Yealm estuary, opposite Newton Ferrers.

CRAB COTTAGE, NOSS MAYO. Charming fisherman's cottage, 50 yards from the quay. Fantastic walks, beaches and dog-friendly pubs on the doorstep. Close to the South Devon Coastal Path. Sleeps 5. Phone 01425 471372 for a brochure. [£15 per pet, per week]
website: www.crab-cottage.co.uk

Ottery St Mary

Pleasant little town in East Devon, within easy reach of the sea. Many interesting little buildings including 11th century parish church. Birthplace of poet Coleridge.

MRS A. FORTH, FLUXTON FARM, OTTERY ST MARY EX11 1RJ (01404 812818). Charming 16th Century farmhouse. B&B from £25. Peace and quiet. Cat lovers' paradise. Masses of dog walks. AA ◆◆ [🐾 pw!]
website: www.fluxtonfarm.co.uk

Paignton

Popular family resort on Torbay with long, safe sandy beaches and small harbour. Exeter 25 miles, Newton Abbott 9, Torquay 3.

J. AND E. BALL, DEPARTMENT P.W., HIGHER WELL FARM HOLIDAY PARK, STOKE GABRIEL, TOTNES TQ9 6RN (01803 782289). Within 4 miles Torbay beaches and 1 mile of River Dart. Central for touring. Dogs on leads. Tourist Board Graded Park ★★★★. [pw! Pets £2 per night, £15 per week in statics, free in tents and tourers]

CHRISTINE CLARK & LLOYD HASTIE, AMBER HOUSE HOTEL, 6 ROUNDHAM ROAD, PAIGNTON TQ4 6EZ (01803 558372). All en suite; ground floor rooms. Good food. Highly recommended. Non-smoking. A warm welcome assured to pets and their families.
e-mail: enquiries@amberhousehotel.co.uk   website: www.amberhousehotel.co.uk

Plymouth

Historic port and resort, impressively rebuilt after severe war damage. Large naval docks at Devonport. Beach of pebble and sand.

THE CRANBOURNE, 278/282 CITADEL ROAD, THE HOE, PLYMOUTH PL1 2PZ (01752 263858/ 661400/224646; Fax: 01752 263858). Convenient for Ferry Terminal and City Centre. All bedrooms with colour TV and tea/coffee. Licensed bar. Keys provided for access at all times. Under personal supervision. Pets by arrangement. AA ★★★ [🐾]
e-mail: cran.hotel@virgin.net   website: www.cranbournehotel.co.uk

CHURCHWOOD VALLEY, WEMBURY BAY, NEAR PLYMOUTH PL9 0DZ (01752 862382). Relax in one of our comfortable log cabins, set in a peaceful wooded valley near the beach. Enjoy wonderful walks in woods and along the coast. Abundance of birds and wildlife. Up to two pets per cabin. [Pets £5 per week each]
e-mail: churchwoodvalley@btconnect.com   website: www.churchwoodvalley.com

A useful index of towns/counties appears at the back of this book

Salcombe

Fishing and sailing centre in sheltered position. Fine beaches and coastal walks nearby.

BOLBERRY FARM COTTAGES, BOLBERRY, NEAR SALCOMBE, DEVON TQ7 3DY (01548 561384). HAZEL AND SEAN HASSALL. Luxury Barn conversion cottages. Private gardens. Close to coastal path and pet-friendly beaches. Dog wash. Short Breaks out of season. The Pet Holiday Specialist. [🐾]
e-mail: info@bolberryfarmcottages.co.uk   website: www.bolberryfarmcottages.co.uk

PORT LIGHT, BOLBERRY DOWN, MALBOROUGH, NEAR SALCOMBE TQ7 3DY (01548 561384 or 07970 859992). A totally unique location set amidst acres of National Trust coastline. Luxury en suite rooms. Superb home-cooked fare, specialising in local seafood. Licensed bar. Pets welcome throughout the hotel. Short Breaks throughout the year. Contact: Sean and Hazel Hassall. [🐾]
e-mail: info@portlight.co.uk   website: www.portlight.co.uk

Seaton

Bright East Devon resort near Axe estuary. Shingle beach and chalk cliffs; good bathing, many lovely walks in vicinity. Exeter 23 miles, Sidmouth 11.

MILKBERE COTTAGE HOLIDAYS, 3 FORE STREET, SEATON EX12 2LE (Brochure: 01297 22925 / Bookings: 01297 20729). Specialising in coast/country holidays on the Devon/Dorset border. Cottages, bungalows, houses, apartments and caravans, ideally situated for walking and exploring the Jurassic Coast. [Pets £20 per week.] VisitBritain ★★★/★★★★★.
e-mail: info@milkberehols.com   website: www.milkberehols.com

AXEVALE CARAVAN PARK, COLYFORD ROAD, SEATON EX12 2DF (0800 0688816). A quiet, family-run park with 68 modern and luxury caravans for hire. Laundry facilities, park shop. All caravans have a shower, toilet, fridge and TV. Relaxing atmosphere. ETC ★★★★ [Pets £10 per week]
website: www.axevale.co.uk

Sidmouth

Sheltered resort, winner of many awards for its floral displays. Good sands at Jacob's Ladder beach.

OTTERFALLS HOLIDAY COTTAGES & LODGES, NEW ROAD, UPOTTERY, HONITON EX14 9QD (FREECALL 0808 145 2700; Fax: 01404 861706). Luxurious fully equipped self-catering cottages and lodges set in 120 acres. Fishing lakes, heated indoor pool. Wonderful walking, including special pet "off-lead" walkways. [pw! Pets £30 per week]
e-mail: hols@otterfalls.co.uk   website: www.otterfalls.co.uk

OAKDOWN TOURING AND HOLIDAY CARAVAN PARK, WESTON, SIDMOUTH EX10 0PD (01297 680387; Fax: 01297 680541). Sidmouth's multi-award-winning touring and holiday caravan park. Welcome to Oakdown, set near the "Jurassic Coast" World Heritage Site, and a winner of "Caravan Holiday Park of The Year" in the Excellence in England Awards 2007. Oakdown is level, sheltered and landscaped into groves to give privacy. Our luxurious amenities include aids for the disabled. Enjoy our Field Trail to the famous Donkey Sanctuary. Free colour brochure with pleasure. ETC ★★★★★, David Bellamy Gold Award, Loo of the Year Award, Best of British, Excellence in England 2007.
e-mail: enquiries@oakdown.co.uk   website: www.oakdown.co.uk

LEIGH FARM SELF-CATERING COTTAGES, WESTON, SIDMOUTH EX10 0PH. Cottages and Bungalows 150 yards from National Trust Valley leading to Coastal Path and beach. Lovely cliff top walks and level walks around nearby Donkey Sanctuary fields. ETC ★★★★ Contact: Geoff & Gill Davis (01395 516065; Fax: 01395 579582). [pw! Pets £18 per week]
e-mail: leigh.farm@virgin.net   website: www.streets-ahead.com/leighfarm

Tavistock

Birthplace of Sir Francis Drake and site of a fine ruined Benedictine Abbey. On edge of Dartmoor, 13 miles north of Plymouth

MRS P.G.C. QUINTON, HIGHER QUITHER, MILTON ABBOT, TAVISTOCK PL19 0PZ (01822 860284). Modern self-contained barn conversion. Own private garden. Terms from £195 inc. linen, coal and logs. Electricity metered. [pw! 🐾]

Thurlestone

Village resort above the cliffs to the north of Bolt Tail, 4 miles west of Kingsbridge.

CUTAWAY COTTAGE, THURLESTONE, KINGSBRIDGE TQ7 3NF. Self-catering cottage within a fenced garden in the middle of the village. Private road, 5 minutes to pub and shop, 20 minutes' walk to beaches & sea, Ideal for children, dog walkers and bird watchers. Phone PAT on 01548 560688 [🐾]

Tiverton

Market town on River Exe, 12 miles north of Exeter.

NEWHOUSE FARM COTTAGES, WITHERIDGE, TIVERTON EX16 8QB (01884 860266). Eight well equipped Grade II Listed stone barns, with accommodation ranging from a one bedroom cottage to a five bedroom barn. 23 acre grounds, heated indoor pool and games room. website: www.newhousecottages.com

Torquay

Popular resort on the English Riviera with a wide range of attractions and entertainments. Yachting and watersports centre with 10 superb beaches and coves.

RED HOUSE HOTEL AND MAXTON LODGE HOLIDAY APARTMENTS, ROUSDOWN ROAD, CHELSTON, TORQUAY TQ2 6PB (01803 607811; Fax: 01803 605357). Choose either the friendly service and facilities of a hotel or the privacy and freedom of self-catering apartments. The best of both worlds! AA/ETC ★★ Hotel & ★★★ Self-catering. [🐾 in flats; £3 per night in hotel]
e-mail: stay@redhouse-hotel.co.uk   website: www.redhouse-hotel.co.uk

THE DOWNS HOTEL, BABBACOMBE DOWNS ROAD, TORQUAY TQ1 3LN (01803 328543). A warm welcome awaits you from resident proprietor Stuart Lewton and family. Totally non-smoking. All rooms en suite with tea/coffee making, colour TV, telephone. Sea view and balcony rooms available. ETC ★★★ [Pets £5 per night].
e-mail: manager@downshotel.co.uk   website: www.downshotel.co.uk

Torrington

Pleasant market town on River Torridge. Good centre for moors and sea. Exeter 36 miles, Okehampton 20, Barnstaple 12, Bideford 7.

RICH AND DIANA JONES, STOWFORD LODGE, LANGTREE, GREAT TORRINGTON EX38 8NU (01805 601540). Sleep 4/6. Picturesque and peaceful. Four delightful cottages set within 6 acres of private land with heated indoor pool. Magnificent countryside. Convenient North Devon coast and moors. Phone for brochure. VisitBritain ★★★ [Pets £15 per week, pw!]
e-mail: enq@stowfordlodge.co.uk   website: www.stowfordlodge.co.uk

Totnes

Town at tidal estuary of River Dart, 7 miles west of Torquay

MRS ANNE TORR, DOWNE LODGE, BROADHEMPSTON, TOTNES TQ9 6BY (Tel & Fax: 01803 812828; Mobile; 07772318746).) Woodland dog walking on doorstep. Cottage available with one or three bedrooms. En suite B&B available. No smoking. Beautiful, quiet position convenient for Dartmoor and the coast. [🐾]
e-mail: info@downelodge.co.uk   website: www.downelodge.co.uk

🐾   Indicates that pets are welcome free of charge.

£   Indicates that a charge is made for pets: nightly or weekly.

Symbols

pw!   Shows some special provision for pets; exercise facility, feeding or accommodation arrangement.

⌂   Indicates separate pets accommodation.

Woolacombe

Favourite resort with long, wide stretches of sand. Barnstaple 15 miles, Ilfracombe 6.

SUNNYMEADE COUNTRY HOTEL, WEST DOWN, NEAR WOOLACOMBE EX34 8NT (01271 863668; Fax: 01271 866061). Small country hotel set in beautiful countryside. A few minutes away from Ilfracombe, Exmoor and Woolacombe's Blue Flag Beach. 10 en suite rooms, 4 on the ground floor. Deaf accessible. Pets welcome – dogs are free. [🐕 pw!]
website: www.sunnymeade.co.uk

MRS JOYCE BAGNALL, CHICHESTER HOUSE, THE ESPLANADE, WOOLACOMBE EX34 7DJ (01271 870761). Holiday apartments on sea front. Fully furnished, sea and coastal views. Watch the sun go down from your balcony. Open all year. SAE Resident Proprietor. [Pets £12 per week, pw!]

MRS VIVIEN LAWRENCE, COVE COTTAGE, SHARP ROCK, MORTEHOE, WOOLACOMBE EX34 7EA (01271 870403). First floor flat overlooking Barricane beach where dogs permitted, (10 minute walk) Sea views, garden. Well equipped. C.H. included early/late season. Open all year. Sleeps 5 + cot. Resident proprietor. Terms £200-£500. ETC ★★ [Pets £1 per night].
e-mail: vlawrence05@aol.com

EUROPA PARK, BEACH ROAD, WOOLACOMBE (01271 871425). Static caravans, chalets, camping, surf lodges and surf cabins. Full facilities. Pets welcome. Indoor heated swimming pool, sauna, 24-hour shop.
e-mail: holidays@europapark.co.uk   website: www.europapark.co.uk

Yelverton

Small town on western edge of Dartmoor, Tavistock 5 miles..

EGGWORTHY FARM, SAMPFORD SPINEY, YELVERTON PL20 6LJ (Tel & Fax: 01822 852142). Moorland and valley walking within yards or just relax in the garden. Comfortable rooms, one double en suite, one family suite with private bathroom. Non-smoking. Pets welcome. Open all year except Christmas. Terms from £23-£30. ETC ★★★ [Pets £3 per night]
e-mail: eggworthyfarm@aol.com   website: www.eggworthyfarm.co.uk

Please note

All the information in this book is given in good faith in the belief that it is correct. However, the publishers cannot guarantee the facts given in these pages, neither are they responsible for changes in policy, ownership or terms that may take place after the date of going to press. Readers should always satisfy themselves that the facilities they require are available and that the terms, if quoted, still apply.

Visit the FHG website
www.holidayguides.com
for details of the wide choice of accommodation
featured in the full range of FHG titles

Bridport, Burton Bradstock, Charmouth

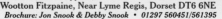

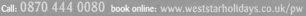

Powerstock, Sherborne, Studland Bay

FREE or REDUCED RATE entry to Holiday Visits and Attractions – see our
READERS' OFFER VOUCHERS on pages 371-390

Looking for holiday accommodation?

for details of hundreds of properties
throughout the UK including
comprehensive coverage of all areas of Scotland try:

www.holidayguides.com

Swanage, Wareham

Visit the FHG website
www.holidayguides.com
for details of the wide choice of accommodation
featured in the full range of FHG titles

West Bexington, Weymouth

DORSET COASTAL COTTAGES (0800 9804070). Carefully selected, traditional cottages in or near villages within ten miles of World Heritage Coast. Many are thatched; open fires or logburners; over half welcome dogs. Available all year. [Pets £15 per week]
website: www.dorsetcoastalcottages.com

Blandford

Handsome Georgian town that rose from the ashes of the 1731 fire; rebuilt with chequered brick and stone. Also known as Blandford Forum.

ANVIL INN & RESTAURANT, PIMPERNE, BLANDFORD DT11 8UQ (01258 453431; Fax: 01258 480182). A typical Old English hostelry offering good old-fashioned English hospitality. Full à la carte menu with mouthwatering desserts in the charming restaurant with log fire, delicious desserts, bar meals, specials board. All bedrooms with private facilities. Ample parking. ETC/AA ★★★★ [Pets £5 per night]
e-mail: theanvilinn@btconnect.com   website: www.anvilinn.co.uk

FREE or REDUCED RATE entry to Holiday Visits and Attractions – see our
READERS' OFFER VOUCHERS on pages 371-390

Bournemouth

One of Britain's premier holiday resorts with miles of golden sand, excellent shopping and leisure facilities. Lively entertainments include Festival of Lights at the beginning of September.

Self-contained two-bedroom apartments in quiet avenue, one minute from clean, sandy beaches and five minutes from shops. Sleeps 2-5. Includes linen. Fully equipped kitchen, cooker, fridge/freezer, microwave, colour TV, washing machine, tumble dryer. Toilet and shower. Central heating. Parking. Terms from £200. Contact: MRS HAMMOND, STOURCLIFFE COURT, 56 STOURCLIFFE AVENUE, SOUTHBOURNE, BOURNEMOUTH BH6 3PX (01202 420698). [Pets £2 per night, £10 weekly]

ALUM DENE HOTEL, 2 BURNABY ROAD, ALUM CHINE, BOURNEMOUTH BH4 8JF (01202 764011) Renowned for good old fashioned hospitality and friendly service. Come and be spoilt at our licensed hotel. All rooms en suite, colour TV. Some have sea views. 200 metres sea. Parking. Christmas House party. No charge for pets. [🐾]
e-mail: alumdenehotel@hotmail.co.uk   website: alumdenehotel.com

MIKE AND LYN LAMBERT, 16 FLORENCE ROAD, BOURNEMOUTH BH5 1HF (01202 304925). Modern Holiday Apartments sleeping up to ten persons, close to sea and shops. Clean, well-equipped flats. Car park. Phoneor e-mail for brochure. [Pets from £35 per week]
website: www.selfcateringbournemouth.co.uk

HOLIDAY FLATS AND FLATLETS a short walk to golden, sandy beaches. Most with private bathrooms. Cleanliness and comfort assured. Dogs welcome. Contact: M DE KMENT, 4 CECIL ROAD, BOURNEMOUTH BH5 1DU (07788 952394). [Pets £25 per week]

ANNE & RICHARD REYNOLDS, THE VINE HOTEL, 22 SOUTHERN ROAD, SOUTHBOURNE, BOURNEMOUTH BH6 3SR (01202 428309). A small, family, award-winning non-smoking Hotel only three hundred yards from dog-friendly beach and shops. All rooms en suite with tea/coffee making facilities and colour TV. Residential licence with attractive bar. Full central heating. Forecourt parking. Open all year. FHG Diploma, South West Tourism ★★★ [🐾]
website: www.vinehotel.co.uk

LANGTRY MANOR, DERBY ROAD, EAST CLIFF, BOURNEMOUTH BH1 3QB (01202 553887). A rare gem of a hotel where the building, food, service and history blend to form something quite exceptional. Midweek and weekend breaks. Pets welcome by arrangement. Bournemouth Tourism 'Best Small Hotel'. [🐾]
website: www.langtrymanor.co.uk

SOUTHBOURNE GROVE HOTEL, 96 SOUTHBOURNE ROAD, SOUTHBOURNE, BOURNEMOUTH BH6 3QQ (01202 420503; Fax: 01202 421953). Friendly, family-run hotel with beautiful garden and ample guest parking. Close to beach and shops. Excellent food served in spacious restaurant. En suite, four-poster suite, ground floor and large family rooms available, all with colour TV and tea/coffee facilities. B&B from £22 per night, £122 per week. This is a no smoking hotel. [🐾]

BILL AND MARJORIE TITCHEN, WHITE TOPPS HOTEL, 45 CHURCH ROAD, SOUTHBOURNE, BOURNEMOUTH BH6 4BB (01202 428868). Situated in quiet position close to lovely walks and beach. Dogs essential. Free parking. [🐾 pw!]
e-mail: thedoghotel@aol.com   website: www.whitetopps.co.uk

Bridport

Market town of Saxon origin noted for rope and net making. Harbour at West Bay has sheer cliffs rising from the beach

LANCOMBES HOUSE, WEST MILTON, BRIDPORT DT6 3TN (01308 485375). Four cottages and farmhouse, two with enclosed gardens. Set in 9 acres in an area ideal for walking, riding and outdoor pursuits. Children and dogs welcome. Open all year. ETC ★★★ [Pets £10 per week].
website: www.lancombes-house.co.uk

MRS S. NORMAN, FROGMORE FARM, CHIDEOCK, BRIDPORT DT6 6HT (01308 456159). The choice is yours - Bed and Breakfast in charming farmhouse, OR self-catering Cottage equipped for five, pets welcome. Brochure and terms free on request. [1st dog free, 2nd dog £3 per night, £15 per week]

GOLDEN ACRE, EYPE, NEAR BRIDPORT DT6 6AL (01308 421521). Private peaceful park. Close to beach. Chalet bungalows (1 or 2 bedrooms), sleep 2-4. Wonderful walks, on the Jurassic Coast. Pets free, house-trained owners welcome! [🐾]

Burton Bradstock

Village near coast, 3 miles SE of Bridport.

MRS JOSEPHINE PEARSE, TAMARISK FARM, BEACH ROAD, WEST BEXINGTON, DORCHESTER DT2 9DF (01308 897784). Self Catering properties sleep 4/7. Overlooking Chesil Beach: four large (MIMOSA FOR WHEELCHAIR DISABLED M3 (1); GRANARY LODGE DISABLED-FRIENDLY M1 and two small Cottages (ETC 3/4 Stars). Part of organic farm with arable, sheep, cattle, horses and market garden with organic vegetables, meat and wholemeal flour available. Good centre for touring, sightseeing, walking. Glorious sea views, very quiet. Lovely place for dogs. Terms from £255 to £960. Please telephone for details. [🐕]
e-mail: holidays@tamariskfarm.com   website: www.tamariskfarm.com

Charmouth

Small resort on Lyme Bay, 3 miles Lyme Regis. Sandy beach backed by undulating cliffs where many fossils are found. Good walks.

MR F. LOOSMORE, MANOR FARM HOLIDAY CENTRE, CHARMOUTH, BRIDPORT DT6 6QL (01297 560226). All units for four to six people. Ten minutes' level walk to beach, many fine local walks. Swimming pools, licensed bar with family room, shop, launderette. Sporting facilities nearby. Children and pets welcome. SAE for colour brochure. [Pets £3 per night, £20 per week]

Christchurch

Residential town near coast, 5 miles east of Bournemouth.

COUNTRY HOLIDAY CHALET on small, quiet, secluded woodland park within National Park. Sleeps four. Fenced private garden. Dogs welcome. Car parking. £175 to £350 per week. BH & HPA Member. Write enclosing SAE or telephone: MRS L.M. BOWLING, OWLPEN CARAVANS LTD, OWLPEN, 148 BURLEY ROAD, BRANSGORE, NEAR CHRISTCHURCH, DORSET BH23 8DB (01425 672875; mobile 07860 547391). [🐕 pw!]
website: www.owlpen-caravans.co.uk

Dorchester

Busy market town steeped in history. Roman remains include Amphitheatre and villa.

CHURCHVIEW GUEST HOUSE, WINTERBOURNE ABBAS, DORCHESTER DT2 9LS (Tel & Fax: 01305 889296). Beautiful 17th Century Licensed Guest House set in the heart of West Dorset, character bedrooms, delightful period dining room, two lounges and bar. Non-smoking. B&B £31–£39 pp. B&BEM £48–£54. Short breaks available. ETC ◆◆◆◆ Silver Award. [🐕]
e-mail: stay@churchview.co.uk   website: www.churchview.co.uk

GRACE COTTAGE. Charming cottage with enclosed garden. Lounge/dining room, study/bedroom, two bedrooms, well-equipped kitchen, two bathrooms. Pub nearby. Non-smokers only. Good touring centre. ETC ★★★. Apply: MRS WILLIS, 46 FLEET STREET, BEAMINSTER, DORSET DT8 3EH   (01308 863868).[🐕]
e-mail: nickywillis@tesco.net

MRS JACOBINA LANGLEY, THE STABLES B&B, HYDE CROOK (OFF A37), FRAMPTON DT2 9NW (01300 320075; Fax: 01300 321718). Comfortable country house in 20 acres with uninterrupted country views. Guest accommodation in separate wing, fully double-glazed, with central heating. Dogs most welcome (must have own beds and be kept under control; kennels can be provided). [pw! £3.50 per night]
e-mail: coba.stables@tiscali.co.uk   website: www.framptondorset.com

GREYGLES, MELCOMBE BINGHAM, NEAR DORCHESTER. Spacious, well-equipped house just 10 miles from Dorchester. Sleep 7. Heating, electricity, linen and towels incl. No smoking. ETC ★★★★ Booking: P. SOMMERFELD, 22 TIVERTON ROAD, LONDON NW10 3HL (020 8969 4830; Fax: 020 8960 0069). [🐕]
e-mail: enquiry@greygles.co.uk   website: www.greygles.co.uk

Lulworth (near)

Village on coast 4 miles from Wool.

MRS L. S. BARNES, LUCKFORD WOOD HOUSE, EAST STOKE, WAREHAM BH20 6AW (01929 463098; Mobile: 07888719002). Peaceful surroundings, delightful scenery. B&B classic farmhouse with style. Breakfast served in conservatory, dining room or garden. Also our camping and caravanning site nearby includes showers, toilets. Caravan and boat storage available. Near Lulworth Cove, Studland, Tank Museum and Monkey World. Open all year. From £35pp per night. [Pets £5 per night, £30 per week]
e-mail: info@luckfordleisure.co.uk   website: www.luckfordleisure.co.uk

Lyme Regis

Picturesque little resort with harbour, once the haunt of smugglers. Shingle beach with sand at low tide. Fishing, sailing and water ski-ing in Lyme Bay. Taunton 28 miles, Dorchester 24, Seaton 8.

JON SNOOK AND DEBBY SNOOK, WESTOVER FARM COTTAGES, WOOTTON FITZPAINE, NEAR LYME REGIS DT6 6NE (01297 560451/561395). Within walking distance of the sea. Four beautiful cottages, sleep 6/7, with large secluded gardens. Car parking. Logs available, linen supplied. 3 bedrooms. Well behaved pets welcome. ETC ★★★/★★★★ [Pets £18 per week]
e-mail: wfcottages@aol.com   website: www.westoverfarmcottages.co.uk

Poole

Flourishing port and market town. Three museums with interesting collections and lively displays.

SANDFORD HOLIDAY PARK, WESTSTAR HOLIDAY PARKS (0870 444 0080). Award-winning holiday park near Poole in a beautiful woodland setting and close to stunning sandy beaches. Dogs most welcome! Booking online. Quote WP. ETC ★★★★ [Pets £35 per week, pw!]
website: www.weststarholidays.co.uk/pw

Powerstock

Village 4 miles north east of Bridport.

MRS M. PREECE, THREE HORSESHOES INN, POWERSTOCK DT6 3TF (01308 485328). Victorian Inn tucked away in a peaceful part of West Dorset. Dogs welcome in three spacious en suite double rooms. Excellent cuisine. Log fires. [🐾]
e-mail: info@threehorseshoesinn.com   website: www.threehorseshoesinn.com

Sherborne

Town with abbey and two castles, one of which was built by Sir Walter Raleigh with lakes and gardens by Capability Brown.

WHITE HORSE FARM, MIDDLEMARSH, SHERBORNE DT9 5QN. The Willows sleeps 4-6; Toad Hall sleeps 4; Badger's sleeps 2; Ratty's sleeps 2/4; Moley's sleeps 2. Character self-catering holiday cottages in rural location. Well-equipped and comfortable. Digital TV, video, free films. 2 acres of paddock, garden and duck pond. Inn 100 yards. ETC ★★★/★★★★. AUDREY & STUART WINTERBOTTOM (01963 210222) [pw! 🐾]
e-mail: enquiries@whitehorsefarm.co.uk   website: www.whitehorsefarm.co.uk

Studland Bay

Unspoilt seaside village at south western end of Poole Bay, 3 miles north of Swanage.

THE MANOR HOUSE HOTEL, STUDLAND BAY BH19 3AU (01929 450288; Fax: 01929 452255). National Trust hotel set in 20 acres on cliffs overlooking Studland Bay. Superb food and accommodation. Log fires and four-posters. Tennis, horse-riding, golf and walking. [Pets £3.50]
e-mail: info@themanorhousehotel.com   website: www.themanorhousehotel.com

THE KNOLL HOUSE, STUDLAND BH19 3AW (01929 450450). Country house hotel within National Trust reserve. Golden beach. 100 acre grounds. Family suites of connecting rooms, six lounges. Tennis, golf, swimming, games rooms, health spa. See our Full Page Advertisement under Studland Bay. [Pets £5 per night, including food]
e-mail: info@knollhouse.co.uk   website: www.knollhouse.co.uk

Swanage

Traditional family holiday resort set in a sheltered bay ideal for water sports. Good base for a walking holiday.

DORSET COTTAGE HOLIDAYS. Self-catering cottages, town houses, bungalows and apartments. All within 10 miles of Heritage Coastline and sandy beaches. Excellent walking in idyllic countryside. Short breaks from £80, weekly from £135 (per cottage). Open all year. Free brochure tel: 01929 553443. [🐾]
e-mail: enq@dhcottages.co.uk   website: www.dhcottages.co.uk

MRS M. STOCKLEY, SWANAGE BAY VIEW HOLIDAY PARK, 17 MOOR ROAD, SWANAGE BH19 1RG (01929 424154). 4/5/6-berth Caravans. Pets welcome. Easter to October. Colour TV. Shop. Parking space. Rose Award Park [🐾]

THE LIMES, 48 PARK ROAD, SWANAGE BH19 2AE (01929 422664). Small and friendly, with en suite rooms, TV, tea/coffee making facilities. Children and pets welcome. Credit cards accepted. ETC ★★★ [🐾]
e-mail: info@limeshotel.net   website: www.limeshotel.net

Wareham

Picturesque riverside town almost surrounded by earthworks, considered pre-Roman. Nature reserves of great beauty nearby. Weymouth 19 miles, Bournemouth 14, Swanage 10, Poole 6.

CATRIONA AND ALISTAIR MILLER, CROMWELL HOUSE HOTEL, LULWORTH COVE BH20 5RJ (01929 400253/400332; Fax: 01929 400566). Comfortable family-run hotel, set in secluded gardens with spectacular sea views. Heated swimming pool, 20 en suite bedrooms. Restaurant, bar wine list. Self-catering. Disabled access. ETC/AA ★★ [🐾]

West Bexington

Seaside village with pebble beach. Chesil beach stretches eastwards. Nearby is Abbotsbury with its Benedictine Abbey and famous Swannery. Dorchester 13 miles, Weymouth 13, Bridport 6.

GORSELANDS CARAVAN PARK, DEPT PW, WEST BEXINGTON-ON-SEA DT2 9DJ (01308 897232; Fax: 01308 897239). Holiday Park. Fully serviced and equipped 4/6 berth caravans. Shop and launderette on site. Glorious sea views. Good country and seaside walks. One mile to beach. Holiday apartments with sea views and private garden. Pets most welcome. Colour brochure on request. ETC ★★★★, David Bellamy Silver Award. [🐾]
e-mail: info@gorselands.co.uk   website: www.gorselands.co.uk

Weymouth

Set in a beautiful bay with fine beaches and a picturesque 17th century harbour, Weymouth has a wide range of entertainment and leisure facilities.

CHARM PROPERTIES, WEYMOUTH. Charm Properties offers high quality, fully furnished self-catering accommodation in Weymouth and Portland, sleeping between 2-8 persons. Cleanliness and parking a priority. (01305 786514; Fax: 01305 786556). [🐾]
e-mail: contactus@charmproperties.co.uk   website: www.charmproperties.co.uk

GLENTHORNE, CASTLE COVE, 15 OLD CASTLE ROAD, WEYMOUTH DT4 8QB (01305 777281; Mobile: 07831 751526). Secluded beachfront B&B in elegant Victorian villa and well equipped apartments with panoramic sea views of Olympic sailing area. Extensive gardens, heated pool, play areas, dog friendly beach, coastal path. Parking. Contact OLIVIA NURRISH. [pw! 🐾]
e-mail: info@glenthorne-holidays.co.uk   website: www.glenthorne-holidays.co.uk

🐾	Indicates that pets are welcome free of charge.
£	Indicates that a charge is made for pets: nightly or weekly.
pw!	Shows some special provision for pets; exercise facility, feeding or accommodation arrangement.
⌂	Indicates separate pets accommodation.

Symbols

Bibury, Bourton-on-the-Water, Broadwell, Chalford, Clearwell (Forest of Dean)

Nailsworth, Newnham-on Severn, Stow-on-the-Wold, Stroud

Bibury

Village on the River Colne, 7 miles NE of Cirencester.

CAROLINE MANN, HARTWELL FARM COTTAGES, READY TOKEN, NEAR BIBURY, CIRENCESTER
GL7 5SY (01285 740210). Two comfortable, fully equipped cottages with country views. Ideally
located for touring. Stabling available. Glorious walks, excellent pubs. Children and well-behaved
dogs welcome. ETC ★★★★ [pw! Pets £15 per week]
e-mail: ec.mann@btinternet.com   website: www.selfcateringcotswolds.com

Bourton-on-the-Water

Delightfully situated on the River Windrush which is crossed by miniature stone bridges. Stow-on-the-Wold 4 miles.

STRATHSPEY, LANSDOWNE, BOURTON-ON-THE-WATER GL54 2AR (01451 810321; mobile: 07889
491993). Tastefully furnished bedrooms with TV, refreshment tray, hairdryer, clock radio. Pleasant
tranquil garden. Five minutes' walk from centre of village. Open all year. Terms from £25pppn. Pets
welcome by prior arrangement. AA ★★★ [🐾]
e-mail: bookings@strathspey.org.uk   website: www.strathspey.org.uk

CHESTER HOUSE HOTEL, VICTORIA STREET, BOURTON-ON-THE-WATER GL54 2BU (01451 820286).
All rooms en suite, all with central heating, colour TV, phone, tea/coffee making facilities. Wheelchair
friendly. Ideal for touring Cotswolds. [🐾]
e-mail: info@chesterhousehotel.com   website: www.chesterhousehotel.com

Broadwell

Village near the border of Oxfordshire, 1 mile north of Stow-on-the-Wold.

ROSE'S COTTAGE, BROADWELL, COTSWOLDS (01451 830007). Delightful country cottage,
tastefully decorated and furnished. Well-equipped kitchen, lounge with TV, comfortable furniture,
bedroom, and a large bathroom. Marvellous walking area. ETC ★★★★ [🐾]

Chalford

Village 4 miles south east of Stroud.

ROS SMITH, THE OLD COACH HOUSE, EDGECOMBE HOUSE, TOADSMOOR, BRIMSCOMBE,
STROUD GL5 2UE (01453 883147). Romantic 18th century Coach House in the heart of the
Cotswolds. Sleeps max. 2 couples + 1 child. Outdoor heated swimming pool and bubbling hot tub.
Free private kennel facilities (optional). Breaks £125-£635. Brochure. [[🐾 ⌂]
website: www.doggybreaks.co.uk

Clearwell (Forest of Dean)

Village 2 miles south of Coleford in the ancient Forest of Dean.

TUDOR FARMHOUSE HOTEL & RESTAURANT, CLEARWELL, NEAR COLEFORD GL16 8JS (Freephone
0800 7835935; Tel: 01594 833046; Fax: 01594 837093). Charming 13th Century farmhouse hotel in
extensive grounds, ideal for dog walking. 22 en suite bedrooms including Four Posters and Cottage
Suite. Award-winning restaurant. WTB ★★★, AA ★★ and Two Rosettes. [Pets £5 per night].
e-mail: info@tudorfarmhousehotel.co.uk   website: www.tudorfarmhousehotel.co.uk

Fairford

Small town 8 miles east of Cirencester.

THE BULL HOTEL, MARKET PLACE, FAIRFORD GL7 4AA (01285 712535/712217; Fax: 01285 713782). Ideal for holding conferences and wedding receptions. Restaurant offers à la carte menu and fine wines. 22 fully equipped bedrooms with sloping roofs and oak beams. Four-poster and family rooms available. Opened January 2007 Cotswold Therapy Room. ETC/AA ★★ [Pets £5 per night, £20 per week]
e-mail: info@thebullhotelfairford.co.uk   website: www.thebullhotelfairford.co.uk

Forest of Dean

Formerly a royal hunting ground, this scenic area lies between the rivers Severn and Wye.

WHARTON LODGE COTTAGES, WESTON-UNDER-PENYARD, NEAR ROSS-ON-WYE HR9 7JX (Tel & Fax: 01989 750140). Two elegantly furnished, fully equipped self-catering retreats overlooking the Herefordshire countryside sleeping 2, 3 or 4 guests. Fully inclusive rates. One well behaved dog by arrangement. Tourist Board ★★★★★.
e-mail: ncross@whartonlodge.co.uk   website: www.whartonlodge.co.uk

DRYSLADE FARM, ENGLISH BICKNOR, COLEFORD GL16 7PA (Tel & Fax: 01594 860259). Daphne and Phil warmly welcome you and your dogs for B&B at their 18th century farmhouse on family working farm. Situated in Royal Forest of Dean and close to Symonds Yat with ample walking. Excellent breakfast. Terms from £27-£35. AA ★★★★ Highly Commended. [🐾]
website: www.drysladefarm.co.uk

THE SPEECH HOUSE, COLEFORD, FOREST OF DEAN GL16 7EL (01594 822607; Fax: 01594 823658). A friendly Hotel set in the heart of the Forest of Dean. The perfect place to get away from it all. 37 en suite bedrooms. Lavish restaurant. Beauty suite. AA/RAC ★★★ [Pets £10 per stay]
e-mail: relax@thespeechhouse.co.uk   website: www.thespeechhouse.co.uk

Meysey Hampton

Award-winning village 6 miles east of Cirencester, 12 miles north west of Swindon.

THE MASONS ARMS, 28 HIGH STREET, MEYSEY HAMPTON, NEAR CIRENCESTER GL7 5JT (Tel: 01285 850164; Fax: 01285 850194). 17th century inn beside village green. Excellent food and drink with daily 'specials'; comfortable bedrooms with en suite facilities, TV. tea/coffee. AA/ETC ◆◆◆
e-mail: info@masonsarmscotswolds.co.uk   website: www.masonsarmscotswolds.co.uk
Lydney

ANTHONY & INEZ MIDGLEY, HIGHBURY COACH HOUSE, BREAM ROAD, LYDNEY GL15 5JH (01594 842 339 or 07834 408 550). Come and stay in one or more of the three spacious flats in the Coach House of Highbury House, situated on the southern edge of the Royal Forest of Dean. EnjoyEngland ★★★. [🐾]
e-mail: info@highburycoachhouse.co.uk   website: www.highburycoachhouse.co.uk

Nailsworth

Hilly town 4 miles south of Stroud

THE LAURELS, INCHBROOK, NAILSWORTH GL5 5HA (01453 834021; Fax: 01453 835190). A lovely rambling house, cottage and secluded garden where dogs and their owners are encouraged to relax and enjoy. Ideally situated for touring all parts of the Cotswolds and West Country; splendid walks. Brochure. [🐾]
e-mail: laurelsinchbrook@tiscali.co.uk   website: www.laurelsinchbrook.co.uk

Newnham-on-Severn

Town on right bank on River Severn, 10 miles south-west of Gloucester.

SWAN HOUSE GUEST HOUSE, HIGH STREET, NEWNHAM-ON-SEVERN GL14 1BY (01594 516504). 17th century Grade II Listed house, tastefully furnished and decorated, near Forest of Dean. All rooms en suite. Choice of delicious breakfasts using fresh local produce. Garden for relaxing. On bus routes. Children and pets welcome. AA ◆◆◆◆ [Pets £8 per stay].
e-mail: stay@swanhousenewnham.co.uk   website: www.swanhousenewnham.co.uk

Painswick

Beautiful little Cotswold town with characteristic stone-built houses.

MISS E. WARLAND, HAMBUTTS MYND, EDGE ROAD, PAINSWICK GL6 6UP (01452 812352; Fax: 01452 813862). Bed and Breakfast in an old Converted Corn Mill. Very quiet with superb views. Three minutes to the centre of the village. Central heating. One double room, one twin, one single, all with TV. From £30 to £55 per night per room, 10% discount for 4 nights or more. ALL ROOMS EN SUITE. ETC ★★★ [🐾]
e-mail: ewarland@aol.com

Stow-on-the-Wold

Charming Cotswold hill-top market town with several old inns and interesting buildings. Birmingham 45 miles, Gloucester 26, Stratford-upon-Avon 21, Cheltenham 18, Chipping Norton 9.

THE OLD STOCKS HOTEL THE SQUARE, STOW-ON-THE-WOLD GL54 1AF (01451 830666; Fax: 01451 870014). Ideal base for touring this beautiful area. Tasteful guest rooms (including three 'garden' rooms) with modern amenities. Mouth-watering menus. Special bargain breaks also available. HETB/AA ★★ [Pets £5 per stay]
e-mail: fhg@oldstockshotel.co.uk   website: www.oldstockshotel.co.uk

THE LIMES, EVESHAM ROAD, STOW-ON-THE-WOLD GL54 1EN (01451 830034/831056). Large Country House. Attractive garden, overlooking fields, 4 minutes town centre. Television lounge. Central heating. Car park. Bed and Breakfast from £25 to £30 pppn. Twin, double or family rooms, all en suite. Children and pets welcome. AA ◆◆◆, Tourist Board Listed. [🐾]
e-mail: thelimes@zoom.co.uk   website: www.cotswolds.info/webpage/thelimes-stow.htm

Stroud

Cotswold town on River Frome below picturesque Stroudwater Hills, formerly renowned for cloth making. Bristol 32 miles, Bath 29, Chippenham 25, Cheltenham 14, Gloucester 9.

DOWNFIELD HOTEL, CAINSCROSS ROAD, STROUD GL5 4HN (01453 764496). Easy to find – just 5 miles from M5 – and easy to park. Ideal location for exploring Cotswolds. Comfortable lounges, home-cooked evening meal, cosy bar – all at sensible prices. Dogs and children most welcome. ETC/AA ◆◆◆ [🐾]
e-mail: downfield@downfieldhotel.co.uk   website: www.downfieldhotel.co.uk

MRS A. RHOTON, HYDE CREST, CIRENCESTER ROAD, MINCHINHAMPTON GL6 8PE (01453 731631). Beautiful country house with enclosed acre garden. All rooms on ground floor opening on to patios and lawns. 500 acres of commons, plus country walks nearby. AA ★★★★ [pw! 🐾]
e-mail: stay@hydecrest.co.uk   website: www.hydecrest.co.uk

MRS UNA PEACEY, THE WITHYHOLT GUEST HOUSE, PAUL MEAD, EDGE, NEAR STROUD GL6 6PG (01452 813618: Fax: 01452 812375) Modern guesthouse in Gloucestershire close to Gloucester Cathedral, Tetbury, Stroud. Many lovely country walks. En suite bedrooms, large lounge. Large garden. ETC ◆◆◆◆ [🐾]

🐾   Indicates that pets are welcome free of charge.

£   Indicates that a charge is made for pets: nightly or weekly.

pw!   Shows some special provision for pets; exercise facility, feeding or accommodation arrangement.

⌂   Indicates separate pets accommodation.

Symbols

Bath, Blue Anchor, Brean, Cheddar

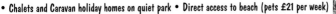

Visit the FHG website
www.holidayguides.com
for details of the wide choice of accommodation
featured in the full range of FHG titles

Duddings
COUNTRY COTTAGES

VB ★★★★

Thatched longhouse and 12 cottages for 2-12 persons, beautifully converted from old stone barns and stables. Original beams and exposed stonework retain the character of the buildings. Two miles from the picturesque village of Dunster in the Exmoor National Park.

Luxury Cottages
Indoor Heated Pool
Tennis Court

Colour brochure from Duddings
Timberscombe Dunster, Somerset TA24 7TB

Telephone: 01643 841123
Web Site: www.duddings.co.uk
Email: richard@duddings.co.uk

As resident owners, we personally guarantee immaculate presentation of cottages on arrival. Each cottage has tasteful decor with matching, highest quality fabrics and is fully central heated. Amenities include comfortable lounges with colour TV/video/DVD, fully fitted modern kitchens with fridge-freezer, cooker and microwave. Our facilities include heated indoor pool, hard tennis court, putting green, pool and table tennis, trampoline, football net and play centre. Trout stream in 8.5 acres for fishing and picnics. Families and pets welcome, walking, riding, beaches nearby. Short breaks available off season, open all year.
Full details and plans of the cottages together with up to date prices and availablity can be found on our website, or please call for brochure.

Looking for holiday accommodation?
for details of hundreds of properties
throughout the UK including
comprehensive coverage of all areas of Scotland try:
www.holidayguides.com

Exmoor, Minehead, Porlock

Porlock, Quantock Hills, Taunton, Watchet, Weston-Super-Mare

Please mention **Pets Welcome!**
when making enquiries about accommodation featured in these pages

Weston-Super-Mare

Bath

The best-preserved Georgian city in Britain, Bath has been famous since Roman times for its mineral springs. It is a noted centre for music and the arts, with a wide range of leisure facilities.

DAVID & JACKIE BISHOP, TOGHILL HOUSE FARM, FREEZING HILL, WICK, NEAR BATH BS30 5RT (01225 891261; Fax: 01225 892128). Luxury barn conversions on working farm 3 miles north of Bath. Each equipped to very high standard, bed linen provided. Also en suite B&B accommodation in 17th century farmhouse. [pw! Pets £2 per night, £8 per week]
website: www.toghillhousefarm.co.uk

Blue Anchor

Hamlet two miles west of Watchet. Beautiful beaches, and rocks and cliffs of geological interest.

PRIMROSE HILL HOLIDAYS, WOOD LANE, BLUE ANCHOR TA24 6LA (01643 821200). Award-winning, spacious, comfortable accommodation in a terrace of four bungalows. Private gardens with panoramic views. A dog-friendly beach is a 10-minute walk away, with other lovely walks from your doorstep. Open all year. Fully whelchair accessible. ETC ★★★★ [Pets £15 per week].
e-mail: info@primrosehillholidays.co.uk   website: www.primrosehillholidays.co.uk

Brean

Coastal village with extensive sands. To north is the promontory of Brean Down. Weston-Super-Mare 9 miles.

BEACHSIDE HOLIDAY PARK, COAST ROAD, BREAN SANDS TA8 2QZ (FREEPHONE 08000 190322; Tel: 01278 751346; Fax: 01278 751683). Chalets and Caravan holiday homes on quiet park. Direct access to beach (dogs allowed). Full facilities. Colour TV. Golf courses nearby. Bars and restaurants nearby. Free brochure. [Pets £3 per night, £21 per week]
website: www.beachsideholidaypark.co.uk

WESTWARD RISE HOLIDAY PARK, SOUTH ROAD, BREAN, NEAR BURNHAM ON-SEA TA8 2RD (01278 751310). Highly Recommended Luxury 2/6 berth Chalet bungalows. 2 double bedrooms, shower, toilet, TV, fridge, cooker, duvets and linen. Open all year. Call for free brochure. [Pets £15 per week.]
website: www.westwardrise.com

Cheddar

Picturesque little town in the Mendips, famous for its Gorge and unique caves. Cheese-making is a speciality. Good touring centre. Bath 24 miles, Burnham-on-sea 13, Weston-Super-Mare 11.

SUNGATE HOLIDAY APARTMENTS, CHURCH STREET, CHEDDAR, SOMERSET BS27 3RA. Ideally situated for walking, cycling and touring the Mendips and the West Country. Competitively priced for short or longer holidays. For full details contact Mrs M. FIELDHOUSE (01934 842273/742264) ETC ★★★ [Quote for Pets].
e-mail: enquiries@sungateholidayapartments.co.uk   web: www.sungateholidayapartments.co.uk

BROADWAY HOUSE HOLIDAY TOURING CARAVAN & CAMPING PARK, CHEDDAR BS27 3DB (01934 742610; Fax: 01934 744950). Holiday caravans for hire; premier touring and camping pitches. Heated pool, adventure playground, pub, shop, launderette. Superb range of activities - skateboard park, BMX track. ETC ★★★★
e-mail: info@broadwayhouse.uk.com   website: www.broadwayhouse.uk.com

Dunster

Pretty village with interesting features, including Yarn Market, imposing 14th century Castle. Priory Church and old houses and cottages. Minehead 3 miles.

DUDDINGS COUNTRY COTTAGES, TIMBERSCOMBE DUNSTER TA24 7TB (01643 841123) Thatched longhouse and 12 cottages for 2-12 persons, beautifully converted from old stone barns and stables. Two miles from the village of Dunster in the Exmoor National Park. Pets and families welcome. Open all year. Visit Britain ★★★★ Self Catering. [pw!, Pets £20 per week].
e-mail: richard@duddings.co.uk   website: www.duddings.co.uk

THE YARN MARKET HOTEL, HIGH STREET, DUNSTER TA24 6SF (01643 821425; Fax: 01643 821475). An ideal location for walking and exploring Exmoor. Family-run hotel with a friendly, relaxed atmosphere, home cooking, en suite rooms with colour TV and tea making facilities. Non-smoking. Mid-week breaks a speciality – Pets Welcome. ETC ★★★ Hotel [pw! 🐾]
e-mail: yarnmarket.hotel@virgin.net   website: www.yarnmarkethotel.co.uk

Exford

Fine touring centre for Exmoor and North Devon, on River Exe. Dulverton 10 miles.

LEONE & BRIAN MARTIN, RISCOMBE FARM HOLIDAY COTTAGES, EXFORD, EXMOOR NATIONAL PARK TA24 7NH (01643 831480). Beside River Exe – centre of Exmoor National Park – close to coast. Four charming self-catering cottages. Dogs and horses welcome. Stabling available. VB ★★★★ [Pets £2.50 per night, £15 per week.]
website: www.riscombe.co.uk (with up-to-date vacancy info.)

MRS P. EDWARDS, WESTERMILL FARM, EXFORD, MINEHEAD TA24 7NJ (01643 831238; Fax: 01643 831216). Cottages in grass paddocks (Disabled Category 2), with woodburners. Separate campsite by river. Way-marked walks. Wonderful for dogs and owners. ETC up to ★★★★ [pw! Pets £2 per night (camp), £15 per week in cottages].
e-mail: pw@westermill.com   website: www.westermill.com

STILEMOOR, EXFORD, EXMOOR NATIONAL PARK TA24 7NA. Charming cosy centrally heated detached bungalow with enclosed garden, superb views, walking, fishing, riding. Sleeps 6. ETC ★★★★. JOAN ATKINS, 2 EDGCOTT COTTAGE, EXFORD, MINEHEAD TA24 7QG (Tel & Fax: 01643 831564; mobile: 078914 37293) [Pets £15 per week]
e-mail: info@stilemoorexmoor.co.uk   website: www.stilemoorexmoor.co.uk

Exmoor

265 square miles of unspoiled heather moorland with deep wooded valleys and rivers, ideal for a walking, pony trekking or fishing holiday.

JENNY COPE, NORTH DOWN FARM, PYNCOMBE LANE, WIVELISCOMBE, TAUNTON TA4 2BL (Tel & Fax: 01984 623730). Traditional working farm. All rooms en suite, furnished to high standard. Log fires. Central heating. B&B £31pppn. BB&EM: 7 nights £250pp, 3-night B&B and evening meal £125pp. Dogs welcome. ETC ◆◆◆◆ Silver Award. [£5 per pet per visit].
e-mail: jennycope@btinternet.com   website: www.north-down-farm.co.uk

WESTERCLOSE HOUSE, WITHYPOOL, EXMOOR NATIONAL PARK TA24 7QR (01643 831302). Moorland cosy cottages including two bungalows in grounds of old hunting lodge overlooking Barle Valley. Dogs and horses welcome. Shop and pub 300 metres. ETC ★★★★ [pw! Dogs £12 per week]
website: www.westerclose.co.uk

THE PACK HORSE, ALLERFORD, NEAR PORLOCK TA24 8HW (Tel & Fax: 01643 862475). Self-catering apartments and cottage within picturesque National Trust village. Immediate access to the beautiful surrounding countryside. Stabling available. Open all year. ETC ★★★/★★★★ [Pets £10 per visit]
e-mail: holidays@thepackhorse.net   website: www.thepackhorse.net

THE CROWN HOTEL, EXFORD TA24 7PP (01643 831554; Fax: 01643 831665). Situated in rural England. All bedrooms with bath, colour television, hairdryer. Excellent cuisine and fine wines. Bargain Breaks. Superb dog holiday country. Small charge for dogs and horses. AA ★★★ and Two Rosettes. [pw! Pets £7.50 per week 🐾]
e-mail: info@crownhotelexmoor.co.uk   website: www.crownhotelexmoor.com

PENNY & ROGER WEBBER, HINDON ORGANIC FARM, SELWORTHY, NEAR MINEHEAD, EXMOOR TA24 8SH (01643 705244) Idyllic award-winning organic working farm. Own produce. Quality accommodation in 18th century farmhouse, also self-catering cottage. Organic cooked breakfasts. Farm shop.
email: hindonfarm@hindonfarm.plus.com   website: www.hindonfarm.co.uk

WOODCOMBE LODGES, BRATTON, NEAR MINEHEAD TA24 8SQ (Tel & Fax: 01643 702789). Four self-catering lodges in a tranquil rural setting on the edge of Exmoor National Park, standing in a beautiful 2½ acre garden with wonderful views. [Pets £10 per week]
e-mail: nicola@woodcombelodge.co.uk   website: www.woodcombelodge.co.uk

JANE STYLES, WINTERSHEAD FARM, SIMONSBATH TA24 7LF (01643 831222). Five tastefully furnished and well-equipped cottages situated in the midst of beautiful Exmoor. Pets welcome, stabling and grazing, DIY livery. Colour brochure on request. ETC ★★★★ [Dogs £15 per week, Horses £20 per week.]
website: www.wintershead.co.uk

Minehead

Neat and stylish resort on Bristol Channel. Sandy bathing beach, attractive gardens, golf course and good facilities for tennis, bowls and horse riding. Within easy reach of the beauties of Exmoor.

MINEHEAD 16TH CENTURY THATCHED COTTAGES. Rose Ash - Sleeps 2, prettily furnished, all electric. Willow - Inglenook, oak panelling, electricity, gas, CH, Sleeps 6. Little Thatch - Sleeps 5, Inglenook, Cosy location, Electricity. Gas, CH. Private car park. Enclosed gardens. Pets welcome. SAE: MR T. STONE, TROYTES FARMSTEAD, TIVINGTON, MINEHEAD TA24 8SU (01643 704531). [🐾]

Porlock

Small resort near coast at foot of a steep hill.

CASTLE HOTEL, PORLOCK TA24 8PY (01643 862504). Fully licensed, family-run hotel in centre of lovely Exmoor village. 9 en suite bedrooms, all centrally heated. Bar snacks and meals. Well-behaved children and pets welcome. [🐾]

SHIP'S MEWS, PORLOCK. Four quality open-plan apartments, former stables, and one spacious family house. All with sea views, parking, easy access, garden or outside space. Linen provided. Pets most welcome. Open all year. To find out more view website or phone 07979 278466 (mobile).
website: www.shipsmews.co.uk

THE COTTAGE, PORLOCK, MINEHEAD TA24 8PU (Tel & Fax: 01643 862996). Bed and Breakfast, Dinner on request. Superior en suite rooms, all facilities. Annexe for guests with dogs with room only option. Credit Cards. AA ★★★★
e-mail: cottageporlock@aol.com   website: www.cottageporlock.co.uk

Mr R. CONNOR, THE SHIP INN, HIGH STREET, PORLOCK TA24 8QD (01643 862507). Thatched 13th century family-run inn within walking distance of sea and moor. Genuine old bar with stone floor and log fire. Home cooked food. Six real ales, three ciders. Four B&B bedrooms, all en suite. [Pets £5 per stay]
e-mail: mail@shipinnporlock.co.uk   website: www.shipinnporlock.co.uk

Quantock Hills

Granite and limestone ridge running north-west and south-east from Quantoxhead and Kingston.

THE OLD CIDER HOUSE, 25 CASTLE STREET, NETHER STOWEY TA5 1LN (01278 732228). In picturesque, historic village at the foot of the Quantocks. All en suite; licensed dining. Own car parking, secluded garden. B&B from £30pppn. Wonderful dog-walking country; only 4 miles from coast. EnjoyEngland ★★★★ Guest Accommodation. [Pets £15.50 per week].
e-mail: info@theoldciderhouse.co.uk   website: www.theoldciderhouse.co.uk

Taunton

County capital in Vale of Taunton Deane. Museum, Civic Centre, remains of Norman castle.

FARTHINGS HOTEL & RESTAURANT, HATCH BEAUCHAMP, TAUNTON TA3 6SG (01823 480664; Fax: 01823 481118). Nestled in the midst of the wild and fertile countryside of Somerset, just 3 miles from the M5 and Taunton. An elegant Georgian Hotel with beautiful grounds and gardens, orchards, roses, and our own poultry for your breakfast eggs. AA ★★ Two Rosettes
e-mail: info@farthingshotel.co.uk   website: www.farthingshotel.co.uk

Watchet

Small port and resort with rocks and sands. Good centre for Exmoor and the Quantocks. Bathing, boating, fishing, rambling. Tiverton 24 miles, Bridgwater 19, Taunton 17, Dunster 6.

MRS K. MUSGRAVE, CROFT HOLIDAY COTTAGES, THE CROFT, ANCHOR STREET, WATCHET TA23 0BY (01984 631121) Courtyard of six cottages/bungalows situated in a quiet backwater of the small harbour town of Watchet. Parking, central heating. TV, DVD, washing machine, fridge/freezer, microwave. Use of heated indoor pool. Sleeps 2-6 persons. £170-£675 per property per week. ETC ★★★★ [Pets £15 per week]
e-mail: croftcottages@talk21.com   website: www.cottagessomerset.com

Wells

England's smallest city. West front of Cathedral built around 1230, shows superb collection of statuary.

INFIELD HOUSE, 36 PORTWAY, WELLS BA5 2BN (01749 670989; Fax: 01749 679093). Richard and Heather invite you and your dog (if older than one year) to visit England's smallest city. Wonderful walks on Mendip Hills. No smoking. Bountiful breakfasts, dinners by arrangement. AA ◆◆◆◆ [🐾]
website: www.infieldhouse.co.uk

Weston-Super-Mare

Popular resort on the Bristol Channel with a wide range of entertainments and leisure facilities. An ideal base for touring the West Country.

SOMERSET COURT COTTAGES, WICK ST LAWRENCE, NEAR WESTON-SUPER-MARE BS22 7YR (01934 521383). Converted stone cottages in mediaeval village. 1, 2 or 3 beds. Some with four-posters, luxury whirlpool/spa baths. Superb centre for touring West Country. Short Breaks available. £200-£660 per week. [Pets £2 per night]
e-mail: peter@somersetcourtcottages.co.uk   website: www.somersetcourtcottages.co.uk

MR C. G. THOMAS, ARDNAVE HOLIDAY PARK, KEWSTOKE, WESTON-SUPER-MARE BS22 9XJ (01934 622319). Caravans - De luxe. 2-3 bedrooms, shower, toilet, colour TVs, all bedding included. Parking. Dogs welcome. Graded ★★★. [🐾 pw!]

BRAESIDE HOTEL, 2 VICTORIA PARK, WESTON-SUPER-MARE BS23 2HZ (01934 626642). Delightful, family-run Hotel, close to shops, beach and park. Parking available. All rooms en suite, colour TV, tea/coffee making. November to March THIRD NIGHT FREE. ETC/AA ◆◆◆◆ (Awarded in 2005) [🐾]
e-mail: enquiries@braesidehotel.com   website: www.braesidehotel.com

Grittleton

Village 6 miles north west of Chippenham.

THE NEELD ARMS INN, THE STREET, GRITTLETON SN14 6AP (01249 782470; Fax: 01249 782358). 17th century inn offering comfortable accommodation and home-cooked food; four-poster available. Children and pets welcome. Convenient for Bath, Stonehenge, Cotswolds. ETC ◆◆◆
e-mail: info@neeldarms.co.uk   website: www.neeldarms.co.uk

Salisbury

13th century cathedral city, with England's highest spire at 404ft. Many fine buildings.

MR A. SHERING, SWAYNES FIRS FARM, GRIMSDYKE, COOMBE BISSETT, SALISBURY SP5 5RF (01725 519240). Small working farm with cattle, poultry, geese and duck ponds. Spacious rooms, all en suite with colour TV. Ideal for visiting the many historic sites in the area. ETC ★★★ [Pets £6 per night]
e-mail: swaynes.firs@virgin.net   website: www.swaynesfirs.co.uk

Warminster

Former market town on the western edge of the Salisbury Plain. Well known for UFO sightings. Westbury 4 miles, Trowbridge 8 Miles.

SPINNEY FARMHOUSE, THOULSTONE, CHAPMANSLADE, WESTBURY BA13 4AQ (01373 832412). Enjoy farm fresh food in a warm, friendly, family atmosphere. Off A36, 16 miles from Bath. All rooms with washbasins, tea/coffee making. TV lounge. No smoking. Children and pets welcome. [🐾]

Chesham

Town on south side of Chiltern Hills. Ideal walking area.

PAT & GEORGE ORME, 49 LOWNDES AVENUE, CHESHAM HP5 2HH (01494 792647). B&B in detached house, 10 minutes from the Underground. Private bathroom, tea/coffee, TV. Good walking country - Chiltern Hills three minutes. ETC ◆◆◆ [🛏]
e-mail: bbormelowndes@tiscali.co.uk

Milton Keynes

Purpose-built new city, home to the Open University. Midway between London, Birmingham, Leicester, Oxford and Cambridge.

SWAN REVIVED HOTEL, HIGH STREET, NEWPORT PAGNELL, MILTON KEYNES MK16 8AR (01908 610565; Fax: 01908 210995). Delightful 16thC former coaching inn, extensively modernised to provide 40 comfortable guest rooms, two bars, à la carte restaurant, meeting rooms and banqueting facilities. Pets very welcome. [🛏]
e-mail: info@swanrevived.co.uk   website: www.swanrevived.co.uk

Looking for holiday accommodation?
for details of hundreds of properties
throughout the UK visit:

www.holidayguides.com

Please note
All the information in this book is given in good faith in the belief that it is correct. However, the publishers cannot guarantee the facts given in these pages, neither are they responsible for changes in policy, ownership or terms that may take place after the date of going to press. Readers should always satisfy themselves that the facilities they require are available and that the terms, if quoted, still apply.

Lyndhurst, New Forest, Petersfield, Ringwood

Ashurst

Three miles north-east of Lyndhurst.

WOODLANDS LODGE HOTEL, BARTLEY ROAD, ASHURST, WOODLANDS SO40 7GN ((023) 80 292257; Fax: (023) 80 293090). Luxury Hotel offering peace and tranquillity. 16 bedrooms, all en suite with whirlpool bath, TV, hairdryer, telephone etc. Award winning Restaurant. Direct access to Forest. ETC/AA ★★★ [Pets £5 per night].
e-mail: reception@woodlands-lodge.co.uk   website: www.woodlands-lodge.co.uk

Lymington

Residential town and yachting centre 15 miles east of Bournemouth.

HONEYSUCKLE HOUSE, 24 CLINTON ROAD, LYMINGTON SO41 9EA (Tel & Fax: 01590 676635). Ground floor double room/single, en suite, non-smoking. Woodland walk, park, quay and marinas nearby. B&B from £30.00 pppn. [🐾]
e-mail: skyblue@beeb.net   website: http://explorethenewforest.co.uk/honeysuckle.htm

MRS P. J. ELLIS, EFFORD COTTAGE, EVERTON, LYMINGTON SO41 0JD (01590 642315; Fax: 01590 641030). Outstanding B&B with old world charm in proprietor's own Georgian home. Excellent touring centre for New Forest and South Coast. All rooms en suite with luxury facilities. B&B from £25-£35pppn. No children. AA ★★★★, Michelin. [PW! Pets from £2 per night]
e-mail: effordcottage@aol.com   website: www.effordcottage.co.uk

Lyndhurst

Good base for enjoying the fascinating New Forest as well as the Hampshire coastal resorts. Bournemouth 20 miles, Southampton 9.

ORMONDE HOUSE HOTEL, SOUTHAMPTON ROAD, LYNDHURST SO43 7BT (023 8028 2806, Fax: 023 8028 2004). Opposite open forest, easy drive to Exbury Gardens and Beaulieu. Elegant, family-run Two Star Hotel with pretty, en suite rooms with CTV, phone and beverage making. Superior rooms and ground floor suites, all with kingsize bed and some with whirlpool bath. Bar, lounge and delicious dinners available. AA ★★. [Pets £3.50 per night, max. 2 per room]
e-mail: enquiries@ormondehouse.co.uk   website: www.ormondehouse.co.uk

THE CROWN HOTEL, LYNDHURST, NEW FOREST S043 7NF (023 8028 2922; Fax: 023 8028 2751). A mellow, Listed building in the centre of the village, an ideal base for exploring the delights of the New Forest with your canine friend(s). Free parking, quiet garden, three star luxury and animal loving staff. [Pets £5.00 per night].
e-mail: reception@crownhotel-lyndhurst.co.uk   website: www.crownhotel-lyndhurst.co.uk

New Forest

Area of heath and woodland of nearly 150 square miles, formerly Royal hunting grounds.

MRS E.E. MATTHEWS, THE ACORNS, OGDENS, NEAR FORDINGBRIDGE SP6 2PY (01425 655552). Luxury two bedroomed residential-type caravan. Sleeps 4/6. Maintained to high standard, kitchen, showeroom, sitting/diningroom, outside laundry area, own garden. Lovely New Forest setting. Non-smoking, ample parking. Children over five years. Well-behaved dogs welcome (max. 2). Terms £185 - £350, Easter to mid-October. [pw! Pets £10 each per week].
e-mail: acornshols@btopenworld.com   website: www.dogscome2.co.uk

THE WATERSPLASH HOTEL, THE RISE, BROCKENHURST SO42 7ZP (01590 622344). Prestigious New Forest family-run country house hotel set in large garden. Noted for fine personal service, accommodation and traditional English cuisine at its best. All rooms en suite. Luxury four-poster with double spa bath. Swimming pool. Short walk to open forest. AA ★★ Colour brochure available.[🐾]
e-mail: bookings@watersplash.co.uk   website: www.watersplash.co.uk

MRS J. PEARCE, ST. URSULA, 30 HOBART ROAD, NEW MILTON BH25 6EG (01425 613515). Excellent facilities and warm welcome for well behaved pets and owners! Ground floor suite suitable for disabled guests, plus single and twin rooms. Bed & Breakfast from £27.50. ◆◆◆◆ [🐾]

Petersfield

Market town situated on the northern border of the South Downs within an Area of Outstanding Natural Beauty, 11 miles north east of Portsmouth.

LANGRISH HOUSE, LANGRISH, PETERSFIELD GU32 1RN (01730 266941).17th century house in idyllic country location. All bedrooms en suite and non-smoking. Small, cosy restaurant; weddings and conferences catered for.
e-mail: frontdesk@langrishhouse.co.uk   website: www.langrishhouse.co.uk

Ringwood

Busy market town, centre for trout fishing, trekking and rambling. Bournemouth 13 miles.

MRS DYSON, THE HIGH CORNER INN, LINWOOD, RINGWOOD, HANTS BH24 3QY (01425 473973, Fax: 01425 483052). Seven en suite bedrooms deep in the heart of The New Forest. Real ales, home-cooked food, Sunday carvery and log fires. Pets welcome.

Isle of Wight

The Isle of Wight has several award-winning beaches, including Blue Flag winners, all of which are managed and maintained to the highest standard. Sandown, Shanklin and Ryde offer all the traditional delights; or head for Compton Bay where surfers brave the waves, fossil hunters admire the casts of dinosaur footprints at low tide, kitesurfers leap and soar across the sea and paragliders hurl themselves off the cliffs

Newport is the commercial centre of the Island with many famous high street stores and plenty of places to eat and drink. Ryde has a lovely Victorian Arcade lined with shops selling books and antiques. Cowes is great for sailing garb and Godshill is a treasure chest for the craft enthusiast.

The Island's diverse terrain makes it an ideal landscape for walkers and cyclists of all ages and abilities. Pony trekking and beach rides are also popular holiday pursuits and the Island's superb golf courses, beautiful scenery and temperate climate combine to make it the perfect choice for a golfing break.

With up to 350 daily ferry crossings, the Isle of Wight has to be the UK's most accessible Island, and once there, it's easy to get around. There's a comprehensive bus network and a regular train service, which operates between Ryde and Shanklin and connects with the Isle of Wight Steam Railway.

ISLAND COTTAGE HOLIDAYS Charming individual cottages in lovely rural surroundings and close to the sea. Over 55 cottages situated throughout the Isle of Wight. Beautiful views, attractive gardens, delightful country walks. All equipped to a high standard and graded for quality by the Tourist Board. For a brochure please telephone 01929 480080. ETC ★★★ to ★★★★★.
e-mail: enq@islandcottageholidays.com   website: www.islandcottageholidays.com

Bonchurch

One mile north-east of Ventnor.

MRS J. LINES, ASHCLIFF HOLIDAY APARTMENT, BONCHURCH PO38 1NT (01983 853919). Self-contained ground floor apartment (sleeps 2) adjoining Victorian house. Large south-facing gardens. Sea views. Large private car park. Pets welcome to use garden. ETC ★★★★ [🐾]

LAKE HOTEL SHORE ROAD, LOWER BONCHURCH PO38 1RF (01983 852613). Lovely country house hotel in a beautiful quiet two-acre garden. First class food and service, all in a relaxed and friendly atmosphere. All rooms en suite. Car ferry inclusive prices available. ETC ★★★★
e-mail: fhg@lakehotel.co.uk   website: www.lakehotel.co.uk

A. EVANS, "THE WATERFALL", SHORE ROAD, BONCHURCH, VENTNOR PO38 1RN (01983 852246). Spacious, self-contained Flat. Sleeps 3 adults. Colour TV. Sun verandah and garden. The beach, the sea and the downs. [🐾]
e-mail: benbrook.charioteer@virgin.net

Carisbrooke

Village adjoining Newport. Of interest is Carisbrooke Castle with its battlements, keep and museum.

MRS V.A. SKEATS, THE MOUNT, 1 CALBOURNE ROAD, CARISBROOKE, NEAR NEWPORT PO30 5AP (01983 524359/522173). Two bedroom bungalow. Lovely enclosed garden. Pets welcome. Fully equipped. Sleeps 2/6. Private parking. Excellent touring position. Also two bedroom bungalow near Cowes. [Pets £10 per week].

Cowes

Yachting centre with yearly regatta since 1814. Newport 4 miles.

SUNNYCOTT CARAVAN PARK, COWES PO31 8NN (01983 292859). Small, quiet, family-run park close to Cowes. All caravans have full cooker, microwave, fridge and colour TV. Shop and laundry room on site. We welcome pets. Short breaks arranged. ETC ★★★★ [Pets £10 per week]
e-mail: info@sunnycottcaravanpark.co.uk   website: www.sunnycottcaravanpark.co.uk

Freshwater

Two kilometres south of Totland. South-west of Farringford, formerly the home of Tennyson.

MR AND MRS B. MOSCOFF, SEAHORSES, VICTORIA ROAD, FRESHWATER PO40 9PP (Tel & Fax: 01983 752574). Peaceful 19th century rectory set in two-and-a-half acres of lovely gardens. Good area for walking, golfing, sailing, paragliding and bird watching. Double and family rooms, all en suite. TV lounge, log fires. B&B pppn: £27 low season, £29 mid season, £31 high season. Children half price. [🐾 pw!]
e-mail: seahorses-iow@tiscali.co.uk   website: www.seahorsesisleofwight.com

Ryde

Popular resort and yachting centre, fine sands, pier. Shanklin 9 miles, Newport 7, Sandown 6.

HILLGROVE PARK, FIELD LANE, ST HELENS, NEAR RYDE PO33 1UT (01983 872802). Family-run Caravan Park. Select site 10 minutes sea, 3 minutes bus stop. Many local walks, heated swimming pool. Phone for brochure. Pets welcome (only one per unit). ETC ★★★★★ Holiday Park. [Pets £3.00 per night, £20.00 per week]
website: www.hillgrove.co.uk

Totland Bay

Small resort 3 miles south-west of Yarmouth Bay.

COUNTRY GARDEN HOTEL, CHURCH HILL, TOTLAND BAY PO39 OET (Tel & Fax: 01983 754521). All en suite, garden and seaview rooms available; TV, phone, duvets, feather/down pillows, fridge, hairdryer etc. Special winter, spring, autumn rates. [pw! Pets £4 per day]
e-mail: countrygardeniow@aol.com   website: www.thecountrygardenhotel.co.uk

SENTRY MEAD HOTEL, MADEIRA ROAD, TOTLAND BAY PO39 0BJ (01983 753212; Fax: 01983 754710). This beautiful Victorian villa is set in its own spacious gardens in the tranquil surroundings of West Wight. Just 150 yards from the beach, and with scenic downland walks on the doorstep, this is the perfect place to relax and unwind. All bedrooms en suite. ETC/AA ★★★ Silver Award [Pets £3 per day, £18 per week]
e-mail: info@sentrymead.co.uk   website: www.sentrymead.co.uk

Ventnor

Well-known resort with good sands, downs, popular as a winter holiday resort. Nearby is St Boniface Down, the highest point on the island. Ryde 13 miles, Newport 12, Sandown 7, Shanklin 4.

MRS B. HART, THE HILLSIDE, MITCHELL AVENUE, VENTNOR PO38 1DR (01983 852271; Fax: 01983 855310). Peaceful and relaxed atmosphere. Home cooking . All rooms en suite and individually furnished and decorated. Residential Licence. Dogs very welcome. Open all year. AA ★★★★ [🐾]
e-mail: hillside-hotel@btconnect.com   website: www.hillside-hotel.co.uk

VENTNOR HOLIDAY VILLAS, WHEELERS BAY ROAD, VENTNOR PO38 1HR (01983 852973). Apartments and Villas on south facing hillside leading down to a small rocky bay. Apartments open all year, villas and caravans April to October. Write or phone for a brochure. Pets welcome in villas. ETC ★/★★ [Pets £20 per week]
e-mail: sales@ventnorholidayvillas.co.uk   website: www.ventnorholidayvillas.co.uk

CASTLEHAVEN CARAVAN SITE, NITON, NEAR VENTNOR PO38 2ND (01983 730495). Island's most southerly six-berth, two-bedroomed caravans, all overlooking the Channel. Small, friendly site. Unspoilt seashore/countryside setting. On the shore. Kiosk serving breakfasts/evening meals by arrangement.
website: www.castlehaven.me.uk

Yarmouth

Coastal resort situated 9 miles west of Newport. Castle built by Henry VIII for coastal defence.

THE ORCHARDS HOLIDAY CARAVAN & CAMPING PARK, NEWBRIDGE, YARMOUTH PO41 0TS (Dial-a-brochure 01983 531331; Fax: 01983 531666). Luxury holiday caravans, most with central heating and double glazing. Excellent facilities including indoor pool with licensed cafe. Dog exercise areas. Coarse fishing; ideal walking, cycling and golf. Open late February to New Year. located in an Area of Outstanding Natural Beauty. Spectacular views.[Pets £1/£2 per night]
e-mail: info@orchards-holiday-park.co.uk   website:www.orchards-holiday-park.co.uk

Visit the FHG website
www.holidayguides.com
for details of the wide choice of accommodation
featured in the full range of FHG titles

Ashford, Broadstairs, Folkestone

A useful index of towns/counties appears on pages 391-396

FREEDOM HOLIDAY HOMES (01580 720770). More than 130 Self-catering properties, many welcoming pets, bring the whole family along and give then a taste of freedom.
e-mail: mail@freedomholidayhomes.co.uk   website: www.freedomholidayhomes.co.uk

GARDEN OF ENGLAND COTTAGES IN KENT & EAST SUSSEX, CLAYFIELD HOUSE, 50 ST JOHNS ROAD, TUNBRIDGE WELLS, KENT TN4 9NY (01892 510117). Pets welcome in many of our holiday homes, and go free with every well-behaved owner. All properties VisitBritain quality assured. On-line booking and availability. [🐾]
e-mail: holidays@gardenofenglandcottages.co.uk   website: www.gardenofenglandcottages.co.uk

Ashford

Market town on Great Stour River, 13 miles south-west of Canterbury.

Luxury pine lodges, superior self-catering accommodation overlooking two lakes in beautiful Kent countryside. Rough shooting and coarse fishing on our farms. Weeks or short breaks. Contact: ASHBY FARMS LTD, PLACE FARM, KENARDINGTON, ASHFORD TN26 2LZ (01233 733332; Fax: 01233 733326). [Pets £10 per stay]
e-mail: info@ashbyfarms.com   website: www.ashbyfarms.com

Broadstairs

Quiet resort, once a favourite of Charles Dickens. Good sands and promenade.

THE HANSON, 41 BELVEDERE ROAD, BROADSTAIRS CT10 1PF (01843 868936). Small, friendly licensed Georgian Hotel. Home comforts; children and pets welcome. Attractive bar. SAE. [pw! Pets £1 per night, £5 per week]
website: www.hansonhotel.co.uk

FREE or REDUCED RATE entry to Holiday Visits and Attractions – see our
READERS' OFFER VOUCHERS on pages 371-390

Folkestone

A traditional holiday resort and channel port, 14 miles east of Ashford.

WYCLIFFE HOTEL, 63 BOUVERIE ROAD WEST, FOLKESTONE CT20 2RN. (Tel & Fax: 01303 252186) Friendly, family hotel. Clean, comfortable and affordable. Based centrally and close to all amenities. A short distance from the Channel Tunnel and Dover. Off-street parking. Please write or call for our brochure. Pets and Children welcome.[Pets £3 per night].
e-mail: sapsford@wycliffehotel.freeserve.co.uk   website: www.wycliffehotel.com

St Margaret's Bay

4 miles north-east of Dover

DEREK AND JACQUI MITCHELL, REACH COURT FARM COTTAGES, REACH COURT FARM, ST MARGARET'S BAY, DOVER CT15 6AQ (Tel & Fax: 01304 852159). Situated in the heart of the Mitchell family farm, surrounded by open countryside, these five luxury self-contained cottages are very special. The cottages are set around the old farmyard, which has been attractively set to lawns and shrubs, with open views of the rural valley both front and back. ETC ★★★★
e-mail: enquiries@reachcourtfarmcottages.co.uk website: www.reachcourtfarmcottages.co.uk

Sevenoaks

Town on North Downs, 21 miles south east of London.

GOLDING HOP FARM COTTAGE, PLAXTOL, NEAR SEVENOAKS TN15 0PS (01732 885432). Three Star cottage on 13-acre cobnut farm in Bourne Valley. Sleeps 5 plus cot. Children and pets welcome. Open all year. £240-£430 pw. [Pets £12 per week].
e-mail: info@goldinghopfarm.com   website: www.goldinghopfarm.com

Ware (near Sandwich)

Rural location 3 miles from Sandwich, 9 miles from Canterbury.

DOREEN ADY, HAWTHORN FARM COTTAGES, WARE, NEAR SANDWICH (01304 813560). Four converted two-bedroom cottages, sleeping 4-5. Ideally situated for relaxing or exploring the Kent coastline. Children's play field. Ample parking. Pets welcome by arrangement. ETC ★★★/★★★★. [pw! Pets £20 per week]
e-mail: hawthornfarmcottages@dsl.pipex.com   www.hawthornfarmcottages.co.uk

Looking for holiday accommodation?
for details of hundreds of properties
throughout the UK visit:
www.holidayguides.com

🐾 Indicates that pets are welcome free of charge.

£ Indicates that a charge is made for pets: nightly or weekly.

pw! Shows some special provision for pets; exercise facility, feeding or accommodation arrangement.

⌂ Indicates separate pets accommodation.

Symbols

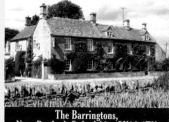

Burford

Small Cotswold Town on River Windrush, 7 miles west of Witney.

THE INN FOR ALL SEASONS, THE BARRINGTONS, NEAR BURFORD OX18 4TN (01451 844324). Family-run and owned Hotel based on traditional 16th century English Coaching Inn. Ideal base for touring, walking and garden visiting. From £70.00pppn DB&B. [pw! Pets £5 per night, £20 per week] e-mail: sharp@innforallseasons.com   website: www.innforallseasons.com

Oxford

City 52 miles from London. University dating from 13th century. Many notable buildings.

MR B. CRONIN, NANFORD GUEST HOUSE, 137 IFFLEY ROAD, OXFORD OX4 1EJ (01865 244743; Fax: 01865 249596). Period guest house located five minutes on foot from the University of Oxford. Wide range and number of rooms, all with private shower and toilet. [🐾] e-mail: b.cronin@btinternet.com   website: www.nanfordguesthouse.com

Tackley/Kidlington

Village 3 miles north-east of Woodstock; approximately 5 miles north of Oxford.

JUNE AND GEORGE COLLIER, 55 NETHERCOTE ROAD, TACKLEY, KIDLINGTON, OXFORD OX5 3AT (01869 331255; mobile: 07790 338225). Bed and Breakfast in Tackley. An ideal base for touring, walking, cycling and riding. Central for Oxford, The Cotswolds, Stratford-on-Avon, Blenheim Palace. Woodstock four miles. There is a regular train and bus service with local Hostelries serving excellent food. ETC ★★★ [🐾 ⌂] e-mail: colliers.bnb@virgin.net   website: www.colliersbnb.co.uk

Thame

Town on River Thame 9 miles south-west of Aylesbury. Airport at Haddenham.

MS. JULIA TANNER, LITTLE ACRE, TETSWORTH, NEAR THAME OX9 7AT (01844 281423; mobile: 07798 625252). A small country house retreat offering every comfort, set in several private acres. Most rooms en suite. Twin en suite £25pppn, king/double en suite £27.50pppn, family room (3 sharing) £75 per night. Prices include a full English breakfast. A perfect place to relax - your dog will love it. Three minutes Junction 6 M40. Also self-catering accommodation. [Pets £3 per night. pw! Bring dog basket with you.] website: www.little-acre.co.uk

Kingston-upon-Thames

Chase Lodge Hotel
An Award Winning Hotel
with style & elegance, set in tranquil surroundings
at affordable prices.

10 Park Road Hampton Wick Kingston-Upon-Thames KT1 4AS   Pets welcome

Tel: 020 8943 1862 . Fax: 020 8943 9363

E-mail: info@chaselodgehotel.com Web: www.chaselodgehotel.com & www.surreyhotels.com

Quality en suite bedrooms
Close to Bushy Park
Buffet-style Full Continental Breakfast
A la carte menu
Licensed bar
Wedding Receptions
Honeymoon suite
available with jacuzzi & steam area
20 minutes from Heathrow Airport
Close to Kingston town centre & all major
transport links.

AA ◆◆◆◆ Les Routiers   All Major Credit Cards Accepted

Kingston-upon-Thames

Market town, Royal borough and administrative centre of Surrey. Kingston is ideally placed for London and environs.

CHASE LODGE HOTEL, 10 PARK ROAD, HAMPTON WICK, KINGSTON-UPON-THAMES KT1 4AS (020 8943 1862; Fax: 020 8943 9363). Award-winning hotel offering quality en suite bedrooms. Easy access to town centre and major transport links. A la carte menu, licensed bar. ETC/AA ◆◆◆◆ [🐾] e-mail: info@chaselodgehotel.com websites: www.chaselodgehotel.com & www.surreyhotels.com

Peaslake

Village 4 miles north of Cranleigh.

THE HURTWOOD INN HOTEL, WALKING BOTTOM, PEASLAKE, NEAR GUILDFORD GU5 9RR (01306 730851; Fax: 01306 731390). Privately run hotel with 22 en suite bedrooms, bar, restaurant; weddings and functions catered for. In heart of Surrey Hills, with miles of beautiful walks on the doorstep. ETC ★★★. [🐾] e-mail: sales@hurtwoodinnhotel.com   website: www.hurtwoodinnhotel.com

Seaford

BEACH COTTAGE • Claremont Road, Seaford, East Sussex

BN25 2OO

Well equipped, three-bedroomed terraced cottage on seafront. Sleeps 5. Central heating,
open fire and woodburner. South-facing patio overlooking sea.
Downland walks (wonderful for dogs), fishing, golf, wind-surfing, etc.
Details from: Julia Lewis, 47 Wandle Bank, London SW19 1DW
Tel: 020 8542 5073 • e-mail: cottage@beachcottages.info • www.beachcottages.info

Chiddingly

Charming village, 4 miles north-west of Hailsham. Off the A22 London-Eastbourne road.

Adorable, small, well-equipped cottage in grounds of Tudor Manor. Two bedrooms, sleeps 4-6. Full
central heating. Colour TV. Fridge/freezer, laundry facilities. Large safe garden. Use indoor heated
swimming pool, sauna/jacuzzi and tennis. From £395 to £750 per week inclusive. ETC ★★★.
Contact: EVA MORRIS, "PEKES", 124 ELM PARK MANSIONS, PARK WALK, LONDON SW10 0AR (020
7352 8088; Fax: 020 7352 8125). [2 dogs free, extra dog £7 (max. 4) pw!].
e-mail: pekes.afa@virgin.net   website: www.pekesmanor.com

Fairlight

Village 3 miles east of Hastings

JANET & RAY ADAMS, FAIRLIGHT COTTAGE, WARREN ROAD, FAIRLIGHT TN35 4AG (01424
812545). Country house in idyllic location with clifftop walks. Tasteful en suite rooms, comfortable
guest lounge. Delicious breakfasts. No smoking. Dogs stay with owners. ETC ◆◆◆◆ [🐾]

Polegate

Quiet position, 5 miles from the popular seaside resort of Eastbourne. London 58 miles, Lewes 12.

MRS P. FIELD, 20 ST JOHN'S ROAD, POLEGATE BN26 5BP (01323 482691). Homely private house.
Quiet location; large enclosed garden. Parking space. Ideally situated for walking on South Downs
and Forestry Commission land. All rooms, washbasins and tea/coffee making facilities. Bed and
Breakfast. Pets very welcome. [pw!]

Rottingdean/Brighton

Picturesque seaside resort in historic conservation village 5 km from Brighton city..

KILCOLGAN PREMIER BUNGALOWS (020 7250 3678) Well appointed three-bedroom properties
sleeping 5/6. Beautiful secluded garden. Terms from £550 to £900 per week fully inclusive. Location
should appeal to those seeking a quality retreat. VB ★★★★★ [Pets £35 per week].
e-mail: jc.stgeorge@virgin.net   website: www.holidaybungalowsbrightonuk.com

Rye

Picturesque hill town with steep cobbled streets. Many fine buildings of historic interest. Hastings 12 miles, Tunbridge Wells 28.

FLACKLEY ASH HOTEL, PEASMARSH, RYE TN31 6YH (01797 230651). Georgian Country House Hotel in beautiful grounds. Indoor swimming pool and Leisure Centre. Beauty and massage. Visit Rye and the castles and gardens of East Sussex and Kent. AA/RAC ★★★ [Pets £8.50 per night]
e-mail: enquiries@flackleyashhotel.co.uk   website: www.flackleyashhotel.co.uk

MRS JANE APPERLY, BRANDY'S COTTAGE, CADBOROUGH FARM, RYE TN31 6AA (01797 225426; Fax: 01797 224097).Newly converted cottage provides luxurious and spacious accommodation for two people. Private courtyard. One small well-behaved dog and children over 12 welcome. No-smoking. Short breaks available. ETC ★★★★ [🐕]
e-mail: apperly@cadborough.co.uk   website: www.cadborough.co.uk

JEAKE'S HOUSE, MERMAID STREET, RYE TN31 7ET (01797 222828; Fax: 01797 222623). Dating from 1689, this Listed building has oak-beamed and panelled bedrooms overlooking the marsh. TV, radio, telephone. Book-lined bar. £45-£62 per person. ETC/AA ★★★★★ [Pets £5 per night]
e-mail: stay@jeakeshouse.com   website: www.jeakeshouse.com

Seaford

On the coast midway between Newhaven and Beachy Head.

BEACH COTTAGE, CLAREMONT ROAD, SEAFORD BN25 2QQ. Well-equipped, three-bedroomed ter-raced cottage on seafront. CH, open fire and woodburner. South-facing patio overlooking sea. Downland walks (wonderful for dogs), fishing, golf, wind-surfing, etc. Details from JULIA LEWIS, 47 WANDLE BANK, LONDON SW19 1DW (020 8542 5073). [pw! 🐕]
e-mail: cottage@beachcottages.info   website: www.beachcottages.info

THE SILVERDALE, 21 SUTTON PARK ROAD, SEAFORD BN25 IRH (01323 491849). We don't just accept dogs, we welcome them. Only a few minutes from seafront and parks. Delightful small dining room and bar. All rooms individually decorated. SEEDA award winner 2003, Clean Catering Award winner for 15 years. AA Pet Friendly Establishment of the Year 2005. ETC/AA ★★★★ [🐕].
e-mail: silverdale@mistral.co.uk   website: www.silverdaleseaford.co.uk

Please note

Pet-Friendly
Pubs, Inns& Hotels
on pages 360-369
Please note that these establishments may not feature in the main section of this book

Arundel, Chichester, Eastergate, Selsey, Worthing

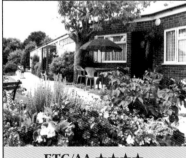

Arundel

Arundel lies between Chichester and Brighton, 5 miles from Littlehampton on the south coast. Magnificent Arundel Castle with its impressive grounds overlooks the River Arun, and the town is also home to the Wildfowl and Wetlands Trust where thousands of rare and migratory birds can be seen.

MRS VICKI RICHARDS, WOODACRE, ARUNDEL ROAD, FONTWELL, ARUNDEL BN18 0QP (01243 814301). Bed & Breakfast in traditional family home. Ideal for Chichester, Goodwood and seaside. Clean, spacious rooms, two on ground floor. ETC ★★★★
e-mail: wacrebb@aol.com　　　　　　　website: www.woodacre.co.uk

Chichester

County town 9 miles east of Havant. Town has cathedral and 16th century market cross.

SPIRE COTTAGE, CHURCH LANE, HUNSTON, CHICHESTER PO20 1AJ (01243 778937). Stylish bed and breakfast accommodation in a friendly and relaxed atmosphere. Excellent facilities. Village pub and two golf courses. [Dogs £5 per night]
e-mail: jan@spirecottage.co.uk　　　　　　website: www.spirecottage.co.uk

Eastergate

Village between the sea and South Downs. Fontwell Park nearby. Bognor Regis 5 miles south.

WANDLEYS CARAVAN PARK, EASTERGATE PO20 6SE (01243 543235 or 01243 543384 evenings/weekends). You will find peace, tranquillity and relaxation in one of our comfortable holiday caravans. All have internal WC and shower. Dogs welcome. Many historic and interesting places nearby. Telephone for brochure. [🐾]

Selsey

Seaside resort 8 miles south of Chichester. Selsey Bill is headland extending into the English Channel.

ST ANDREWS LODGE, CHICHESTER ROAD, SELSEY PO20 0LX (01243 606899; Fax: 01243 607826). 10 bedrooms, all en suite, with direct dial telephones and modem point, some on ground floor. Spacious lounges with log fire; licensed bar for residents only. Wheelchair accessible room. Dogs welcome in rooms overlooking large garden. Apply for brochure and prices. ETC/AA ★★★★ [🐾]
e-mail: info@standrewslodge.co.uk　　　　website: www.standrewslodge.co.uk

Worthing

Residential town and seaside resort with 5 miles seafront. Situated 10 miles west of Brighton.

CAVENDISH HOTEL, 115 MARINE PARADE, WORTHING BN11 3QG (01903 236767; Fax: 01903 823840). Ideal base for touring Sussex villages and the rolling South Downs. All rooms are en suite, have TV, direct-dial telephone and tea/coffee facilities. No charge for dogs belonging to readers of Pets Welcome! AA/RAC ★★ [🐾].
e-mail: reservations@cavendishworthing.co.uk　　　website: www.cavendishworthing.co.uk

Visit the FHG website
www.holidayguides.com
for details of the wide choice of accommodation
featured in the full range of FHG titles

Burwell

Burwell

One of the largest villages in Cambridgeshire, with over 60 listed buildings of interest, and the 15th century Church of St Mary's. Ideal area for walkers, fishing enthusiasts and nature lovers.

THE MEADOW HOUSE, 2A HIGH STREET, BURWELL, CAMBRIDGE CB5 0HB (01638 741926; Fax: 01638 741861). Modern house in two acres of wooded grounds offering superior Bed and Breakfast. Variety of en suite accommodation. All rooms have TV, central heating and tea/coffee facilities. No smoking. Family rate on request. ETC ◆◆◆◆
e-mail: hilary@themeadowhouse.co.uk   website: www.themeadowhouse.co.uk

Ely

Magnificent Norman Cathedral dating from 1083. Ideal base for touring the fen country of East Anglia.

MRS C. H. BENNETT, STOCKYARD FARM, WISBECH ROAD, WELNEY PE14 9RQ (01354 610433; Fax: 01354 610422). Comfortable converted farmhouse, rurally situated between Ely and Wisbech. Conservatory breakfast room, TV lounge. Free range produce. Miles of riverside walks. No smoking. B&B from £22.50. [🐾 pw!]

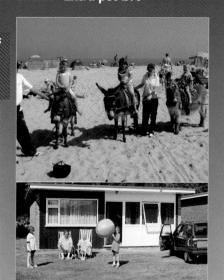

We have more than 330 self-catering cottages to choose from.

Sweeping beaches, pretty countryside and many rural footpaths make Norfolk the perfect destination for you and your discerning pets.

Telephone: 01603 871872
Email: info@norfolkcottages.co.uk
www.norfolkcottages.co.uk

Norfolk Country Cottages

SOWERBYS
holiday cottages

North Norfolk Coastal Cottages
Over 90 much loved second homes sleeping from 2 to 16, many with sea views. Tailor-made short breaks available.
Please call us on 01328 730880
www.sowerbysholidaycottages.co.uk

Looking for holiday accommodation?
for details of hundreds of properties
throughout the UK visit:

www.holidayguides.com

Pet-Friendly
Pubs, Inns& Hotels
on pages 360-369
Please note that these establishments may not feature in the main section of this book

Cromer, Dereham, East Dereham

Pet welcome free of charge

Comfortable, well-equipped chalets situated on beautiful, landscaped, quiet site. Ideally placed for walks to adjacent woods, cliffs and sandy beaches. 10 minutes' walk to town. Golf course and local shops nearby. Plenty of local places of interest to visit. One twin, one double room, bathroom, colour TV, microwave, well-equipped kitchenette. Children welcome.

Short Breaks in Spring/Autumn 2 nights or more from £80
Spring/Autumn £140-£210 per week
June-September £230-£305 per week

DETAILS FROM: MRS I. SCOLTOCK, SHANGRI-LA, LITTLE CAMBRIDGE, DUTON HILL, DUNMOW, ESSEX CM6 3QU • TEL: 01371 870482

Kings Chalet Park
Cromer, Norfolk
Sleep 2-4
Open March to October

KING'S CHALET PARK
Enquiries to: Stenson Guest House, 32 Overstrand Road, Cromer, Norfolk NR27 0AJ

Families Welcome & Pets Free of Charge

Well-equipped Chalets sleeping 2 to 6; shower/ bathroom, microwave, TV. Tourist Board and NNH/GHA Approved. One Twin, one Double bedroom, bed sofa in lounge. Well-equipped kitchenette.

Quiet site adjacent to woods, Golf Club and beach. Local shops nearby or pleasant 10 minutes' walk into town.

Telephone: 01263 511308

Scarning Dale
Dale Road, Scarning, East Dereham NR19 2QN
Tel: 01362 687269

A warm welcome awaits you. 16th Century house in 25 acres of landscaped gardens, paddocks and woodland. Excellent home cooking (à la carte and table d'hôte). Indoor heated swimming pool and full size snooker table. Good access Norfolk and Suffolk. Self-catering cottages also available. Dogs welcome in self-catering cottages. Grazing and Stables available.
Tariff: Single £50 – £60; Double £90 – £100.

Stay in the peaceful, tranquil heart of Norfolk's most beautiful countryside. All rooms tastefully decorated in country style, with full en suite facilities, TVs, tea/coffee making facilities, etc. Overlooking 12 acres of landscaped meadows with its own private fishing lakes. Bed and Breakfast from £36.
Bartles Lodge, Church Street, Elsing, Dereham NR20 3EA Tel: 01362 637177

Holly Farm Cottages, High Common, Cranworth, Norfolk IP25 7SX
Two comfortable, single-storey cottages each sleeping 1-4. Fully equipped, including TV/video, dishwasher, washing machine, central heating. Enclosed garden. Ample car parking. Uninterrupted views of beautiful countryside, peaceful lanes for walking/cycling. Local golf and fishing. Convenient for Norwich, North Norfolk Coast and Broads.
www.hollyfarmcottages.co.uk
Tel: 01362 821468　　　　　　　e-mail: jennie.mclaren@btopenworld.co

FREE or REDUCED RATE entry to Holiday Visits and Attractions – see our
READERS' OFFER VOUCHERS on pages 371-390

Fakenham, Foxley, Great Yarmouth, King's Lynn

King's Lynn, Mundesley-on-Sea, North Walsham

Readers are requested to mention this FHG
guidebook when seeking accommodation

The Lifeboat Inn

16th Century Smugglers' Ale House

Ship Lane, Thornham, Norfolk PE36 6LT

Tel: 01485 512236 • Fax: 01485 512323
e-mail: lifeboatinn@maypolehotels.com

THE LIFEBOAT INN has been a welcome sight for the weary traveller for centuries – roaring open fires, real ales and a hearty meal awaiting. The Summer brings its own charm – a cool beer, gazing over open meadows to the harbour, and rolling white horses gently breaking upon Thornham's sandy beach.

Dogs are welcome in all our bars and we provide the sort of breakfast that will enable you to keep up with your four-legged friend on the way to the beach!

Guests arriving at reception are greeted by our grand old fireplace in the lounge – ideal for toasting your feet after a day walking the coastal path – if you can coax your sleeping dog out of prime position! The restaurant (AA Rosette) opens every evening offering a varied selection of dishes to suit all tastes. Our extensive bar snack menu is also available if guests wish their pets to join them in the bar.

There are numerous and varied walks along miles of open beaches, across sweeping sand dunes, through pine woods or along chalk and sandstone cliff tops. It is truly a walker's paradise – especially if you're a dog.

We hope you will come and visit us. For our brochure and tariff which includes details of breaks please ring 01485 512236 **or visit our website**

www.maypolehotels.com/lifeboatinn

★★★★ **Poppyland Holiday Cottages & Touring Park Welcomes Dogs**

Poppyland is situated on The Green in the middle of the picturesque village of Thorpe Market, in North Norfolk, just 4 miles south of the well known fishing port of Cromer and approximately 16 miles north of the ancient city of Norwich. The location is ideal for guests who want to just relax with their friend away from the daily pressures on a quiet holiday, or use the cottage as a base to visit local places of interest. The two holiday cottages have their own private entrances and gardens. The touring park (adults only) is situated in an acre of landscaped garden surrounded by trees. There is a public house /hotel opposite which serves excellent food.

Tel: 01263 833219 • e-mail: poppylandjc@netscape.net • www.poppyland.com

---

HOLIDAY IN OUR ENGLISH COUNTRY GARDEN

Two acres in rural Norfolk. Ten spacious family-run bungalows and 7-bedroom farmhouse. Games room, heated pool, children's play area, fishing, boating, riding and golf nearby. Near River Staithe with access to Broads. Parking. Licensed bar. For details/colour brochure contact: **F.G. Delf, Thurne Cottage, The Staithe, Thurne, Norfolk NR29 3BU Tel: 01692 670242 or 01493 844568 •** www.norfolkbroads.co.uk/hederahouse

---

Bolding Way Holidays in Weybourne, North Norfolk

Bed & Breakfast for up to 6 and Self-catering (for 2) are available throughout the year. Weybourne is located in an Area of Outstanding Natural Beauty and on the Heritage Coast. Well behaved pets are welcome in both. Both with fenced gardens. Excellent local walks. The Stables, Bolding Way, Weybourne, Holt Norfolk NR25 7SW   Phone: 01263 588 666
e-mail: holidays@boldingway.co.uk • www.boldingway.co.uk

Winterton-on-Sea

Go BLUE RIBAND for quality inexpensive self-catering holidays where your dog is welcome – choice of locations all in the borough of Great Yarmouth. Detached 3 bedroom bungalows, seafront bungalows, detached Sea-Dell chalets and modern sea front caravans. Free colour brochure: DON WITHERIDGE, BLUE RIBAND HOUSE, PARKLANDS, HEMSBY, GREAT YARMOUTH NR29 4HA (01493 730445). [pw! First pet free when booking through Pets Welcome!, 2nd pet £10 per week]. website: www.BlueRibandHolidays.co.uk

NORFOLK COUNTRY COTTAGES (01603 871872). We have more than 330 self-catering cottages to choose from. Sweeping beaches, pretty countryside and many rural footpaths make norfolk the perfect destination for you and your discerning pets.
e-mail: info@norfolk.cottages.co.uk   website: www.norfolkcottages.co.uk/pw

SOWERBYS HOLIDAY COTTAGES. North Norfolk Coastal Cottages. Over 90 much loved second homes sleeping from 2 to 16, many with sea views. Tailor-made short breaks available. Please call us on 01328 730880
website: www.sowerbysholidaycottages.co.uk

Bacton-on-Sea

Village on coast. 5 miles from North Walsham.

CASTAWAYS HOLIDAY PARK, PASTON ROAD, BACTON-ON-SEA NR12 0JB (01692 650436 and 650418). In peaceful village with direct access to sandy beach. Modern caravans, Pine Lodges and Flats, with all amenities. Licensed club, entertainment, children's play area. Ideal for discovering Norfolk. [Pets £17 per week]
website: www.castawaysholidaypark.co.uk

Caister-on-Sea

Historic site with Roman ruins and 15th century Caister Castle with 100 foot tower.

Superior brick-built, tiled roof cottages. Adjacent golf course. Lovely walks on dunes and coast. 2-4 night breaks early/late season, Christmas and New Year. Terms from £69 to £345. SAND DUNE COTTAGES, TAN LANE, CAISTER-ON-SEA, GREAT YARMOUTH NR30 5DT (01493 720352; mobile: 07785 561363). ETC ★★ [Pets £15 per week]
e-mail: sand.dune.cottages@amserve.net
website: www.eastcoastlive.co.uk/sites/sanddunecottages.php

ELM BEACH CARAVAN PARK, MANOR ROAD, CAISTER-ON-SEA NR30 5HG (Freephone: 08000 199 360). Small, quiet park offering 4-6 berth, fully equipped caravans, most with sea views. Entertainment supplied free of charge by neighbouring parks. Pets very welcome. [Pets £25 per week]
e-mail: enquiries@elmbeachcaravanpark.com   website: www.elmbeachcaravanpark.com

Cromer

Attractive resort built round old fishing village. Norwich 21 miles.

CLIFTONVILLE HOTEL, SEAFRONT, CROMER NR27 9AS (01263 512543; Fax: 01263 515700). Ideally situated on the Norfolk coast. Beautifully restored Edwardian Hotel. 30 en suite bedrooms all with sea view. Executive suites. Seafood Bistro, à la carte Restaurant. AA ★★★ [pw! pets £4 per night] e-mail: reservations@cliftonvillehotel.co.uk   website: www.cliftonvillehotel.co.uk

KINGS CHALET PARK, CROMER. Comfortable well-equipped chalets on quiet site; ideally placed for woodland and beach walks. 10 minutes' walk to town, shops nearby. Details from MRS I. SCOLTOCK, SHANGRI-LA, LITTLE CAMBRIDGE, DUTON HILL, DUNMOW, ESSEX (01371 870482). [one pet free]

KINGS CHALET PARK, CROMER NR27 0AJ (01263 511308) . Well-equipped chalets sleeping 2 to 6; shower/bathroom, microwave and TV. 1 Twin, 1 Double bedroom, bed sofa in lounge, well-equipped kitchenette. Quiet site adjacent to woods, golf club and beaches. Local shops nearby. Pleasant 10 minutes' walk to town. Tourist Board and NNH/GHA Approved. Families welcome. [🐕]

Dereham

Situated 16 miles west of Norwich. St Nicholas Church has 16th century bell tower.

SCARNING DALE, SCARNING, EAST DEREHAM NR19 2QN (01362 687269). Self-catering cottages (not commercialised) in grounds of owner's house. On-site indoor heated swimming pool and full-size snooker table. B&B for six also available in house (sorry no pets in house). Grazing and Stables available.

BARTLES LODGE, CHURCH STREET, ELSING, DEREHAM NR20 3EA (01362 637177). Stay in the peaceful, tranquil heart of Norfolk's most beautiful countryside. All rooms en suite, TVs, tea/coffee making facilities, etc. [pw! Pets £2 per night, £10 per week]

East Dereham

Site of 7th Century nunnery. Archaeogical Museum at Bishop Banner's Cottages, with distinctive fruit and flower plaster work.

HOLLY FARM COTTAGES, HIGH COMMON, CRANWORTH IP25 7SX (01362 821468). 2 single-storey cottages each sleeping 1-4. TV/video, dishwasher, washing machine, central heating. Enclosed garden. Ample car parking. Peaceful lanes for walking/cycling. Local golf and fishing. Use of field for pony/horse. [🐕]
e-mail: jennie.mclaren@btopenworld.com   website: www.hollyfarmcottages.co.uk

Fakenham

Agricultural centre on River Wensum 23 miles north-west of Norwich.

VERE LODGE, SOUTH RAYNHAM, NEAR FAKENHAM NR21 7HE (01328 838261; Fax: 01328 838300). 14 superbly equipped cottages with leisure centre and heated indoor pool. 8 acres of lawns, paddock and woodland, with Norfolk's vast beaches nearby. [pw! Pets £6 per night, £29.50 per week]
e-mail: major@verelodge.co.uk   website: www.idylliccottages.co.uk

FoxleySelf-catering Cottages (2/3 bedrooms) on working farm. All fully equipped, with central heating. 20 miles from coast, 15 from Broads. Mature woodland nearby. Fishing in owner's lake. Indoor heated swimming pool. ETC ★★/★★★★. MOOR FARM STABLE COTTAGES, FOXLEY NR20 4QP (Tel & Fax: 01362 688523). [Pets £10 per week]
e-mail: enquiry@moorfarmstablecottages.co.uk   website: www.moorfarmstablecottages.co.uk

Great Yarmouth

Traditional lively seaside resort with a wide range of amusements, including the Marina Centre and Sealife Centre.

CAREFREE HOLIDAYS, CHAPEL BRIERS, YARMOUTH ROAD, HEMSBY, GREAT YARMOUTH NR29 4NJ (01493 732176). A wide selection of superior chalets for live-as-you-please holidays near Great Yarmouth and Norfolk Broads. All amenities on site. Parking. Children and pets welcome. [Pets £20 per week, free in June.]

King's Lynn

Ancient market town and port on the Wash with many beautiful medieval and Georgian buildings.

MRS J. E. FORD, 129 LEZIATE DROVE, POTT ROW, KING'S LYNN PE32 1DE (01553 630356). Detached bungalow sleeps 4. In quiet village close to Sandringham and beaches. Facilities include colour TV, video, microwave, fridge/freezer, washing machine, off road parking, dog run. [🐴]

MRS G. DAVIDSON, HOLMDENE FARM, BEESTON, KING'S LYNN PE32 2NJ (01328 701284). 17th century farmhouse situated in central Norfolk within easy reach of the coast and Broads. Sporting activities available locally, village pub nearby. One double room, one twin and one single. Pets welcome. Bed and Breakfast from £22.50pp; Evening Meal from £15. Weekly terms available and child reductions. Two self-catering cottages. Sleeping 4/8. Terms on request. ETC ★★★ [🐴] e-mail: holmdenefarm@farmersweekly.net   website: www.northnorfolk.co.uk/holmdenefarm

Mundesley-on-Sea

Small resort backed by low cliffs. Good sands and bathing. Norwich 20 miles, Cromer 7.

HOLIDAY PROPERTIES (MUNDESLEY) LTD, 6a PASTON ROAD, NORWICH NR11 8BN (01263 720719). Self-catering holiday chalets on three pretty sites in village on North Norfolk coast, close to sandy beach, and village amenities. All chalets are heated with fully equipped kitchens, colour TVs. Sleep 4-6. Low season short breaks. VisitBritain 1-3 stars. [Pets £10 per week]. e-mail: info@holidayprops.co.uk   website: www.holidayprops.co.uk

KILN CLIFFS CARAVAN PARK, CROMER ROAD, MUNDESLEY NR11 8DF (01263 720449). Peaceful family-run site situated around an historic brick kiln. Six-berth caravans for hire, standing on ten acres of grassy cliff top. All caravans fully equipped (except linen) and price includes all gas and electricity. [Pets £5 per week].

ANNE & ALAN CUTLER, WHINCLIFF BED & BREAKFAST, CROMER ROAD, MUNDESLEY NR11 8DU (01263 721554). Clifftop house, sea views and sandy beaches. Rooms with colour TV and tea-making. Families and pets welcome. Open all year round. [🐴] e-mail: whincliff@freeuk.com   website: http://whincliff.freeuk.com

47 SEAWARD CREST, MUNDESLEY. West-facing brick built chalet on private site with lawns, flowers and parking. Large lounge/dining room, kitchenette, two bedrooms, bathroom. Beach and shops nearby. Pets most welcome. SAE please: MRS DOAR, 4 DENBURY ROAD, RAVENSHEAD, NOTTS. NG15 9FQ (01623 798032). [🐴]

North Walsham

Market town 14 miles north of Norwich, traditional centre of the Norfolk reed thatching industry.

MRS. G. FAULKNER, DOLPHIN LODGE, 3 KNAPTON ROAD,TRUNCH, NORTH WALSHAM NR28 0QE (01263 720961). Friendly-run bungalow accommodation. B&B in village setting two-and-a-half miles from beaches. Many rural walks. Easy reach of all Norfolk attractions including Norfolk Broads. All rooms en suite, tea/coffee facilities, TVs, hairdryers etc. ETC ◆◆◆ [🐴] e-mail: dolphin.lodge@btopenworld.com   website: www.dolphinlodges.net

Norwich

Historuc city with Cathedral, Castle, shops, restaurants and lots to see and do. Many medieval streets and lanes, with attractive timbered houses.

SIMON & HEATHER MOSS, OAKBROOK GUEST HOUSE, FRITH WAY, GREAT MOULTON, NORWICH NR15 2HE (01379 677359; Mobile: 07885 351212). Former village school with views over the quiet Tas Valley. Warm, comfortable en suite rooms of various sizes and prices. Ideal touring base for East Anglia. Long stay discounts. [Pets £5]. e-mail: oakbrookhouse@btinternet.com   website: www.oakbrookhouse.co.uk

A useful index of towns/counties appears at the back of this book

Thornham

Village 4 miles east of Hunstanton. Site of Roman signal station.

THE LIFEBOAT INN, SHIP LANE, THORNHAM PE36 6LT (01485 512236; Fax: 01485 512323). A welcome sight for the weary traveller for centuries. Dogs welcome. Restaurant (one AA rosette). Bird watching and walking along miles of open beaches. Please ring for brochure and tariff. [Pets £5 per week.]
e-mail: lifeboatinn@maypolehotels.com　website: www.maypolehotels.com/lifeboatinn

Thorpe Market

Village 4 miles south of Cromer.

POPPYLAND HOLIDAY COTTAGES & TOURING PARK, THE GREEN, THORPE MARKET NR11 8AJ (01263 833219). Ideal for guests who want to relax. Two holiday cottages with private entrances and gardens. Touring park (adults only) in landscaped gardens surrounded by trees. Excellent food nearby.[🐾]
e-mail: poppylandjc@netscape.net　　　　　　　website: www.poppyland.com

Thurne

Idyllic Broadland village. Great Yarmouth 10 miles.

HEDERA HOUSE AND PLANTATION BUNGALOWS, THURNE NR29 3BU (01692 670242 or 01493 844568). Adjacent river, seven bedroomed farmhouse, 10 competitively priced bungalows in peaceful gardens. Outdoor heated pool. Enjoy boating, fishing, walking, touring, nearby golf, horseriding, sandy beaches and popular resorts.
website: www.norfolkbroads.co.uk/hederahouse

Weybourne

Located in an Area of Outstanding Natural Beauty and part of the Heritage Coastline. Sheringham and Holt 4 miles.

BOLDING WAY HOLIDAY COTTAGES, THE STABLES, WEYBOURNE, HOLT NR25 7SW (01263 588666). Bed & Breakfast for up to 6 and Self-catering (for 2). In an Area of Outstanding Natural Beauty and on the Heritage Coast. Well behaved pets welcome. Both with fenced gardens. Excellent local walks. Open all year. [🐾]
e-mail: holidays@boldingway.co.uk　　　　　　website: www.boldingway.co.uk

Winterton-on-Sea

Good sands and bathing. Great Yarmouth 8 miles.

WINTERTON VALLEY HOLIDAYS. A selection of modern superior fully appointed holiday chalets in a choice of locations near Great Yarmouth. Enjoy panoramic views from WINTERTON, a quiet and picturesque 35-acre estate, while CALIFORNIA has all the usual amenities, with free entry to the pool and clubhouse. Pets are very welcome at both sites. For colour brochure: 15 KINGSTON AVENUE, CAISTER-ON-SEA NR30 5ET (01493 377175).
website: www.wintertonvalleyholidays.co.uk

🐾　Indicates that pets are welcome free of charge.

£　Indicates that a charge is made for pets: nightly or weekly.

pw!　Shows some special provision for pets; exercise facility, feeding or accommodation arrangement.

⌂　Indicates separate pets accommodation.

Symbols

Aldeburgh, Bungay, Bury St Edmunds

Bury St Edmunds, Cratfield, Dunwich, Hadleigh, Henley

Visit the FHG website
www.holidayguides.com
for details of the wide choice of accommodation
featured in the full range of FHG titles

Please note

All the information in this book is given in good faith in the belief that it is correct. However, the publishers cannot guarantee the facts given in these pages, neither are they responsible for changes in policy, ownership or terms that may take place after the date of going to press. Readers should always satisfy themselves that the facilities they require are available and that the terms, if quoted, still apply.

SUFFOLK SECRETS (01502 722717). Many of our 130 self-catering properties warmly welcome pets. With our heritage coast, wonderful countryside and relaxed atmosphere, Suffolk is the ideal destination for pet owners.
e-mail: holidays@suffolk-secrets.co.uk   website: www.suffolk-secrets.co.uk

Aldeburgh

Coastal town 6 miles south-east of Saxmundham. Annual music festival at Snape Maltings.

WENTWORTH HOTEL, ALDEBURGH IP15 5BD (01728 452312). Country House Hotel overlooking the sea. Immediate access to the beach and walks. Two comfortable lounges with log fires and antique furniture. Refurbished bedrooms with all facilities and many with sea views. Restaurant specialises in fresh produce and sea food. ETC Silver Award. AA ★★★ Two Rosettes. [Pets £2 per day]
e-mail: stay@wentworth-aldeburgh.co.uk   website: www.wentworth-aldeburgh.com

Bungay

Attractive town in the Waveney Valley, with a wealth of historic sites. Town centre has a Roman well, a Saxon church, and the remains of a Norman castle and Benedictine priory. 14 miles south east of Norwich.

ANNIE'S COTTAGE, SUFFOLK. Peaceful, rural location in open countryside. 2 bedrooms, sleeps 4. Large lounge/dining room, woodburning stove. Linen and towels provided. Electricity included. Enclosed private garden. Well equipped mobile home also available. Contact: LYNNE MORTON, HILL FARM HOLIDAYS, ILKETSHALL ST JOHN, BECCLES NR34 8JE. (01986 781240). [🐾]
website: www.hillfarmholidays.com

Bury St Edmunds

This prosperous market town on the River Lark lies 28 miles east of Cambridge.

THE ICKWORTH HOTEL, HORRINGER, BURY ST EDMUNDS IP29 5QE(Tel: 01284 735350; Fax: 01284 736300). Warm and welcoming hotel situated in the rolling green acres of Ickworth parkland. Elegant, individually styled bedrooms. Dogs welcome – specific dietary requirements catered for; doggy massage available.
e-mail: ickworth@ickworthhotel.com   www.luxuryfamilyhotels.com

REDE HALL FARM PARK, REDE, BURY ST EDMUNDS IP29 4UG (01284 850695; Fax: 01284 850345). Two well equipped cottages, ideal for touring East Anglia and the coast. Totally non-smoking. Hot Tub Spa available for exclusive use (inclusive). Well behaved dogs welcome. ETC ★★★★ [🐾 ▢]
website: www.redehallfarmpark.co.uk

RAVENWOOD HALL COUNTRY HOUSE HOTEL AND RESTAURANT, ROUGHAM, BURY ST EDMUNDS IP30 9JA (01359 270345; Fax: 01359 270788). 16th century heavily beamed Tudor Hall set in seven acres of perfect dog walks. Individually furnished en suite bedrooms; renowned restaurant; relaxing inglenook fires. AA ★★★, AA 2 Rosettes. [🐾 pw!]
e-mail: enquiries@ravenwoodhall.co.uk   website: www.ravenwoodhall.co.uk

Cratfield

Village 5 miles West of Halesworth.

POACHERS FARM, HOLIDAY COTTAGE, CRATFIELD. Light and spacious cottage with views across open farm land. Situated on edge of village, pub nearby. Sleeps up to 6 plus sofa bed. 30 minutes to Southwold and coast. Fully fenced garden. Pets welcome. For brochure phone: MRS JANE BREWER, LODGE COTTAGE, LAXFIELD ROAD, CRATFIELD, HALESWORTH IP19 0QG (01986 798830 or 07788853884).[🐾]
e-mail: janebrewer@ukonline.co.uk

Readers are requested to mention this FHG
guidebook when seeking accommodation

Dunwich

Small village on coast, 4 miles south west of Southwold.

MR & MRS COLE, THE CLOSE, MIDDLEGATE BARN, DUNWICH IP17 3DP (01728 648244). Situated in a quiet, private road 200 yards from the sea. Ideal for walking/birdwatching. Furnished and equipped to a high standard. Centrally heated; available all year. Short Breaks available in low season, telephone for availability and brochure. [🐾]
e-mail: middlegate@aol.com

Hadleigh

Historic town on River Brett with several buildings of interest including unusual 14th century church. Bury St Edmunds 20 miles, Colchester 14, Sudbury 11, Ipswich 10.

EDGE HALL, 2 HIGH STREET, HADLEIGH IP7 5AP (01473 822458). Treacle invites you to stay in her master's comfortable lodge house. Well behaved owners will enjoy the perfect walks and super breakfasts. Twin/double £80 per night, single £55. Self-catering also available. ETC/AA ★★★★★ [Pets £5 per night, £10 per week]
website: www.edgehall.co.uk

Henley

Vilage 4 miles north of Ipswich.

WAYNE & SUE LEGGETT, DAMERONS FARM HOLIDAYS, HENLEY, IPSWICH IP6 0RU (01473 832454 or 07881 824083). Five cottages, each sleeping 1-6. The Old Dairy has a high level of accessibility for disabled visitors; three others have ground floor bedrooms and bathrooms. Games room with table tennis, pool and table football. Short Breaks out of season.
www.dameronsfarmholidays.co.uk

Kessingland

Little seaside place with expansive beach, safe bathing, wildlife park, lake fishing. To the south is Benacre Broad, a beauty spot. Norwich 26 miles, Adleburgh 23, Lowestoft 5.

Comfortable well-equipped bungalow on lawned site overlooking beach, next to Heritage Coast. Panoramic sea views. Easy beach access. Unspoiled walking area. ETC ★★ MRS L.G. SAUNDERS, 159 THE STREET, ROCKLAND ST MARY, NORWICH NR14 7HL (01508 538340). [Pets £10 per week].

Quality seaside bungalows in lawned surrounds overlooking the sea. Open all year, central heating, colour TV, parking, bed-linen, microwave, video recorder, heat and light included. Sleep 1/6. Direct access to award-winning beach. Pets very welcome. APPLY– KNIGHTS HOLIDAY HOMES, 198 CHURCH ROAD, KESSINGLAND, SUFFOLK NR33 7SF (FREEPHONE 0800 269067).
e-mail: info@knightsholidays.co.uk   website: www.knightsholidays.co.uk

Laxfield

Village 6 miles North of Framlingham.

LODGE COTTAGE, LAXFIELD. Pretty 16C thatched cottage retaining some fine period features. Sleeps 4. Pets welcome. Fenced garden. 1 mile from village. 30 minutes to Southwold and coast. Rural, quiet and relaxing. ETC ★★★★. For brochure phone: MRS JANE BREWER, LODGE COTTAGE, LAXFIELD ROAD, CRATFIELD, HALESWORTH IP19 0QG (01986 798830 or 07788853884). [Pets £10 per week].
e-mail: janebrewer@ukonline.co.uk

Long Melford

Village in the beautiful countryside of Suffolk, in the River Stour valley, just north of Sudbury, beside the A314 road to Bury St Edmunds.

THE BLACK LION HOTEL & RESTAURANT, THE GREEN, LONG MELFORD CO10 9DN (01787 312356). The Georgian Black Lion Hotel overlooks the famous green, and the cosy bar and restaurant offer a range of innovative dishes. 10 en suite bedrooms refurbished to luxury status. Idyllic dog walks. [🐾]
e-mail: enquiries@blacklionhotel.net   website: www.blacklionhotel.net

Lowestoft

Resort town on the North Sea coast, 38 miles north east of Ipswich.

BROADLAND HOLIDAY VILLAGE, OULTON BROAD, LOWESTOFT NR33 9JY (01502 573033). Discover the delights of the Forgotten Norfolk Broad with your faithful friend. Stay in cosy brick bungalows or pine lodges. Indoor heated pool. The perfect holiday for the whole family! [Pets £30 per week].
website: www.broadlandvillage.co.uk

Nayland

Small town on River Stour, 6 miles north of Colchester.

GLADWINS FARM, HARPER'S HILL, NAYLAND CO6 4NU (01206 262261). Self-catering cottages (sleep 2-8) and B&B set in 22 acres of Suffolk countryside. Indoor heated pool, sauna, hot tub, tennis court and playground. Loads of dog walking. [Pets £20 per week] ETC ★★★★/★★★★★.
e-mail: gladwinsfarm@aol.com   website: www.gladwinsfarm.co.uk

Orford

Village on River Ore, 9 miles east of Woodbridge.

THE CROWN AND CASTLE, ORFORD, WOODBRIDGE IP12 2LJ (01394 450205). Comfortable and very dog-friendly hotel situated close to 12th century castle in historic and unspoilt village of Orford. Honest good food served in award-winning Trinity Restaurant. [Pets £10 per night]
e-mail: info@crownandcastle.co.uk   website: www.crownandcastle.co.uk

Saxmundham

Small town 18 miles NE of Ipswich.

SWEFFLING HALL FARM, SWEFFLING, SAXMUNDHAM IP17 2BT (Tel & Fax: 01728 663644). In a quiet location. One double and one family room with en suite/private bathrooms. Ideal for walking/cycling and Heritage Coast. Open all year. Always a warm welcome. ETC ◆◆◆ [pw! 🐾 🏠]
e-mail: stephenmann@suffolkonline.net

Sudbury

Birthplace of Thomas Gainsborough, with a museum illustrating his career. Colchester 13 miles.

Situated in small, picturesque village within 15 miles of Sudbury, Newmarket Racecourse and historic Bury St Edmunds. Bungalow well equipped to accommodate 4 people. All facilities. Car essential, parking. Children and pets welcome. Terms from £71 to £141 per week. For further details send SAE to MRS M. WINCH, PLOUGH HOUSE, STANSFIELD, SUDBURY CO10 8LT (01284 789253). [🐾]

Visit the FHG website
www.holidayguides.com
for details of the wide choice of accommodation
featured in the full range of FHG titles

Ashbourne, Barlow, Buxton

·COUNTRY INN·

Mary and Martin Stelfox welcome you to a family-run 17th century Inn and Motel set in five acres, five miles from Alton Towers and close to Dovedale and Ashbourne. We specialise in family breaks, and special diets and vegetarians are catered for. All rooms have private bathrooms, colour TV, direct-dial telephone, tea-making facilities and baby listening service. Ideal for touring Stoke Potteries, Derbyshire Dales and Staffordshire Moorlands. Open Christmas and New Year. 'Staffs Good Food Winners 2003/2004'.

Restaurant open all day, non-residents welcome

e-mail: info@dogandpartridge.co.uk

Tel: 01335 343183 • www.dogandpartridge.co.uk

Swinscoe, Ashbourne DE6 2HS

THROWLEY HALL FARM • ILAM, ASHBOURNE DE6 2BB (01538 308202/308243)

Self-catering accommodation in farmhouse for up to 12 and cottages for five and seven people (ETC ★★★★). Also Bed and Breakfast in farmhouse (ETC ◆◆◆◆). Central heating, en suite rooms. No Smoking. TV, tea/coffee facilities in rooms. Children and pets welcome. Near Alton Towers and stately homes.

Mill Farm Holiday Cottages & Caravan Site

Five fully equipped converted cottages on 50 acres conservation land. Eight fishing lakes, trout/coarse, fishing free with cottages. Pub with meals 200 yards. Spacious parking area. Ideal base for walking. Laundry room and telephone. Dogs accepted.

Rex & Œnone Ward, Holiday Cottages, Mill Farm, Crow Hole, Barlow, Dronfield, Sheffield S18 5TJ • Tel: 0114 289 0543 • www.barlowlakes.co.uk

---

Alison Park Hotel 3 Temple Road, Buxton SK17 9BA • 01298 22473

Situated close to the Pavilion Gardens and within a few minutes' walk of the Opera House. • 17 bedrooms, all with either en suite or private bathroom. • Full English or Continental breakfast, full dinner menu and an extensive wine list; lunches, bar meals & dinner available to non-residents. • Vegetarian and special diets catered for. • Lounge with colour TV. • All bedrooms have tea & coffee makers, colour TV etc. • Wheelchair ramp access. • Ground floor bedrooms. • Lift to all floors. • Conference facilities. • Licensed.

Fax: 01298 72709 • e-mail: reservations@alison-park-hotel.co.uk • www.alison-park-hotel.co.uk

---

Please mention **Pets Welcome!**

when making enquiries about accommodation featured in these pages

Buxton, Peak District National Park

PEAK COTTAGES (0114 262 0777). Quality self-catering accommodation in the Derbyshire Dales and Peaks. Whether you are a walker, climber, potholer, antiquarian, historian, naturalist, gardener or sportsman – Derbyshire has it all. Pets Welcome. Telephone for colour brochure.　　[Pets £12 per week.]
website: www.peakcottages.com

Ashbourne

Market town on River Henmore, close to its junction with River Dove. Several interesting old buildings. Birmingham 42 miles, Nottingham 29, Derby 13.

MRS M.M. STELFOX, DOG AND PARTRIDGE COUNTRY INN, SWINSCOE, ASHBOURNE DE6 2HS (01335 343183). 17th century Inn offering ideal holiday accommodation. Many leisure activities available. All bedrooms with washbasins, colour TV, telephone and private facilities. ETC/AA ★★ [★, pw!]
e-mail: info@dogandpartridge.co.uk　　　　　　website: www.dogandpartridge.co.uk

MRS M.A. RICHARDSON, THROWLEY HALL FARM, ILAM, ASHBOURNE DE6 2BB (01538 308202/ 308243). Self-catering accommodation in farmhouse for up to 12 and cottages for five and seven people. Also Bed and Breakfast in farmhouse. Central heating, en suite rooms, TV, tea/coffee facilities in rooms. No smoking. Children and pets welcome. Near Alton Towers and stately homes. ETC ★★★★ *SELF-CATERING*, ETC ◆◆◆◆. [Pets £5 per week.]

MR & MRS LENNARD, WINDLEHILL FARM, SUTTON ON THE HILL, ASHBOURNE DE6 5JH (Tel & Fax: 01283 732377). Converted beamed barns on small organic farm - the Chop House sleeps 6 and has a fenced garden, the Hayloft sleeps 2 and is a first floor apartment. Well behaved pets welcome. ETC ★★★★ [pw! Pets £10 per week minimum]
e-mail: windlehill@btinternet.com   website: www.windlehill.btinternet.co.uk

Barlow

Situated on B6051 road, 4 miles north east of Chesterfield.

REX & ŒNONE WARD, HOLIDAY COTTAGES, MILL FARM, CROW HOLE, BARLOW, DRONFIELD, SHEFFIELD S18 5TJ (0114 289 0543). Five fully equipped converted cottages. Eight fishing lakes, trout/coarse, fishing free with cottages. Pub with meals 200 yards.Ideal base for walking. [Dogs £10 per week].
e-mail: cottages@barfish.fsnet.co.uk   website: www.barlowlakes.co.uk

Buxton

Well-known spa and centre for the Peak District. Beautiful scenery and good sporting amenities. Leeds 50 miles, Matlock 20, Macclesfield 12.

ALISON PARK HOTEL, 3 TEMPLE ROAD, BUXTON SK17 9BA (01298 22473; Fax: 01298 72709). Situated close to the Pavilion Gardens. 17 bedrooms, all en suite or private bathroom. Lunches, bar meals and dinner available to non-residents. Wheelchair ramp access; ground floor bedrooms. Licensed. [🅗]
e-mail: reservations@alison-park-hotel.co.uk   website: www.alison-park-hotel.co.uk

PRIORY LEA HOLIDAY FLATS. Close to Poole's Cavern Country Park. Fully equipped. Full central heating. Sleep 2/6. Cleanliness assured. Terms from £90-£275. Open all year. Short Breaks available. ETC ★★/★★★. MRS GILL TAYLOR, 50 WHITE KNOWLE ROAD, BUXTON SK17 9NH (01298 23737). [pw! Pets £1 per night.]

THE DEVONSHIRE ARMS, PEAK FOREST, NEAR BUXTON SK17 8EJ (01298 23875) Situated in a village location in the heart of the Peak District. All rooms en suite with tea/coffee and colour TV. Meals served every day. Excellent walking area. ETC ★★★ [🅗]
website: www.devarms.com

Peak District National Park

A green and unspoilt area at the southern end of the Pennines, covering 555 square miles.

WHEELDON TREES FARM, EARL STERNDALE, BUXTON SK17 0AA (01298 83219). Relax and unwind with your dog(s) in our 18thC barn conversion. Seven cosy, well equipped holiday cottages sleeping 2-5. [🅗]
website: www.wheeldontreesfarm.co.uk

BIGGIN HALL, PEAK PARK (01298 84451). Close Dove Dale. 17th century hall sympathetically restored. Bathrooms en suite, log fires, C/H comfort, warmth and quiet. Fresh home cooking. Beautiful uncrowded footpaths. Brochure on request. ETC ★★
website: www.bigginhall.co.uk

🅗   Indicates that pets are welcome free of charge.

£   Indicates that a charge is made for pets: nightly or weekly.

pw!   Shows some special provision for pets; exercise facility, feeding or accommodation arrangement.

⌂   Indicates separate pets accommodation.

Symbols

Hay-on-Wye, Kington, Ledbury, Pembridge, Ross-on-Wye

Readers are requested to mention this FHG
guidebook when seeking accommodation

Great Malvern

Fashionable spa town in last cenury with echoes of that period.

KATE AND DENIS KAVANAGH, WHITEWELLS FARM COTTAGES, RIDGEWAY CROSS, NEAR MALVERN WR13 5JR (01886 880607; Fax: 01886 880360). Charming converted Cottages, sleep 2–6. Fully equipped with colour TV, microwave, barbecue, fridge, iron, etc. Linen, towels also supplied. One cottage suitable for the disabled with full wheelchair access. Short breaks, long lets, large groups. ETC ★★★★ [pw! Pets £10 per week.] Also see Display Advert..
e-mail: info@whitewellsfarm.co.uk   website: www.whitewellsfarm.co.uk

Hay-on-Wye

Small market town 15 miles north east of Brecon.

BASKERVILLE ARMS HOTEL, CLYRO, NEAR HAY-ON-WYE HR3 5RZ (01497 820670). Delightfully placed comfortable retreat with well appointed en suite bedrooms. Tasty, home-cooked food in bar and restaurant, using the best local produce. Special break rates. AA ★★
e-mail: info@baskervillearms.co.uk   website: www.baskervillearms.co.uk

Kington

Town on River Arrow, close to Welsh border, 12 miles north of Leominster.

THE ROCK COTTAGE, HUNTINGTON, KINGTON. Secluded, stone-built cottage near Offa's Dyke footpath. Ideal for touring, birdwatching, golf and pony trekking. Sleeps 4/6. Fully equipped kitchen, lounge with wood-burner. Central Heating. Spacious garden. Children and pets welcome. Details from MRS C. WILLIAMS, RADNOR'S END, HUNTINGTON, KINGTON HR5 3NZ (01544 370289). [🐕]
website: www.the-rock-cottage.co.uk

Ledbury

Town 12 miles east of Hereford with many timbered houses.

CHURCH FARM, CODDINGTON, LEDBURY HR8 IJJ (01531 640271). Black and white 16th-century Farmhouse on a working farm close to the Malvern Hills — ideal for touring and walking. Two double and one twin bedrooms. Excellent home cooking. Warm welcome assured. Open all year. From £35 to £36 pppn. Single supplement. AA ★★★★ [🐕]
website: www.dexta.co.uk

Leominster

Known as "The Town in the Marches", this historic market town is located in the heart of the beautiful border countryside and possesses some fine examples of architecture throughout the ages, such as The Priory Church and Grange Court. Ludlow 9½ miles, Hereford 12 miles.

CLIVE & CYNTHIA PRIOR, MOCKTREE BARNS, LEINTWARDINE, LUDLOW SY7 0LY (01547 540441). Gold Award winning cottages around sunny courtyard. Sleep 2-6. Comfortable, well-equipped. Friendly owners. Dogs and children welcome. Non-Smoking. Lovely country walks. Ludlow, seven miles. Brochure. NAS Level 1 Accessibility. VB ★★★ [🐕] See also colour advertisement page 226
e-mail: mocktreebarns@care4free.net   website: www.mocktreeholidays.co.uk

Pembridge

Tiny medieval village surrounded by meadows and orchards.

MRS N. OWENS, THE GROVE, PEMBRIDGE, LEOMINSTER HR6 9HP (01544 388268). Two flats (sleep 4), each superbly equipped. All linen and towels included. Ideal base for touring; lovely walks on farm. Pets welcome under strict control. Terms from £185 pw. ETC ★★★ [Pets £5 per week, pw!]
e-mail: nancy@grovedesign.co.uk

Ross-on-Wye

An attractive town standing on a hill rising from the left bank on the Wye. Cardiff 47 miles, Gloucester 17.

THE ARCHES GUEST HOUSE, WALFORD ROAD, ROSS-ON-WYE HR9 5PT (01989 563348). All rooms en suite with colour TV and beverage making facilities. Centrally heated. Bed and Breakfast. Family room available, also ground floor room. Pets welcome. ETC ◆◆◆ [🐕]
e-mail: the.arches@which.net

THE INN ON THE WYE, KERNE BRIDGE, GOODRICH, NEAR ROSS-ON-WYE HR9 5QS (01600 890872; Fax: 01600 890594). Beautifully restored 18th century coaching inn, near Goodrich Castle on the banks of the River Wye. All bedrooms en suite. Peaceful country walks, ideal base for touring. RAC ◆◆◆, AA (Awaiting Grading).
e-mail: theinnonthewye@kernebridge.freeserve.co.uk   website: www.theinnonthewye.co.uk

LEA HOUSE, LEA, ROSS-ON-WYE HR9 7JZ (Tel & Fax: 01989 750652). Double/family en suite; twin/double en suite; twin private bath - all individually styled with TV and beverage tray. Secluded garden. Dogs very welcome. AA ★★★★ [Dogs £6 per stay]. See Display Advert.
e-mail: enquiries@leahouse.co.uk   website: www.leahouse.co.uk

Leicestershire & Rutland
Market Harborough, Melton Mowbray

Market Harborough

Town on River Welland 14 miles south-east of Leicester.

BROOK MEADOW HOLIDAYS. Three self-catering chalets, farmhouse Bed and Breakfast, Carp fishing, camping and caravan site with electric hookups. Phone for brochure. ETC ★★★ to ★★★★. MRS MARY HART, WELFORD ROAD, SIBBERTOFT, MARKET HARBOROUGH LE16 9UJ (01858 880886). [🐾 camping, £5 per night B&B, £12 Self-catering]
e-mail: brookmeadow@farmline.com   website: www.brookmeadow.co.uk

Melton Mowbray

Old market town, centre of hunting country. Large cattle market. Church and Ann of Cleves' House are of interest. Kettering 29 miles, Market Harborough 22, Nottingham 18, Leicester 15.

SYSONBY KNOLL HOTEL, ASFORDBY ROAD, MELTON MOWBRAY LE13 0HP (01664 563563; Fax: 01664 410364.). Family-run hotel on edge of market town. Grounds of five acres with river frontage. Superb food, comfortable accommodation and a genuine welcome for pets. No charge for dogs, please see website for further details. ETC/AA ★★★ [🐾]
website: www.sysonby.com

Horncastle

Market town once famous for annual horse fairs. 13th century Church is noted for brasses and Civil War relic

LITTLE LONDON COTTAGES, TETFORD, HORNCASTLE. Three very well-equipped properties standing in own gardens on our small estate. Lovely walks. Short breaks and special offers. ETC ★★★★/★★★★★. Contact: MRS S.D. SUTCLIFFE, THE MANSION HOUSE, LITTLE LONDON, TETFORD, HORNCASTLE LN9 6QL (01507 533697; mobile: 07767 321213). [🐾]
e-mail: debbie@sutcliffell.freeserve.co.uk   website: www.littlelondoncottages.co.uk

Langton-by-Wragby

Village located south-east of Wragby.

MISS JESSIE SKELLERN, LEA HOLME, LANGTON-BY-WRAGBY, LINCOLN LN8 5PZ (01673 858339). Ground floor accommodation in chalet-type house. Central for Wolds, coast, fens, historic Lincoln. Market towns, Louth, Horncastle, Boston, Spilsby, Alford, Woodhall Spa. Two double bedrooms. Washbasin, TV; bathroom, toilet adjoining; lounge with colour TV, separate dining room. Drinks provided. Children welcome reduced rates. Car almost essential, parking. Numerous eating places nearby. B&B from £25 per person (double/single let). Open all year. Pets welcome free. Tourist Board Listed [🐾]

Mablethorpe

Coastal resort 11 miles from Louth.

MRS GRAVES, GRANGE FARM, MALTBY-LE-MARSH, ALFORD LN13 0JP (01507 450267). Farmhouse B&B and country cottages set in ten idyllic acres of Lincolnshire countryside. Peaceful base for leisure, walking and sightseeing. Private fishing lakes. Many farm animals. Brochure available. [Pets £4 per night B&B, £30 per week in cottages] *[🏠]*
website: www.grange-farmhouse.co.uk

A useful index of towns/counties appears on pages 391-396

Edwinstowe

Crow Hollow Cottage, Near Edwinstowe. Recently refurbished farm cottage stands in its own hedged garden. Close to Sherwood Forest and its numerous attractions. Many NT properties nearby. Explore the local area on horseback, or by foot, car or bicycle. DIY stabling at adjacent Broomhill Grange. Village shops 2 miles. ETC ★★★

Contact Helen Proctor (01636 677847; mobile 07976 829066) • e-mail: shp18@lineone.net • www.crowhollow.co.uk

Burton Joyce

Residential area 4 miles north-east of Nottingham.

MRS V. BAKER, WILLOW HOUSE, 12 WILLOW WONG, BURTON JOYCE, NOTTINGHAM NG14 5FD (0115 931 2070 or 07816 347706). Large Victorian house, authentically furnished, in quiet village near beautiful stretch of River Trent. Four miles city. Close to station/bus stop. Bright, clean rooms. TV. Parking. En suite available. From £24 pppn. Good local eating. Please phone first for directions. [🐾]

Edwinstowe

Village 2 miles west of Ollerton.

CROW HOLLOW COTTAGE, NEAR EDWINSTOWE. Recently refurbished farm cottage stands in its own hedged garden. Close to Sherwood Forest and its numerous attractions. Explore the local area on horseback, or by foot, car or bicycle. DIY stabling at adjacent Broomhill Grange. Contact Helen Proctor (01636 677847; mobile 07976 829066). ETC ★★★
e-mail: shp18@lineone.net　　　website: www.crowhollow.co.uk

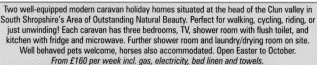

Bishop's Castle

Small town in the hills on the Welsh Border, 8 miles from Craven Arms.

BROADWAY HOUSE, CHURCHSTOKE, POWYS SY15 6DU (01588 620770). 17th century Lodge and 18th century Coach House in the grounds of a Regency gentleman's residence on Wales/England border. Picturesque views. Linen and fuel included. Open all year. Sleep five and two. WTB ★★★★★ Self-Catering. [🐾]
e-mail: enqs@bordercottages.co.uk   website: www.bordercottages.co.uk

Church Stretton

Delightful little town in lee of Shropshire Hills. Walking and riding country. Facilities for tennis, bowls, gliding and golf. Knighton 22 miles, Bridgnorth 19, Ludlow 15, Shrewsbury 12.

MRS C.F. BRANDON-LODGE, NORTH HILL FARM, CARDINGTON, CHURCH STRETTON SY6 7LL (01694 771532). Rooms with a view! B&B in beautiful Shropshire hills. TV in rooms, tea etc. Ideal walking country. From £25 per person; en suite available. AA ★★★★ [pw! Pets £2.00 per night, 🐕]
e-mail: cbrandon@btinternet.com   website: www.virtual-shropshire.co.uk/northhill/

Craven Arms

Surrounded by hills, Craven Arms is home to the Shropshire Hills Discovery Centre where you can experience virtual balloon rides and meet the "hairy mammoth". Beautiful Stokesey Castle lies just outside the town. Ludlow 6½ miles, Shrewsbury 19 miles.

Two well-equipped modern caravan holiday homes in Area of Outstanding Natural Beauty. Perfect for walking, cycling, riding, or just unwinding! Each has three bedrooms, TV, shower room with flush toilet, and kitchen with fridge and microwave. Well behaved pets welcome, horses also accommodated. Open Easter to October. THE ANCHORAGE, ANCHOR, NEWCASTLE ON CLUN, CRAVEN ARMS, SHROPSHIRE SY7 8PR (01686 670737). [Pets £10 per week].

Grinshill

Village 7 miles north of Shrewsbury.

THE INN AT GRINSHILL, HIGH STREET, GRINSHILL, NEAR SHREWSBURY SY4 3BL (01939 220410). Situated 7 miles north of Shrewsbury, this warm, friendly inn offers the highest standards of food, refreshment and accommodation. Dogs on leads are welcome in the bar.
info@theinnatgrinshill.co.uk   website: www.theinnatgrinshill.co.uk

Ludlow

Lovely and historic town on Rivers Teme and Corve with numerous old half-timbered houses and inns. Worcester 29 miles, Shrewsbury 27, Hereford 24, Bridgnorth 19, Church Stretton 16.

HENWICK HOUSE, GRAVEL HILL, LUDLOW SY8 1QU (01584 873338). Warm, comfortable Georgian coach house, good traditional English Breakfast. Easy walking distance from town centre and local inns. Lots of nice local walks. TV, tea/coffee making facilities. One double, two twin, and one single room, all en suite. B&B from £28 pppn. ETC ◆◆◆ [🐾]

THE MOOR HALL, NEAR LUDLOW SY8 3EG (01584 823209; Fax: 08707 492202). Built in 1789, a splendid example of the Georgian Palladian style. Breathtaking views, 5 acre garden. B&B from £30 pppn. AA ★★★★ [🐾]
e-mail: info@moorhall.co.uk   website: www.moorhall.co.uk

CLIVE & CYNTHIA PRIOR, MOCKTREE BARNS, LEINTWARDINE, LUDLOW SY7 0LY (01547 540441). Gold Award winning self-catering cottages around sunny courtyard. Sleep 2-6. Comfortable, well-equipped. Friendly owners. Dogs and children welcome. Non-Smoking. Lovely country walks. Ludlow, seven miles. Brochure. NAS Level 1 Accessibility. VB ★★★ [🐾] See also colour advertisement page 226.
e-mail: mocktreebarns@care4free.net   website: www.mocktreeholidays.co.uk

SALLY AND TIM LOFT, GOOSEFOOT BARN, PINSTONES, DIDDLEBURY, CRAVEN ARMS, SHROPSHIRE SY7 9LB (01584 861326). Four delightful cottages thoughtfully converted and equipped to the highest standard. All with en suite facilities and garden or seating area. One cottage with disabled access. Situated in a secluded valley and ideally located to explore the beautiful South Shropshire countryside. Sleep 2-6. ETC ★★★★ [🐾]
e-mail: sally@goosefoot.freeserve.co.uk   website: www.goosefootbarn.co.uk

Oswestry

Borderland market town. Many old castles and fortifications. Shrewsbury 16, Vyrnwy 18.

PEN-Y-DYFFRYN COUNTRY HOTEL, NEAR RHYDYCROESAU, OSWESTRY SY10 7JD (01691 653700). Picturesque Georgian Rectory quietly set in Shropshire/ Welsh Hills. 12 en suite bedrooms, four with private patios. 5-acre grounds. No passing traffic. Johansens recommended. Dinner, Bed and Breakfast from £80.00 per person per day. AA ★★★. [🐾 pw!]
e-mail: stay@peny.co.uk   website: www.peny.co.uk

Leek

One cosy three bedroomed cottage which sleeps six, with four-poster. Also delightful flat which sleeps up to four. Both fully equipped and carpeted throughout; CD and DVD players. Electricity and linen inclusive, laundry room. Ideal base for Alton Towers, Potteries and Peak District. Terms £180 to £350.
EDITH & ALWYN MYCOCK, 'ROSEWOOD COTTAGE and ROSEWOOD FLAT', LOWER BERKHAMSYTCH FARM, BOTTOM HOUSE, NEAR LEEK ST13 7QP
Tel & Fax: 01538 308213 • www.rosewoodcottage.co.uk

Leek

Village 10 miles from Stoke-on-Trent.

EDITH & ALWYN MYCOCK, 'ROSEWOOD COTTAGE and ROSEWOOD FLAT', LOWER BERKHAMSYTCH FARM, BOTTOM HOUSE, NEAR LEEK ST13 7QP (Tel & Fax: 01538 308213). Cosy three bedroomed cottage with four-poster, sleeps six; also flat, sleeps up to four. Fully equipped and carpeted. Electricity and linen inclusive, laundry room. Ideal base for Alton Towers, Potteries and Peak District. Terms £180 to £350. [Pets £6.50 per week]
website: www.rosewoodcottage.co.uk

CLIFTON CRUISERS, CLIFTON WHARF, VICARAGE HILL, CLIFTON, RUGBY, WARWICKSHIRE CV23 0DG (01788 543570; Fax: 01788 579799). Varied choice of boat layouts and accommodation to satisfy the requirements of most family and holiday groups (sleeping 2-8). Starting base centrally situated on the waterway network. [Pets £20 per week]
e-mail: info@cliftoncruisers.com   website: www.cliftoncruisers.com

Stratford-upon-Avon

Historic town famous as Shakespeare's birthplace and home. Birmingham 24, Warwick 8.

RIVERSIDE CARAVAN PARK, TIDDINGTON ROAD, STRATFORD-UPON-AVON CV37 7BE (01789 292312). Luxury Caravans, sleep 6. Fully equipped kitchens, bathroom/ shower/WC. Also two riverside Cottages, all modern facilities to first-class standards. Private fishing. On banks of River Avon. [Pets £15 weekly.]
website: www.stratfordcaravans.co.uk

Warwick

Town on the River Avon, 9 miles south-west of Coventry, with medieval castle and many fine old buildings.

DAVID & PATRICIA CLAPP, CROFT GUESTHOUSE, HASELEY KNOB, WARWICK CV35 7NL (Tel & Fax: 01926 484447). All bedrooms en suite or with private bathroom, some ground floor. Non-smoking. Picturesque rural setting. Central for NEC, Warwick, Stratford, Stoneleigh and Coventry. B&B single £40, double/twin £60. ETC/AA ★★★★ [Dogs £3 per night]
e-mail: david@croftguesthouse.co.uk   website: www.croftguesthouse.co.uk

Droitwich, Great Malvern, Worcestershire

FREE or REDUCED RATE entry to Holiday Visits and Attractions – see our

READERS' OFFER VOUCHERS on pages 371-390

Droitwich

Town 6 miles north-east of Worcester. Former spa status due to saline springs.

MRS SALLI HARRISON, MIDDLETON GRANGE, SALWARPE, DROITWICH SPA WR9 0AH (01905 451678; Fax: 01905 453978). Traditional 18th century country house surrounded by picturesque gardens. Children welcome. Babysitting service. Dogs and cats by arrangement. All rooms en suite. M5 motorway six minutes. Worcester 10 minutes. ETC ◆◆◆◆ *SILVER AWARD*. [Pets £5 per night].

Great Malvern

Fashionable spa town in last century with echoes of that period.

MALVERN HILLS HOTEL, WYNDS POINT, MALVERN WR13 6DW (01684 540690). Enchanting family-owned and run hotel nestling high in the hills. Direct access to superb walking with magnificent views. Oak-panelled lounge, log fire, real ales, fine food and friendly staff. Great animal lovers. AA ★★ [Pets £5 per night].
website: www.malvernhillshotel.co.uk

KATE AND DENIS KAVANAGH, WHITEWELLS FARM COTTAGES, RIDGEWAY CROSS, NEAR MALVERN WR13 5JR (01886 880607; Fax: 01886 880360). Charming converted Cottages, sleep 2–6. Fully equipped with colour TV, microwave, barbecue, fridge, iron, etc. Linen, towels also supplied. One cottage suitable for the disabled with full wheelchair access. Short breaks, long lets, large groups. ETC ★★★★ [pw! Pets £10 per week.] Also see Display Advert..
e-mail: info@whitewellsfarm.co.uk   website: www.whitewellsfarm.co.uk

ANN AND BRIAN PORTER, CROFT GUEST HOUSE, BRANSFORD, WORCESTER WR6 5JD (01886 832227). 16th-18th century country house. 10 minutes from Worcester, Malvern and M5. Non-smoking house. Family Room. Bedrooms have en suite (3), colour TV, tea and coffee tray, hairdryer, radio alarm. Dinners available. Dogs welcome. AA ◆◆◆ [🐾]
e-mail: hols@crofthousewr6.fsnet.co.uk   website: www.croftguesthouse.com

Worcester

Cathedral city on River Severn, 24 miles south-west of Birmingham.

MOSELEY FARM BED & BREAKFAST, MOSELEY ROAD, HALLOW, WORCESTER WR2 6NL (01905 641343; Fax: 01905 641416). Spacious 17th century former farmhouse with countryside views. Two en suite family rooms and two standard rooms, with colour TV, radio alarm clocks and tea/coffee making facilities. Room only weekdays. Full breakfast at weekends.[🐾]
e-mail: moseleyfarm@aol.com   website: www.moseleyfarmbandb.co.uk

Looking for holiday accommodation?
for details of hundreds of properties
throughout the UK visit:

www.holidayguides.com

RECOMMENDED COTTAGE HOLIDAYS. 1st choice for dream cottages at very competitive prices in all holiday regions of beautiful Britain. Pets welcome. All properties inspected. Free brochure - call 01751 475547.
website: www.recommended-cottages.co.uk

DALES HOLIDAY COTTAGES . See the best of the Dales, Coast and Wolds. A wide range of cottages to choose from, all personally inspected. Pets welcome. Free brochure. Call 0870 909 9500 or visit our website.
website: www.dalesholcot.com

East Yorkshire
Beverley, Bridlington, Kilnwick Percy, Driffield

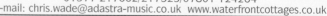

Beverley

Popular medieval market and county town in the East Riding of Yorkshire, 8 miles from Kingston upon Hull, 10 miles from Market Weighton and 12 from Hornsea.

ROBEANNE HOUSE, DRIFFIELD LANE, SHIPTONTHORPE, YORK YO43 3PW (01430 873312). Family B&B, country location, 18 miles from historic York. Ideal for coast, Moors, racing, Beverley, Cycle Route 66 and Wolds Way. Beautiful country house and gardens. All rooms en suite. Contact: JEANNE WILSON. AA ★★★ [pw! Pets £5 per night]
e-mail: enquiries@robeannehouse.co.uk   website: www.robeannehouse.co.uk

Bridlington

Traditional family resort with picturesque harbour and a wide range of entertainments and leisure facilities. Ideal for exploring the Heritage coastline and the Wolds.

THE TENNYSON, 19 TENNYSON AVENUE, BRIDLINGTON YO15 2EU (01262 604382). Small, non-smoking, family hotel offering all usual amenities. B&B from £26pppn. All rooms en suite. Located within easy walking distance of town centre, North Beach and cliff walks. AA ★★★ [Pets £2.50 per night].
website: www.thetennysonhotel.co.uk

Driffield

Town 11 miles south west of Bridlington.

Old Cobbler's Cottage, North Dalton. Pretty cottage with garden looking over village mere with its ducks and fish. Good walking area and easy access to York and coast. Open fire. First-class restaurants and pubs within 20 yards. For details contact (01377 217662/217523/07801 124264). ETC ★★★ [🐾]
e-mail:chris.wade@adastra-music.co.uk   website: www.waterfrontcottages.co.uk

Kilnwick Percy

Located 2 miles east of Pocklington

PAWS-A-WHILE, KILNWICK PERCY, POCKLINGTON YO42 1UF (01759 301168; Mobile: 07711 866869). Small family B & B set in forty acres of parkland twixt York and Beverley. Golf, walking, riding. Pets and horses most welcome. Brochure available. ETC ★★★★ [pw! 🐾]
e-mail: paws.a.while@lineone.net   website: www.pawsawhile.net

---

Pet-Friendly
Pubs, Inns & Hotels
on pages 360-369
Please note that these establishments may not feature in the main section of this book

Austwick, Bentham, , Clapham, Coverdale, Danby

FHG Guides

publish a large range of well-known accommodation guides.

We will be happy to send you details or you can use the order form

at the back of this book.

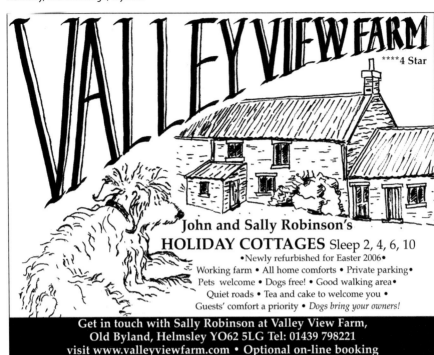

Malham, Northallerton, Pickering, Port Mulgrave, Ripon, Scalby Nabs (Scarborough)

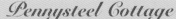

Looking for holiday accommodation?
for details of hundreds of properties
throughout the UK visit:

www.holidayguides.com

FHG Guides

publish a large range of well-known accommodation guides.
We will be happy to send you details or you can use the order form
at the back of this book.

INGRID FLUTE HOLIDAY ACCOMMODATION AGENCY. Established 1970. Over 200 cottages, bungalows, chalets and apartments throughout Whitby, Scarborough, North Yorkshire Moors and Ryedale. For a free brochure contact 01723 376777.
website: www.ingridflute.co.uk

Austwick

Village 4 miles north west of Settle.

WOOD VIEW GUEST HOUSE, AUSTWICK LA2 8BB (015242 51190). Grade II Listed building overlooking the green in picturesque village in the Yorkshire Dales National Park. All rooms en suite and non-smoking, with private parking. VB ★★★★ [🐾]
e-mail: woodview@austwick.org   website: www.woodviewbandb.com

Bentham

Quiet village amidst the fells. Good centre for rambling and fishing. Ingleton 5 miles north-east.

MRS L. J. STORY, HOLMES FARM, LOW BENTHAM, LANCASTER LA2 7DE (015242 61198). Cottage conversion in easy reach of Dales, Lake District and coast. Central heating, fridge, TV, washer, games room. ETC ★★★★. [🐾]
e-mail: lucy@holmesfarmcottage.co.uk   website: www.holmesfarmcottage.co.uk

Clapham

Situated in beautiful countryside within the Yorkshire Dales National Park, 6 miles north west of Settle, just off the A65.

DAVID & JACKIE KINGSLEY, ARBUTUS GUEST HOUSE, RIVERSIDE, CLAPHAM (NEAR SETTLE) LA2 8DS (015242 51240). Restored Georgian vicarage in a delightful setting. All rooms en suite, or private facilities. TV, tea/coffee. Central heating. Open all year round. Pets welcome. ETC ★★★★ [🐾]
e-mail: info@arbutus.co.uk   website: www.arbutus.co.uk

Coverdale

Located in the Yorkshire Dales National Park, famous for Middleham Castle, Richard III and the Forbidden Corner..

MRS JULIE CLARKE, MIDDLE FARM, WOODALE, COVERDALE, LEYBURN DL8 4TY (01969 640271). Peacefully situated farmhouse away from the madding crowd. B&B with optional Evening Meal. Home cooking. Pets sleep where you prefer. Ideally positioned for exploring the beautiful Yorkshire Dales. [🐾 pw!]
e-mail: j-a-clarke@hotmail.co.uk

Danby

Village on River Esk 12 miles west of Whitby.

THE FOX & HOUNDS INN, AINTHORPE, DANBY YO21 2LD (01287 660218; Fax: 01287 660030). Residential 16th Century Coaching Inn. Comfortable en suite bedrooms available. Enjoy our real ales or quality wines. Special mid-week breaks available Oct - May. Open all year. ETC ★★★★ [Pets £2.50 per night.]
e-mail: info@foxandhounds-ainthorpe.com   website: www.foxandhounds-ainthorpe.com

Grassington

Wharfedale village in attractive moorland setting. Ripon 22 miles, Skipton 9.

JERRY AND BEN'S HOLIDAY COTTAGES. Four comfortable properties sleeping 2, 4, 6, and 10 near Grassington in Yorkshire Dales National Park. Wooded mountain becks, waterfalls, rocky crags and accessible hill and footpath walking. Brochure from: MRS FIONA HOOLE, JERRY AND BEN'S HOLIDAY COTTAGES, HEBDEN, SKIPTON BD23 5DL (01756 752369). [Pets £10 per week]
e-mail: Fiona@jerryandbens.co.uk   website: www.jerryandbens.co.uk

FORESTERS ARMS, MAIN STREET, GRASSINGTON, SKIPTON BD23 5AA (01756 752349; Fax: 01756 753633). The Foresters Arms is situated in the heart of the Yorkshire Dales and provides an ideal centre for walking or touring. Within easy reach of York and Harrogate. ETC ★★★ [🐾]

Harrogate

Charming and elegant spa town set amid some of Britain's most scenic countryside. Ideal for exploring Herriot Country and the moors and dales. York 22 miles, Bradford 19, Leeds 16.

ROSEMARY HELME, HELME PASTURE LODGES & COTTAGES, OLD SPRING WOOD, HARTWITH BANK, SUMMERBRIDGE, HARROGATE HG3 4DR (01423 780279, Fax: 01423 780994). Country accommodation for owners and dogs and numerous walks in unspoilt Nidderdale. Central for Harrogate, York, Herriot and Bronte country. National Trust area. ETC ★★★★, ETC Category 1 for Disabled Access. [pw! Pets £5 per night, £25 per week.]
e-mail:helmepasture@btinternet.com   website: www.helmepasture.co.uk

RUDDING HOLIDAY PARK, FOLLIFOOT, HARROGATE HG3 1JH (01423 870439; Fax: 01423 870859). Luxury cottages and lodges sleeping two to seven people. All equipped to a high standard. Pool, licensed bar, golf and children's playground in the Parkland. Illustrated brochure available. ETC ★★★ [🐾]
e-mail: holiday-park@ruddingpark.com   website: www.ruddingpark.com

Hawes

12 miles north-west on the Hawes to Kirkby Stephen road.

SIMONSTONE HALL, HAWES, WENSLEYDALE DL8 3LY (01969 667255; Fax: 01969 667741). Facing south across picturesque Wensleydale. All rooms en suite with colour TV. Fine cuisine. Extensive wine list. Friendly personal attention. A relaxing break away from it all. AA ★★ [£12 per stay]
e-mail: e-mail@simonstonehall.demon.co.uk   website: www.simonstonehall.co.uk

COCKLAKE HOUSE, MALLERSTANG CA17 4JT (017683 72080). Charming, High Pennine Country House B&B in unique position above Pendragon Castle in Upper Mallerstang Dale offering good food and exceptional comfort to a small number of guests. Two double rooms with large private bathrooms. Three acres riverside grounds. Dogs welcome. [🐾]

STONE HOUSE HOTEL, SEDBUSK, HAWES DL8 3PT (01969 667571). This fine Edwardian country house has spectacular views and serves delicious Yorkshire cooking with fine wines. Comfortable en suite bedrooms, some ground floor. Phone for details. [🐾]
website: www.stonehousehotel.com

Helmsley

A delightful stone-built town on River Rye with a large cobbled square. Thirsk 12 miles.

JOHN & SALLY ROBINSON'S VALLEY VIEW FARM, OLD BYLAND, HELMSLEY, YORK YO62 5LG (01439 798221). Fully equipped self-catering cottages on working farm in North Yorks moors. Ideal for touring Yorkshire, or just walking the hills and lanes around. Rural peace and tranquillity. Dogs free. Kennel and run available. ETC ★★★★ [🐾]
website: www.valleyviewfarm.com

Knaresborough

Town on escarpment above the River Nidd, 3 miles NE of Harrogate..

NEWTON HOUSE, KNARESBOROUGH. Winner of the AA Pet Friendly Award – pets genuinely welcomed and lots of great walks nearby. Spacious and comfortable, newly refurbished ensuite accommodation and great breakfasts. AA ★★★★ Highly Commended, AA Breakfast Award. Contact MARK & LISA WILSON, NEWTON HOUSE, 5-7 YORK PLACE, KNARESBOROUGH HG5 0AD (Tel: 01423 863539). [🐾]
e-mail: newtonhouse@btinternet.com   website: www.newtonhouseyorkshire.com

GALLON HOUSE 47 KIRKGATE, KNARESBOROUGH HG5 8BZ (01423 862102). Overlooking the beautiful Nidd Gorge, Gallon House offers award-winning accommodation and superb fresh food. Two double and one twin bedrooms, all en suite. Licensed. ETC/AA ◆◆◆◆ Gold Award. [🐾]
e-mail: gallon-house@ntlworld.com   website: www.gallon-house.co.uk

Leyburn

Small market town, 8 miles south-west of Richmond, standing above the River Ure in Wensleydale.

BARBARA & BARRIE MARTIN, THE OLD STAR, WEST WITTON, LEYBURN DL8 4LU (01969 622949). Former 17th century Coaching Inn now run as a guest house. Oak beams, log fire, home cooking. En suite B&B from £25 pppn. ETC ◆◆◆. [🐴]
e-mail: enquiries@theoldstar.com   website: www.theoldstar.com

GOLDEN LION HOTEL, MARKET PLACE, LEYBURN DL8 5AS (01969 622161; Fax: 01969 623836). Excellent accommodation in this splendid hotel at the gateway to Wensleydale. En suite bathrooms, TV, telephone, radio and tea/coffee makers. Lift to all floors. ETC ★. [🐴]
e-mail: info@goldenlionleyburn.co.uk

Malham

Village in upper Airedale, 5 miles east of Settle, across the moors.

MR C. SHARP, MIRESFIELD FARM, MALHAM, SKIPTON BD23 4DA (01729 830414). In beautiful gardens bordering village green and stream. Excellent food. 11 bedrooms, all with private facilities. Full central heating. Two well-furnished lounges and conservatory. B&B from £24pppn. ETC ◆◆◆ [🐴 pw!]

Northallerton

Town 14 miles south of Darlington.

JULIE & JIM GRIFFITH, HILL HOUSE FARM, LITTLE LANGTON, NORTHALLERTON DL7 0PZ (01609 770643). Sleep 2/4. Four well-equipped cottages, cosily heated for year round appeal. Centrally located between Dales and Moors. Weekly rates from £175 incl. Short breaks available. Golf 2 miles, shops 3 miles, pub food 1.5 miles. Pets welcome. ETC ★★★★ [🐴]
e-mail: info@hillhousefarmcottages.com   website: www.hillhousefarmcottages.com

Pickering

Pleasant market town on southern fringe of North Yorkshire Moors National Park with moated Norman Castle. Bridlington 31 miles, Whitby 20, Scarborough 16, Helmsley 13, Malton 3.

MRS ELLA BOWES, BANAVIE, ROXBY ROAD, THORNTON-LE-DALE, PICKERING YO18 7SX (01751 474616). Large stone-built semi-detached house set in Thornton-le-Dale. Ideal for touring. One family bedroom and two double bedrooms, all en suite. All with TV, shaver points, central heating and tea-making facilities. Open all year. Car park, cycle shed. B&B from £26pppn. Welcome Host and Hygiene Certificate held. ETC ★★★★ [🐴]
e-mail: info@banavie.uk.com   website: www.banavie.uk.com

THE WHITE SWAN INN AT PICKERING (01751 472288). 16th century inn with a buzz. Dog friendly with excellent: service, rooms, food and wine. "...consistently brilliant.." Please phone or visit our website for a brochure. ETC ★★★, AA Rosette [Pets £12.50 per visit].
e-mail: welcome@white-swan.co.uk   website: www.white-swan.co.uk

Port Mulgrave

Located 1km north of Hinderwell.

NORTH YORK MOORS NATIONAL PARK. Stone Cottage (sleeps) 4 in North York Moors National Park. Sea view, near Cleveland coastal footpath. Log fire, non-smoking. Whitby 9 miles. Brochure available (01642 613888). [🐴]

A useful index of towns/counties appears at the back of this book

Ripon

Town 10 miles north of Harrogate. Cathedral in a mixture of styles, Racecourse 2 miles south east.

Five ground floor en suite rooms round a pretty courtyard. All rooms are full of character: oak beams etc., with modern facilities, all with views of the countryside. Private fishing lake. Terms from £65 to £75. AA ★★★★ Details from MRS L. HITCHEN, ST GEORGE'S COURT, OLD HOME FARM, HIGH GRANTLEY, RIPON HG4 3PJ (01765 620618). [🐾]

Scalby Nabs (Scarborough)

Small town and suburb 2 miles north west of Scarborough.

EAST FARM COUNTRY COTTAGES, SCALBY NABS, SCALBY, SCARBOROUGH (01723 353635). Single-storey two-bedroom stone cottages (no steps/stairs) in national Park; only 5 minutes from Scarborough. All completely non-smoking. Ideal base for walking or touring. VisitBritain ★★★ [Pets from £10 per week.]
e-mail: joeastfarmcottages@hotmail.co.uk   website: www.eastfarmcountrycottages.co.uk

Scarborough

Very popular family resort with good sands. York 41 miles, Whitby 20, Bridlington 17, Filey 7.

HARMONY GUEST HOUSE, 13 PRINCESS ROYAL TERRACE, SOUTH CLIFF, SCARBOROUGH YO11 2RP (01723 373562). Child/veggie/doggie friendly Guest House. Local produce, home-cooked, no "boil in the bag'. 4 bedrooms, all en suite. Informal atmosphere. Open all year. B&B £22pppn, BBEM £32. [🐾].
e-mail: harmonyguesthouse@hotmail.com   website: www.theharmonyguesthouse.co.uk

RAVEN HALL COUNTRY HOUSE HOTEL & GOLF COURSE, RAVENSCAR, SCARBOROUGH YO13 0ET (01723 870353; Fax: 01723 870072). This imposing hotel offers oustanding accommodation, superb, typically Yorkshire cuisine and an impressive range of leisure facilities including a 9-hole golf course. A family holiday paradise. AA ★★★ [pw! Pets £5 per night.]
e-mail: enquiries@ravenhall.co.uk   website: www.ravenhall.co.uk

SUE AND TONY HEWITT, HARMONY COUNTRY LODGE, LIMESTONE ROAD, BURNISTON, SCARBOROUGH YO13 0DG (0800 2985840). A peaceful retreat set in two acres of private grounds with 360° panoramic views of the National Park and sea. An ideal centre for walking or touring. En suite centrally heated rooms with superb views. Non-smoking, licensed, private parking facilities. B&B from £27 to £36. ETC ★★★★
website: www.harmonylodge.net

Skipton

Airedale market town, centre for picturesque Craven district. Fine Castle (14th cent). York 43 miles, Manchester 42, Leeds 26, Harrogate 22, Settle 16.

Over 250 super self-catering Cottages, throughout the Yorkshire Dales, York, Moors, Lancashire, Peak and Lake District. For our fully illustrated brochure apply: HOLIDAY COTTAGES (YORKSHIRE) LTD, WATER STREET, SKIPTON BD23 1PB (01756 700872). [🐾]
e-mail: p@holidaycotts.co.uk   website: www.holidaycotts.co.uk

BECK HALL, MALHAM BD23 4DJ (01729 830332). 18th century B&B on the Pennine Way, log fires and huge breakfasts. Midweek and 4-night specials. Ideal for exploring the Yorkshire Dales. AA ◆◆◆, WELCOME HOST. [🐾]
e-mail: simon@beckhallmalham.com   website: www.beckhallmalham.com

THE CONISTON HOTEL, CONISTON COLD, SKIPTON BD23 4EB (01756 748080; Fax: 01756 749487). Set in a stunning 1400 acre estate, an ideal base for guests wishing to explore the Yorkshire Dales. 50 en suite bedrooms with full facilities. Special rates for leisure breaks and family rooms. ETC ★★★ Silver Award, AA ★★★ & Rosette. [pw! Pets £10 per stay]
e-mail: sales@theconistonhotel.com   website: www.theconistonhotel.com

Staithes

Fishing village surrounded by high cliffs on North Sea coast, 9 miles north west of Whitby.

PENNYSTEEL COTTAGE, STAITHES. Old fisherman's cottage overlooking picturesque harbour. Ideal for walking and touring. Sleep 3 + 2 children. Electricity, heating, bed linen incl. One well-behaved pet welcome. ETC ★★★ For details contact CHRIS WADE (01377 217662/217523/07801 124264) [🐕]
e-mail: chris.wade@adastra-music.co.uk   website: www.waterfrontcottages.co.uk

Thirsk

Market town with attractive square. Excellent touring area. Northallerton 3 miles.

POPLARS HOLIDAY COTTAGES AND BED & BREAKFAST, THIRSK. The Poplars stands in two acres of lovely gardens with a field for dog walking. We have old brick cottages and new lodges, with bed and breakfast in the Poplars House. Contact AMANDA RICHARDS, THE POPLARS, CARLTON MINIOTT, THIRSK YO7 4LX (01845 522712). ETC ★★★★, Silver Award. [Pets £5 per night B&B, £5 per week SC]
website: www.poplars-cottages.co.uk

GOLDEN FLEECE HOTEL, MARKET PLACE, THIRSK YO7 1LL (01845 523108; Fax: 01845 523996). Characterful Coaching Inn offering good food and up to date facilities. All rooms are en suite, with satellite TV, phone, trouser press, hairdryer. ETC/AA ★★ [🐕]
e-mail: reservations@goldenfleecehotel.com   website: www.goldenfleecehotel.com

MR A. BOWYER, GLEN FREE, HOLME-ON-SWALE, SINDERBY, NEAR THIRSK YO7 4JE (01845 567331). Our old Lodge Bungalow surrounded by countryside with lovely gardens is ideal for walking and touring the Dales. One double and one family room with all the facilities you would expect. From £20pppn.
e-mail: alan.bowyer@fsmail.net   website: www.glenfree.co.uk

FOXHILLS HIDEAWAYS, FELIXKIRK, THIRSK YO7 2DS (01845 537575). 4 Scandinavian log cabins, heated throughout, linen provided. A supremely relaxed atmosphere on the edge of the North York Moors National Park. Open all year. Village pub round the corner. [🐕]

Whitby

Charming resort with harbour and sands. Of note is the 13th century ruined Abbey. Stockton-on-Tees 34 miles, Scarborough 20, Saltburn-by-the-Sea 19.

THE SEACLIFFE HOTEL, WEST CLIFF, WHITBY YO21 3JX (Freephone 0800 0191747). A very warm-hearted, family-run hotel overlooking the beach. Children and dogs welcome. Enjoy fine ales and delicious "Heartbeat Country" cooking in our own "Aidensfield Arms" traditional licensed bar or sample superb seafoods and fine wines in the Candleight restaurant (booking advised). VisitBritain ◆◆◆◆. [🐕]
e-mail: stay@seacliffehotel.co.uk   website: www.seacliffehotel.co.uk

WHITE ROSE HOLIDAY COTTAGES, NEAR WHITBY. Quality cottages and bungalows offering a warm and friendly welcome. Sleep 1-9. Private parking. Ideal for coast and country. APPLY: MRS J. ROBERTS (PW), 5 BROOK PARK, SLEIGHTS, NEAR WHITBY YO21 1RT (01947 810763) [Pets £5, pw!] ETC ★★★-★★★★.
website: www.whiterosecottages.co.uk

MRS JILL McNEIL, SWALLOW HOLIDAY COTTAGES, LONG LEAS FARM, HAWSKER, WHITBY YO22 4LA (01947 603790). Discover historic Whitby, pretty fishing villages, way-marked walks. Four cottages, one or two bedrooms. Private parking. Children and dogs welcome. Weekly rates from £195 to £500. Please phone or write for a brochure. ETC ★★★★ [🐕]

🐕   Indicates that pets are welcome free of charge.

£   Indicates that a charge is made for pets: nightly or weekly.

pw! Shows some special provision for pets; exercise facility, feeding or accommodation arrangement.

⌂   Indicates separate pets accommodation.

York

Historic cathedral city and former Roman Station on River Ouse. Magnificent Minster and 3 miles of ancient walls. Facilities for a wide range of sports and entertainments. Horse-racing on Knavesmire. Bridlington 41 miles, Filey 41, Leeds 24, Harrogate 22.

ASCOT HOUSE, 80 EAST PARADE, YORK YO31 7YH (01904 426826; Fax: 01904 431077). Attractive Victorian villa with easy access to city centre. Family and double rooms en suite. Comfortable residents' lounge, dining room. Single room £30-£70, double room £60-£76. Free private enclosed car park. ETC/AA ★★★★, ETC Silver Award. [🐾]
e-mail: admin@ascothouseyork.com   website: www.ascothouseyork.com

MRS M. S. A. WOODLIFFE, MILL FARM, YAPHAM, POCKLINGTON, YORK YO42 1PH (01759 302172). WOLDS VIEW HOLIDAY COTTAGES. Granville Lodge (sleeps 6-8), Parlour (sleeps 6), Barn (sleeps 4), Stables (sleeps 3) and Courtyard (sleeps 4). Full details on request. [Pets by arrangement].

ST GEORGE'S, 6 ST GEORGE'S PLACE, YORK YO24 1DR (01904 625056). Family-run guest house in quiet cul-de-sac near racecourse. All rooms en suite with colour TV, tea/coffee making facilities. Private parking. Pets welcome by arrangement. From £60 double room, £65 for four-poster room. ETC/AA ★★★ [🐾]
e-mail: sixstgeorg@aol.com   website: www.stgeorgesyork.com

YORK LAKESIDE LODGES, MOOR LANE, YORK YO24 2QU (01904 702346; Fax: 01904 701631). Self-catering pine lodges. Mature parkland setting. Large fishing lake. Nearby superstore with coach to centre every 10 mins. ETC ★★★★ [pw! Pets £18 per week]
e-mail: neil@yorklakesidelodges.co.uk   website: www.lakesidelodges.co.uk

HIGH BELTHORPE, BISHOP WILTON, YORK YO42 1SB (01759 368238; Mobile: 07786 923330). Set on an ancient moated site at the foot of the Yorkshire Wolds, this comfortable Victorian farmhouse offers huge breakfasts, private fishing and fabulous walks. Dogs and owners will love it! Open all year except Christmas. Prices from £25. ETC ◆◆◆ [pw! 🐾]
website: www.holidayswithdogs.com

Wortley

Wortley

Village famous for the Wortley Top Forge, dating back to the Industrial Revolution, and as the birthplace of the notorious highwayman Swift Nick. 2 miles from Stocksbridge.

PENNINE EQUINE HOLIDAY COTTAGES, COTE GREEN FARM, WORTLEY. An ideal location to spend time with your horse, mountain bike or walking boots. Two comfortably furnished cottages (each sleeps 6/8). Well equipped, bed linen provided. Non-smoking. Dogs not allowed, but kennels available. Livery and stabling for visitors' horses. CONTACT: BROMLEY FARM, WORTLEY, SHEFFIELD S35 7DE (0114 284 7140) [Kennels £2 per night, Stabling (not incl. feeding) £40 per week] website: www.pennine-equine.co.uk

West Yorkshire

Bingley

Bingley

Town on River Aire 5 miles north-west of Bradford.

THE FIVE RISE LOCKS HOTEL & RESTAURANT, BECK LANE, BINGLEY BD16 4DD (01274 565296). Large Victorian house in tranquil area, but close main roads, tourist sites. Good views, individual decor, informal style. Historic canal locks and excellent walking (dogs and humans) close by. AA/VisitBritain ★★★★.
e-mail: info@five-rise-locks.co.uk   website: www.five-rise-locks.co.uk

Visit the FHG website
www.holidayguides.com
for details of the wide choice of accommodation
featured in the full range of FHG titles

Bishop Auckland, Castleside, Teesdale, Waterhouses, Weardale

Pet-Friendly
Pubs, Inns& Hotels
on pages 360-369
Please note that these establishments may not feature in the main section of this book

Bishop Auckland

Town on right bank of River Wear, 9 miles south-west of Durham. Castle, of varying dates, residence of the Bishop of Durham.

ALISON & KEITH TALLENTIRE, LOW LANDS FARM, LOW LANDS, COCKFIELD, BISHOP AUCKLAND DL13 5AW (01388 718251; mobile: 07745 067754). Two self-catering cottages on a working livestock farm. Each sleeps up to 4, plus cot. Prices from £160-£340. Call for a brochure. Pets and children most welcome. ETC ★★★★ ETC CATEGORY 3 DISABLED ACCESSIBILITY (one cottage). [Pets £10 per week]
e-mail: info@farmholidaysuk.com   website: www.farmholidaysuk.co

Castleside

A suburb 2 miles south-west of Consett.

DAVID BLACKBURN AND IRENE MORDEY, BEE COTTAGE FARMHOUSE, CASTLESIDE, CONSETT DH8 9HW (01207 508224). Charming farmhouse with stunning views. You will be most welcome. Ideal for Newcastle, Durham, Beamish etc. Bed and Breakfast; dinner available, licensed. Great for pets. VisitBritain ★★★★ [pw! 🐕]
e-mail: beecottage68@aol.com   website: www.beecottage.co.uk

Teesdale

Admin district of the County of Durham. Ideal area for all outdoor .

FROG HALL COTTAGE (Tel & Fax: 01833 622215). Traditional cottage, magnificent views. Rare flora and fauna near Nature Reserve on award-winning environmental farm. Sheep and cows peer over your garden wall. Guided walks arranged.[🐕]
e-mail: kath.herdship@btinternet.com   website: www.herdship.co.uk

Waterhouses

6 miles west of Durham.

MRS P. A. BOOTH, IVESLEY EQUESTRIAN CENTRE, IVESLEY, WATERHOUSES, DURHAM DH7 9HB (0191 373 4324; Fax: 0191 373 4757). Beautifully furnished comfortable country house set in 220 acres in Durham but very quiet and rural. Excellent dog exercising facilities. En suite bedrooms. Excellent food. Licensed. Fully equipped Equestrian Centre adjacent. [Pets £2 per night].
e-mail: ivesley@msn.com   website: www.ridingholidays-ivesley.co.uk

Weardale

A designated Area of Outstanding Natural Beauty, 10 miles from the market town of Alston.

NEWFIELD HOUSE AND RAINWALKER HOUSE WEARDALE, NORTH PENNINES (01207 504828). Area of Outstanding Natural Beauty. Super holiday cottages, sleep 5/6. Ideal base for touring Lakes etc. Log burners, Aga, Sky/DVD. From £155-£450 per week all inclusive. [🐕]
website: www.cottageguide.co.uk/rainwalker

Alnmouth, Alnwick, Bamburgh, Belford

Warkworth

NORTHUMBERLAND COTTAGES LTD. A local booking agency, with over 25 years of living and loving Northumberland. Based in the heart of the area between Alnwick and the beautiful sandy beaches of the Heritage Coastline. Choose from our selection of inland and coastal cottages. Telephone 01665 589434 or check availability online. [Pets £10 per week]
e-mail: enquiries@northumberlandcottages.com   website: www.northumberlandcottages.com

Alnmouth

Seaside village situated at the mouth of the River Aln.

SADDLE HOTEL & GRILL, 24/25 NORTHUMBERLAND STREET, ALNMOUTH NE66 2RA (01665 830476). Friendly, family-run hotel, on the Northumberland coast. Fully licensed, home-cooked meals a speciality. All bedrooms en suite. Children and pets most welcome. ETC ★★. [🐾]

Alnwick

Picturesque market town in the heart of Northumberland which is famous for its unsspoilt beauty, long sandy beaches, and numerous stately homes and gardens. Berwick-upon-Tweed and the Scottish Border 32 miles, Alnmouth 5 miles.

ROCK FARMHOUSE B&B, ROCK, ALNWICK NE66 3SE (01665 579367). Spacious farmhouse in tranquil surroundings. Ideally situated to explore Northumbria. Relaxed and friendly. Large superior bedrooms. Large children's play area. Pets welcome.
e-mail: stay@rockfarmhouse.co.uk   website: www.rockfarmhouse.co.uk

Bamburgh

Village on North Sea coast with magnificent castle. Grace Darling buried in churchyard

THE MIZEN HEAD HOTEL, BAMBURGH NE69 7BS (01668 214254; Fax: 01668 214104). A warm welcome awaits owners and pets alike at the Mizen Head. Close to the beautiful Northumbrian coastline and just a short drive from many lovely walks in the Ingram Valley. The hotel boasts log fires, live music, good food and real ales.
e-mail: reception@themizenheadhotel.co.uk   website: www.themizenheadhotel.co.uk

Belford

Village 14 miles south-east of Berwick-upon-Tweed.

MRS PHYL CARRUTHERS, BLUEBELL FARM, BELFORD NE70 7QE (01668 213362). In a quiet central position in the village of Belford, three miles from the Heritage Coast and within easy walking distance of all village amenities. Sleep 4-6. Each cottage is very well equipped, with gas-fired central heating; living/dining/kitchen areas are open plan.
e-mail: phyl.carruthers@virgin.net

ETIVE COTTAGE, WARENFORD, NEAR BELFORD NE70 7HZ. Well-equipped two-bedroomed cottage with double glazing, central heating. Open views to coast. Fenced garden; secure parking. Welcome pack. Regional Winner, Winalot Best Place to Stay 2004. Brochure: JAN THOMPSON (Tel & Fax: 01668 213233). [🐾]
e-mail: janet.thompson1@homecall.co.uk

Berwick-upon-Tweed

Border town at mouth of River Tweed 58 miles north west of Newcastle and 47 miles south east of Edinburgh. Medieval town walls, remains of a Norman Castle.

FRED AND LYNDA MILLER, COBBLED YARD HOTEL, 40 WALKERGATE, BERWICK-UPON-TWEED TD15 1DJ (01289 308 407; Fax: 01289 330 623) Situated in centre of town and yet near to scenic walks. En suite rooms. Own restaurant and Bar. Car park. Bring this advert for Pets Free of Charge. [🐾]
e-mail:cobbledyardhotel@berwick35.fsnet.co.uk   website : www.cobbledyardhotel.com

FRIENDLY HOUND COTTAGE, FORD COMMON, BERWICK-UPON-TWEED TD15 2QD (01289 388554) Set in a quiet country location, one mile from the picturesque village of Ford but only 15 minutes from Holy Island, Berwick and Bamburgh. Come and enjoy our quality accommodation, excellent breakfasts, friendly hospitality and our warm welcome. VB ★★★★ [🐾]
website: www.friendlyhoundcottage.co.uk

2, THE COURTYARD, BERWICK-UPON-TWEED. Secluded Self catering Townhouse in heart of old Berwick. Planted courtyard garden and sunny verandah. Historic ramparts 400 yards, golf course, beaches. Ideal for exercising pets. Contact: J. MORTON, 1, THE COURTYARD, CHURCH STREET, BERWICK -UPON-TWEED, TD15 1EE (01289 308737). ETC ★★★ [pw! 🐾]
e-mail: jvm@patmosphere.uklinux.net   website: www.berwickselfcatering.co.uk

Corbridge

Small town on the north bank of the River Tyne, 3 miles west of Hexham. Nearby are remains of Roman military town of Corstopitum.

MR & MRS MATTHEWS, THE HAYES GUEST HOUSE, NEWCASTLE ROAD, CORBRIDGE NE45 5LP (01434 632010). Stone-built stables in grounds of large country house converted into two self-catering cottages, each accommodating 4/5. ETC ★★★ [Pets £12.50 per week]
e-mail: camon@surfree.co.uk   website: www.hayes-corbridge.co.uk

Haltwhistle

Small market town about one mile south of Hadrian's Wall.

KATH AND BRAD DOWLE, SAUGHY RIGG FARM, TWICE BREWED, HALTWHISTLE NE49 9PT (01434 344120). Close to the best parts of Hadrian's Wall. A warm welcome and good food. All rooms en suite. Parking. TV. Central heating. Children and pets welcome. Open all year. Prices from £20 pppn. ETC ◆◆◆◆
e-mail: kathandbrad@aol.com   website: www.saughyrigg.co.uk

A.D. & S.M. SAUNDERS, SCOTCHCOULTHARD, HALTWHISTLE NE49 9NH (01434 344470). Situated in 178 acres within Northumberland National Park, fully equipped self-catering cottages (sleep 2/7). Linen, towels, all fuel incl. Heated indoor pool, games room. Rare breed farm animals. Children and dogs welcome. [🐾]
e-mail: scotchcoulthard@hotmail.co.uk   website: www.scotchcoulthard.co.uk

Hexham

Market town on south bank of the River Tyne, 20 miles west of Newcastle-upon-Tyne.

BATTLESTEADS HOTEL & RESTAURANT, WARK, HEXHAM NE48 3LS (01434 230209). Excellent bar meals and à la carte menus; good choice wines and beers. 17 en suite bedrooms including ground floor with disabled access. Pets very welcome. B&B from £40-£45pppn. ★★★★ Inn. [Pets £5 per night].
e-mail: info@battlesteads.com   website: www.battlesteads.com

Morpeth

Market town on River Wansbeck, 14 miles north of Newcastle-upon-Tyne.

MICKLEWOOD PARK, LONGHIRST, MORPETH (01670 794530). Self-catering houses set in 75 acres. An ideal base from which to explore historic Northumberland. We cater for groups and families who are explorers and sports enthusiasts, or who simply enjoy relaxing breaks. [🐾]
website: www.micklewoodpark.co.uk

Warkworth

Village on River Coquet near North Sea coast north-west of Amble with several interesting historic remains.

BIRLING VALE is an attractive stone built detached house in secluded garden. Fully equipped, two double bedrooms, one twin, cot. Free central heating. Close to sandy beaches, trout and salmon rivers and many places of interest. Well-trained dogs welcome. Weekly rates from £130 Low Season, £250 Mid Season, £510 High Season. SAE to MRS J. BREWIS, THE MASTER'S HOUSE, SHILBOTTLE, NEAR ALNWICK NE66 2JB (01665 575222). [🐾]

Balterley, Chester

Balterley

Small village two miles west of Audley.

MR & MRS HOLLINS, BALTERLEY GREEN FARM, DEANS LANE, BALTERLEY, NEAR CREWE CW2 5QJ (01270 820214). 145-acre farm in quiet and peaceful surroundings. Within easy reach of Junction 16 on the M6. Bed and Breakfast from £25pp. Also cottage for self-catering. Caravans and tents welcome. [pw! Pets £2 per night]

Chester

Former Roman city on the River Dee, with well-preserved walls and beautiful 14th century Cathedral. Liverpool 25 miles

THE EATON HOTEL, CITY ROAD, CHESTER CH1 3AE (01244 320840; Fax: 0870 6221691). Ideally located for you and your dog, in the heart of Chester, with parking, and bordering the Shropshire Union Canal towpath. [🐾]
website: www.eatonhotelchester.co.uk

MRS ANNE ARDEN, NEWTON HALL, TATTENHALL, CHESTER CH3 9NE (01829 770153; Fax: 01829 770655). Part 16thC country house on a family-run farm, surrounded by beautiful scenery, with views of Beeston and Peckforton Castles. Ideal for a quiet, relaxing holiday. Chester 15 minutes' drive. ETC ★★★★ [🐾]
e-mail: saarden@btinternet.com   website: www.newtonhallfarm.co.uk

Ambleside

Ambleside

Ambleside, Appleby-in-Westmorland, Bassenthwaite, Borrowdale

Brampton, Broughton-in-Furnesss, Carlisle, Cartmel

Farlam Hall Hotel Brampton, Cumbria CA8 2NG

Tel: 016977 46234 • Fax: 016977 46683

Standing in four acres of gardens, with its own lake, Farlam Hall has that indefinable quality that makes a stay here something really special. Fine quality cuisine, individually decorated and well-equipped guest rooms. Ideal touring centre for the Lakes, Borders & Hadrian's Wall.

e-mail: farlam@relaischateaux.com • www.farlamhall.co.uk

AA ★★★
Inspectors' Choice
Two Rosettes, Relais & Chateaux

Woodend Cottages • between the Eskdale and Duddon Valleys
Visit our website at www.woodendhouse.co.uk or phone 019467 23277
Woodend is remote and surrounded by hills and moorland, with views towards Scafell Pike. The cottages and house offer cosy accommodation for two to six people.
SHORT BREAKS AVAILABLE OUT OF SEASON.

www.lakedistrictcottages.co.uk Two well-equipped cottages and two caravans in excellent walking area. Wildlife/birdwatchers paradise. Private fishing lake. Ancient woodlands, quiet, relaxing, warm welcome. Established 1968. ETC ★★★

J. JACKSON, THORNTHWAITE FARM, WOODLAND HALL, WOODLAND, BROUGHTON-IN-FURNESS LA20 6DF
Tel & Fax: 01229 716340 • e-mail: info@lakedistrictcottages.co.uk

---

NEW PALLYARDS, HETHERSGILL, CARLISLE CA6 6HZ • 01228 577308
One modern bungalow, 3/4 bedrooms, sleeps 8. Two lovely cottages on farm. Bed and Breakfast, Half Board. En suite double/family, twin/single rooms. Disabled welcome. Won the National Award for the Best Breakfast in Britain and have been filmed for BBC TV. ETC ◆◆◆◆ / ETC ★★★★
B&B from £25.00, Dinner £14.00 • DB&B weekly rate £170.00 - £180.00.
Self Catering £150.00 - £672.00
e-mail: newpallyards@btinternet.com • www.4starsc.co.uk

GRAHAM ARMS HOTEL
Longtown, Near Carlisle, Cumbria CA6 5SE

A warm welcome awaits at this 180-year-old former Coaching Inn. Situated six miles from the M6 (J44) and Gretna Green, The Graham Arms makes an ideal overnight stop or perfect touring base for the Scottish Borders, English Lakes, Hadrian's Wall and much more. 16 comfortable en suite bedrooms, including four-poster and family rooms with TV, radio etc. Meals and snacks served throughout the day. Friendly 'local's bar' and new 'Sports bar' serving real ale, extra cold lagers, cocktails and a fine selection of malt whiskies. Secure courtyard parking for cars, cycles and motorcycles. Beautiful woodland and riverside walks. Pets welcome with well behaved owners!

Visit our website on www.grahamarms.com • Tel: 01228 791213 • Fax: 01228 794110
Email: office@grahamarms.com • Website: www.grahamarms.com
Bed and full traditional breakfast £32– £36.   Special rates for weekend and midweek breaks.   AA ★★

Seven cottages sleeping 2-6. Set behind a large Georgian house set in parkland on the side of Hamps Fell. Beautiful garden, great walks.
Pets and children welcome. Open all year. Please telephone for details.
Contact: MR M. AINSCOUGH, LONGLANDS AT CARTMEL, CARTMEL LA11 6HG • 015395 36475 • Fax: 015395 36172
e-mail: longlands@cartmel.com • www.cartmel.com

Readers are requested to mention this FHG
guidebook when seeking accommodation

Cockermouth, Coniston

Coniston, Eskdale, Grange over Sands, Grasmere

Pet-Friendly
Pubs, Inns & Hotels
on pages 360-369
Please note that these establishments may not feature in the main section of this book

Keswick

Keswick, Kirkby-in-Furness, Kirkby Lonsdale, Kirkby Stephen

Kirkoswald

Lamplugh, Langdale, Little Langdale

Visit the FHG website
www.holidayguides.com
for details of the wide choice of accommodation
featured in
the full range of FHG titles

Pet-Friendly
Pubs, Inns& Hotels
on pages 360-369
Please note that these establishments may not feature in the main section of this book

Penrith, Ravenstonedale, Silloth-on-Solway, Ullswater

Ullswater, Windermere

DALES HOLIDAY COTTAGES. See the best of the Lake District and Eden Valley. A wide range of cottages to choose from, all personally inspected. Pets welcome. Free brochure. Call 0870 909 9500 or visit our website.
website: www.dalesholcot.com

RECOMMENDED COTTAGE HOLIDAYS. 1st choice for dream cottages at very competitive prices in all holiday regions of beautiful Britain. Pets welcome. All properties inspected. Free brochure - call 01751 475547. [🐾]
website: www.recommended-cottages.co.uk

Ambleside

Popular centre for exploring Lake District at northern end of Lake Windermere. Picturesque Stock Ghyll waterfall nearby, lovely walks. Associations with Wordsworth. Penrith 30 miles, Keswick 17, Windermere 5.

SMALLWOOD HOUSE HOTEL, COMPSTON ROAD, AMBLESIDE LA22 9DJ (015394 32330). Where quality and the customer come first. En suite rooms, car parking, leisure club membership. ETC ◆◆◆◆ [Pets £3 per night]
website: www.smallwoodhotel.co.uk

2 LOWFIELD, OLD LAKE ROAD, AMBLESIDE. Ground floor garden flat half a mile from town centre; sleeps 4. Lounge/diningroom, kitchen, bathroom/WC, two bedrooms, one with en suite shower. Linen supplied. Children and pets welcome. Parking. Terms from £140 to £240 per week. Contact: MR P. F. QUARMBY, 3 LOWFIELD, OLD LAKE ROAD, AMBLESIDE LA22 0DH (Tel & Fax: 015394 32326) [🐾]
e-mail: paulfquarmby@aol.com

THE OLD VICARAGE, VICARAGE ROAD, AMBLESIDE LA22 9DH (015394 33364). 'Rest a while in style'. Quality B&B set in tranquil wooded grounds in the heart of the village. Car park. All rooms en suite. Kettle, clock/radio, TV. Heated indoor pool, sauna, hot tub, sun lounge and rooftop terrace. Special breaks. Friendly service where your pets are welcome. Telephone IAN OR HELEN BURT. [🐾]
website: www.oldvicarageambleside.co.uk

GREENHOWE CARAVAN PARK, GREAT LANGDALE, AMBLESIDE LA22 9JU (015394 37231; Fax: 015394 37464). Permanent Caravan Park with Self Contained Holiday Accommodation. An ideal centre for Climbing, Fell Walking, Riding, Swimming, or just a lazy holiday. ETC ★★★★ [Pets £6 per night, £30 per week]
website: www.greenhowe.com

KIRKSTONE FOOT, KIRKSTONE PASS ROAD, AMBLESIDE LA22 9EH (015394 32232; Fax: 015394 32805). Superior cottage and apartment complex, set in peaceful gardens, adjoining the Lakeland fells and village centre. Open all year. ETC ★★★★/★★★★★ [pw! Pets £5.00 per night.]
e-mail: enquiries@kirkstonefoot.co.uk   website: www.kirkstonefoot.co.uk

BETTY FOLD, HAWKSHEAD HILL, AMBLESIDE LA22 0PS (015394 36611). Ground floor apartment sleeping four. Private entrance. Set in peaceful and spacious grounds, ideal for walkers and families with pets. Open all year. [pw! Pets £2 per night.]
e-mail: csalisbury@bettyfold.fsnet.co.uk   website: www.bettyfold.co.uk

LYNDALE GUEST HOUSE LAKE ROAD, AMBLESIDE LA22 0DN (015394 34244) Nestled midway between Lake Windermere and Ambleside village, with superb views of Loughrigg Fell and the Langdales beyond. Excellent base for walking, touring, or just relaxing. [🐾]
website: www.lyndale-guesthouse.co.uk

Appleby-in-Westmorland

Located in the Eden Valley, ideal for walking, riding, fishing and cycling. Annual events include The Gypsy Horse Fair and the Jazz Festival.

KEITH AND DIANE BUDDING, SCALEBECK HOLIDAY COTTAGES, SCALEBECK, GREAT ASBY, APPLEBY CA16 6TF (01768 351006; Fax: 01768 353532). Comfortable and well-equipped self-catering accommodation in the tranquil and picturesque Eden Valley. Sleep 2/5. No smoking. ETC ★★★★ [pw! £20 per week]
e-mail: mail@scalebeckholidaycottages.com

Bassenthwaite

Village on Bassenthwaite Lake with traces of Norse and Roman settlements.

BROOK HOUSE COTTAGE HOLIDAYS, NEAR KESWICK CA12 4QP (Tel & Fax: 017687 76393). Delightful cottages in attractive hamlet near Keswick (sleep 2-10). Excellent food at village pub. Ideally for Skiddaw, Bassenthwaite Lake, Keswick and Cockermouth. Farmhouse B&B also available.
e-mail: stay@amtrafford.co.uk   website: www.holidaycottageslakedistrict.co.uk
www.bedandbreakfast-lakedistrict.co.uk

SKIDDAW VIEW HOLIDAY HOME PARK, BOTHEL, NEAR BASSENTHWAITE CA7 2JG (016973 20919). Quality lodge, cottage and holiday home accommodation for 2-5 in peaceful, relaxing surroundings. Please telephone for brochure and prices. ETC ★★★★ [pw!🐾]
e-mail: office@skiddawview.com   website: www.skiddawview.co.uk

Borrowdale

Scenic valley of River Derwent, splendid walking and climbing country.

MARY MOUNT HOTEL, BORROWDALE, NEAR KESWICK CA12 5UU (017687 77223). Set in 4½ acres of gardens and woodlands on the shores of Derwentwater. 2½ miles from Keswick in picturesque Borrowdale. Superb walking and touring. All rooms en suite with colour TV and tea/coffee making facilities. Licensed. Brochure on request. ETC ★★ [pw! £6.50 per 2/3 nights , £10 per week.]
e-mail: mawdsley1@aol.com   website: www.marymounthotel.co.uk

Brampton

Market town with cobbled streets. Octagonal Moat Hall with exterior staircases and iron stocks.

FARLAM HALL HOTEL, BRAMPTON, CUMBRIA CA8 2NG (016977 46234; Fax: 016977 46683). Standing in four acres of gardens, with its own lake, Farlam Hall offers fine quality cuisine and individually decorated guest rooms. Ideal touring centre for the Lakes, Borders and Hadrian's Wall. AA Three Stars Inspectors' Choice and Two Rosettes, Relais & Chateaux. [🐾]
e-mail: farlam@relaischateaux.com   website: www.farlamhall.co.uk

Broughton-in-Furness

Village 8 miles NW of Ulverston.

PAUL SANDFORD, WOODEND COTTAGES, WOODEND, ULPHA, BROUGHTON-IN-FURNESS LA20 6DY Woodend is remote and surrounded by hills and moorland, with views towards Scafell Pike. The cottages and house offer cosy accommodation for two to six people. Short breaks available out of season.
website: www.woodendhouse.co.uk

J. JACKSON, THORNTHWAITE FARM, WOODLAND HALL, WOODLAND, BROUGHTON-IN-FURNESS LA20 6DF (Tel & Fax: 01229 716340). Two well-equipped cottages and two caravans in excellent walking area. Wildlife/birdwatchers paradise. Private fishing lake. Ancient woodlands, quiet, relaxing, warm welcome. Established 1968. ETC ★★★ [Pets £15 per week]
e-mail: info@lakedistrictcottages.co.uk   website: www.lakedistrictcottages.co.uk

Carlisle

Important Border city and former Roman station on River Eden. Castle is of historic interest, also Tullie House Museum and Art Gallery. Good sports facilities inc. football and racecourse. Kendal 45 miles, Dumfries 33, Penrith 18.

NEW PALLYARDS, HETHERSGILL, CARLISLE CA6 6HZ (01228 577308). Relax and see beautiful North Cumbria and the Borders. Self-catering accommodation in one Bungalow, 3/4 bedrooms; two lovely Cottages on farm. Also Bed and Breakfast or Half Board – en suite rooms. ETC ◆◆◆◆/★★★★ [Pets from £10 per week]
e-mail: newpallyards@btinternet.com   website: www.4starsc.co.uk

GRAHAM ARMS HOTEL, ENGLISH STREET, LONGTOWN, CARLISLE CA6 5SE (01228 791213; Fax: 01228 794110). 16 bedrooms en suite, including four-poster and family rooms, all with tea/coffee facilities, TV and radio. Secure courtyard locked overnight. Pets welcome with well-behaved owners. AA ★★ [🐾]
e-mail: office@grahamarms.com   website: www.grahamarms.com

Cartmel

Village 4 miles south of Newby Bridge.

RATHER SPECIAL COTTAGES. Seven cottages sleeping 2-6. Set behind a large Georgian house set in parkland on the side of Hamps Fell. Beautiful garden, great walks. Pets and children welcome. Open all year. Please telephone for details. ETC ★★★★. Contact: MR M. AINSCOUGH, LONGLANDS AT CARTMEL, CARTMEL LA11 6HG (015395 36475; Fax: 015395 36172). [★]
e-mail: longlands@cartmel.com　　　　　website: www.cartmel.com

Cockermouth

Market town and popular touring centre for Lake District and quiet Cumbrian coast. On Rivers Derwent and Cocker. Penrith 30 miles, Carlisle 26, Whitehaven 14, Keswick 12.

ROSE COTTAGE GUEST HOUSE, LORTON ROAD, COCKERMOUTH CA13 9DX (Tel & Fax: 01900 822189). Family-run guest house on the outskirts of Cockermouth. Warm, friendly atmosphere. Parking. All rooms en suite with colour TV, tea/coffee, central heating. Pets welcome. Ideal base for visiting both Lakes and coast. ETC ◆◆◆◆ [★]
website: www.rosecottageguest.co.uk

THE DERWENT LODGE, EMBLETON, NEAR BASSENTHWAITE, COCKERMOUTH CA13 9YA (017687 76606). A warm welcome awaits you and your pet. Choose from luxury self-catering apartments or en suite hotel rooms/suites. New for August 2007 indoor pool and fitness suite. Ideal for touring Western Lakes and coast.
info@derwent_lodge@yahoo.co.uk　　　　　website: www.derwentlodge.co.uk

THE MANOR HOUSE, OUGHTERSIDE, ASPATRIA, CUMBRIA CA7 2PT (016973 22420). 18th century manor farmhouse retaining many original features and several acres of land. Spacious en suite rooms, tea/coffee making facilities, TV and lots of little extras. All pets and children welcome. Inspection Commended. [★]
e-mail: richardandjudy@themanorhouse.net　　　　　website: www.themanorhouse.net

Coniston

Village 8 miles south-west of Ambleside, dominated by Old Man of Coniston (2635ft).

LAKELAND HOUSE, TILBERTHWAITE AVENUE, CONISTON LA21 8ED (015394 41303). Village centre guest house, hearty breakfasts, from £25 per person. Two self-catering cottages also available, sleeping two to six - one with lake views, one with four-poster. [Pets £10 per week]
e-mail: info@lakelandhouse.co.uk　　　　　website: www.lakelandhouse.co.uk

THE COPPERMINES AND CONISTON LAKES COTTAGES (015394 41765). Unique Lakeland cottages for 2 – 30 of quality and character in stunning mountain scenery. Log fires, exposed beams. Pets welcome! ★★★ - ★★★★ Book online. [Pets £25 per stay]
website: www.coppermines.co.uk

BROCKLEBANK GROUND HOLIDAY COTTAGES, TORVER, CONISTON LA21 8BS (015394 49588). Three luxury cottages in a quiet rural setting, sleeping 2,4 & 7. Excellent walking from the door. Dog-friendly pubs 600 yards. Short breaks available. Prices from £275. ETC ★★★★. [★]
e-mail: info@brocklebankground.com　　website: www.brocklebankground.com

WATERHEAD HOTEL, CONISTON LA21 8AJ (015394 41244; Fax: 015394 41193). Situated alongside Coniston Water, The Waterhead Hotel makes a perfect retreat. 22 en suite bedrooms, Mountain View Restaurant, lounge bar with views across the Lake. Non smoking. Ideal base for outdoor activities, also lake cruises and historic houses. [Pets £5.00 per night, £20 per week].
website: www.classic-hotels.net

★　　Indicates that pets are welcome free of charge.

£　　Indicates that a charge is made for pets: nightly or weekly.

pw!　Shows some special provision for pets; exercise facility, feeding or accommodation arrangement.

⌂　　Indicates separate pets accommodation.

Symbols

Eskdale

Lakeless valley, noted for waterfalls and ascended by a light-gauge railway. Tremendous views. Roman fort. Keswick 35 miles, Broughton-in-Furness 10 miles.

THE BOOT INN (FORMERLY THE BURNMOOR INN), BOOT, ESKDALE CA19 1TG (019467 23224). Nine en suite bedrooms. Dogs welcome to be in the bar with you for lunch and dinner. We do not make a charge for well behaved dogs. Special breaks available all year. Call for a brochure. [🐾]
e-mail: enquiries@bootinn.co.uk   website:www.bootinn.co.uk

FISHERGROUND FARM, ESKDALE. Traditional hill farm, with a stone cottage and three pine lodges, ideal for walkers, nature lovers, dogs and children. Games room, raft pool and adventure playground. Good pubs nearby. IAN & JENNIFER HALL, ORCHARD HOUSE, APPLETHWAITE, KESWICK CA12 4PN (017687 73175) [🐾]
e-mail: holidays@fisherground.co.uk   website: www.fisherground.co.uk

Grange-over-Sands

Charming Edwardian resort set between Lake District Fells and Morecambe Bay.

HAMPSFELL HOUSE HOTEL, HAMPSFELL ROAD, GRANGE-OVER-SANDS LA11 6BG (015395 32567). In two acres of private grounds, just a few minutes' walk from the town centre. The nine en suite bedrooms are well appointed. Enjoy the best of fresh Cumbrian produce in the elegant dining room. From £35pppn. Ideal base for exploring the Lake District. AA ★★ [Pets £3 per night]. enquiries@hampsfellhouse.co.uk   website: www.hampsfellhouse.co.uk

Grasmere

Village famous for Wordsworth associations; the poet lived in Dove Cottage (preserved as it was), and is buried in the churchyard. Museum has manuscripts and relics.

GRASMERE HOTEL, BROADGATE, GRASMERE LA22 9TA (015394 35277). Charming 13 bedroomed Country House Hotel, with ample parking and a licensed lounge. All rooms recently refurbished with en suite facilities. Award-winning restaurant overlooking gardens, river and surrounding hills. Special breaks throughout the year. AA/ETC ★★ Silver Award.[Pets £5 per stay]. e-mail: enquiries@grasmerehotel.co.uk   website: www.grasmerehotel.co.uk

LAKE VIEW COUNTRY HOUSE & SELF-CATERING APARTMENTS, GRASMERE LA22 9TD (015394 35384/35167). Luxury B&B or 3 Self-Catering apartments in unrivalled, secluded location in the village with wonderful views and lakeshore access. All B&B rooms en suite, some with whirlpool baths. Ground floor accommodation available. No smoking. Featured in "Which?" Good B&B Guide.

Hawkshead

Quaint village in Lake District between Coniston Water and Windermere. The 16th century Church and Grammar School, which Wordsworth attended, are of interest. Ambleside 5 miles.

HIDEAWAYS, THE SQUARE, HAWKSHEAD LA22 0NZ (015394 42435). Cottages in and around Hawkshead. Great walks and lakes for swimming, dog friendly pubs, open fires to lie in front of... owners will enjoy it too. [Pets £15 per week].
e-mail: bookings@lakeland-hideaways.co.uk   website: www.lakeland-hideaways.co.uk

SAWREY HOUSE COUNTRY HOTEL & RESTAURANT, NEAR SAWREY, HAWKSHEAD LA22 0LF (015394 36387; Fax: 015394 36010). Quality family-run hotel in three acres of peaceful gardens with magnificent views across Esthwaite Water. Excellent food, warm friendly atmosphere. Lounge, bar. Pets welcome. Non-smoking. AA Red Rosette for food. AA ◆◆◆◆◆. [Pets £10 per night.]
website: www.sawreyhouse.com

THE KINGS ARMS HOTEL, HAWKSHEAD, AMBLESIDE LA22 0NZ (015394 36372). Join us for a relaxing stay amidst the green hills and dales of Lakeland, and we will be delighted to offer you good food, homely comfort and warm hospitality in historic surroundings. We hope to see you soon! Self-catering cottages also available.[🐾, pets £20 per week s/c]
website: www.kingsarmshawkshead.co.uk

Ireby

A peaceful and uncrowded village just outside The Lake District National Park. Wigton 7 miles, Carlisle 18 miles.

2 MOOT HALL, IREBY CA7 1DU (01423 360759; Mobile: 07774 420996) Lovely cottage, part of 16th century Moot Hall in unspoilt village; delightful walks in Uldale Fells and northern Lake District. Sleeps 4. Linen/fuel/electricity incl. Open all year. Reductions for PAT, Assistance and Rescue Dogs. [🐾]
e-mail: david.boyes1@virgin.net   website: www.irebymoothall.co.uk

Kendal

Market town and popular centre for touring the Lake District. Of historic interest is the Norman castle, birthplace of Catherine Parr. Penrith 25 miles, Lancaster 22, Ambleside 13.

MRS HELEN JONES, PRIMROSE COTTAGE, ORTON ROAD, TEBAY CA10 3TL (015396 24791). Adjacent M6 J38 (10 miles north of Kendal). Excellent rural location for North Lakes and Yorkshire Dales. Superb facilities, jacuzzi bath, king and four-poster beds. One acre garden. Self-contained ground floor flat and 3 purpose-built self-catering bungalows for disabled guests, with electric bed, jacuzzi and large, wheel-in bathroom. Pets welcome, very friendly. VisitBritain★★★★ Guest Accommodation. [🐾]
e-mail: info@primrosecottagecumbria.co.uk   website: www.primrosecottagecumbria.co.uk

MRS L. HODGSON, PATTON HALL FARM, KENDAL LA8 9DT (01539 721590). 2 Modern caravans, fully double glazed, gas central heating. Double and twin bedrooms, kitchen, spacious lounge/dining area, toilet and shower. Traditional working farm set in 140 acres of beautiful countryside. [Pets £10/£15 per week].
e-mail: stay@pattonhallfarm.co.uk   website: www.pattonhallfarm.co.uk

ANNE TAYLOR, RUSSELL FARM, BURTON-IN-KENDAL, CARNFORTH, LANCS. LA6 1NN (01524 781334). Bed, Breakfast and Evening Meal offered. Ideal centre for touring Lakes and Yorkshire Dales. Good food, friendly atmosphere on working dairy farm. Modernised farmhouse. Guests' own lounge. [🐾]
e-mail: miktaylor@farming.co.uk

MIREFOOT COTTAGES, MIREFOOT, KENDAL, CUMBRIA LA8 9AB (Tel: 01539 720015). 5 Star, pet friendly, self-catering cottages in a superb rural location in the Lake District National Park. Both cottages sleep 2. Fully equipped with TV (Freeview), DVD, WiFi, gas central heating. Tennis court, private parking. VB ★★★★★ [🐾]
e-mail: booking@mirefoot.co.uk   website: www.mirefoot.co.uk

STONECROSS MANOR HOTEL, MILNTHORPE ROAD, KENDAL LA9 5HP (01539 733559; Fax: 01539 736386). Stonecross Manor offers easy access to town, ample parking, local cuisine, conference and banquet facilities, indoor swimming pool, and four-poster bedrooms. [Pets £10 per night].
e-mail: info@stonecrossmanor.co.uk   website: www.stonecrossmanor.co.uk

FHG Guides

publish a large range of well-known accommodation guides.

We will be happy to send you details or you can use the order form

at the back of this book.

Please note

All the information in this book is given in good faith in the belief that it is correct. However, the publishers cannot guarantee the facts given in these pages, neither are they responsible for changes in policy, ownership or terms that may take place after the date of going to press. Readers should always satisfy themselves that the facilities they require are available and that the terms, if quoted, still apply.

Keswick

Famous Lake District resort at north end of Derwentwater with Pencil Museum and Cars of the Stars Motor Museum. Carlisle 30 miles, Ambleside 17, Cockermouth 12.

LOW BRIERY HOLIDAYS (017687 72044). A peaceful and scenic riverside location just outside Keswick. A choice of cottages, timber lodges and holiday caravans to suit all budgets. ETC ★★★★ [Pets £20 per week]
website: www.keswick.uk.com

COLEDALE INN, BRAITHWAITE, NEAR KESWICK CA12 5TN (017687 78272). Friendly, family-run Victorian Inn in peaceful situation. Warm and spacious en suite bedrooms with TV. Children and pets welcome. Open all year. ETC ◆◆◆ [🐾]
website: www.coledale-inn.co.uk

ROYAL OAK HOTEL, BORROWDALE, KESWICK CA12 5XB (017687 77214). Traditional Lakeland hotel with friendly atmosphere. Home cooking, cosy bar, comfortable lounge and some riverside rooms. Winter and Summer discount rates. Brochure and Tariff available. AA ★ Hotel. [🐾]
e-mail: info@royaloakhotel.co.uk   website: www.royaloakhotel.co.uk

WOODSIDE, PENRITH ROAD, KESWICK CA12 4LJ (017687 73522). Friendly family-run establishment. All our rooms are en suite. We have ample private parking and large gardens. Non-smoking. Dogs welcome. [🐾]
website: www.woodsideguesthouse.co.uk

CRAGSIDE GUEST HOUSE, 39 BLENCATHRA STREET, KESWICK CA12 4HX (Tel & Fax: 017687 73344). Quiet, comfortable guest house close to the centre of Keswick. All rooms en suite, tastefully decorated, centrally heated and have clock radio, colour TV and tea/coffee making facilities. AA ★★★★ [🐾]
e-mail: wayne-alison@cragside39blencathra.fsnet.co.uk
website: www.SmoothHound.co.uk/hotels/cragside

DERWENT WATER MARINA, PORTINSCALE, KESWICK CA12 5RF Lakeside self-catering apartments. Three apartments sleep 2 plus folding bed for occasional use, one apartment sleeps 6. Superb views over the lake and fells. Includes TV, heating and bed linen. Non-smoking. Watersports and boat hire available on site. (017687 72912) for brochure. [🐾]
e-mail: info@derwentwatermarina.co.uk   website: www.derwentwatermarina.co.uk

RICKERBY GRANGE, PORTINSCALE, KESWICK CA12 5RH (017687 72344). Delightfully situated in quiet village. Licensed. Imaginative home-cooked food, attractively served. Open all year. VisitBritain ★★★★ Guest Accommodation. [Pets £2.50 per night, £15 per week]
e-mail: stay@rickerbygrange.co.uk   website: www.rickerbygrange.co.uk

KESWICK COTTAGES, 8 BEECHCROFT, BRAITHWAITE, KESWICK CA12 5TH (017687 78555). Cottages and apartments in and around Keswick. Properties are well maintained and clean. From a one bedroom cottage to a four bedroom house. Children and pets welcome. [Pets £10 per week]
e-mail: info@keswickcottages.co.uk   website: www.keswickcottages.co.uk

Warm, comfortable houses and cottages in Keswick and beautiful Borrowdale, welcoming your dog. Inspected and quality graded. LAKELAND COTTAGE HOLIDAYS, KESWICK CA12 4QX (017687 76065; Fax: 017687 76869). [Pets £15 per week]
e-mail: info@lakelandcottages.co.uk   website: www.lakelandcottages.co.uk

OVERWATER HALL, OVERWATER, NEAR IREBY, NEAR KESWICK CA7 1HH (017687 76566). Elegant Country House Hotel in spacious grounds. Dogs very welcome in your room. 4 night mid-week breaks from £600 per room, inclusive of Dinner and Breakfast for two people. Mini breaks also available all year. Award-winning restaurant. See also advertisement on page 266 [pw! 🐾]
e-mail: welcome@overwaterhall.co.uk   website: www.overwaterhall.co.uk

---

🐾   Indicates that pets are welcome free of charge.

£   Indicates that a charge is made for pets: nightly or weekly.

pw!   Shows some special provision for pets; exercise facility, feeding or accommodation arrangement.

⌂   Indicates separate pets accommodation.

Symbols

Kirkby-in-Furness

Small coastal village (A595). 10 minutes to Ulverston, Lakes within easy reach. Ideal base for walking and touring.

JANET AND PETER, 1 FRIARS GROUND, KIRKBY-IN-FURNESS LA17 7YB (01229 889601). "Sunset Cottage", self-catering 17th century two/three bedroom character cottage with garden. Original features. Panoramic views over sea/mountains; Coniston/Windermere 30 minutes. Non-smoking. Open all year. VisitBritain ★★★★ [Pets £15 per pet]
e-mail: enquiries@southlakes-cottages.com   website: www.southlakes-cottages.com

Kirkby Lonsdale

Georgian buildings and quaint cottages. Riverside walks from medieval Devil's Bridge.

MRS PAULINE BAINBRIDGE, ULLATHORNS FARM, MIDDLETON, KIRKBY LONSDALE LA6 2LZ (015242 76214). 17th Century farmhouse on a working farm situated in the Lune Valley. B&B from £25. Children and well-behaved pets welcome. Non-smoking. VisitBritain ◆◆◆◆ [🐾]
e-mail: pauline@ullathorns.co.uk   website: www.ullathorns.co.uk

THE SNOOTY FOX, KIRKBY LONSDALE (01524 271308). Charming Jacobean Inn, offering 9 en suite rooms, award-winning restaurant and lounge bar, the perfect base from which to explore both the Lake District and Yorkshire Dales. AA/ETC ★★ [🐾]
e-mail: snootyfoxhotel@talktalk.net   website: www.thesnootyfoxhotel.co.uk

Kirkby Stephen

5 miles south on B6259 Kirkby Stephen to Hawes road.

COCKLAKE HOUSE, MALLERSTANG CA17 4JT (017683 72080). Charming, High Pennine Country House B&B in unique position above Pendragon Castle in Upper Mallerstang Dale offering good food and exceptional comfort to a small number of guests. Two double rooms with large private bathrooms. Three acres riverside grounds. Dogs welcome. [🐾]

Kirkoswald

Village in the Cumbrian hills, lying north west of the Lake District. Ideal for touring. Penrith 7 miles.

SECLUDED COTTAGES WITH PRIVATE FISHING, KIRKOSWALD CA10 1EU (24 hour brochure line 01768 898711, manned most Saturdays). Quality cottages, clean, well equipped and maintained. Centrally located for Lakes, Pennines, Hadrian's Wall, Borderland. Enjoy the Good Life in comfort. Pets' paradise. Guests' coarse fishing. Bookings/enquiries 01768 898711. ETC ★★★ [pw! £2.50 per pet per night, £14 per week].
e-mail: info@crossfieldcottages.co.uk   website: www.crossfieldcottages.co.uk

Lamplugh

Hamlet 7 miles south of Cockermouth.

FELLDYKE COTTAGE HOLIDAYS, LAMPLUGH. Visiting the Western Lakes? Then why not stay in this lovely 19th century cottage. Sleeps 4, short breaks can be arranged. Pets are welcome. Open all year. Contact MRS A. WILSON (01946 861151). VB ★★★★ [pw!🐾]   .
e-mail: dockraynook@talk21.com   website: www.felldykecottageholidays.co.uk

Langdale

Dramatic valley area to the west of Ambleside, in the very heart of the National Park.

WHEELWRIGHTS HOLIDAY COTTAGES, ELTERWATER, NEAR AMBLESIDE LA22 9HS (015394 38305; Fax: 015394 37618). Some of the loveliest cottages in the Lake District with stunning scenery on their doorsteps are ready to welcome you and your pets. Prices vary. Please visit our website. ETC ★★★ - ★★★★★ [🐾]
e-mail: enquiries@wheelwrights.com   website: www.wheelwrights.com

THE BRITANNIA INN, ELTERWATER, AMBLESIDE LA22 9HP (015394 37210; Fax: 015396 78075). 500-year-old traditional lakeland inn. Extensive, home-cooked menu, real ales, cosy bars, log fires. Comfortable, high quality en suite accommodation. Well-behaved pets welcome. ETC ★★★ [🐾]
e-mail: info@britinn.co.uk   website: www.britinn.co.uk

Little Langdale

Hamlet 2 miles west of Skelwith Bridge. To west is Little Langdale Tarn, a small lake.

HIGHFOLD COTTAGE, LITTLE LANGDALE. Very comfortable Lakeland cottage, ideally situated for walking and touring. Superb mountain views. Sleeps 5. Personally maintained. Pets welcome. Weekly £240–£490. VB ★★★. MRS C.E. BLAIR, 8 THE GLEBE, CHAPEL STILE, AMBLESIDE LA22 9JT (015394 37686). [🐾]
website: www.highfoldcottage.co.uk

Loweswater

A small hamlet situated between the lakes Loweswater and Crummock Water, in the Lake District National Park. Cockermouth 6 miles.

SCALE HILL, LOWESWATER, COCKERMOUTH CA13 9UX (01900 85232). With walking distance of Loweswater, Crummock Water, Buttermere. Four posters, bed linen, daily newspapers. Good food and real ales served at local country inns. Open February to December. See also advert on p269. [Pets £25 per week].
e-mail: thompson@scalehillloweswater.co.uk   website: www.scalehillloweswater.co.uk

Penrith

Market town and centre for touring Lake District. Of interest are 14th century castle, Gloucester Arms (1477) and Tudor House. Excellent sporting facilities. Windermere 27 miles, Keswick 18.

LYVENNET COTTAGES, THE MILL, KINGS MEABURN, PENRITH CA10 3BU (01931 714661/714226; Fax: 01931 714598) Four different cottages in and around the small farming village of Kings Meaburn in beautiful unspoilt 'Lyvennet Valley'. Ideal touring centre for the Lakes and Dales. ETC ★★★★
website: www.lyvennetcottages.co.uk

THE TROUTBECK INN, TROUTBECK, PENRITH CA11 0SJ (Tel: 017684 83635 Fax: 017684 87071) Close to the shores of lovely Ullswater, this friendly and well-appointed inn enjoys sweeping fell views and is a haven for a variety of outdoor pursuits, Excellent varied food and real ales. Tastefully furnished en suite bedrooms. Three self-catering cottages. ETC ★★★★/◆◆◆◆ [Pets £5-£15 per week].
e-mail: info@thetroutbeckinn.co.uk   website: www.thetroutbeck-inn.co.uk

CARROCK COTTAGES. Four recently renovated, award-winning, stone-built cottages set on the fringe of the Lakeland Fells. Games room, spa facilities. Home cooked meals service. Ideal for fell walking. Excellent restaurants nearby. A warm welcome guaranteed. ETC ★★★★★ Contact MALCOLM OR GILLIAN (01768 484111; Fax: 01768 488850). [Pets £20 per week each].
e-mail: info@carrockcottages.co.uk   website: www.carrockcottages.co.uk

Ravenstonedale

Conservation village in the Eden Valley, 5 miles from Kirkby Stephen.

MRS D. METCALFE, FELLVIEW, HIGH GREENSIDE, RAVENSTONEDALE, KIRKBY STEPHEN CA17 4LU (015396 23671). At foot of Howgills, 18th century farmhouse. En suite accommodation. Colour TV, tea/coffee facilities, own entrance. Dogs welcome. B&B £21. 3 nights £54. [🐾]
website: www.farmhousebandbcumbria.com

THE BLACK SWAN HOTEL, RAVENSTONEDALE, KIRKBY STEPHEN CA17 4NG (015396 23204). A welcoming hotel and village inn, perfect for touring the Lakes and Yorkshire Dales. Riverside garden, own 9-hole golf course. 10 en suite bedrooms, excellent home-cooked food, wines and ales. [🐾 pw!]
enquiries@blackswanhotel.com   website: www.blackswanhotel.com

Silloth-on-Solway

Solway Firth resort with harbour and fine sandy beach. Mountain views. Golf, fishing. Penrith 33 miles, Carlisle 23, Cockermouth 17.

MR AND MRS M.C. BOWMAN, TANGLEWOOD CARAVAN PARK, CAUSEWAY HEAD, SILLOTH CA7 4PE (016973 31253). Friendly country site, excellent toilet and laundry facilities. Tourers welcome or hire a luxury caravan. Open 1st March - January 31st. Telephone or e-mail for a brochure. AA *THREE PENNANTS.* [🐕]
e-mail: tanglewoodcaravanpark@hotmail.com   website: www.tanglewoodcaravanpark.co.u

Ullswater

Lake stretching for 7 miles with attractive Lakeside walks.

LAND ENDS CABINS, WATERMILLOCK, NEAR ULLSWATER CA11 0NB (017684 86438). Only 1.5 miles from Ullswater, our four detached log cabins have a peaceful fellside location in 25-acre grounds with two pretty lakes. Doggy heaven! Sleep 2-5. ETC ★★★ [🐕]
e-mail: infolandends@btinternet.com   website: www.landends.co.uk

FELL VIEW HOLIDAYS, FELL VIEW, GLENRIDDING, PENRITH CA11 0PJ (017684 82795). Sleep 2-5. Lovely, comfortable, well equipped accommodation in an idyllic location between Glenridding and Patterdale. Magnificent views of the surrounding fells. Short Breaks available out of season.
e-mail: enquiries@fellviewholidays.com   website: www.fellviewholidays.com

Wasdale

Hamlet 1 mile north east of Wast Water

THE BRIDGE INN, SANTON BRIDGE, HOLMROOK CA19 1UX (019467 26221; Fax: 019467 26026). Award-winning country inn providing good food and accommodation. 16 en suite bedrooms. Ideal for exploring the Western Lakes and fells. Well behaved dogs welcome. [Pets £5 per stay].
e-mail: info@santonbridgeinn.com   website: www.santonbridgeinn.com

Windermere

Famous resort on lake of same name, the largest in England. Magnificent scenery. Car ferry from Bowness, one mile distant. Kendal 9 miles.

LOW SPRINGWOOD HOTEL, THORNBARROW ROAD, WINDERMERE LA23 2DF (015394 46383). Millie and Lottie (Boxers) would like to welcome you to their peaceful Hotel in its own secluded gardens. Lovely views of Lakes and Fells. All rooms en suite with colour TV etc. Some four-posters. Brochure available. [🐕 pw!]

WATERMILL INN & BREWERY, INGS, NEAR STAVELEY, KENDAL LA8 9PY (01539 821309; Fax: 01539 822309). Shelly and friends (Dogs) welcome you to the award-winning Inn. 16 real ales. Cosy fires, en suite rooms, excellent bar meals. Doggie water and biscuits served in the bar. Good doorstep dog walking. ETC ◆◆◆. [Pets £3 per night (includes donation to Dogs' Trust].
e-mail: all@watermillinn.co.uk   website: www.watermillinn.co.uk

LANGDALE CHASE HOTEL, WINDERMERE LA23 1LW (015394 32201). Magnificent country house hotel with grounds sloping to the edge of Lake Windermere. Panoramic views, log fires, excellent food and friendly professional staff all ensure a memorable stay. [🐕]
e-mail: sales@langdalechase.co.uk   website: www.langdalechase.co.uk

Hundreds of self-catering holiday homes in a variety of wonderful locations, all well equipped and managed by our caring staff. Pets welcome. Free leisure club membership. For brochure, contact: LAKELOVERS, BELMONT HOUSE, LAKE ROAD, BOWNESS-ON-WINDERMERE LA23 3BJ. (015394 88855; Fax: 015394 88857). ETC ★★★ - ★★★★★ [Pets £15.00 per week.]
e-mail: bookings@lakelovers.co.uk   website: www.lakelovers.co.uk

THE FAMOUS WILD BOAR (08458 504 604). Nestled in the beautiful Gilpin Valley, former coaching Inn set within its own private 72 acres of woodland. Excellent restaurant with local produce and real ales. Windermere Golf Club and Leisure Club nearby. [Pets £15.00 per night.]
e-mail: wildboar@elhmail.co.uk   website: www.elh.co.uk

Blackburn, Blackpool, Clitheroe, Pilling, Southport

Blackburn

Industrial town on River Darwen and on Leeds and Liverpool Canal.

THE BROWN LEAVES COUNTRY HOTEL, LONGSIGHT ROAD, COPSTER GREEN, NEAR BLACKBURN BB1 9EU (01254 249523; Fax: 01254 245240). Situated on the A59 halfway between Preston and Clitheroe, five miles from Junction 31 on M6 in beautiful Ribble Valley. All rooms ground floor, en suite facilities, satellite TV, tea-making and hairdryer. Guests' lounge and bar lounge. Car parking. Pets by arrangement. All credit cards welcome. [🐶]
website: www.brownleavescountryhotel.co.uk

Blackpool

Famous resort with fine sands and many attractions and vast variety of entertainments. Blackpool Tower (500ft). Three piers. Manchester 47 miles, Lancaster 26, Preston 17, Fleetwood 8.

THE BRAYTON, 7-8 FINCHLEY ROAD, GYNN SQUARE, BLACKPOOL FY1 2LP (01253 351645). Quiet licensed hotel overlooking Gynn gardens and the promenade. Full 'restaurant style' menu served daily. Dogs most welcome. Open all year. ETC ◆◆◆ [🐶]
e-mail: info@the-brayton-hotel.com   website: www.the-brayton-hotel.com

Clitheroe

Town above River Ribble valley, 10 miles north east of Blackburn.

THE ASSHETON ARMS, DOWNHAM, NEAR CLITHEROE BB7 4BJ (01200 441227). A traditional country pub in the beautiful Ribble Valley. Food to suit all tastes, variety of modern and traditional beers. Children and dogs welcome. Totally non-smoking.
website: www.assheton-arms.co.uk

Pilling

Village 3 miles north east of Pressall.

BERYL AND PETER RICHARDSON, BELL FARM, BRADSHAW LANE, SCRONKEY, PILLING, PRESTON PR3 6SN (01253 790324).18th century farmhouse with one family room, one double and one twin. All en suite, and centrally heated. Full English breakfast is served. Open all year except Christmas and New Year. [🐶]
website: www.bellfarm.co.uk

Southport

Elegant seaside resort with Victorian feel. Amusement park, zoo and Birkdale championship golf course.

THE GARDEN COURT, 22 BANK SQUARE, SOUTHPORT PR9 0DG (Tel & Fax: 01704 530219). Victorian town house overlooking Central Promenade, Theatre, Marine Lake and Floral Hall Conference Centre. All attractions within easy walking distance. En suite bedrooms, some four-poster. Friendly, comfortable accommodation from £25 B&B pppn. [🐶]
website: www.gardencourtsouthport.co.uk

CRIMOND HOTEL & RESTAURANT, KNOWSLEY ROAD, SOUTHPORT PR9 0HN (01704 536456; Fax: 01704 548643). Situated close to the town centre, this hotel can cater for all your needs with free use of indoor swimming pool and health club nearby. Open all year. Table d'hôte service. Full central heating. ETC ★★ [Pets £1 per night].
website: www.crimondhotel.com

Scotland

Scotland • Regions

SHETLAND
ISLANDS

WESTERN
ISLES

MORAY

ABERDEENSHIRE

HIGHLAND

14

ANGUS

PERTH AND KINROSS

13

ARGYLL
AND BUTE

STIRLING

FIFE

9

2 6 8

1 11

3 5 7 10 EAST LOTHIAN

4 12

NORTH AYRSHIRE

S. LANARKSHIRE

EAST
AYRSHIRE

SCOTTISH
BORDERS

SOUTH
AYRSHIRE

DUMFRIES
AND GALLOWAY

1.	Inverclyde	8.	Falkirk
2.	West Dunbartonshire	9.	Clackmannanshire
3.	Renfrewshire	10.	West Lothian
4.	East Renfrewshire	11.	City of Edinburgh
5.	City of Glasgow	12.	Midlothian
6.	East Dunbartonshire	13.	Dundee City
7.	North Lanarkshire	14.	Aberdeen City

CAMPING & CARAVANNING CLUB (0845 130 7632). Visit one of our award-winning UK Club Sites. Our sites have dog walking areas for you and your dog to explore. A friendly welcome will be given to you and your pet on our sites, joining is great value for money. QUOTE REF NO 0716
website: www.campingandcaravanningclub.co.uk

SCOTLAND COTTAGES. See the best of the Highlands, Lochs and Borders. Almost 100 cottages to choose from, all personally inspected. Pets welcome. Free brochure. Call 0870 4059 599 or visit our website.
website: www.scotland-cottages.co.uk

Aberdeen, Banff & Moray

Fochabers, Glenlivet, Rattray Head, Turriff

Fochabers

Village on east bank of River Spey, 8 miles east of Elgin.

RED LION TAVERN, 65-67 HIGH STREET, FOCHABERS IV32 7DU (01343 820455). Pets on holiday in Scotland - ideal for Whisky, Castle and Coastal Trails. All rooms non-smoking and en suite. Full restaurant menu and packed lunches available. Children welcome.
e-mail: reception@redlionfochabers.co.uk

Glenlivet

Located 8 miles north of Tomintoul. Distilleries and State forest.

BEECHGROVE COTTAGES, GLENLIVET. Traditional stone cottages set amidst beautiful surroundings near rivers Avon and Livet. All modernised and very comfortable. Fishing available. Ideal for exploring Highlands, Castle and Whisky Trails, walking, skiing, golf. Contact: THE POST OFFICE, TOMNAVOULIN, BALLINDALLOCH AB37 9JA (01807 590220) [🐕]
website: www.beechgrovecottages.co.uk

Grantown-on-Spey

Market town 19 miles south of Forres.

MR AND MRS J. R. TAYLOR, MILTON OF CROMDALE, GRANTOWN-ON-SPEY PH26 3PH (01479 872415). Fully modernised Cottage with large garden and views of River Spey and Cromdale Hills. Golf, tennis and trekking within easy reach. Fully equipped except linen. Two double bedrooms. Shower, refrigerator, electric cooker, colour television. Car desirable. Open March to October. £120 per week. Children and pets welcome. [🐕]

Rattray Head

Fishing port on the north east coast 27 miles north of Aberdeen. The most easterly town on the Scottish mainland. Arbuthnot Museum features displays on local history.

SAND DUNES & SECLUDED 11-MILE BEACH. Eco-hostel, B&B and holiday flat. Homely, relaxing, non-smoking retreat on generally sunny, dry, midge-free coast. Suit nature lovers, cyclists, walkers, even giant dogs. Washroom for clothes, kit and pets. Veggie breakfast option. ROB & VAL, LIGHTHOUSE COTTAGES, RATTRAY HEAD, PETERHEAD AB42 3HA (01346 532236) [pw! 🐕]
website: www.rattrayhead.net

Stonehaven

Fishing port on east coast, 13 miles south of Aberdeen.

MRS AILEEN PATON, 'WOODSIDE OF GLASSLAW', STONEHAVEN AB39 3XQ (01569 763799). Modern bungalow with six centrally heated en suite bedrooms with colour TV and hospitality trays. Stonehaven two miles. Accessible for disabled guests.

Turriff

Small town in agricultural area, 9 miles south of Banff.

SIMON PEARSE, COUNTRY COTTAGES, FORGLEN ESTATE, TURRIFF AB53 4JP (01888 562918). Estate on the beautiful Deveron River. Sandy beaches only nine miles away, Turriff two miles. 6 cottages sleeping 4–9. From £209 weekly. Open all year. Ideal for top golf courses, free brown trout fishing. Well-behaved dogs welcome. [🐕]
e-mail: reservations@forglen.co.uk   website: www.forglen.co.uk

Readers are requested to mention this FHG
guidebook when seeking accommodation

Finavon

Located on the River South Esk, 5 miles north east of Forfar.

BRAEHEAD COTTAGE, FINAVON, BY FORFAR DD8 3PX (01307 850715). The Dog-friendly B&B!! We offer a very warm welcome to our guests and their four-legged friends. Three guest rooms, all with en suite shower rooms. Outside enclosed area and ample car parking. Our two Golden Retrievers and Newfoundland love making new friends. [pw! 🐕]
e-mail: braeheadbandb@btinternet.com   website: www.braeheadbandb.co.uk

Readers are requested to mention this FHG
guidebook when seeking accommodation

Looking for holiday accommodation?
for details of hundreds of properties
throughout the UK including
comprehensive coverage of all areas of Scotland try:

www.holidayguides.com

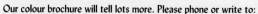

Tarbert, Taynuilt

Appin

Mountainous area bounded by Loch Linnhe, Glen Creran and Glencoe.

MRS J PERY, ARDTUR, APPIN PA38 4DD (01631 730223 or 01626 834172). Two adjacent cottages in secluded surroundings. Ideal for hill walking, climbing, pony trekking, boating and fly fishing. Shop one mile; sea 200 yards; car essential; pets allowed.[🐾]
e-mail: pery@btinternet.com   website: www.selfcatering-appin-scotland.com

Ballachulish

Impressively placed village at entrance to Glencoe and on Loch Leven. Magnificent mountain scenery including Sgorr Dhearg (3362ft). Good centre for boating, climbing and sailing. Glasgow 89 miles, Oban 38, Fort William 14, Kinlochleven 9.

Cottages and Chalets in Natural Woodland sleeping two to six people. The Glencoe area is lovely for walking and perfect for nature lovers too. Regret no smokers. No VAT. Brochure available. APPLY: HOUSE IN THE WOOD HOLIDAYS, GLENACHULISH, BALLACHULISH PH49 4JZ (01855 811379). Pets welcome. [🐾]

Cairndow

Village at mouth of Kinglas Water on Loch Fyne in Argyll, near head of Loch.

Two comfortable holiday cottages at the head of the longest sea loch in Scotland, in lovely walking country. Sleep four and eight. Linen and electricity included. STB ★★★ Self Catering. MRS DELAP, ACHADUNAN, CAIRNDOW, ARGYLL PA26 8BJ (Tel & Fax: 01499 600238). website: www.argyllholidaycottages.com

CAIRNDOW STAGECOACH INN, CAIRNDOW PA26 8BN (01499 600286; Fax: 01499 600220). 14 well-appointed en suite bedrooms. Excellent cuisine in Stables Restaurant and lounge meals all day. Amenities include lochside beer garden, sauna, multi-gym and solarium. STB ★★★ Inn. website: www.cairndow.com

Please mention **Pets Welcome!**
when making enquiries about accommodation featured in these pages

Dalmally

Small town in Glen Orchy to the south-west of Loch Awe, with romantic Kilchurn Castle (14th century). Edinburgh 98 miles, Glasgow 69, Ardrishaig 42, Oban 25, Inveraray 16.

ROCKHILL WATERSIDE COUNTRY HOUSE, ARDBRECKNISH, BY DALMALLY PA33 1BH (01866 833218). 17th century guest house on waterside with spectacular views over Loch Awe. Five delightful rooms with all modern facilities. First-class home cooking with much home-grown produce.

Dunoon

Town and resort in Argyll, 4 miles west of Gourock across Firth of Clyde.

ABBOTS BRAE HOTEL, WEST BAY, DUNOON PA23 7QJ (01369 705021; Fax: 01369 701191). Small welcoming hotel at the gateway to the Western Highlands with breathtaking views. Comfortable, spacious, en suite bedrooms, quality home cooking and select wines. [🐾]
e-mail: info@abbotsbrae.co.uk   website: www.abbotsbrae.co.uk

Isle of Gigha

A tranquil island, one of the Inner Hebrides just of the west coast of Scotland. A haven for birds and wildlife.

GIGHA HOTEL, ISLE OF GIGHA PA41 7AA (01583 505254; Fax: 01583 505244). Beautiful, tranquil island. Explore the white sandy bays and lochs; famous Achamore Gardens. Easy walking, bike hire, birds, wildlife and wild flowers. Dog-friendly. Holiday cottages also available. [🐾]
website: www.gigha.org.uk

Loch Goil

Six mile long loch stretching from Lochgoilhead to Loch Long.

DARROCH MHOR, CARRICK CASTLE, LOCH GOIL PA24 8AF (01301 703249; Fax: 01301 703348). Five self-catering Chalets on the shores of Loch Goil in the heart of Argyll Forest Park. Fully equipped except linen. Colour TV, fitted kitchen, carpeted. Pets very welcome. Open all year. [🐾]
e-mail: chalets@murray-s.fslife.co.uk   website: www.argyllchalets.com

Oban

Popular Highland resort and port, yachting centre, ferry services to Inner and Outer Hebrides. Sandy bathing beach at Ganavan Bay. McCaig's Tower above town is Colosseum replica built in 1890s.

LAGNAKEIL HIGHLAND LODGES, LERAGS, OBAN, ARGYLL PA34 4SE (01631 562746; Fax: 01631 570225). Our Timber Lodges and four cottages are set in a tranquil, scenic wooded glen overlooking Loch Feochan, only 3 miles from the picturesque harbour town of Oban: "Gateway to the Isles". Fully equipped Lodges to a high standard, including linen and towels, country pub a short walk. OAP. discount. Free loch fishing. Special Breaks from £49 per lodge per night, weekly from £225. Sleep 2-10 comfortably. Our colour brochure will tell lots more. VisitScotland ★★★/★★★★ Self-Catering. [Pets £15 per week].
e-mail: info@lagnakeil.com   website: www.lagnakeil.co.uk

MRS LINDA BATTISON, COLOGIN COUNTRY CHALETS, LERAGS GLEN, BY OBAN PA34 4SE (01631 564501; Fax: 01631 566925). Cosy timber chalets, sleep two to six, all conveniences. Situated on farm, wildlife abundant. Games room, launderette, licensed bar serving home-cooked food. Free fishing. Playpark. Live entertainment. STB ★★★/★★★★ Self-Catering [pw! Pets £15 per week.]
e-mail: cologin@west-highland-holidays.co.uk   website: www.west-highland-holidays.co.uk

WILLOWBURN HOTEL, CLACHAN SEIL, BY OBAN PA34 4TJ (01852 300276). Peaceful, relaxing, informal and addictive. Superb setting overlooking the Sound of Seil. Walk, fish, birdwatch or simply just laze. Completely non-smoking. Tempted? Bring your owners too! STB ★★★★ Small Hotel, AA ★★ [🐾]
website: www.willowburn.co.uk

TRALEE BAY HOLIDAYS, BENDERLOCH, BY OBAN PA37 1QR (01631 720255/217). Overlooking Ardmucknish Bay. The wooded surroundings and sandy beaches make Tralee the ideal destination for a self-catering lodge or caravan holiday anytime of the year. STB ★★★★★ [Pets £15 per week] e-mail: tralee@easynet.co.uk   website: www.tralee.com

MRS STEWART, GLENVIEW, SOROBA ROAD, OBAN PA34 4JF (01631 562267). Small family-run guest house, 10 minutes' walk from train, boat and bus terminal. A warm welcome awaits you all year round. [🐕]

Well-equipped Scandinavian chalets in breathtaking scenery near Oban. Chalets sleep 4–7, are widely spaced and close to Loch Tralaig. Car parking. From £200 per week per chalet. Available April to October. STB ★★ & ★★★ Self Catering. APPLY – ANNE & ROBIN GREY, ELERAIG HIGHLAND LODGES, KILNINVER, BY OBAN PA34 4UX (01852 200225) [🐕] e-mail: robingrey@eleraig.co.uk   website: www.scotland2000.com/eleraig

Tarbert

Fishing port on isthmus connecting Kintyre to the mainland.

WEST LOCH HOTEL, BY TARBERT, LOCH FYNE PA29 6YF (01880 820283; Fax: 01880 820930). Family-run, 18th century coaching inn, well situated for a relaxing holiday. It is renowned for outstanding food. Excellent for hill-walking and enjoying the wide variety of wildlife. Attractions include castles, distilleries, gardens and sandy beaches. STB ★★ Inn. [🐕] e-mail: westlochhotel@btinternet.com   website: www.westlochhotel.co.uk

DUNMORE COURT, KILBERRY ROAD, NEAR TARBERT PA29 6XZ (01880 820654). Five cottages sleeping 2-8. Wonderful walks and scenery, peace and quiet. Winter breaks available. Easy access to island ferries. Terms from £250-£600. Open all year. ASSC member. STB ★★ SELF CATERING. [🐕 e-mail: bookings@dunmorecourt.com   website: www.dunmorecourt.com

Peaceful, unspoilt West Highland estate. Traditional cottages, with open fires; some with a dinghy in summer. Sleep 4–10. Pets welcome. Walks, pony trekking, golf nearby. APPLY SOPHIE JAMES, SKIPNESS CASTLE, BY TARBERT PA29 6XU (01880 760207; Fax: 01880 760208). STB ★★/★★★[🐕] e-mail: sophie@skipness.freeserve.co.uk

Taynuilt

Village in Argyll 1km south west of Bonawe.

JENIFER MOFFAT, AIRDENY CHALETS, TAYNUILT PA35 1HY (01866 822648). Three 3-bedroom chalets (STB ★★★★) and four 2-bedroom chalets (STB ★★★), furnished to a very high standard. Ideal for walking, cycling, fishing, bird watching, touring, or just relaxing. Dogs welcome. Open all year. [Pets £10 per week]. e-mail: jenifer@airdenychalets.co.uk   website www.airdenychalets.co.uk

Visit the FHG website
www.holidayguides.com
for details of the wide choice of accommodation
featured in
the full range of FHG titles

Ayr

Popular family holiday resort with sandy beaches. Excellent shopping, theatre, racecourse.

HORIZON HOTEL, ESPLANADE, AYR KA7 1DT (01292 264384; Fax: 01292 264011). Highly recommended for golf breaks; special midweek rates. Coach parties welcome. Lunches, dinners and bar suppers served. Phone now for free colour brochure. [🐕]
e-mail: reception@horizonhotel.com   website: www.horizonhotel.com

Catacol (Isle of Arran)

Location on north side of Catacol Bay on north-west coast of Arran.

CATACOL BAY HOTEL, CATACOL, LOCHRANZA KA27 8HN (01770 830231; Fax: 01770 830350). Comfortable, friendly, small country house hotel where good cooking is our speciality. Extensive bar menu, meals are served from noon until 10pm. Centrally heated. Open all year. Details of Special Breaks and brochure on request. Children and pets welcome. [🐕]
e-mail: catbay@tiscali.co.uk   website: www.catacol.co.uk

Jedburgh, Kelso, Selkirk, West Linton

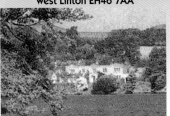

Jedburgh

Small town on Jed water, 10 miles north-east of Hawick. Ruins of abbey founded in 1138.

GLENBANK HOUSE HOTEL, CASTLEGATE, JEDBURGH TD8 6BD (01835 862258). Set in its own grounds with ample private parking and beer garden. Licensed restaurant and bar. All rooms en suite with TV. Open to non-residents. Reduced rates for children. [🐴]
e-mail: enquiries@glenbankhotel.co.uk   website: www.glenbankhotel.co.uk

ALAN & CHRISTINE SWANSTON, FERNIEHIRST MILL LODGE, JEDBURGH TD8 6PQ (01835 863279). A chalet style guest house set in grounds of 25 acres. All rooms en suite with tea/coffee making facilities. Licensed for residents. Well behaved pets (including horses) welcome by arrangement. VisitScotland ★, AA ★★. [🐴]
e-mail: ferniehirstmill@aol.com   website: www.ferniehirstmill.co.uk

Kelso

Market town 18 miles north-west of Hawick and 20 miles south-west of Berwick-upon-Tweed.

PLUM BRAES BARN Three lovely cottages, standing in an elevated position with wonderful views, on an organic farm in a peaceful setting two miles from the beautiful market town of Kelso. River walk perfect for picnics, birdwatching and fishing. EDMONSTON HOUSE (sleeps 4-10) is a chalet style farmhouse nearby, with commanding views. Contact: Maggie Stewart, Cliftonhill Farm, Kelso TD5 7QE (01573 225028) STB ★★★/★★★★ Self Catering.
e-mail: maggie@plumbraesbarn.com   websites: www.plumbraesbarn.co.uk
www.plumbraesbarn.com

WESTWOOD HOUSE, OVERLOOKING SCOTLAND'S FAMOUS RIVER TWEED. Enclosed and secluded riverside cottage with walled gardens and own private island. Sleeps 2-8 persons plus child, from £375 per week. 2 person discounts. For brochure contact: DEBBIE CRAWFORD, PIPPIN HEATH FARM, HOLT, NORFOLK NR25 6SS (07788 134832). [🐴]

Selkirk

Town on hill above Ettrick Water, 9 miles north of Hawick.

THE GARDEN HOUSE, WHITMUIR, SELKIRK TD7 4PZ (01750 721728; Fax: 01750 720379). Comfortable, warm modern farm house B&B. Spacious bedrooms, private bathrooms. Good home cooking. Fishing, walking, cycling and horse riding nearby. Grazing available. Open all year. [🐴]
e-mail: whitmuir@btconnect.com   website: www.whitmuirfarm.co.uk

West Linton

Village on east side of Pentland hills, 7 miles south-west of Penicuick. Edinburgh 18 miles.

MRS C. M. KILPATRICK, SLIPPERFIELD HOUSE, WEST LINTON EH46 7AA (01968 660401). Two lovely cottages on hideaway country estate near Edinburgh. Sleep 4/6. Available all year. Perfect dog-friendly location. STB ★★★/★★★★ [🐴]
e-mail: cottages@slipperfield.com   website: www.slipperfield.com

Please note

All the information in this book is given in good faith in the belief that it is correct. However, the publishers cannot guarantee the facts given in these pages, neither are they responsible for changes in policy, ownership or terms that may take place after the date of going to press. Readers should always satisfy themselves that the facilities they require are available and that the terms, if quoted, still apply.

Castle Douglas, Drummore, Dumfries, Gatehouse-of-Fleet, Moffat

FHG Guides
publish a large range of well-known accommodation guides.
We will be happy to send you details or you can use the order form
at the back of this book.

Castle Douglas

Old market town at the northern end of Carlingwalk Loch, good touring centre for Galloway

Readers are requested to mention this FHG
guidebook when seeking accommodation

Drummore

Coastal location, 4 miles north of Mull of Galloway.

MULL OF GALLOWAY, DRUMMORE. A few short steps from the beach. STB 3/4-Star cottages; non-smoking cottages available. Tranquil and unspoiled village. Logan Botanical Gardens, golf, fishing, birdwatching nearby. Unrestricted beaches. ASSC. Contact SALLY COLMAN (01776 840631). [£15 per pet].
website: www.harbourrow.co.uk

Dumfries

County town of Dumfries-shire and a former seaport. Dumfries contains many interesting buildings including an 18th century windmill containing a camera obscura. Robert Burns lived in the town before his death in 1796.

DAVID & GILL STEWART, AE FARM COTTAGES, GUBHILL FARM, DUMFRIES DG1 1RL (01387 860648). Modern accommodation in old stone buildings on a traditional farm, overlooking a peaceful valley. Beautiful views, plentiful wildlife and endless paths on the doorstep. Between Dumfries, Moffat and Thornhill. STB ★★★ SELF CATERING, CATEGORY ONE DISABILITY. [🐾]
e-mail: gill@gubhill.co.uk

Gatehouse of Fleet

Small town near mouth of Water of Fleet, 6 miles north-west of Kirkcudbright

RUSKO HOLIDAYS, GATEHOUSE OF FLEET, CASTLE DOUGLAS DG7 2BS (01557 814215). Spacious farmhouse and three charming, cosy cottages near beaches, hills, gardens, castles and golf course. Walking, fishing, tennis. Pets, including horses, welcome. Sleep 2-12. Rates £225-£1329. STB ★★ to ★★★★ Self-Catering. Disabled Awards. [First pet free, second pet £20.00 per week]
e-mail: info@ruskoholidays.co.uk   website: www.ruskoholidays.co.uk

Moffat

At head of lovely Annandale, grand mountain scenery. Good centre for rambling, climbing, angling and golf. The 'Devil's Beef Tub' is 5 miles, Edinburgh 52, Peebles 33, Dumfries 21.

BARNHILL SPRINGS COUNTRY GUEST HOUSE, MOFFAT DG10 9QS (01683 220580). Early Victorian country house overlooking some of the finest views of Upper Annandale. Comfortable accommodation, residents' lounge with open fire. Situated on the Southern Upland Way half-a-mile from A74/M74 Moffat Junction. Pets free of charge. Bed & Breakfast from £27; Evening Meal (optional) from £18. STB ★★ Guest House, AA ★★. [pw! 🐾]

ANNANDALE ARMS HOTEL, HIGH STREET, MOFFAT DG1O 9HF (01683 220013; Fax: 01683 221395). A warm welcome is offered at the Annandale Arms to dogs with well-mannered and house-trained owners. Excellent restaurant and a relaxing panelled bar. Large private parking area. £95 per room for two; £55 per room for one. STB ★★★ [pw! 🐾]
e-mail: pw@annandalearmshotel.co.uk   website: www.annandalearmshotel.co.uk

Portpatrick

Historic harbour village on southernmost tip of Scotland. Excellent beach with launching ramp, good fishing. Stranraer six miles.

G&S COTTAGES. Three cottages a few minutes' walk from the sea on the beautiful Galloway coast. Modern fittings and decor; fully equipped. Linen provided. Decking and barbecue facilities. Contact: GRAHAM AND SUE FLETCHER, 468 OTLEY ROAD, LEEDS LS16 8AE (0113 230 1391/07976 671926)
e-mail: info@gscottages.co.uk   website: www.gscottages.co.uk

Thornhill

Small town on River Nith 13 miles north-west of Dumfries. Site of Roman signal station lies to the south.

HOPE COTTAGE, THORNHILL DG3 5BJ (01848 331510; Fax: 01848 331810). Pretty stone cottage in the peaceful conservation village of Durisdeer. Well-equipped self-catering cottage with large secluded garden. Sleeps 6. Towels, linen, heating and electricity included. Phone MRS S. STANNETT for brochure. STB ★★★★ [🐾]
e-mail: a.stann@btinternet.com   website: www.hopecottage.co.uk

Gartocharn/Loch Lomond

Village 4 miles east of Balloch, near Loch Lomond.

ANGUS & SALLY MACDONELL, MARDELLA FARMHOUSE, OLD SCHOOL ROAD, GARTOCRAN, DUNBARTONSHIRE G83 8SD (01389 830428). This peaceful, scenic location on a quiet country lane in magnificent countryside is ideal for you and your pets. Excellent place for walking and touring. [🐕]

Edinburgh & Lothians
Rosewell

Rosewell

Village 4 miles south west of Dalkeith.

HUNTER HOLIDAY COTTAGES, THORNTON FARM, ROSEWELL, EDINBURGH EH24 9EF (0131 448 0888; Fax: 0131 440 2082). A range of cottages in beautiful countryside only eight miles from Edinburgh city centre. Recently renovated, with modern facilities sleeping four to ten plus. Contact MARGOT CRICHTON. [Pets £10 per week].
e-mail: info@edinburghcottages.com website: www.edinburghcottages.com

Lower Largo

Village on the bay, 2 miles NE of Leven. Birth place of Alexander Selkirk of Robinson Crusoe fame.

THE CRUSOE HOTEL, Main Street, Lower Largo, NEAR ST ANDREWS KY8 6BT. (01333 320759; Fax: 01333 320865). Old-world ambience with fine harbour views. En suite accommodation, outstanding cuisine, free house. Excellent centre for sailing, golf, birdwatching, wind surfing, coastal walks. STB ★★★ Hotel. [🐾]
email: relax@crusoehotel.co.uk   website: www.crusoehotel.co.uk

St Andrews

Home of golf - British Golf Museum has memorabilia dating back to the origins of the game. Remains of castle and cathedral. Sealife Centre and beach Leisure Centre. Excellent sands. Ideal base for exploring the picturesque East Neuk.

COBWEBS. Self-catering for five people, situated opposite the University, just 3 minutes from the Castle Sands and 10 from the famous links. Our secluded, secure walled garden is perfect for you and your pets. Telephone 01764 685485 or e-mail FRANCES from the web page.
website: www.heartofstandrews.co.uk

MR & MRS PATRICK WEDDERBURN, ST ANDREWS COUNTRY COTTAGES, MOUNTQUHANIE ESTATE, FREEPOST, CUPAR KY15 4BR (01382 330318; Fax: 01382 330480). Quality self-catering houses and cottages in St Andrews and on a tranquil Country Estate. Central heating, TV, phone. Enclosed gardens. STB ★★★ to ★★★★★ Self Catering. [pw! Dogs £15 per week, Cats F.O.C.].
e-mail: enquiries@standrews-cottages.com   website: www.standrews-cottages.com

Drumnadrochit, Fort William, Glencoe, Invermoriston

Readers are requested to mention this FHG
guidebook when seeking accommodation

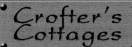

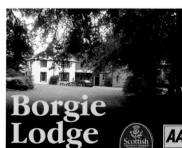

Aviemore (Inverness-shire)

Scotland's leading ski resort in Spey valley with superb sport and entertainment facilities. All-weather holiday centre.

PINE BANK CHALETS, DALFABER ROAD, AVIEMORE PH22 1PX (01479 810000). Cosy Log Cabins and 6 Quality Chalets, situated near the River Spey. Superb Family/Activity Holidays by mountains. Ideal skiing, walking, fishing and golf. Sky TV. Short breaks available. Pets welcome. Open all year. ASSC Member. Brochure. [Pets £20 per week.]
e-mail: pinebankchalets@btopenworld.com   website: www.pinebankchalets.co.uk

CAIRNGORM HIGHLAND BUNGALOWS, GLEN EINICH, 29 GRAMPIAN VIEW, AVIEMORE, INVERNESS-SHIRE PH22 1TF. (01479 810653, Fax: 01479 810262). Well equipped bungalows ranging from one to four bedrooms. Open all year. Leisure facilities nearby. Children and pets welcome. Phone for brochure. [🐾]
e-mail: linda.murray@virgin.net   website: www.cairngorm-bungalows.co.uk

Beauly (Inverness-shire)

Town at head of Beauly Firth, 11 miles west of Inverness.

FRANK & JULIET SPENCER-NAIRN, CULLIGRAN COTTAGES, GLEN STRATHFARRAR, STRUY, NEAR BEAULY IV4 7JX (Tel & Fax: 01463 761285). Pure magic! Come for a spell in a chalet or cottage and this glen will cast one over on you! Nature Reserve with native woodlands and wildlife. Brochure. (March - November). Terms from £189 to £489. [🐾]
e-mail: info@culligrancottages.co.uk   website: www.culligrancottages.co.uk

Boat of Garten (Inverness-shire)

Village on River Spey, 5 miles north east of Aviemore.

ANNE MATHER, THE TREEHOUSE SELF-CATERING LODGE, BOAT OF GARTEN (0131-337 7167). Unique lodge in woodland setting, yet minutes from local amenities. Fully equipped, superb log-burning fire. Sleeps 7. Perfect for an active or a relaxing break. Pets welcome. [🐾]
e-mail: fhg@treehouselodge.plus.com   website: www.treehouselodge.co.uk

Carrbridge (Inverness-shire)

Village on River Dulnain, 7 miles north of Aviemore. Landmark Visitor Centre has exhibition explaining history of local environment.

THE PINES COUNTRY GUESTHOUSE, DUTHIL, CARRBRIDGE PH23 3ND (01479 841220). Relax and enjoy our Highland hospitality, woodland setting; all rooms en suite. Traditional or vegetarian home cooking. B&B from £25 daily; DB&B from £236 weekly. Children and pets welcome. AA ★★★ [🐕]
website: www.thepines-duthil.co.uk

Contin (Ross-shire)

Village 2 miles south west of Strathpeffer.

COUL HOUSE HOTEL, CONTIN, BY STRATHPEFFER IV14 9ES (01997 421487; Fax: 01997 421945). Privately owned and operated 20-bedroom Country House Hotel with miles of forest walks, many log fires, and great food. Both you and your dog are made to feel most welcome.
e-mail: stay@coulhousehotel.com   website: www.coulhousehotel.com

Drumnadrochit (Inverness-shire)

Village on the shores of Loch Ness with "Monster" visitor centre. Sonar scanning cruises.

CAROL HUGHES, GLENURQUHART LODGES, BY DRUMNADROCHIT IV63 6TJ (01456 476234; Fax: 01456 476286). Situated between Loch Ness and Glen Affric in a spectacular setting ideal for walking, touring or just relaxing in this tranquil location. Four spacious chalets all fully equipped for six people, set in wooded grounds. Owner's hotel adjacent where guests are most welcome in the restaurant and bar. [Pets £10 per week.]
e-mail: carol@glenurquhartlodges.co.uk   website: www.glenurquhart-lodges.co.uk

Fort William (Inverness-shire)

Small town at foot of Ben Nevis, ideal base for climbers and hillwalkers.

THE CLAN MACDUFF HOTEL, FORT WILLIAM PH33 6RW (01397 702341; Fax: 01397 706174). This family-run hotel overlooks Loch Linnhe, two miles south of Fort William, excellent for touring the West Highlands. All rooms have TV, hair dryer, hospitality tray and private facilities. B&B from £27.50pppn. Three nights DB&B from £118.50 (Spring/Autumn). STB ★★★ Hotel. Phone or write for colour brochure and tariff. [🐕]
website: www.clanmacduff.co.uk

LINNHE LOCHSIDE HOLIDAYS, CORPACH, FORT WILLIAM PH33 7NL (01397 772376; Fax: 01397 772007). Linnhe is unique and one of the most beautiful lochside parks in Britain. Close to Ben Nevis and Fort William. Excellent facilities. Pets welcome. Open 31 March - 31 October. Colour brochure. (Pets £5 per night, £25 per week).
e-mail: relax@linnhe-lochside-holidays.co.uk   website: www.linnhe-lochside-holidays.co.uk

Glencoe (Inverness-shire)

Valley of River Coe, running west to Loch Leven, 3 miles east of Ballachulish. Site of notorious massacre in 1692.

INCHREE CENTRE, NEAR FORT WILLIAM PH33 6SE (Tel & Fax: 01855 821287). Between Ben Nevis and Glencoe. 8 self-catering chalets, 4 or 6 berth. Pub and Restaurant on site. Discount for couples. Short-stay breaks available most of the year. [Pets £2.50 per night, £15 per week]
e-mail: reception@inchreecentre.co.uk   website: www.inchreecentre.co.uk

Invermoriston (Inverness-shire)

Village on River Moriston, running from Loch Cluanie to Loch Ness.

INVERMORISTON HOLIDAY CHALETS, Glenmoriston IV63 7YF (01320 351254; Fax: 01320 351343). Spectacular location by Loch Ness. Comfortable, well equipped self catering chalets in spacious grounds. Few minutes' walk to the village. Excellent base for touring, walking, fishing etc. Pets welcome in some chalets. [Pets £20 per week]
e-mail: ihc@ipw.com   website: www.invermoriston-holidays.com

Kincraig (Inverness-shire)

Attractive Highland village close to Loch Insh and Glenfeshie, midway between Aviemore and Kingussie.

NICK & PATSY THOMPSON, INSH HOUSE GUESTHOUSE AND SELF-CATERING COTTAGES, KINCRAIG, NEAR KINGUSSIE PH21 1NU (01540 651377). B&B in 1827 Telford Manse and two timber s/c cottages in superb rural location. Ideal for many outdoor activities and good touring base. Dogs and children welcome. STB ★★★ [🐾]
e-mail: inshhouse@btinternet.com   website: www.kincraig.com/inshhouse

Kingussie (Inverness-shire)

Tourist centre on the River Spey 48 miles south of Inverness.

COLUMBA HOUSE HOTEL AND GARDEN RESTAURANT, MANSE ROAD, KINGUSSIE PH21 1JF (01540 661402). Quiet Highland retreat offering highest standards of hospitality, care and accommodation. Candlelit Garden Restaurant. Ground-floor rooms with own front doors, perfect for doggie holidays. STB ★★★ [pw! Pets £3 per night, £10 per week]
e-mail: myra@columbahousehotel.com   website: www.columbahousehotel.com

Kinlochbervie (Sutherland)

Village on north side of Loch Inchard.

THE KINLOCHBERVIE HOTEL, KINLOCHBERVIE, SUTHERLAND IV27 4RP (01971 521 275; Fax: 01971 521 438). Friendly, family-run hotel in one of the most stunning areas of North West Scotland. Supremely comfortable guest rooms from £30 pp for bed & breakfast.
e-mail: klbhotel@aol.com   website: www.kinlochberviehotel.com

Lochcarron (Ross-shire)

Village on north shore of Loch Carron 2 miles below the head of the loch. Known for its ties and tartans.

THE COTTAGE, STROMECARRONACH, LOCHCARRON WEST, STRATHCARRON. Small, stone-built Highland cottage, double bedroom, shower room, open plan kitchen/living room, fully equipped. Panoramic views over Loch Carron and the mountains. For further details please phone. MRS A.G. MACKENZIE, STROMECARRONACH, LOCHCARRON WEST, STRATHCARRON IV54 8YH (01520 722284) [🐾]
website: www.lochcarron.org

Loch Ness (Inverness-shire)

Home of 'Nessie', extending for 23 miles from Fort Augustus to south of Inverness.

JUSTINE HUDSON, WILDSIDE HIGHLAND LODGES, WILDSIDE, WHITEBRIDGE, INVERNESS IV2 6UN. (01456 486373; Fax: 01456 486371). Charming riverside lodges. Log fires and mountain views. Sleep 2 to 8 people. Pets welcome. Free fishing. STB ★★★★ Self-catering. [Pets £15 per booking].
e-mail: info@wildsidelodges.com   website: www.wildsidelodges.com

WILDERNESS COTTAGES. Self-catering cottages all around Loch Ness plus small selection of West coast properties. Pets welcome. Please see website for details or for a brochure contact: GORDON & CORINNE ROBERTS, ROEBUCK COTTAGE, ERROGIE IV2 6UH (01456 486358). [1 dog free, extra dogs £10 each per week] STB★★★/★★★★/★★★★★ SELF CATERING
e-mail: corinne@wildernesscottages.co.uk   website: www.wildernesscottages.co.uk

Nethy Bridge (Inverness-shire)

Popular Strathspey resort on River Nethy with extensive Abernethy Forest to the south. Impressive mountain scenery. Grantown-on-Spey 5 miles.

BALNAGOWAN MILL AND WOODLARK, NETHY BRIDGE. Comfortable, modern 3 bedroom cottages in secluded locations in the Cairngorms National Park. Woodland and riverside walks on the doorstep. Ideal for pets. Furnished to a high standard with full central heating. £250-£500 per week incl. of electricity and bed linen. VisitScotland ★★★/★★★★. ASSC MEMBER. Contact PAULA FRASER, 33 ARGYLE GROVE, DUNBLANE FK15 9DT (01786 824957) [🐾]
e-mail: paulajfraser@aol.com

MONDHUIE CHALETS & B&B, NETHY BRIDGE, INVERNESS-SHIRE PH25 3DF (01479 821062). Situated in the country between Aviemore and Grantown-on-Spey, two comfortable, self-catering chalets, or you can have Dinner, B&B in the house. A warm welcome awaits you. Pets welcome. Red squirrels seen daily. Free internet access[🐾]
e-mail: david@mondhuie.com   website: www.mondhuie.com

Poolewe (Ross-shire)

Village lying between Lochs Ewe and Maree with the river Ewe flowing through.

POOLEWE, WESTER ROSS. (01445 781765) Dogs welcome in N/S Bed & Breakfast. Convenient for local beaches and Torridon Mountains. Please phone or e-mail for further information. STB ★★★ B&B
e-mail: dgeorge@globalnet.co.uk   website: www.davidgeorge.co.uk

MR A. URQUHART, CROFTERS COTTAGES, 15 CROFT, POOLEWE IV22 2JY (01445 781 268). Two traditional cottages situated in a scenic and tranquil area, ideal for a "get away from it all" holiday. Comfortably furnished with all mod cons. [🐾]
e-mail: crofterscottages@btopenworld.com   website:www.crofterscottages.co.uk

Rhiconich (Sutherland)

Locality at the head of Loch Inchard on west coast of Sutherland District.

RHICONICH HOTEL, SUTHERLAND, N. W. HIGHLANDS IV27 4RN (01971 521224; Fax: 01971 521732). She's your best friend so why leave her at home, bring her to Rhiconich Hotel, she'll be made equally as welcome as you will. A place where we put service, hospitality and really fresh food as a priority, but why don't you come and see for yourself? For further details contact Ray Fish. STB ★★★ [🐾]
e-mail: rhiconichhotel@aol.com   website: www.rhiconichhotel.co.uk

Spean Bridge (Inverness-shire)

Village on River Spean at foot of Loch Lochy. Site of WWII Commando Memorial.

RIVERSIDE LODGES, INVERGLOY, SPEAN BRIDGE PH34 4DY (01397 712684). The ultimate Highland location. Three lodges, each sleep 6 in 12 acres of woodland garden on Loch Lochy. Free fishing. Open all year. Pets welcome. Brochure on request. [🐾]
e-mail: enquiries@riversidelodge.org.uk   website: www.riversidelodge.org.uk

CORRIEVIEW LODGES, SPEAN BRIDGE PH34 4DX (01397 712395). Two lodges 10 miles north of Fort William, an ideal base for couples, families (and dogs). Each has two bedrooms, and upstairs open-plan lounge/kitchen/dining area. Balcony with views to Nevis Mountain Range. VisitScotland ★★★★ [Pets £10 per week].
e-mail: fantasticviews@corrieviewlodges.com   website: www.corrieviewlodges.com

Tongue (Sutherland)

Village near north coast of Caithness District on east side of Kyle of Tongue.

BORGIE LODGE HOTEL, SKERRAY, TONGUE KW14 7TH (Tel & Fax: 01641 521332). Set in a secluded Highland glen lies Borgie Lodge. Try pony trekking, fishing and forest walks. Open fires and fine dining. STB ★★★★ [🐾]
e-mail: info@borgielodgehotel.co.uk   website: www.borgielodgehotel.co.uk

Whitebridge (Inverness-shire)

Hamlet in the heart of the Scottish Highlands, 4 miles from Loch Ness and 9 miles from Fort Augustus.

WHITEBRIDGE HOTEL, WHITEBRIDGE, SOUTH LOCH NESS IV2 6UN (01456 486226; Fax: 01456 486413). Peaceful location with magnificent mountain views and excellent walks. Friendly locals' bar with home-cooked food. 12 en suite rooms. B&B from £30pppn. AA ★★[🐾]
e-mail: info@whitebridgehotel.co.uk   website: www.whitebridgehotel.co.uk

Biggar

Small town set round broad main street. Gasworks museum, puppet theatre seating 100, street museum displaying old shop fronts and interiors. Peebles 13 miles.

CARMICHAEL COUNTRY COTTAGES, CARMICHAEL ESTATE, BY BIGGAR ML12 6PG (01899 308336; Fax: 01899 308481). Our stone cottages nestle in the woods and fields of our historic family-run estate. Ideal homes for families, pets and dogs. 15 cottages, 32 bedrooms. STB ★★/★★★★ Self catering. Open all year. £225 to £595 per week. [pw! ⛵]
e-mail: chiefcarm@aol.com   website: www.carmichael.co.uk/cottages

Harthill

Village 5 miles south-west of Bathgate.

MRS STEPHENS, BLAIRMAINS FARM, HARTHILL ML7 5TJ (01501 751278; Fax: 01501 753383). Attractive farmhouse on small farm. Ideal for touring. Children welcome. Bed and Breakfast from £20; weekly rates available. Reduced rates for children. Open all year. [⛵]
e-mail: heather@blairmains.freeserve.co.uk   website: www.blairmains.co.uk

Looking for holiday accommodation?
for details of hundreds of properties
throughout the UK visit:

www.holidayguides.com

The FHG Directory of Website Addresses
on pages 000-000 is a useful quick reference guide for
holiday accommodation with e-mail and/or website details

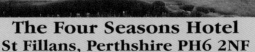

Aberfeldy

Small town standing on both sides of Uriar Burn near its confluence with the River Tay. Pitlochry 8 miles.

LOCH TAY LODGES, REMONY, ACHARN, ABERFELDY PH15 2HR (01887 830209). Enjoy hill walking, golf, sailing or touring. Salmon and trout fishing available. Log fires. Pets welcome. Walks along loch shore from house. STB ★★★ SELF CATERING in village close to Loch. For brochure, contact MRS P. W. DUNCAN MILLAR at above address. [🐾]
e-mail: remony@btinternet.com   website: www.lochtaylodges.co.uk

Killin

Village at confluence of Rivers Dochart and Lochay at head of Loch Tay.

GILL & DAVE HUNT, THE STEADING, WESTER LIX, KILLIN FK21 8RD (01567 820 990 & 07747 862641). Both cottages decorated and equipped to a high standard, and have washing machines, freezers, oven, Sky TV etc; one with sauna. Well-behaved pets welcome by arrangement. [Pets £15 per week for first pet, then £5 per pet for others]
e-mail: gill@westerlix.net   website: www.westerlix.net

Kinloch Rannoch

Village at foot of Loch Rannoch.

KILVRECHT CAMP SITE, KINLOCH RANNOCH, PERTHSHIRE (01350 727284; Fax: 01350 727811). Secluded campsite on a level open area in quiet, secluded woodland setting. Fishing available for brown trout on Loch Rannoch. Several trails begin from campsite. Please write, fax or telephone for further information. [🐾]
e-mail: hamish.murray@forestry.gsi.gov.uk

Pitlochry

Popular resort on River Tummel in beautiful Perthshire Highlands. Excellent golf, loch and river fishing. Famous for summer Festival Theatre; distillery, Highland Games.

JACKY & MALCOLM CATTERALL, "TULLOCH", ENOCHDHU, BY KIRKMICHAEL, PITLOCHRY PH10 7PW (01250 881404). Former farmhouse offers comfortable accommodation and good food. Peace and quiet guaranteed. B&B from £22; Dinner if required from £12. Haven for wildlife and dogs. Large paddock for walking. STB ★★★ [🐾]
e-mail: maljac@tulloch83.freeserve.co.uk   website: www.maljac.com

St Fillans

Village at foot of Lochearn, 5 miles west of Comrie.

THE FOUR SEASONS HOTEL, ST FILLANS PH6 2NF (01764 685333). Ideal holiday venue for pets and their owners. Spectacular Highland scenery, walking, fishing, watersports. Wonderful food. Full details on request. STB ★★★ Hotel, AA ★★★ and 2 Red Rosettes, Which? Hotel Guide, Johansens, Best Loved Hotels. [🐾]
e-mail: sham@thefourseasonshotel.co.uk   website: www.thefourseasonshotel.co.uk

Pet-Friendly
Pubs, Inns & Hotels
on pages xxx-xxx
Please note that these establishments may not feature in the main section of this book

Torlochan

"Torlochan", Isle of

Torlochan is a small working croft situated in the centre of the
Isle of Mull, with panoramic views over Loch na Keal.
An ideal place where you can relax and enjoy the
antics of our horses, Kuni Kuni pigs and a variety
of poultry, including white doves.
We have two comfortable and spacious log cabins which are
well fitted. They can sleep 4-6 people. We also have a smaller
log cabin for bed and breakfast.

Self catering from £330 per week. Short breaks from
£45 per night off season. B&B £22 per person.
A friendly welcome awaits you.
PETS FREE OF CHARGE

Mull

Torlochan

Situated in the centre of Mull, 20 minutes from Tobermory and 25 minutes from Craignure.

TORLOCHAN, GRULINE, ISLE OF MULL PA71 6HR (Tel & Fax: 01680 300380). Situated in centre of
Mull. Panoramic views over Loch na Keal. Croft of 33 acres, Two Log Cabins for self-catering and
en suite Bed & Breakfast. Friendly welcome awaits. [🐾]
e-mail: torlochan@btopenworld.com   website: www.torlochan.com

Orkney Islands

Kirkwall

Point of Ness Caravan & Camping Site • Stromness

Stromness is a small, picturesque town with impressive views of the hills of Hoy. The site is one
mile from the harbour in a quiet, shoreline location. Many leisure activities are available close
by, including fishing, sea angling, golf and a swimming & fitness centre. **For details contact:**
Department of Education & Recreation Services, Orkney Islands Council,
Kirkwall, Orkney KW15 1NY • Tel: 01856 873535 ext. 2404   Graded "Very Good" by VisitScotland

Kirkwall

*An old traditional stone built port and Orkney's second main town, situated on the south western tip of the mainland on the shores of
Hamnavoe.*

POINT OF NESS CARAVAN & CAMPING SITE, STROMNESS. The site is one mile from the harbour
in a quiet, shoreline location. Many leisure activities are available close by, including fishing, sea
angling, golf and a swimming & fitness centre. For details contact: DEPARTMENT OF EDUCATION
& RECREATION SERVICES, ORKNEY ISLANDS COUNCIL, KIRKWALL, ORKNEY KW15 1NY (01856
873535 ext. 2404).

🐾   Indicates that pets are welcome free of charge.

£   Indicates that a charge is made for pets: nightly or weekly.   **Symbols**

pw! Shows some special provision for pets; exercise facility, feeding or accommodation arrangement.

⌂   Indicates separate pets accommodation.

Breakish

Location 2 miles east of Broadford on the Isle of Skye.

TIGH HOLM COTTAGES, SCULAMUS MOSS, BREAKISH IV42 8QB (01471 820077). Two modern well-appointed cottages for four people. Five minutes' walk to shoreline with stunning views. Near Broadford, seven miles from Skye Bridge. [🐾]
e-mail: tigh.holm@byconnect.com   website: www.tigh-holm-cottges.com

Staffin

Crofting and fishing village on rocky coast around Staffin bay, 12 miles north of Portree.

IAN STRATTON & DOREEN HARBEN, GLENVIEW HOTEL, CULNACNOC, STAFFIN IV51 9JH (01470 562248). Traditional island house, ideally situated for exploring North East Skye. Comfortable en suite bedrooms. Restaurant renowned for fresh seafood and traditional home cooking. Pets most welcome. Which? Best B&B. [🐾]
e-mail: enquiries@glenviewskye.co.uk   website: www.glenviewskye.co.uk

Wales

Looking for Holiday Accommodation?

for details of hundreds of properties throughout the UK, visit our website

www.holidayguides.com

CAMPING & CARAVANNING CLUB (0845 130 7632). Visit one of our award-winning UK Club Sites. Our sites have dog walking areas for you and your dog to explore. A friendly welcome will be given to you and your pet on our sites, joining is great value for money. QUOTE REF NO 0716 website: www.campingandcaravanningclub.co.uk

RECOMMENDED COTTAGE HOLIDAYS. 1st choice for dream cottages at very competitive prices in all holiday regions of beautiful Britain. Pets welcome. All properties inspected. Free brochure - call 01751 475547.
website: www.recommended-cottages.co.uk

MR P.W. REES, "QUALITY COTTAGES', CERBID, SOLVA, HAVERFORDWEST, PEMBROKESHIRE SA62 6YE (01348 837871). Cottages set in all coastal areas, unashamed luxury, highest residential standards. Dishwashers, microwaves, washing machines. Log fires. Linen supplied. Pets welcome. [pw! 🐕]
website: www.qualitycottages.co.uk

Pet-Friendly
Pubs, Inns & Hotels
on pages 360-369
Please note that these establishments may not feature in the main section of this book

Please mention **Pets Welcome!**
when making enquiries about accommodation featured in these pages

Criccieth, Dulas Bay, Ffestiniog, Trearddur Bay

MR P.W. REES, "QUALITY COTTAGES', CERBID, SOLVA, HAVERFORDWEST, PEMBROKESHIRE SA62 6YE (01348 837871). Cottages set in all coastal areas, unashamed luxury, highest residential standards. Dishwashers, microwaves, washing machines. Log fires. Linen supplied. Pets welcome. [pw! ✝]
website: www.qualitycottages.co.uk

Bala

Natural touring centre for Snowdonia. Narrow gauge railway runs along side of Bala lake, the largest natural lake in Wales. Golf, sailing, fishing, canoeing.

TY GWYN - two-bedroomed luxury caravan in private grounds. Situated just two miles from Bala in beautiful country area, ideal for walking, sailing, fishing and canoeing. Only 30 miles from seaside. Contact: MRS A. SKINNER, TY GWYN, RHYDUCHAF, BALA LL23 7SD (01678 521267). [✝]

Barmouth

Modern seaside resort with two miles of sandy beaches. Surrounding hills full of interesting archaeological remains.

LAWRENNY LODGE, BARMOUTH LL42 1SU (01341 280466). Eight bedroom guest accommodation (seven en suite) overlooking the harbour and estuary and only five minutes from town centre. All rooms have TV and tea/coffee making facilities. Varied restaurant menu, residential licence and private car park. [✝]
e-mail: enquiries@lawrennylodge.co.uk   website: www.lawrennylodge.co.uk

PARC CAERELWAN, TALYBONT, BARMOUTH LL43 2AX (0800 136892 or 01341 247 236/891). Relax at our quiet, family-run holiday park. Caravan-bungalows and caravans at very affordable prices. Indoor heated pool, sauna etc. Shop, off-licence and launderette. Pets welcome. WTB ★★★★ [Pets £9 per week]
website: www.parccaerelwan.co.uk

ISLAWRFFORDD CARAVAN PARK, TAL-Y-BONT, GWYNEDD LL43 2BQ (01341 247269; Fax: 01341 242639). On the Snowdonia coastline, just north of Barmouth, our park offers a limited number of caravans for hire; touring caravan field and camping also available. Facilities include: shop, laundry, indoor heated pool, jacuzzi, sauna, bar, amusements, food bars. [Pets £2 per night, £25 perweek].
e-mail: info@islawrffordd.co.uk   website: www.islawrffordd.co.uk

Beaumaris

Elegant little town dominated by castle built by Edward I in 13th century. Museum of Childhood has Victorian toys and music boxes.

MR P.W. REES, "QUALITY COTTAGES', CERBID, SOLVA, HAVERFORDWEST, PEMBROKESHIRE SA62 6YE (01348 837871). Cottages set in all coastal areas, unashamed luxury, highest residential standards. Dishwashers, microwaves, washing machines. Log fires. Linen supplied. Pets welcome. [pw! 🐾]
website: www.qualitycottages.co.uk

Beddgelert

Village at confluence of Rivers Colwyn and Glaslyn, 12 miles from Caernarfon, 4 miles from Snowdon

COLWYN GUEST HOUSE, CAERNARFON ROAD, BEDDGELERT LL55 4UY (01766 890276). A charming well appointed 18th century Listed guest house in the heart of Snowdonia National Park. Pets welcome with well behaved owners. WTB ★★★ *GUEST HOUSE*. [Pets £2.50 per night]
e-mail: colwynguesthouse@tiscali.co.uk   website: www.beddgelertguesthouse.co.uk

SYGUN FAWR COUNTRY HOUSE, BEDDGELERT, GWYNEDD LL55 4NE (Tel & Fax: 01766 890258). All rooms en suite with tea/coffee facilities, hairdryer and radio alarm. Superb views. Four-course dinner using local produce, interesting wine list. Cosy bar, conservatory. Only a short walk from the village. [Pets £4 per night.]
e-mail: sygunfawr@aol.com   website: ww.sygunfawr.co.uk

Bodorgan

A rural area in South West Anglesey.

CROESO. Comfortable three-bedroomed house. Enclosed garden. Near beaches, common, forest. Fully equipped, bedding and electricity inclusive. Colour TV/video, microwave. Dogs and children welcome. £210-£390 per week. WTB ★★★ [🐾] Contact: MRS J. GUNDRY, FARMYARD LODGE, BODORGAN, ANGLESEY LL62 5LW (01407 840977).

Caernarfon

Historic walled town and resort, ideal for touring Snowdonia. Museums, Segontium Roman Fort, magnificent 13th century castle. Old harbour, sailing trips.

PLAS-Y-BRYN CHALET PARK, BONTNEWYDD, NEAR CAERNARFON LL54 7YE (01286 672811). Two miles from Caernarfon. It offers safety, seclusion and beautiful views of Snowdonia. Ideally positioned for touring. Well behaved pets always welcome. WTB ★★★★ [Pets £20 per week].
website: www.plasybrynholidayscaernarfon.co.uk

Criccieth

Popular family resort with safe beaches divided by ruins of 13th century castle. Salmon and sea trout fishing. Festival of Music and Arts in the summer.

MRS A. M. JONES, RHOS COUNTRY COTTAGES, CRICCIETH, PORTHMADOG LL52 0PB (01758 720047 or 0776 986 4642). Superb collection of secluded country cottages with private gardens. Private fishing and rough shooting by arrangement. Open all year. VisitWales ★★★★★ [🐾]
e-mail: cottages@rhos.freeserve.co.uk   website: www.rhos-cottages.co.uk

MRS ANN WILLIAMS, TYDDYN HEILYN, CHWILOG, CRICCIETH LL53 6SW (01766 810441). Comfortably renovated Welsh stone cottage. Double-glazed, centrally heated and enjoying mild Gulf Stream climate. Ample grounds with enclosed garden with doggy walk. One mile tree lined walk to beach. [🐾]

A warm welcome awaits you in comfortable self-catering cottages. Easily accessible to numerous attractions, or enjoy tranquillity of countryside. Short breaks available. Pets welcome. MRS M. WILLIAMS, GAERWEN FARM, YNYS, CRICCIETH, GWYNEDD LL52 0NU (01766 810324).[🐾]
e-mail: gaerwen@btopenworld.com

PARC WERNOL PARK, CHWILOG, PWLLHELI LL53 6SW (01766 810506). Peaceful and quiet, ideal for touring. Self-catering holidays – 1,2 & 3 bedroom cottages, 2 and 3 bedroom caravans and chalets. Colour brochure. [Pets £10 per week.]
website: www.wernol.com

MR P.W. REES, "QUALITY COTTAGES', CERBID, SOLVA, HAVERFORDWEST, PEMBROKESHIRE SA62 6YE (01348 837871). Cottages set in all coastal areas, unashamed luxury, highest residential standards. Dishwashers, microwaves, washing machines. Log fires. Linen supplied. Pets welcome. [pw! 🐾]
website: +

Dulas Bay

On north-east coast of Anglesey, between Amlwch and Moelfre.

MRS G. McCREADIE, DERI ISAF, DULAS BAY LL70 9DX (01248 410536; Mobile: 07721 374471). Victorian Country House in 20 acres of woodland, gardens and fields. Family, twin and double rooms, all en suite. Pets welcome. Stabling/grazing available. WTB ★★★★ Country House [Dogs £2.50 per night]
e-mail: mccreadie@deriisaf.freeserve.co.uk   website: www.angleseyfarms.com/deri.htm

Ffestiniog

Asmall village in Gwynedd, North Wales, lying south of Blaenau Ffestiniog, 9 miles east of Porthmadoc.

PLAS BLAENDDOL, LLAN FFESTINIOG LL41 4PH (01766 762406). Luxury self-catering on private estate in the heart of Snowdonia. Old Bell House sleeps up to 10 and is very suitable for pets. Central location for walking, mountain biking, rafting etc. [Pets £15 per week]
e-mail: snowhols@snowdoniasolutions.co.uk   website: www.plasblaenddol.co.uk

Harlech

Small stone-built town dominated by remains of 13th century castle. Golf, theatre, swimming pool, fine stretch of sands

MR P.W. REES, "QUALITY COTTAGES', CERBID, SOLVA, HAVERFORDWEST, PEMBROKESHIRE SA62 6YE (01348 837871). Cottages set in all coastal areas, unashamed luxury, highest residential standards. Dishwashers, microwaves, washing machines. Log fires. Linen supplied. Pets welcome. [pw! 🐾]
website: www.qualitycottages.co.uk

Llanddona

Village on Anglesey 3 miles north west of Beaumaris.

MR P.W. REES, "QUALITY COTTAGES', CERBID, SOLVA, HAVERFORDWEST, PEMBROKESHIRE SA62 6YE (01348 837871). Cottages set in all coastal areas, unashamed luxury, highest residential standards. Dishwashers, microwaves, washing machines. Log fires. Linen supplied. Pets welcome. [pw! 🐾]
website: www.qualitycottages.co.uk

Morfa Nefyn

Picturesque village 2 miles west of Nefyn.

MR P.W. REES, "QUALITY COTTAGES', CERBID, SOLVA, HAVERFORDWEST, PEMBROKESHIRE SA62 6YE (01348 837871). Cottages set in all coastal areas, unashamed luxury, highest residential standards. Dishwashers, microwaves, washing machines. Log fires. Linen supplied. Pets welcome. [pw! 🐾]
website: www.qualitycottages.co.uk

Porthmadog

Harbour town with mile-long Cob embankment, along which runs Ffestiniog Narrow Gauge Steam Railway to Blaenau Ffestiniog. Pottery, maritime museum, car museum. Good beaches nearby.

MR P.W. REES, "QUALITY COTTAGES', CERBID, SOLVA, HAVERFORDWEST, PEMBROKESHIRE SA62 6YE (01348 837871). Cottages set in all coastal areas, unashamed luxury, highest residential standards. Dishwashers, microwaves, washing machines. Log fires. Linen supplied. Pets welcome. [pw! 🐕]
website: www.qualitycottages.co.uk

Red Wharf Bay

Deep curving bay with vast expanse of sand, very popular for sailing and swimmin

MR P.W. REES, "QUALITY COTTAGES', CERBID, SOLVA, HAVERFORDWEST, PEMBROKESHIRE SA62 6YE (01348 837871). Cottages set in all coastal areas, unashamed luxury, highest residential standards. Dishwashers, microwaves, washing machines. Log fires. Linen supplied. Pets welcome. [pw! 🐕]
website: www.qualitycottages.co.uk

Trearddur Bay

Attractive holiday spot set amongst low cliffs on Holy Island, near Holyhead. Golf, sailing, fishing and swimming.

TREARDDUR HOLIDAY BUNGALOWS, LON ISALLT,TREARDDUR BAY, ANGLESEY LL65 2UP (01407 860494). Comfortable self-catering holiday bungalows sleeping 2-7 near Trearddur's lovely beaches. Locally, beautiful headland walks, fishing, golf and horse riding. Ideal location to explore Anglesey and the North Wales coast. Terms from £100-£580 per week.
e-mail: trearholiday@btconnect.com   website: www.holiday-bungalows.co.uk

CLIFF COTTAGES AND PLAS DARIEN APARTMENTS, TREARDDUR BAY LL65 2UR (01407 860789; Fax: 01407 861150). Fully equipped holiday cottages, sleeping 4/8 plus cot. Near sea. Indoor and outdoor heated pools. Colour television. Choice of centrally heated apartments or stone-built cottages. Own private leisure complex with bowls, saunas, snooker, table tennis; tennis courts. Adjacent golf course. [🐕]
website: www.plasdarien.com

Tywyn

Pleasant seaside resort, start of Talyllyn Narrow Gauge Railway. Sea and river fishing, golf.

WOODLANDS PARK. Delightful chalet where your pet can join in the fun of a family holiday. Phone us for more details. Mercedes and David Morgan. (01568 780912). [🐕]

MR P.W. REES, "QUALITY COTTAGES', CERBID, SOLVA, HAVERFORDWEST, PEMBROKESHIRE SA62 6YE (01348 837871). Cottages set in all coastal areas, unashamed luxury, highest residential standards. Dishwashers, microwaves, washing machines. Log fires. Linen supplied. Pets welcome. [pw! 🐕]
website: www.qualitycottages.co.uk

Visit the FHG website
www.holidayguides.com
for details of the wide choice of accommodation
featured in
the full range of FHG titles

Betws-y-Coed, Colwyn Bay

Looking for holiday accommodation?
for details of hundreds of properties
throughout the UK including
comprehensive coverage of all areas of Scotland try:
www.holidayguides.com

Tyn-y-Groes, Near Conwy

Homely Victorian stone cottage in picturesque Conwy valley. Mountain views. Enjoy walking, mountains, beaches, bird watching. Bodnant Gardens, RSPB reserve and Conwy castle, harbour and marina close by. Victorian Llandudno, Betws-y-Coed, Anglesey, Caernarfon and Snowdon easy distance. Good local food and pubs. Enclosed garden, patio furniture. Parking. Gas fired central heating. Lounge with gas fire, dining room, kitchen, utility.

Brongain

Two double bedded rooms, one small single; blankets/duvet provided. Bathroom with bath, shower, toilet and basin. Colour TV, electric cooker, fridge, microwave, washing machine and tumbler dryer. Terms £210-£325; heating, electricity included. Linen extra. Pets welcome. Open all year. No children under five years..

Mrs G. Simpole, 105 Hay Green Road, Terrington-St-Clement, King's Lynn, Norfolk PE34 4PU

Tel: 01553 828897
Mobile: 0798 9080665

Sychnant Pass House
Sychnant Pass Road, Conwy LL32 8BJ
Tel: 01492 596868 • Fax: 01492 585486
e-mail: bre@sychnant-pass-house.co.uk
www.sychnant-pass-house.co.uk

Millie and Maisie, our lovely collies, would love to welcome your four-legged friends to their home in the hills above Conwy. Sychnant Pass House is a lovely Victorian House set in two acres with a little pond and stream running through it. Step out of our garden and straight onto Snowdonia National Park land where you can walk for miles with your dogs. Just over two miles from the beach and one-and-a-half miles from Conwy, it is an ideal base from which to tour Wales. All our rooms are en suite, our garden rooms have French windows opening into the garden which are ideal for pets. We have a lovely sitting room that you can share with your best friends after dinner which is served in our informal, friendly restaurant, doggie bags are always available. Your four-legged friends and their folk are most welcome here. *Bed & Breakfast from £50 per person*

Hafod Country House

Trefriw, Llanrwst, Conwy Valley LL27 0RQ

Relax in this centuries-old farmhouse. Exceptional food (top grade in the last three WTB inspections), warm hospitality, and a strong sense of style, combine to create a special stay for guests.

As well as some 2½ acres of grounds, there are walks in the woods, beside waterfalls, or along the banks of the River Conwy, where you can exercise your dog.

WTB ★★★★ *Country House*   • AA ★★★★
Guest Accommodation

Tel: 01492 640029 • Fax: 01492 641351
e-mail: hafod@breathemail.net • www.hafod-house.co.uk

Please note

All the information in this book is given in good faith in the belief that it is correct. However, the publishers cannot guarantee the facts given in these pages, neither are they responsible for changes in policy, ownership or terms that may take place after the date of going to press. Readers should always satisfy themselves that the facilities they require are available and that the terms, if quoted, still apply.

TREFRIW • CONWY VALLEY SNOWDONIA

Secluded cottages, log fire and beams
Dogs will love it – a place of their dreams
Plenty of walks around mountains and lakes
Cosy and tranquil – it's got what it takes.
It's really a perfect holiday let
For up to 2-7 people, plus their pet(s).

Apply: Mrs Williams
Tel: 01724 733990 or 07711 217 448 (week lets only)

MR P.W. REES, "QUALITY COTTAGES', CERBID, SOLVA, HAVERFORDWEST, PEMBROKESHIRE SA62 6YE (01348 837871). Cottages set in all coastal areas, unashamed luxury, highest residential standards. Dishwashers, microwaves, washing machines. Log fires. Linen supplied. Pets welcome. [pw! 🐂]
website: www.qualitycottages.co.uk

SEASIDE COTTAGES. MANN'S, SHAW'S AND SNOWDONIA TOURIST SERVICES (01758 701 702). Large selection of self-catering seaside and country cottages, bungalows, farmhouses, caravans etc. offering superb, reasonably priced accommodation for owners and their pets. Please telephone for brochure.
websites: www.mannsholidays.com   www.shaws-holidays.co.uk   www.snowdoniatourist.com

Betws-y-Coed

Popular mountain resort in picturesque setting where three rivers meet. Trout fishing, craft shops, golf, railway and motor museums, Snowdonia National Park Visitor Centre. Nearby Swallow Falls are famous beauty spot.

MRS MORRIS, TY COCH FARM-TREKKING CENTRE, PENMACHNO, BETWS-Y-COED LL25 0HJ (01690 760248). Hill farm in Wales. TV, teamaking, en suite. Set in National Park/Snowdonia. Very quiet and well off the beaten track. A great welcome and good food. Many return visits. £20 B&B. [🐂]
e-mail: cindymorris@tiscali.co.uk

SUMMER HILL NON-SMOKERS' GUEST HOUSE, BETWS-Y-COED LL24 0BL (01690 710306). Quiet location, overlooking river. 150 yards from main road and shops. En suite and standard rooms, tea-making facilities, residents' lounge. Ideal for walkers. B&B from £22-£30. [Pets £1.50 per night.]

Colwyn Bay

Lively seaside resort with promenade amusements. Attractions include Mountain Zoo, Eirias Park; golf, tennis, riding and other sports. Good touring centre for Snowdonia. The quieter resort of Rhos-on-Sea lies at the western end of the bay.

NORTH WALES HOLIDAYS, BRON-Y-WENDON AND NANT-Y-GLYN HOLIDAY PARKS, WERN ROAD, LLANDDULAS, COLWYN BAY LL22 8HG (01492 512903/512282). Cottages with sea views at Bron-Y-Wendon or chalets, cottages and coach house in picturesque valley at Nant-Y-Glyn. 16 units in total. WTB ★★★/★★★★/★★★★★ [Pets £10 per week].
e-mail: stay@northwales-holidays.co.uk   website: www.northwales-holidays.co.uk

---

Looking for holiday accommodation?
for details of hundreds of properties
throughout the UK including
comprehensive coverage of all areas of Scotland try:
www.holidayguides.com

Conwy

One of the best preserved medieval fortified towns in Britain on dramatic estuary setting. Telford Suspension Bridge, many historic buildings, lively quayside (site of smallest house in Britain). Golf, pony trekking, pleasure cruises.

BRONGAIN, TY'N-Y-GROES, CONWY. Homely Victorian stone cottage, picturesque Conwy Valley. Snowdonia Mountain views. Enjoy lakes, mountains, walking, bird watching, beaches, Bodnant, RSPB, Conwy Castle. £210-£325. Contact: MRS G. M. SIMPOLE, 105 HAYGREEN ROAD, TERRINGTON ST CLEMENT, KINGS LYNN, NORFOLK PE34 4PU (01553 828897; Mobile: 0798 9080 665) [pw! 🐾]

SYCHNANT PASS HOUSE, SYCHNANT PASS ROAD, CONWY LL32 8BJ (01492 596868: Fax: 01492 585486). A lovely Victorian House set in two acres with a little pond and stream. Step out of our garden and straight onto Snowdonia National Park land. Walk for miles with your dogs. All rooms en suite. B&B from £50. AA ★★★★★ and Rosette. [🐾]
e-mail: bre@sychnant-pass-house.co.uk   website: www.sychnant-pass-house.co.uk

Conwy Valley

Fertile valley with wood and moor rising on both sides. Many places of interest in the area.

HAFOD COUNTRY HOUSE, TREFRIW, CONWY VALLEY LL27 0RQ (01492 640029; Fax: 01492 641351). Small informal hotel. Over two acres of grounds. Excellent food in restaurant. Short breaks available. Well behaved dogs welcome. Non-smoking. WTB ★★★★ Country House AA ★★★★ Guest Accommodation [Pets £5 per night, £30 per week]
e-mail: hafod@breathemail.net　　　　　　　website: www.hafod-house.co.uk

Secluded cottages with log fire and beams. Dogs will love it. Plenty of walks around mountains and lakes. For 2 - 7 people plus their pet(s). MRS WILLIAMS (01724 733990 or 07711 217 448) week lets only. [🐾]

Llandyrnog

Village 4 miles east of Denbigh.

PENTRE MAWR COUNTRY HOUSE, LLANDYRNOG LL16 4LA (01824 790732) Ancestral home of 400 years with woodland, park and riverside meadows, within easy reach of Chester and coast. Heated swimming pool. All rooms en suite. Pets most welcome. AA ★★★★★ and Dinner Award [🐾]
e-mail: bre@sychnant-pass-house.co.uk　　　　　www.pentremawrhouse.co.uk

Llangollen

Famous for International Music Eisteddfod held in July. Plas Newydd, Valle Crucis Abbey nearby. Standard gauge steam railway; canal cruises; ideal for golf and walking.

THE HAND AT LLANARMON, LLANARMON D.C., CEIRIOG VALLEY, NEAR LLANGOLLEN LL20 7LD (01691 600666). Standing in the glorious Ceiriog Valley, The Hand at Llanarmon radiates charm and character. 13 comfortable en suite bedrooms, log fires, and fabulous food, a wonderful base for most country pursuits. [🐾]
e-mail: reception@thehandhotel.co.uk   website: www.TheHandHotel.co.uk

Rhos-on-Sea

Popular resort at east end of Penrhyn Bay, adjoining Colwyn Bay to the north-west.

SUNNYDOWNS HOTEL, 66 ABBEY ROAD, RHOS-ON-SEA, CONWY LL28 4NU (01492 544256; Fax: 01492 543223). A 3 star luxury family hotel just two minutes' walk to beach and shops. All rooms en suite with colour TV, video & satellite channels, tea/coffee facilities and central heating. Hotel has bar, pool room and car park. A non-smoking hotel. [pets £4.50 per night]
e-mail: sunnydowns-hotel@tinyworld.co.uk　　　website: www.hotelnorthwales.co.uk

---

🐾　　Indicates that pets are welcome free of charge.

£　　Indicates that a charge is made for pets: nightly or weekly.

pw!　Shows some special provision for pets; exercise facility, feeding or accommodation arrangement.

⌂　　Indicates separate pets accommodation.

SIR JOHN'S HILL FARM HOLIDAY COTTAGES
Laugharne, Carmarthenshire SA33 4TD

Old Stables Cottage • Tel: 01994 427001

Wren Cottage & The Farmhouse • Tel: 01994 427667

In one of the finest locations in West Wales with spectacular views of coast and countryside, the three very comfortable cottages are the perfect place for a relaxing break. Here at Sir Johns Hill Farm we specialise in dog-friendly holidays and aim to make their holiday just as good as yours. They will have a great time at the farm which is well away from the main road, and there are lots of great country walks and long sandy beaches nearby too.

www.sirjohnshillfarm.co.uk

Relax in The Farmhouse, one of six traditional cottages set within two acres of secure gardens at **MAERDY COTTAGES**. From this idyllic centre enjoy local walks and famous gardens and discover the beautiful coast and countryside of Carmarthenshire. Each cottage is equipped to give maximum comfort...two cottages are fully wheelchair accessible, and all are ideal for families of all ages. Home cooked evening meals available. Open all year. Brochure and enquiries:

Maerdy Cottages, Taliaris, Llandeilo, Carmarthenshire SA19 7DA • 01550 777448

WTB ★★★★ - ★★★★★ e-mail: enquiries@maerdyholidaycottages.co.uk • www.maerdyholidaycottages.co.uk

---

Pen Y Banc Cottage, Llanfihangel ar Arth, Llandysul
Lovely isolated, cosy bungalow on owner's organic farm. Ideal for walking and touring Brecon Beacons, Pembrokeshire Coastal Footpath and Black Mountains. Sleeps 4, one double and one twin bedroom. Oil fired, two oven Rayburn cooker in beamed open plan sitting/dining room. All heating/electric costs included in price. Brochure available. Non smoking.

Penny & Graeme Whitaker • Tel: 01559 384515 • Fax: 01559 389034
Gwhit34925@aol.com • www.solutions-factory.co.uk/penybanccottage

---

The Diplomat Hotel Felinfoel Road, Aelybryn, Llanelli SA15 3PJ
Tel: 01554 756156 • Fax: 01554 751649 • AA/WTB ★★★

The Diplomat Hotel offers a rare combination of charm and character, with excellent well appointed facilities to ensure your comfort. Explore the Gower Peninsula and the breathtaking West Wales coastline. Salmon & trout fishing, horse riding, golf, and motor racing at Pembrey are all within reach.

e-mail: reservations@diplomat-hotel-wales.com • www.diplomat-hotel-wales.com

---

Other specialised holiday guides from FHG

Recommended **INNS & PUBS** OF BRITAIN

Recommended **COUNTRY HOTELS** OF BRITAIN

Recommended **SHORT BREAK HOLIDAYS** IN BRITAIN

The GOLF GUIDE, Where to Play, Where to Stay IN BRITAIN & IRELAND

COAST & COUNTRY HOLIDAYS

SELF-CATERING HOLIDAYS IN BRITAIN

BED & BREAKFAST STOPS

CARAVAN & CAMPING HOLIDAYS

CHILDREN WELCOME! Family Holiday & Days Out Guide

BRITAIN'S BEST LEISURE & RELAXATION GUIDE

Published annually: available in all good bookshops or direct from the publisher:
FHG Guides, Abbey Mill Business Centre, Seedhill, Paisley PA1 1TJ
Tel: 0141 887 0428 • Fax: 0141 889 7204
E-mail: admin@fhguides.co.uk • Web: www.holidayguides.com

Laugharne

Village on the River Taf estuary 4 miles south of St Clears, burial place of Dylan Thomas.

SIR JOHN'S HILL FARM HOLIDAY COTTAGES, LAUGHARNE SA33 4TD. OLD STABLES COTTAGE 01994 427001, WREN COTTAGE & THE FARMHOUSE 01994 427667. Specialising in dog-friendly holidays, three very comfortable cottages. In one of the finest locations in West Wales, with spectacular views, lots of great country walks, and long sandy beaches nearby. [pw! £15 per week.] website: www.sirjohnshillfarm.co.uk

Llandeilo

Town on River Towy, 14 miles east of Carmarthen.

MAERDY COTTAGES, TALIARIS, LLANDEILO, CARMARTHENSHIRE SA19 7DA (01550 777448). Six traditional cottages set within two acres of secure gardens. Each cottage is equipped to give maximum comfort, two cottages are fully wheelchair accessible, and all are ideal for families of all ages. Home cooked evening meals available. Open all year. WTB ★★★★ - ★★★★★. [First pet free, others £5 per night, £20 per week].
e-mail: enquiries@maerdyholidaycottages.co.uk　　website: www.maerdyholidaycottages.co.uk

Llandysul

Small town on River Teifi, 12 miles north of Carmarthen.

PENNY AND GRAEME WHITAKER, PEN Y BANC COTTAGE, LLANFIHANGEL AR ARTH, LLANDYSUL SA39 9JX (01559 384515; Fax: 01559 389034). Lovely, isolated, cosy cottage sleeping four in one double and one twin bedroom. Ideal for walking/touring Brecon Beacons, Black Mountains and Pembrokeshire's Coastal Path. Non smoking. Brochure available. [🐾]
e-mail: Gwhit34925@aol.com　　　　　website: www.solutions-factory.co.uk/penybanccottage

Llanelli

Village on the River Taf estuary, 10 mile north-west of Swansea.

THE DIPLOMAT HOTEL, FELINFOEL ROAD, AELYBRYN, LLANELLI SA15 3PJ (01554 756156; Fax: 01554 751649). Privately owned and operated with warmth and generous hospitality. The Diplomat Hotel offers a rare combination of charm and character with excellent well appointed facilities to ensure your comfort and convenience. WTB/AA ★★★ [Pets £5 per night]
e-mail: reservations@diplomat-hotel-wales.com　　website: www.diplomat-hotel-wales.com

Please mention **Pets Welcome!**
when making enquiries about accommodation featured in these pages

Pet-Friendly
Pubs, Inns& Hotels
on pages 360-369
Please note that these establishments may not feature in the main section of this book

MR P.W. REES, "QUALITY COTTAGES', CERBID, SOLVA, HAVERFORDWEST, PEMBROKESHIRE SA62 6YE (01348 837871). Cottages set in all coastal areas, unashamed luxury, highest residential standards. Dishwashers, microwaves, washing machines. Log fires. Linen supplied. Pets welcome. [pw! 🐕] website: www.qualitycottages.co.uk

Aberporth

Popular seaside village offering safe swimming and good sea fishing. Good base for exploring Cardigan Bay coastline.

MR P.W. REES, "QUALITY COTTAGES', CERBID, SOLVA, HAVERFORDWEST, PEMBROKESHIRE SA62 6YE (01348 837871). Cottages set in all coastal areas, unashamed luxury, highest residential standards. Dishwashers, microwaves, washing machines. Log fires. Linen supplied. Pets welcome. [pw! 🐕] website: www.qualitycottages.co.uk

Aberystwyth

Resort at mouth of Rivers Rheidol and Ystwyth on Cardigan Bay, 82 miles from Cardiff.

THE HAFOD HOTEL, DEVIL'S BRIDGE, ABERYSTWYTH SY23 3JL (01970 890232; Fax: 01970 890394). At the head of the Mynach Falls, perfect for exploring some of Wales' most spectacular scenery. Most bedrooms enjoy superb views. Restaurant and a delightful Victorian Tea Room. WTB ★★, AA ★★★ [🐕] pw!
e-mail: hafodhotel@btconnect.com   website: www.thehafodhotel.co.uk

Ciliau Aeron

Village in undulating country just inland from the charming Cardigan Bay resorts of New Quay and Aberaeron. New Quay 12 miles, Aberaeron 6.

MR P.W. REES, "QUALITY COTTAGES', CERBID, SOLVA, HAVERFORDWEST, PEMBROKESHIRE SA62 6YE (01348 837871). Cottages set in all coastal areas, unashamed luxury, highest residential standards. Dishwashers, microwaves, washing machines. Log fires. Linen supplied. Pets welcome. [pw! 🐕] website: www.qualitycottages.co.uk

Lampeter

Small market town on River Teifi, 20 miles north east of Carmarthen.

JEFF & SUE RICE, GAER COTTAGES, CRIBYN, LAMPETER SA48 7LZ (Tel & Fax: 01570 470275). Nine luxury stone cottages in the unspoilt West Wales countryside; eight acre grounds; indoor pool; games room; play area; animals. Coast/mountains. Extensive disabled facilities. £120 - £975 per week. Welcome Host Gold Award, Holiday Care Award. [Pets £15 per week]
e-mail: gaer@bigfoot.com   website: www.selfcateringinwales.co.uk

MR P.W. REES, "QUALITY COTTAGES', CERBID, SOLVA, HAVERFORDWEST, PEMBROKESHIRE SA62 6YE (01348 837871). Cottages set in all coastal areas, unashamed luxury, highest residential standards. Dishwashers, microwaves, washing machines. Log fires. Linen supplied. Pets welcome. [pw! 🐕] website: www.qualitycottages.co.uk

Llangrannog

Pretty little seaside village overlooking a sandy beach. Superb cliff walk to NT Ynys Lochtyn, a secluded promonto

MR P.W. REES, "QUALITY COTTAGES', CERBID, SOLVA, HAVERFORDWEST, PEMBROKESHIRE SA62 6YE (01348 837871). Cottages set in all coastal areas, unashamed luxury, highest residential standards. Dishwashers, microwaves, washing machines. Log fires. Linen supplied. Pets welcome. [pw! 🐕] website: www.qualitycottages.co.uk

Looking for holiday accommodation?

for details of hundreds of properties throughout the UK visit:

www.holidayguides.com

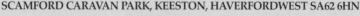

Whitland

MR P.W. REES, "QUALITY COTTAGES', CERBID, SOLVA, HAVERFORDWEST, PEMBROKESHIRE SA62 6YE (01348 837871). Cottages set in all coastal areas, unashamed luxury, highest residential standards. Dishwashers, microwaves, washing machines. Log fires. Linen supplied. Pets welcome. [pw! 🐕]
website: www.qualitycottages.co.uk

Bosherton

Village 4 miles south of Pembroke, bordered by 3 man-made lakes, a haven for wildlife and covered in water lilies in early summer.

MR P.W. REES, "QUALITY COTTAGES', CERBID, SOLVA, HAVERFORDWEST, PEMBROKESHIRE SA62 6YE (01348 837871). Cottages set in all coastal areas, unashamed luxury, highest residential standards. Dishwashers, microwaves, washing machines. Log fires. Linen supplied. Pets welcome. [pw! 🐕]
website: www.qualitycottages.co.uk

Broad Haven

Inlet one mile north of St Govan's Head..

PEMBROKESHIRE NATIONAL PARK. Sleeps 6 + cot. Three-bedroom fully furnished Holiday House. Walking distance sandy beaches and coastal footpath. £140 to £350 per week. MRS L.P. ASHTON, 10 ST LEONARDS ROAD, THAMES DITTON, SURREY KT7 0RJ (020-8398 6349). [🐕]
e-mail: lejash@aol.com   website: www.33timberhill.com

Croes Goch

Hamlet 6 miles north east of St Davids

MR P.W. REES, "QUALITY COTTAGES', CERBID, SOLVA, HAVERFORDWEST, PEMBROKESHIRE SA62 6YE (01348 837871). Cottages set in all coastal areas, unashamed luxury, highest residential standards. Dishwashers, microwaves, washing machines. Log fires. Linen supplied. Pets welcome. [pw! 🐕]
website: www.qualitycottages.co.uk

Croft

place description to follow

CROFT FARM & CELTIC COTTAGES, CROFT NEAR CARDIGAN SA43 3NT (01239 615179). Featured in Daily Mail. Stone barn conversions with luxury indoor heated pool, sauna, spa pool and gym. Colourful gardens, indoor and outdoor play areas. WTB ★★★★★ *SELF CATERING*. Pets welcome. [Pets £28 per week, pw!]
e-mail: info@croft-holiday-cottages.co.uk   website: www.croft-holiday-cottages.co.uk

Fishguard

Small town at end of Fishguard Bay

IVYBRIDGE, DRIM MILL, DYFFRYN, GOODWICK SA64 0FT (01348 875366, Fax: 01348 872338). Stay at Ivybridge, swim in our heated pool or relax in our comfortable guest lounge. En suite rooms, home cooking, large off road carpark. Pets welcome! [Pets £5 per stay].
e-mail: ivybridge5366@aol.com   website: www.ivybridgeleisure.co.uk

Haverfordwest

Administrative and shopping centre for the area; ideal base for exploring National Park. Historic town of narrow streets; museum in castle grounds; many fine buildings.

PEDWAR GWYNT, SQUARE & COMPASS, HAVERFORDWEST SA62 5JJ (01348 837032). Claire and Keith invite you and your dogs to their small, family-owned Bed and Breakfast, within 2 miles of the Pembrokeshire coast between St Davids and Fishguard. £25-£35 pppn. [🐾]
website: www.pedwargwynt.co.uk

NOLTON HAVEN FARM COTTAGES, NOLTON HAVEN, HAVERFORDWEST SA62 3NH (01437 710200). Quality beachfront cottages, sleep 2-6, adjacent sandy beach. Well equipped. Open all year. Winter breaks. [Pets £10 per week].
e-mail: info@havencottages.co.uk   website: www.havencottages.co.uk

CLARE HALLETT, KEESTON HILL COTTAGE, KEESTON, HAVERFORDWEST SA62 6EJ (01437 710440). Two apartments sleeping 4/5 each in cottage with garden. A short walk to our family-run restaurant/bar. Open all year. From £220 to £405 per week. Heating, electricity and linen included. [🐾]
e-mail: enquiries@keestonhillcottage.co.uk

NOLTON HAVEN QUALITY COTTAGES. Sleep 2 to 14. 3,4 & 5 star cottages, some with sea view, some just 30 yards from the beach. Children and pets welcome. Farmhouse B&B also available - seven bedrooms, some en suite. WTB ★★★/★★★★/★★★★★ Self-Catering. Contact: JIM & JOYCE CANTON, NOLTON HAVEN FARMHOUSE, NOLTON HAVEN, HAVERFORDWEST SA62 6NH (01437 710263).
e-mail: PW5@noltonhaven.com   website: www.noltonhaven.com

SCAMFORD CARAVAN PARK, KEESTON, HAVERFORDWEST SA62 6HN (Tel & Fax: 01437 710304). 25 luxurious caravans (shower, fridge, microwave, colour TV). Peaceful park near lovely sandy beaches. Super playground. Launderette. Five touring pitches, hook-ups. Modern shower block. Pets welcome.WTB ★★★★ Holiday Park.
e-mail: holidays@scamford.com   website: www.scamford.com

Lawrenny

Village near River Cresswell estuary, 8 miles south-west of Narberth

MRS VIRGINIA LORT PHILLIPS, KNOWLES FARM, LAWRENNY SA68 0PX (01834 891221). Come and relax with us in our lovely south-facing farmhouse. Listen to the silence and spoil yourselves and your dogs whilst discovering the delights of hidden Pembrokeshire. Walk along the shores of the Estuary which surrounds our organic farm. B&B from £28 to £34 pppn, Dinner on request. WTB ★★★ [First pet free, others £2 per pet per night.]
e-mail: ginilp@lawrenny.org.uk   website: www.lawrenny.org.uk

Llanteg

Hamlet 4 miles south of Whitland.

TONY & JANE BARON, LLANTEGLOS ESTATE, LLANTEG, NEAR AMROTH SA67 8PU (01834 831677 /831371). Self-contained Woodland Lodges. Sleep 6. Children's play area. Licensed bar & entertainment. Visitor attractions. Call for brochure. WTB ★★★★ Self Catering [Pets £5 per night, £30 per week.]
e-mail: llanteglosestate@supanet.com   website: www.llanteglos-estate.com

Llechryd

Village on the A484 3 miles from Cardigan.

CASTELL MALGWYN COUNTRY HOUSE HOTEL, LLECHRYD, CARDIGAN SA43 2QA (01239 682382) Well behaved dogs welcome. Set on the banks of the River Teifi in large grounds. Excellent food in Lily's Restaurant. [🐕]
e-mail: reception@malgwyn.co.uk   website: www.castellmalgwyn.co.uk

Newgale

On St Bride's Bay 3 miles east of Solva. Long beach where at exceptionally low tide the stumps of a submerged forest may be seen.

MR P.W. REES, "QUALITY COTTAGES', CERBID, SOLVA, HAVERFORDWEST, PEMBROKESHIRE SA62 6YE (01348 837871). Cottages set in all coastal areas, unashamed luxury, highest residential standards. Dishwashers, microwaves, washing machines. Log fires. Linen supplied. Pets welcome. [pw! 🐕]
website: www.qualitycottages.co.uk

Newport

Small town at mouth of the River Nyfer, 9 miles south west of Cardigan. Remains of 13th-century castle.

MR P.W. REES, "QUALITY COTTAGES', CERBID, SOLVA, HAVERFORDWEST, PEMBROKESHIRE SA62 6YE (01348 837871). Cottages set in all coastal areas, unashamed luxury, highest residential standards. Dishwashers, microwaves, washing machines. Log fires. Linen supplied. Pets welcome. [pw! 🐕]
website: www.qualitycottages.co.uk

St Brides

Located on St Bride's Bay 7 miles north west of Milford Haven.

ST BRIDE'S BAY COTTAGES (01437 720027). Select quality self-catering holidays in North Pembrokeshire. Sleep 2-11. Short Breaks available. Pets welcome. VisitWales graded.
website: www.sbbc.uk.com

St Davids

Smallest cathedral city in Britain, shrine of Wales' patron saint. Magnificent ruins of Bishop's Palace. Craft shops, farm parks and museums; boat trips to Ramsey Island.

FFYNNON DDOFN, LLANON, LLANRHIAN, NEAR ST DAVIDS. Comfortable, well-equipped cottage with panoramic coastal views. Sleeps 6. Fully carpeted with central heating. Large games room. Open all year. Pets welcome free of charge. Brochure on request from: MRS B. REES WHITE, BRICKHOUSE FARM, BURNHAM RD, WOODHAM MORTIMER, MALDON, ESSEX CM9 6SR (01245 224611). [🐕]
website: www.ffynnonddofn.co.uk

MARION LOVERING, TREMYNYDD FACH, ST DAVID'S SA62 6DB (01437 721677; Fax: 01437 720308). A working sheep farm, whose fields extend down to the sea. Farm B&B (in cosy cottages) and Self-catering (in farmhouse and chalet) available. Spectacular and unspoilt stretch of coastal path abounding with rare species of plants and wildlife. [Pets £10 per week]
e-mail: sheepdog_training@lineone.net   website: www.sheepdogtraining.co.uk

MR P.W. REES, "QUALITY COTTAGES', CERBID, SOLVA, HAVERFORDWEST, PEMBROKESHIRE SA62 6YE (01348 837871). Cottages set in all coastal areas, unashamed luxury, highest residential standards. Dishwashers, microwaves, washing machines. Log fires. Linen supplied. Pets welcome. [pw! 🐕]
website: www.qualitycottages.co.uk

FELINDRE COTTAGES, PORTHGAIN, ST DAVID'S, PEMBROKESHIRE SA62 5BH (01348 831220). Self-catering cottages with panoramic sea and country views. Five minutes' walk from Coastal Path, picturesque fishing village of Porthgain and a great pub! Peaceful location. Short breaks available. One well-behaved dog welcome, except August. WTB graded. [pw! £10 per week]
e-mail: steve@felindrecottages.co.uk   website: www.felindrecottages.co.uk

Saundersfoot

Popular resort and sailing centre with picturesque harbour and sandy beach. Tenby 3 miles

VINE COTTAGE, THE RIDGEWAY, SAUNDERSFOOT SA69 9LA (01834 814422). Coastal village outskirts. Sandy beaches and coast path nearby. Award-winning garden for guests' and dogs' relaxation and exercise. Non-smoking throughout. WTB/AA ★★★★ [pw! Pets £5 per stay.]
e-mail: enquiries@vinecottageguesthouse.co.uk   website: www.vinecottageguesthouse.co.uk

Solva

Picturesque coastal village with sheltered harbour and excellent craft shops. Sailing and watersports; sea fishing, long sandy beach.

MRS M. JONES, LOCHMEYLER FARM GUEST HOUSE, LLANDELOY, PEN-Y-CWM, NEAR SOLVA, ST DAVIDS, PEMBROKESHIRE SA62 6LL (01348 837724; Fax: 01348 837622). Welcome Host Gold Award. 12 en suite luxury bedrooms, four in the cottage suites adjacent to the house. All bedrooms non-smoking, with TV, video and refreshment facilities. Children 14 years and over welcomed. WTB ★★★★★ *FARM*, AA◆◆◆◆◆ [pw! 🐕]

MR P.W. REES, "QUALITY COTTAGES', CERBID, SOLVA, HAVERFORDWEST, PEMBROKESHIRE SA62 6YE (01348 837871). Cottages set in all coastal areas, unashamed luxury, highest residential standards. Dishwashers, microwaves, washing machines. Log fires. Linen supplied. Pets welcome. [pw! 🐕]
website: www.qualitycottages.co.uk

Tenby

Popular resort with two wide beaches. Fishing trips, craft shops, museum. Medieval castle ruins, 13th-century church. Golf, fishing and watersports; boat trips to nearby Caldy Island with monastery and medieval church.

MR P.W. REES, "QUALITY COTTAGES', CERBID, SOLVA, HAVERFORDWEST, PEMBROKESHIRE SA62 6YE (01348 837871). Cottages set in all coastal areas, unashamed luxury, highest residential standards. Dishwashers, microwaves, washing machines. Log fires. Linen supplied. Pets welcome. [pw! 🐕]
website: www.qualitycottages.co.uk

Whitland

Village 6 miles east of Narberth. Whitland Abbey 2 km.

MRS ANGELA COLLEDGE, GWARMACWYDD FARM, LLANFALLTEG, WHITLAND SA34 0XH (01437 563260). Country estate with six character stone cottages, fully furnished and equipped. All linen and electricity included; heated for year-round use. WTB ★★★★ [pw! Pets £10 per week]
website: www.davidsfarm.com

Please note

All the information in this book is given in good faith in the belief that it is correct. However, the publishers cannot guarantee the facts given in these pages, neither are they responsible for changes in policy, ownership or terms that may take place after the date of going to press. Readers should always satisfy themselves that the facilities they require are available and that the terms, if quoted, still apply.

Caer Beris Manor

GWESTY
★★★
HOTEL

★★★

Family-owned three star Country House Hotel set in 27 acres of parkland. Free salmon and trout fishing on River Wye (two rods) and on River Irfon. Superb walking and touring. 18 hole Golf Course nearby. Excellent cuisine.
All rooms en suite with telephone, TV and tea making.
DOGS WELCOME!
DB&B £67pppn; £402 weekly; B&B £54.50pppn.
**Mrs Katharine Smith, Caer Beris Manor, Builth Wells
Powys LD2 3NP • Tel: 01982 552601 • Fax: 01982 552586
e-mail: caerberis@btconnect.com • www.caerberis.co.uk**

• ERWOOD, BUILTH WELLS LD2 3SZ • Tel: 01982 560680 •

Situated in secluded grounds with glorious views of the beautiful Wye Valley. Attractive spacious rooms (one en suite, two sharing guests' own bathroom), have TV, drinks tray, fridge, wash basin. Bacon and sausage from locally reared pigs, free range eggs and home made preserves for breakfast. Two bedrooms with double aspect. FHG Diploma Winner 2004.

OLD VICARAGE e-mail: linda@oldvicwyevalley.co.uk • www.oldvicwyevalley.co.uk   WTB ★★ Farm

Pet-Friendly
Pubs, Inns& Hotels
on pages 360-369
Please note that these establishments may not feature in the main section of this book

Visit the FHG website
www.holidayguides.com
for details of the wide choice of accommodation
featured in
the full range of FHG titles

Garthmyl, Hay-on-Wye, Knighton, Llandrindod Wells, Llanfair Caereinion

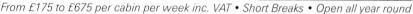

Llanwrtyd Wells, Machynlleth, Presteigne, Rhayader

Readers are requested to mention this FHG
guidebook when seeking accommodation

Builth Wells

Old country town in lovely setting on River Wye amid beautiful hills. Lively markets; host to Royal Welsh Agricultural Show

MRS KATHARINE SMITH, CAER BERIS MANOR, BUILTH WELLS LD2 3NP (01982 552601; Fax: 01982 552586). Family-owned country house hotel set in 27 acres of parkland. Free salmon and trout fishing; golf nearby, superb walking and touring. All rooms en suite. WTB/AA ★★★. [Pets £5 per night, £30 per week].
e-mail: caerberis@btconnect.com   website: www.caerberis.co.uk

MRS LINDA WILLIAMS, OLD VICARAGE, ERWOOD, BUILTH WELLS LD2 3SZ (01982 560680). Situated in secluded grounds with glorious views of the beautiful Wye Valley. Attractive spacious rooms (one en suite, two sharing guests' own bathroom), have TV, drinks tray, fridge, wash basin. Bacon and sausage from locally reared pigs, free range eggs and home made preserves for breakfast. Two bedrooms with double aspect. WTB ★★ Farm, FHG Diploma Winner 2004.[🐾]
e-mail: linda@oldvicwyevalley.co.uk   website: www.oldvicwyevalley.co.uk

Garthmyl

Situated on A483 between Welshpool and Newtown in unspoilt countryside.

Self-catering log cabins set in 30 acres of unspoilt woodland teeming with wildlife. Central heating, colour TV, microwave etc. Pets welcome in certain cabins. From £175-£675 per cabin per week breaks. Apply PENLLWYN LODGES, GARTHMYL, POWYS SY15 6SB (Tel & Fax: 01686 640269) for colour brochure. [Pets £15 per stay]
e-mail: daphne.jones@onetel.net   website: www.penllwynlodges.co.uk

Hay-on-Wye

Small market town at north end of Black Mountains, 15 miles north-east of Brecon.

MRS E. BALLY, LANE FARM, PAINSCASTLE, BUILTH WELLS LD2 3JS (Tel & Fax: 01497 851605). 17th century farm in rural Radnorshire, five miles Hay-on-Wye. Wonderful walking country. Self-catering apartments sleeping 2-14. A warm welcome for you and your pet(s). WTB ★★★ [🐾]
e-mail: lanefarm@onetel.com

Knighton

Town on River TEme, 14 miles west of Ludlow.

Situated three miles from Knighton - self-contained, fully furnished, ground floor accommodation. One twin bedroom + sofa bed in lounge. No smoking. Pets welcome. Open all year - short breaks available. B&B also available. Apply: ROGER & SUE MORRIS, GRAIG COTTAGE, LLANFAIRWATERDINE, KNIGHTON LD7 1TS (01547 529542). VisitWales ★★★. [🐾]
website: thegardenlodgeatgraigcottage.co.uk

Llandrindod Wells

Popular inland resort, Victorian spa town, excellent touring centre. Golf, fishing, bowling, boating and tennis. Visitors can still take the waters at Rock Park Gardens.

THE PARK HOUSE MOTEL, CROSSGATES, LLANDRINDOD WELLS LD1 6RF (01597 851201). In three acres, amidst beautiful countryside near Elan Valley. Static caravans, touring pitches and fully equipped motel units. Licensed restaurant, bar. Pets welcome. [Pets £3 per night, £20 per week. Guide dogs free). [🐾]
e-mail: barr560@btinternet.com   website: www.parkmotel.co.uk

Llanfair Caereinion

Small town on River Banwy, 8 miles west of Welshpool.

MRS ANN REED, MADOG'S WELLS, LLANFAIR CAEREINION, WELSHPOOL SY21 0DE (Tel & Fax: 01938 810446). Three self-catering bungalows, wheelchair accessible. Open all year. WTB 3/4/5 STARS *SELF-CATERING*. [🐾]
e-mail: info@madogswells.co.uk   website: www.madogswells.co.uk

Llangurig

Village on River Wye, 4 miles south-west of Llanidloes. Ideal walking countryside.

MRS J. BAILEY, GLANGWY, LLANGURIG, LLANIDLOES SY18 6RS (01686 440697). Bed, breakfast and evening meals in the countryside. Plenty of walking locally. Also caravan and campsite. Prices on request. [🐕]

Llanwrtyd Wells

The smallest town in Britain full of olde worlde charm and surrounded by spectacular mountain scenery. Ideal for walking, cycling and pony trekking. Llandovery 10 miles.

FOREST CABIN BARGAIN BREAKS (02920 754887). Arguably as like the Canadian Rockies as you will find in this country. High in the majestic mountains and forests of Mid-Wales. Enjoy the sheer exhilaration of mountain air so pure it sparkles like champagne! Pets very welcome. 3 nights from £83, 7 nights from £199.
website: www.victoriawells.org.uk

Machynlleth

Attractive old town with half timbered houses. Ideal for hillside rambles and pony trekking.

PETS WELCOME at The Wynnstay Hotel. Award-winning food, wine and beer. Glorious countryside and miles of sandy beaches. Masses to do and see. WTB/AA ★★★. Good Food Guide & Good Beer Guide Recommended, Les Routiers "Best Wine List in Britain". (01654 702941). [Pets free in kennels, £5 one-off charge in rooms]
e-mail: info@wynnstay-hotel.com   website: www.wynnstay-hotel.com

Presteigne

Attractive old town with half timbered houses. Ideal for hillside rambles and pony trekking.

MRS R. L. JONES, UPPER HOUSE, KINNERTON, NEAR PRESTEIGNE LD8 2PE (01547 560207). Cosy cottage two miles from Offa's Dyke. Central heating, washing machine, microwave, colour TV, inglenook, woodburner, linen included. Sleeps 4 plus cot. Children and pets welcome. WTB 4 Stars. [🐕].

Rhayader

Small market town on River Wye north of Builth Wells. Popular for angling and pony trekking

TYN-Y-CASTELL SELF-CATERING CHALET. Spectacular scenery and magical walks; around the lakes, through the woods, up on the hills. A doggy paradise and the folks will love it too! Our delightful chalet is warm and comfortable and in a lovely rural location. JOAN MORGAN (01982 560402) [🐕]
e-mail: oldbedw@lineone.net   website: www.rhayader.co.uk/tynycastell

OAK WOOD LODGES, LLWYNBAEDD, RHAYADER LD6 5NT (01597 811422). Luxurious self-catering log cabins with spectacular views of the Elan Valley and Cambrian Mountains. Walking, pony trekking, mountain biking, fishing and bird watching in idyllic surroundings. WTB ★★★★ Self-catering. [Pets £20 per week, £13 per short break; additional dogs half price].
website: www.oakwoodlodges.co.uk

🐕   Indicates that pets are welcome free of charge.

£   Indicates that a charge is made for pets: nightly or weekly.

pw!   Shows some special provision for pets; exercise facility, feeding or accommodation arrangement.

◻   Indicates separate pets accommodation.

Symbols

Egerton Grey

Porthkerry, Vale of Glamorgan, Near Cardiff CF62 3BZ
Tel: 01446 711666 • Fax: 01446 711690
e-mail: info@egertongrey.co.uk • www.egertongrey.co.uk ★★★★

AA ★★★

A recommended centre from which to explore the lovely and uncrowded Gower Peninsula and the Brecon Beacons, this stylish and distinguished country house was opened as a small and luxurious hotel in 1988. Only 10 miles from Cardiff, it is set in a secluded, wooded valley in seven acres of gardens, with views down to Porthkerry Park and the sea. The excellent facilities accorded guests include exquisitely furnished bedrooms (all with private bathrooms), two dining rooms, library and magnificent Edwardian drawing room. Only a short stroll away is a well-maintained country park with an 18-hole pitch and putt course. The cuisine is outstanding and dining here by candlelight is a memorable experience. Recommended by many national and international hotel and restaurant guides. *Taste of Wales Cuisine Award*

BEST WESTERN ABERAVON BEACH HOTEL

Modern seafront hotel. A warm Welsh welcome awaits you and your pets. 2 miles of flat promenade and a pet friendly beach. Pets Paradise!! And for you..... comfortable rooms, fine cuisine, leisure centre and many local attractions. Tel: 01639 884949
Neath Port Talbot, Swansea Bay SA12 6QP • www.aberavonbeach.com

AA ★★★

The Wye Valley Hotel • www.wyevalleyhotel.co.uk

WTB ★★

Tintern, Near Chepstow, South Wales NP16 6SQ

Homely hotel in the heart of the Wye Valley, just a short stroll from historic Tintern Abbey. Splendid base for touring. Well furnished en suite rooms. Dogs welcome by arrangement.
Tel: 01291 689441 • Fax: 01291 689440 • e-mail: info@wyevalleyhotel.co.uk

Cwrt-y-Gaer in the Vale of Usk and Wye Valley

One, four or more dogs welcome FREE. Three self-catering units in well converted stone Welsh Longhouse, set in old hilltop fort in 20 acres with fine views across to mountains. Quiet area with good access to many places of interest. Good walking. Open all year. Brochure from **Sue & John Llewellyn, Cwrt-y-Gaer, Wolvesnewton, Chepstow, Monmouthshire NP16 6PR**
Tel: (01291) 650700 • E-mail: john.llewellyn11@btinternet.com
All units are WTB ★★★. One unit is Grade 1 access for the disabled.

www.cwrt-y-gaer.co.uk

CASTLE NARROWBOATS CHURCH ROAD WHARF, GILWERN NP7 0EP (01873 830001). The Monmouthshire & Brecon Canal in South Wales. Discover the beauty of Wales onboard one of our excellent narrowboats. 2-8 berth boats, short breaks available. Pets welcome. For a free colour brochure call Castle Narrowboats:
website: www.castlenarrowboats.co.uk

Abergavenny

Historic market town at south-eastern gateway to Brecon Beacons National Park. Pony trekking, leisure centre; excellent touring base for Vale of Usk.

THE HALF MOON INN, LLANTHONY, NEAR ABERGAVENNY NP7 7NN (01873 890611). Friendly 17th-Century Hotel. Good food and real ale. Wonderful scenery of Black Mountains. Good base. Walking, pony trekking. B&B accommodation. Dogs welcome. [🐾]
e-mail: halfmoon@llanthony.wanadoo.co.uk

Please mention **Pets Welcome!**
when making enquiries about accommodation featured in these pages

Cardiff

City and port at mouth of River Taff. Capital of Wales.

EGERTON GREY COUNTRY HOUSE HOTEL, PORTHKERRY, BARRY, NEAR CARDIFF, VALE OF GLAMORGAN CF62 3BZ (01446 711666; Fax: 01446 711690). Magnificently preserved country house set in seven acres in a secluded valley 10 miles from Cardiff. Ideal for touring South Wales. WTB ★★★★ Hotel, AA ★★★ [🐾]
e-mail: info@egertongrey.co.uk   website: www.egertongrey.co.uk

Gower

Britain's first designated Area of Outstanding Natural Beauty with numerous sandy beaches and lovely countryside to explore.

CULVER HOUSE HOTEL, PORT EYNON, GOWER SA3 1NN (01792 390755). Small, friendly Hotel with fabulous breakfast and quality service. Peacefully situated, with superb coast and countryside. En suite, sea views. WTB ★★ Country Hotel. [Pets £2 per night.]
website: www.culverhousehotel.co.uk

Mumbles

Seaside resort of Swansea to west and north west of Mumbles Head.

MUMBLES & SWANSEA. Seafront ground floor flat. Well-equipped modern conveniences. Ideal for beaches, countryside and local amenities. Personally supervised. Plenty of dog walks! WTB ★★★★. MRS JEAN GRIERSON, 112 MUMBLES ROAD, BLACKPILL, SWANSEA SA3 5AS (01792 402278). [🐾]

Swansea

*Second largest city in Wales with a wide variety of leisure activities and excellent shopping.*e

BEST WESTERN ABERAVON BEACH HOTEL, NEATH PORT TALBOT, SWANSEA BAY SA12 6QP (01639 884949). Modern seafront hotel. A warm Welsh welcome awaits you and your pets. 2 miles of flat promenade and a pet friendly beach. Pets Paradise!! And for you..... comfortable rooms, fine cuisine, leisure centre and many local attractions. AA ★★★.[🐾]
website: www.aberavonbeach.com

Tintern

Village on River Wye, 4 miles North of Chepstow.

BARRY & SUE COOKE, THE WYE VALLEY HOTEL, TINTERN, NEAR CHEPSTOW NP16 6SQ (01291 689441; Fax: 01291 689440). Homely hotel in the heart of the Wye Valley, just a short stroll from historic Tintern Abbey. Splendid base for touring. Well furnished en suite rooms. Dogs welcome by arrangement. WTB ★★.
e-mail: info@wyevalleyhotel.co.uk   website: www.wyevalleyhotel.co.uk

Wye Valley

Scenic area, ideal for relaxation.

MR & MRS J. LLEWELLYN, CWRT-Y-GAER, WOLVESNEWTON, CHEPSTOW NP16 6PR (01291 650700). 1, 4 or more dogs welcome free. Self-catering, attractively converted stone buildings of Welsh Longhouse. 20 acres, super views of Usk Vale. Brochure. Three units (one suitable for disabled). WTB ★★★, Welcome Host Gold Award. [pw! 🐾]
e-mail: john.llewellyn11@btinternet.com   website: www.cwrt-y-gaer.co.uk

www.holidayguides.com

NARROWBOATS

Holidays with Horses

A selection of accommodation where horse and owner/rider can be put up
at the same address – if not actually under the same roof!
We would be grateful if readers making enquiries and/or bookings
from this supplement would mention **Pets Welcome!**

England

Cornwall

CELIA HUTCHINSON,
CARADON COUNTRY COTTAGES, EAST TAPHOUSE, NEAR LISKEARD PL14 4NH
(Tel & Fax: 01579 320355)
e-mail: celia@caradoncottages.co.uk   website: www.caradoncottages.co.uk
Luxury cottages in the heart of the Cornish countryside. Ideal centre for exploring Devon and
Cornwall, coast and moor and Eden Project. Central heating and log burners for cosy off-
season breaks. Meadow and paddock (enclosed). Stabling available.

Cumbria

FARLAM HALL HOTEL
BRAMPTON CA8 2NG.
(016977 46234; Fax: 016977 46683)
e-mail: farlam@relaischateaux.com • website: www.farlamhall.co.uk
Standing in four acres of gardens, with its own lake, Farlam Hall offers fine quality cuisine and
individually decorated guest rooms. Ideal touring centre for the Lakes, Borders and hadrian's
Wall. AA Three Stars Inspectors' Choice and Two Rosettes, Relais & Chateaux.

Durham

MRS P A BOOTH,
IVESLEY EQUESTRIAN CENTRE, IVESLEY, WATERHOUSES DH7 9HB.
(0191 373 4324; Fax: 0191 373 4757)
e-mail: ivesley@msn.com • website: www.ridingholidays-ivesley.co.uk

Beautifully furnished comfortable country house set in 220 acres in Durham but very quiet and rural. Excellent dog exercising facilities. En suite bedrooms. Excellent food. Licensed. Fully equipped Equestrian Centre adjacent.

Oxfordshire

JUNE AND GEORGE COLLIER
55 NETHERCOTE ROAD, TACKLEY, KIDLINGTON, OXFORD OX5 3AT
(01869 331255; mobile: 07790 338225)
e-mail: colliers.bnb@virgin.net   website: www.colliersbnb.co.uk

An ideal base for riding - superb network of Bridleways. Stop-over for Claude Duval route. Close to Blenheim. Regular train and bus service. Local Hostelries serve excellent food. ETC ★★★

Somerset

LEONE & BRIAN MARTIN,
RISCOMBE FARM HOLIDAY COTTAGES, EXFORD,
EXMOOR NATIONAL PARK TA24 7NH
(Tel: 01643 831480)
website: www.riscombe.co.uk (with up-to-date vacancy info.)

Four self-catering stone cottages in the centre of Exmoor National Park. Excellent walking and riding country. Dogs and horses welcome. Open all year. VB ★★★★

WESTERMILL FARM
EXFORD, MINEHEAD TA24 7NJ
(01643 831238; Fax: 01643 831216)
e-mail: pw@westermill.com   website: www.westermill.com

Cottages (Disabled Catergory 2) in grass paddocks. Ideal for children. Stabling and fields for horses. Wonderful for dogs and owners. Separate campsite by river.

Suffolk

MRS JANE BREWER,
LODGE COTTAGE, LAXFIELD ROAD, CRATFIELD, HALESWORTH IP19 0QG
(01986 798830 or 07788 853884)
e-mail: janebrewer@ukonline.co.uk

Pretty 16C thatched cottage retaining some fine period features. Sleeps 4. Pets welcome. Fenced garden. One mile from village. 30 minutes to Southwold and coast. Rural, quiet and relaxing. Brochure.

East Yorkshire

PAWS-A-WHILE
KILNWICK PERCY, POCKLINGTON YO42 1UF
(01759 301168; Mobile: 07711 866869)
e-mail: paws.a.while@lineone.net • website: www.pawsawhile.net

Small family B & B set in forty acres of parkland twixt York and Beverley. Golf, walking, riding. Pets and horses most welcome. Brochure available. ETC ★★★★

South Yorkshire

**PENNINE EQUINE HOLIDAY COTTAGES
COTE GREEN FARM, WORTLEY, SHEFFIELD
(0114 284 7140)
website: www.pennine-equine.co.uk**

Two comfortably furnished cottages attached to main stable building (each sleeps 6/8). Dogs not allowed, but kennels available. Livery and stabling for visitors' horses. 3-mile cross country course within grounds. Riding lessons available. Ample parking for trailers, horse boxes etc. Contact: Bromley Farm, Wortley, Sheffield S35 7DE

Scotland

Dumfries & Galloway

**RUSKO HOLIDAYS,
GATEHOUSE OF FLEET, CASTLE DOUGLAS DG7 2BS
(01557 814215)
e-mail: info@ruskoholidays.co.uk • website: www.ruskoholidays.co.uk**

Spacious, traditional farmhouse and three charming, cosy cottages near beaches, hills and forest park. Lots of off-road riding amid stunning scenery. Stabling and grazing available for your own horse. Beautiful walking and riding country, fishing and tennis. Rates £225-£1329. STB ★★ to ★★★★

Wales

Powys

**MRS E. BALLY
LANE FARM, PAINSCASTLE, BUILTH WELLS LD2 3JS
(Tel & Fax: 01497 851605)
e-mail: lanefarm@onetel.com**

Self-Catering apartments sleeping 2-14. Nine good stables and ample grazing in the heart of rural Radnorshire with wonderful open riding. Some cross-country jumps. WTB ★★★★

Visit the FHG website
www.holidayguides.com
for details of the wide choice of accommodation
featured in the full range of FHG titles

Winalot

At Winalot, we firmly believe that a hearty walk rounds off a good meal for all members of the family - be they two of four legged - which is why we have launched a nationwide campaign to find the best walks in the UK in conjunction with the launch of our new Winalot Roasts.

New Winalot Roasts with Gravy offers dogs the great taste of a roast every day. It's a nutritionally balanced meal which provides comfort, taste, tradition and energy - perfect fuel for a good walk!

Launched by Tim Vincent and his dog Ruby in September, the Winalot Walkies campaign will be judged by Tim to find Britain's Best Walks. Tim loves to get out and about with his dog and enjoy the Welsh country air. He says: 'Walking Ruby is a big part of my day when I go home. I really miss her when I'm in America. Walking with Ruby is a great way for us to bond, especially playing fetch. It teaches her to always come back and is great fun for both of us!"

Walkies Campaign

Peter Neville, Animal Behaviour Therapist confirms the benefits of going on a good walk, he believes it's essential to a good quality of life for owner and dog.

"Fresh air, aerobic exercise, stretching your muscles and expanding your lungs all while enjoying scenery on a regular basis, helps keep us in a good balanced mood and better equipped to deal with the relentless demands of modern life.

"**'Those who play together stay together'** and the more time and effort we invest in helping our dogs to express their natural behaviours in a playful cooperative partnership with us, the closer our relationship will become. Cuddles and fuss are great when we are home from the walk, but out in the fields, owner and dog working and playing together is what really cements that family bond.

"**So a good long walk with the dog gives both dog and owner a huge feel good factor...**exercising, socialising, mood restoring, fun and the sense of co-operating and interacting together as owner and dog have done for thousands of years."

So if you have a favourite walk in your area log onto www.winalot-dog.co.uk/walkies, before the 12th November for your chance of winning a weekend break to a dog friendly hotel, a trophy and a year's supply of Winalot Roasts for your faithful friend. The winner of the Winalot Walkies campaign will be featured in the next edition of the Pets Welcome Guide out next spring.

PURINA

winalot®

APPROVED DOG FRIENDLY

ENGLAND

BERKSHIRE

UNCLE TOM'S CABIN
Hills Lane, Cookham Dean, Berkshire (01628 483339).
Dogs allowed throughout.
Pet Regulars: Flossie and Ollie (Old English Sheepdog). Free dog biscuit pub.

THE GREYHOUND (known locally as 'The Dog')
The Walk, Eton Wick, Berkshire (01753 863925).
Dogs allowed throughout the pub.
Pet Regulars: Harvey (Retriever), retrieves anything, including Beer mats. Tully - German Shepherd.

THE OLD BOOT
Stanford Bingley, Berkshire (01189 744292).
Pets welcome in bar and garden area.
Pet Regulars: Resident dog Skip - Black Labrador.

THE TWO BREWERS
Park Street, Windsor, Berkshire (01753 855426).
Dogs allowed, public and saloon bars.
Pet Regulars: Molly (Newfoundland), Bear (Black Labrador), Rufus (Springer Spaniel), Rosie (Chocolate Labrador), Lilly (English Bulldog), Molly (Fox Terrier), McIntosh (Highland Terrier) and Lulu & Paddy (Cocker Spaniels).

BUCKINGHAMSHIRE

WHITE HORSE
Village Lane, Hedgerley, Buckinghamshire SL2 3UY (01753 643225).
Dogs allowed at tables on pub frontage, beer garden (on leads), public bar.

FROG AT SKIRMETT
Skirmett, Henley-on-Thames, Buckinghamshire RG9 6TG (01491 638996)
Dogs welcome, pet friendly.

GEORGE AND DRAGON
High Street, West Wycombe, Buckinghamshire HP14 3AB (01494 464414)
Pet friendly.

CAMBRIDGESHIRE

YE OLD WHITE HART
Main Street, Ufford, Peterborough, Cambridgeshire (01780 740250).
Dogs allowed in non-food areas.

CHESHIRE

THE GROSVENOR ARMS
Chester Road, Aldford, Cheshire CH3 6HJ (01244 620228)
Pet friendly.
Pet Regulars: resident dog "Sadie" (Labrador).

DRIFTWOOD SPARS HOTEL
Trevaunance Cove, St Agnes, Cornwall (01872 552428).
Dogs allowed everywhere except the restaurant.
Pet Regulars: Buster (Cornish Labrador cross with a Seal) - devours anything.

JUBILEE INN
Pelynt, Near Looe, Cornwall PL13 2JZ (01503 220312).
Dogs allowed in all areas except restaurant; accommodation for guests with dogs.

THE MILL HOUSE INN
Trebarwith Strand, Tintagel, Cornwall PL34 0HD (01840 770200).
Pet friendly.

THE MOLESWORTH ARMS HOTEL
Molesworth Street, Wadebridge, Cornwall PL27 7DP (01208 812055).
Dogs allowed in all public areas.
Pet Regulars: Murthy West (Collie) and Max West (Black Lab).

THE BRITANNIA INN
Elterwater, Ambleside, Cumbria LA22 9HP (015394 37210).
Dogs allowed in all areas except dining room and residents' lounge.
Pet Friendly.

STAG INN
Dufton, Appleby, Cumbria (017683 51608).
Dogs allowed in non-food bar, beer garden, village green plus cottage.
Pet Regulars: Sofie (Labrador) and Jeanie (Terrier).

WATERMILL INN
School Lane, Ings, Near Staveley, Kendal, Cumbria (01539 821309).
Dogs allowed in beer garden, Wrynose bottom bar.
Pet Regulars: Blot (sheepdog), Finn (mongrel) and Pub dogs Shelley and Scarlet (German Shepherds).
Owners cannot walk dogs past pub, without being dragged in! Biscuits and water provided.

THE GEORGE HOTEL
Commercial Road, Tideswell, Near Buxton, Derbyshire SK17 8NU (01298 871382).
Dogs allowed in snug and around the bar, water bowls provided.

DOG AND PARTRIDGE COUNTRY INN & MOTEL
Swinscoe, Ashbourne, Derbyshire (01335 343183).
Dogs allowed throughout, except restaurant.
Pet Regulars: Include Mitsy (57); Rusty (Cairn); Spider (Collie/GSD) and Rex (GSD).

DEVONSHIRE ARMS
Peak Forest, Near Buxton, Derbyshire SK17 8EJ (01298 23875)
Pet friendly.

A useful index of towns/counties appears at the back of this book

DEVON

Julie and Shaun invite you to **The Trout & Tipple**
Dogs welcome, bowls of water and treats available on request. Children welcome.
Non-smoking dining room and games room. Real Ales include
locally brewed Jail Ale and Dartmoor Best. Lunch on Sunday.
Parkwood Road, Tavistock, Devon PL19 0JS
Tel: 01822 618886   www.troutandtipple.co.uk

THE SHIP INN
Axmouth, Devon EX12 4AF (01297 21838).
A predominantly catering pub, so dogs on a lead please.
Pet Regulars: Kym (Boxer), Soxy (cat). Also 2 Japanese Quail, 2 Cockatiels and 2 Rabbits.

BRENDON HOUSE
Brendon, Lynton, North Devon EX35 6PS (01598 741206).
Dogs very welcome and allowed in tea gardens, guest bedrooms by arrangement.
Owner's dogs - Drummer, Piper and Angus (Labradors).

THE BULLERS ARMS
Chagford, Newton Abbot, Devon (01647 432348).
Dogs allowed throughout pub, except dining room/kitchen. "More than welcome".

CROWN AND SCEPTRE
2 Petitor Road, Torquay, Devon TQ1 4QA (01803 328290).
Dogs allowed in non-food bar, family room, lounge. All dogs welcome.
Owner's dogs: Two Jack Russells - Scrappy Doo and Minnie Mouse.

THE JOURNEY'S END INN
Ringmore, Near Kingsbridge, South Devon TQ7 4HL (01548 810205).
Dogs allowed throughout the pub.

THE ROYAL OAK INN
Dunsford, Near Exeter, Devon EX6 7DA (01647 252256).
Dogs allowed in bars, beer garden, accommodation for guests with dogs.
Pet Regulars: Kizi. Resident Dogs - Connie and Posie.

THE POLSHAM ARMS
Lower Polsham Road, Paignton, Devon (01803 558360).
Dogs allowed throughout the pub, must be kept on lead.
Pet Regulars: Patch, owner brings his supply of dog biscuits, and Bracken (German Shepherd).

THE SEA TROUT INN
Staverton, Near Totnes, Devon TQ9 6PA (01803 762274).
Dogs welcome in lounge and public bar, beer garden.
Pet Regulars: Tess (resident dog - spaniel).

Readers are requested to mention this FHG
guidebook when seeking accommodation

THE DEVONSHIRE INN
Sticklepath, Okehampton, Devon EX20 2NW (01837 840626).
Dogs allowed in non-food bar, car park, beer garden, family room and guest rooms.
Pet Regulars: Clarrie and Rosie (Terriers).

THE TROUT & TIPPLE
(A386 - Tavistock to Okehampton Road), Parkwood Road, Tavistock,
Devon PL10 0JS (01822 618886)
Dogs welcome at all times in bar, games room and patio.
Pet regulars include: Connor and Fenrhys (Black Labradors) - sometimes misbehave. Ollie (Black Lab) -
always after food. Border, Chaos and Mischief (Border Collies), Snoopy (Rhodesian Ridgeback) likes his
beef dinners. Also, our own dog - Dave (Lurcher).

DORSET

THE ANVIL HOTEL
Sailsbury Road, Pimperne, Blandford, Dorset DT11 8UQ (01258 453431).
Pets allowed in bar, lounge and bedrooms.

THE SQUARE AND COMPASS
Swanage, Dorset BH19 3LF (01929 439229).
Well-behaved dogs allowed - but beware of the chickens!

DRUSILLA'S INN
Wigbeth, Horton, Dorset (01258 840297).
Well-behaved dogs welcome.

DURHAM

MOORCOCK INN
Hill Top, Eggleston, Teesdale, County Durham DL12 9AU (01833 650395).
Pet friendly.

TAP AND SPILE
27 Front Street, Framwellgate Moor, Durham DH1 5EE (0191 386 5451).
Dogs allowed throughout the pub.

THE ROSE TREE
Low Road West, Shincliff, Durham DH1 2LY (0191-386 8512).
Pets allowed in bar area and garden.
Pet Regulars: "Benson" (Boxer) and "Oliver" (King Charles).

THE SEVEN STARS
High Street North, Shincliff, Durham (0191-384 8454).
Dogs welcome in bar area only.

ESSEX

WHITE HARTE
The Quay, Burnham-on-Crouch, Essex CM0 8AS (01621 782106).
Pets welcome.
Pet Regulars: Resident dog "Tilly" (Collie).

THE OLD SHIP
Heybridge Basin, Heybridge, Maldon, Essex (01621 854150).
Dogs allowed downstairs only, on lead.

GLOUCESTERSHIRE

THE OLD STOCKS HOTEL

The Square, Stow on the Wold, Gloucestershire GL54 1AF (01451 830666).
Dogs allowed in the beer garden, accommodation for dogs and their owners also available.
Pet Regulars: Ben (Labrador) enjoys bitter from the drip trays and Casey (Doberman) often gets carried out as he refuses to leave.

GREATER LONDON

THE PHOENIX

28 Thames Street, Sunbury on Thames, Middlesex (01932 785358).
Dogs allowed on lead in beer garden, family room.

THE TIDE END COTTAGE

Ferry Road, Teddington, Middlesex (0208 977 7762).
Dogs allowed throughout the pub.
Pet Regulars: Mimi (Labrador), Toffee (Terrier), Gracie (Guide Dog) and Fiona.

HAMPSHIRE

THE SUN

Sun Hill, Bentworth, Alton, Hampshire GU34 5JT (01420 562338)
Pets welcome throughout the pub.
Pet Regulars: Willow (Collie), Millie (Setter), Hazel and Purdey (Jack Russells) and "Dilweed" the cat.

HIGH CORNER INN

Linwood, Near Ringwood, Hampshire BH24 3QY (01425 473973).
Dogs, and even horses, are catered for here.

THE CHEQUERS

Ridgeway Lane, Lower Pennington, Lymington, Hants (01590 673415).
Dogs allowed in non-food bar, outdoor barbecue area (away from food).
Pet Regulars: Rusty Boyd - parties held for him. Resident pet - D'for (Labrador).

THE VICTORY

High Street, Hamble-le-Rice, Southampton, Hampshire (023 80 453105).
Dogs allowed.
Pet Regulars: Chester (Boxer).

HERTFORDSHIRE

THE BLACK HORSE

Chorley Wood Common, Dog Kennel Lane, Rickmansworth, Herts (01923 282252).
Dogs very welcome and allowed throughout the pub, on a lead.

THE RED LION

Chenies Village, Rickmansworth, Hertfordshire WD3 6ED (01923 282722).
Pets welcome in bar area only.
Pet Regulars: Resident dog Bobby (Collie mixture), Paddy (Boxer) and Rebel (Golden Lab).

THE ROBIN HOOD AND LITTLE JOHN

Rabley Heath, near Codicote, Hertfordshire (01438 812361).
Dogs allowed in bar, car park tables, beer garden.

KENT

KENTISH HORSE
Cow Lane, Mark Beech, Edenbridge, Kent (01342 850493).
Dogs allowed in reserved area on lead, outside included.

THE SWANN INN
Little Chart, Kent TN27 0QB (01233 840702).
Dogs allowed - everywhere except restaurant.

LINCOLNSHIRE

THE BLUE DOG INN
Main Street, Sewstern, Grantham, Lincs NG33 5QR (01476 860097).
Dogs allowed.
Pet Regulars: Cassie (Scottie) shares biscuits with Hamish (pub dog); Nelson (Terrier), Diesel (Springer Spaniel) and Ted (Spaniel).

MERSEYSIDE

THE SCOTCH PIPER
Southport Road, Lydiate, Merseyside (0151 526 0503).
Dogs allowed throughout the pub.

NORFOLK

THE OLD RAILWAY TAVERN
Eccles Road, Quidenham, Norwich, Norfolk NR16 2JG (01953 888223).
Dogs allowed, must be on lead.
Pet Regulars: Pub dog Flo (German Shepherd).

THE HOSTE ARMS
The Green, Burnham Market, King's Lynn, Norfolk PE31 8HD (01328 738777).
Dogs allowed throughout the pub, except restaurant.
Pet Regulars: "Augustus" and "Sweep" (Black Labradors).

OXFORDSHIRE

THE BELL
Shenington, Banbury, Oxfordshire OX15 6NQ (01295 670274).
Pets allowed throughout.
Pet Regulars: Resident pub dogs "Oliver" (Great Dane).

THE BELL INN
High Street, Adderbury, Oxon (01295 810338).
Dogs allowed throughout the pub and accommodation rooms.
Owner's dogs: Murphy and Dizzy (Lancashire Heelers) and Rika (Rottweiler).

LONGMYND HOTEL
Cunnery Road, Church Stretton, Shropshire SY6 6AG (01694 722244).
Dogs allowed in owners' hotel bedrooms but not in public areas.

SOMERSET

CASTLE OF COMFORT HOTEL
Dodington, Nether Stowey, Bridgwater, Somerset TA5 1LE (01278 741264).
Pet friendly.

THE BUTCHERS ARMS
Carhampton, Somerset (01643 821333).
Dogs allowed in bar. B&B accommodation available.

HOOD ARMS
Kilve, Somerset TA5 1EA (01278 741210)
Pets welcome.

THE SHIP INN
High Street, Porlock, Somerset (01643 862507).
Dogs allowed throughout and in guests' rooms.
Pet Regulars: Include Silver (Jack Russell); Sam (Black Lab) and Max (Staffordshire). Resident Pets include Brit (Spaniel) and Holly (Belgian Shepherd).

SUFFOLK

The Ickworth Hotel, Horringer, Bury St Edmunds IP29 5QE
Tel: 01284 735350 • Fax: 01284 736300
e-mail: ickworth@ickworthhotel.com • www.luxuryfamilyhotels.com

"Overall Winner of Winalot Approved Dog Friendly Award"
Warm and welcoming hotel with more than a dash of style and much comfort situated in the rolling green acres of Ickworth parkland. Elegant, individually styled bedrooms and stunning apartments. Delicious food in Frederick's Restaurant or the less formal Cafe Inferno. Dogs welcome - specific dietary requirements catered for; doggy massage available.

THE KINGS HEAD
High Street, Southwold, Suffolk IP18 6AD (01502 724517).
Well-behaved dogs welcome.

SIX BELLS AT BARDWELL
The Green, Bardwell, Bury St Edmunds, Suffolk IP31 1AW (01359 250820).
Dogs allowed in guest bedrooms by arrnagement but not allowed in bar and restaurant.

FHG Guides
publish a large range of well-known accommodation guides.
We will be happy to send you details or you can use the order form
at the back of this book.

SURREY

THE PLOUGH
South Road, Woking, Surrey GU21 4JL (01483 714105).
Pets welcome in restricted areas. Must be kept on a lead.

THE SPORTSMAN
Mogador Road, Mogador, Surrey (01737 246655).
Adopted dogs congregate at this pub.
Pet Regulars: Meesha (Border Collie) and Max (German Shepherd).

THE CRICKETERS
12 Oxenden Road, Tongham, Farnham, Surrey (01252 333262).
Dogs allowed in beer garden on lead.

SUSSEX

THE FORESTERS ARMS
High Street, Fairwarp, Near Uckfield, East Sussex TN22 3BP (01825 712808).
Dogs allowed in the beer garden and at car park tables, also inside.
Dog biscuits always available.

THE PLOUGH
Crowhurst, Near Battle, East Sussex TN33 9AY (01424 830310).
Dogs allowed in non-food bar, car park tables, beer garden.

QUEENS HEAD
Village Green, Sedlescombe, East Sussex (01424 870228).
Dogs allowed throughout the pub.

THE SLOOP INN
Freshfield Lock, Haywards Heath, West Sussex RH17 7NP (01444 831219).

Dogs allowed in public bar and garden.
THE SPORTSMAN'S ARMS
Rackham Road, Amberley, Near Arundel, West Sussex BN18 9NR (01798 831787).
Dogs allowed in the bar area and B&B accommodation.

WILTSHIRE

THE HORSE AND GROOM
The Street, Charlton, Near Malmesbury, Wiltshire (01666 823904).
Dogs welcome in bar.
Pet Regulars: Troy and Gio (Labradors).

YORKSHIRE

THE FORESTERS ARMS
Kilburn, North Yorkshire YO6 4AH (01347 868386).
Dogs allowed throughout, except restaurant.

NEW INN HOTEL
Clapham, Near Settle, North Yorkshire LA2 8HH (015242 51203).
Dogs allowed in bar, beer garden, bedrooms.

SIMONSTONE HALL

Hawes, North Yorkshire DL8 3LY (01969 667255).
Dogs allowed except dining area.
Dogs of all shapes, sizes and breeds welcome.

THE SPINNEY

Forest Rise, Balby, Doncaster, South Yorkshire DN4 9HQ (01302 852033).
Dogs allowed throughout the pub.
Pet Regulars: Wyn (Labrador) a guide dog and Buster (Staff). Resident dog Paddy (Irish Setter).

THE ROCKINGHAM ARMS

8 Main Street, Wentworth, Rotherham, South Yorkshire S62 7LO (01226 742075).
Pets welcome.
Pet Regulars: Sheeba (Springer Spaniel), Charlie and Gypsy (Black Labradors), Sally (Alsatian) and Rosie (Jack Russell).

THE GOLDEN FLEECE

Lindley Road, Blackley, near Huddersfield, West Yorkshire (01422 372704).
Guide Dogs only.

WALES

ANGLESEY & GWYNEDD

THE BUCKLEY HOTEL

Castle Street, Beaumaris, Isle of Anglesey LL58 8AW (01248 810415).
Dogs allowed throughout the pub, except in the dining room and bistro.
Pet Regulars: Cassie (Springer Spaniel) and Rex (mongrel), dedicated 'companion' dogs, also Charlie (Spaniel).

NORTH WALES

THE WEST ARMS HOTEL

Llanarmon Dyffryn Ceiriog, Llangollen, North Wales LL20 7LD (01691 600665).
Welcome pets.

PEMBROKESHIRE

THE FARMERS

14-16 Goat Street, St David's, Pembrokeshire (01437 721666).
Pets welcome in the pub area.

SEVERN ARMS HOTEL

Penybont, Llandrindod Wells, Powys LD1 5UA (01597 851224).
Dogs allowed in the bar, but not the restaurant, and in the rooms - but not on the beds.

SCOTLAND

ABERDEEN, BANFF & MORAY

THE CLIFTON BAR
Clifton Road, Lossiemouth, Moray (01343 812100).
Dogs allowed in beer garden only.

ARGYLL & BUTE

The Village Inn •• Arrochar, Loch Long, Argyll G83 7AX
A warm welcome on the banks of Loch Long. Open all year round, The Village Inn is perfect for a midweek break or a weekend away, as well as a relaxing daytime or evening meal. 14 en suite bedrooms, tastefully decorated and furnished in traditional style. Excellent selection of ales, beer, wines and spirits. Traditional Scottish Breakfast, bar meals, à la carte evening menu • **Tel: 01301 702279** • **Fax: 01301 702458**
e-mail: villageinn@maclay.co.uk • **www.maclay.com**

CAIRNDOW STAGECOACH INN
Cairndow, Argyll PA26 8BN (01499 600286).
Pets welcome.

THE BALLACHULISH HOTEL
Ballachulish, Argyll PA39 4JY (01855 811606).
Dogs allowed in the lounge and guests' bedrooms, excluding food areas.

EDINBURGH & LOTHIANS

JOHNSBURN HOUSE
Johnsburn Road, Balerno, Lothians EH14 7BB (0131-449 3847).
Pets welcome in bar area only.
Pet Regulars: Resident dog "Topaz" (Great Dane).

LAIRD & DOG
Lasswade, Midlothian (0131-663 9219).
Dogs allowed in bar.
Pet Regulars: Fleetwood (cat). Many pet regulars. Drinking bowls.

PERTH & KINROSS

FOUR SEASONS HOTEL
St Fillans, Perthshire (01764 685333).
Dogs allowed in all non-food areas.

THE MUNRO INN
Main Street, Strathyre, Perthshire FK18 8NA (01877 384333).
Dogs allowed throughout pub, lounge, games room and bedrooms (except restaurant).
Pet Regulars: Residents Jess (black mongrel with brown eyes) and Jules (white lurcher with blue eyes). Bring your dog to visit! Water and dog biscuits always available.

Looking for Holiday Accommodation?

for details of hundreds of properties throughout the UK, visit our website

www.holidayguides.com

371

LEIGHTON BUZZARD RAILWAY
Page's Park Station, Billington Road,
Leighton Buzzard, Bedfordshire LU7 4TN
Tel: 01525 373888
e-mail: info@buzzrail.co.uk
www.buzzrail.co.uk

READERS' OFFER 2008

One FREE adult/child with full-fare adult ticket
Valid 11/3/2008 - 28/10/2008

NOT TO BE USED IN CONJUNCTION WITH ANY OTHER OFFER

BUCKINGHAMSHIRE RAILWAY CENTRE
Quainton Road Station, Quainton,
Aylesbury HP22 4BY
Tel & Fax: 01296 655720
e-mail: bucksrailcentre@btopenworld.com
www.bucksrailcentre.org

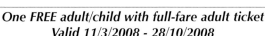

READERS' OFFER 2008

One child FREE with each full-paying adult
Not valid for Special Events

NOT TO BE USED IN CONJUNCTION WITH ANY OTHER OFFER

THE RAPTOR FOUNDATION
The Heath, St Ives Road,
Woodhurst, Huntingdon, Cambs PE28 3BT
Tel: 01487 741140 • Fax: 01487 841140
e-mail: heleowl@aol.com
www.raptorfoundation.org.uk

READERS' OFFER 2008

TWO for the price of ONE
Valid until end 2008 (not Bank Holidays)

NOT TO BE USED IN CONJUNCTION WITH ANY OTHER OFFER

SACREWELL FARM & COUNTRY CENTRE
Sacrewell, Thornhaugh,
Peterborough PE8 6HJ
Tel: 01780 782254
e-mail: info@sacrewell.fsnet.co.uk
www.sacrewell.org.uk

READERS' OFFER 2008

One child FREE with one full paying adult
Valid from March 1st to October 1st 2008

NOT TO BE USED IN CONJUNCTION WITH ANY OTHER OFFER

A 70-minute journey into the lost world of the English narrow gauge light railway. Features historic steam locomotives from many countries.

PETS MUST BE KEPT UNDER CONTROL AND NOT ALLOWED ON TRACKS

Open: Sundays and Bank Holiday weekends 11 March to 28 October. Additional days in summer.

Directions: on A4146 towards Hemel Hempstead, close to roundabout junction with A505.

FHG GUIDES, ABBEY MILL BUSINESS CENTRE, PAISLEY PA1 1TJ • www.holidayguides.com

A working steam railway centre. Steam train rides, miniature railway rides, large collection of historic preserved steam locomotives, carriages and wagons.

Open: Sundays and Bank Holidays April to October, plus Wednesdays in school holidays 10.30am to 4.30pm.

Directions: off A41 Aylesbury to Bicester Road, 6 miles north west of Aylesbury.

FHG GUIDES, ABBEY MILL BUSINESS CENTRE, PAISLEY PA1 1TJ • www.holidayguides.com

Birds of Prey Centre offering audience participation in flying displays which are held 3 times daily. Tours, picnic area, gift shop, tearoom, craft shop.

Open: 10am-5pm all year except Christmas and New Year.

Directions: follow brown tourist signs from B1040.

FHG GUIDES, ABBEY MILL BUSINESS CENTRE, PAISLEY PA1 1TJ • www.holidayguides.com

Farm animals, Shire Horse Centre, 18th century watermill and farmhouse, farm artifacts, caravan and camping,
children's play areas.
Cafe and farm & gift shop.

Open: all year.
9.30am to 5pm 1st March -30th Sept
10am-4pm 1st Oct to 28th Feb

Directions: signposted off both A47 and A1.

FHG GUIDES, ABBEY MILL BUSINESS CENTRE, PAISLEY PA1 1TJ • www.holidayguides.com

THE NATIONAL WATERWAYS MUSEUM

South Pier Road, Ellesmere Port,
Cheshire CH65 4FW
Tel: 0151-355 5017 • Fax: 0151-355 4079
ellesmereport@thewaterwaystrust.org.uk
www.nwm.org.uk/ellesmere

·K·U·P·E·R·A·R·D·

**READERS'
OFFER
2008**

*20% discount on standard admissions.
Valid during 2008.*

NOT TO BE USED IN CONJUNCTION WITH ANY OTHER OFFER

CHINA CLAY COUNTRY PARK

Wheal Martyn, Carthew, St Austell,
Cornwall PL26 8XG
Tel & Fax: 01726 850362
e-mail: info@chinaclaycountry.co.uk
www.chinaclaycountry.co.uk

·K·U·P·E·R·A·R·D·

**READERS'
OFFER
2008**

*TWO for ONE adult entry, saving £7.50.
One voucher per person. Valid until July 2008.*

NOT TO BE USED IN CONJUNCTION WITH ANY OTHER OFFER

GEEVOR TIN MINE

Pendeen, Penzance,
Cornwall TR19 7EW
Tel: 01736 788662 • Fax: 01736 786059
e-mail: bookings@geevor.com
www.geevor.com

·K·U·P·E·R·A·R·D·

**READERS'
OFFER
2008**

*TWO for the price of ONE or £3.75 off a family ticket
Valid 02/01/2008 to 20/12/2008*

NOT TO BE USED IN CONJUNCTION WITH ANY OTHER OFFER

NATIONAL SEAL SANCTUARY

Gweek, Helston,
Cornwall TR12 6UG
Tel: 01326 221361
e-mail: seals@sealsanctuary.co.uk
www.sealsanctuary.co.uk

·K·U·P·E·R·A·R·D·

**READERS'
OFFER
2008**

*TWO for ONE - on purchase of another ticket of
equal or greater value. Valid until December 2008.*

NOT TO BE USED IN CONJUNCTION WITH ANY OTHER OFFER

Can you imagine your family living in a space measuring 6' x 8'? Clamber aboard our collection of narrowboats. New interactive galleries, shop, cafe. Large free car park. Daily boat trips.

Open: 10am to 5pm daily

Directions: Junction 9 off the M53, signposted.

The Country Park covers 26 acres and includes woodland and historic trails, picnic sites, children's adventure trail and award-winning cycle trail. Remains of a Victorian clay works complete with the largest working water wheel in Cornwall. Shop, cafe, exhibitions, museum.

Open: 10am-6pm daily (closed Christmas Day)

Directions: two miles north of St Austell on the B3274. Follow brown tourist signs. 5 minutes from Eden Project.

Geevor is the largest mining history site in the UK in a spectacular setting on Cornwall's Atlantic coast. Guided underground tour, many surface buildings, museum, cafe, gift shop. Free parking.

Open: daily except Saturdays 10am to 4pm

Directions: 7 miles from Penzance beside the B3306 Land's End to St Ives coast road

Britain's leading grey seal rescue centre

Open: daily (except Christmas Day) from 10am

Directions: from A30 follow signs to Helston, then brown tourist signs to Seal Sanctuary.

A collection of cars from film and TV, including Chitty Chitty Bang Bang, James Bond's Aston Martin, Del Boy's van, Fab1 and many more. PETS MUST BE KEPT ON LEAD	**Open:** daily 10am-5pm. Open February half term, Ist April to end November, also weekends in December. **Directions:** in centre of Keswick close to car park.

FHG GUIDES, ABBEY MILL BUSINESS CENTRE, PAISLEY PA1 1TJ • www.holidayguides.com

The oldest working mill in England with 18th century oatmeal machinery running daily. DOGS ON LEADS	**Open:** 11am to 5pm April to Sept. (may be closed Saturdays & Mondays) **Directions:** near inland terminus of Ravenglass & Eskdale Railway or over Hardknott Pass.

FHG GUIDES, ABBEY MILL BUSINESS CENTRE, PAISLEY PA1 1TJ • www.holidayguides.com

A superb family day out in the atmosphere of a bygone era. Explore the recreated period street and fascinating exhibitions. Unlimited tram rides are free with entry. Play areas, woodland walk and sculpture trail, shops, tea rooms, pub, restaurant and lots more.	**Open:** daily April to October 10 am to 5.30pm, weekends in winter. **Directions:** eight miles from M1 Junction 28, follow brown and white signs for "Tramway Museum".

FHG GUIDES, ABBEY MILL BUSINESS CENTRE, PAISLEY PA1 1TJ • www.holidayguides.com

This award-winning Victorian mining museum makes a great day out for all the family. Hands-on activities plus unforgettable mine tour. Green Tourism Gold Award 2007.	**Open:** Easter weekend +April 1st to October 31st 10.30am to 5pm daily. **Directions:** alongside A689, midway between Stanhope and Alston in the heart of the North Pennines.

FHG GUIDES, ABBEY MILL BUSINESS CENTRE, PAISLEY PA1 1TJ • www.holidayguides.com

377

READERS' OFFER 2008

AVON VALLEY RAILWAY
Bitton Station, Bath Road, Bitton,
Bristol BS30 6HD
Tel: 0117 932 5538
e-mail: info@avonvalleyrailway.org
www.avonvalleyrailway.org

One FREE child with every fare-paying adult
Valid May - Oct 2008 (not 'Day Out with Thomas' events)

NOT TO BE USED IN CONJUNCTION WITH ANY OTHER OFFER

READERS' OFFER 2008

THE HOP FARM AT THE KENTISH OAST VILLAGE
Beltring, Paddock Wood,
Kent TN12 6PY
Tel: 01622 872068 • Fax: 01622 870800
e-mail: info@thehopfarm.co.uk
www.thehopfarm.co.uk

Admit one child HALF PRICE with a full paying adult.
Valid until March 2008.

NOT TO BE USED IN CONJUNCTION WITH ANY OTHER OFFER

READERS' OFFER 2008

MUSEUM OF KENT LIFE
Lock Lane, Sandling, Maidstone,
Kent ME14 3AU
Tel: 01622 763936 • Fax: 01622 662024
e-mail: enquiries@museum-kentlife.co.uk
www.museum-kentlife.co.uk

One child FREE with one full-paying adult
Valid during 2008

NOT TO BE USED IN CONJUNCTION WITH ANY OTHER OFFER

READERS' OFFER 2008

DOCKER PARK FARM
Arkholme, Carnforth,
Lancashire LA6 1AR
Tel & Fax: 015242 21331
e-mail: info@dockerparkfarm.co.uk
www.dockerparkfarm.co.uk

One FREE child per one paying adult (one voucher per child)
Valid from January to December 2008

NOT TO BE USED IN CONJUNCTION WITH ANY OTHER OFFER

The Avon Valley Railway offers a whole new experience for some, and a nostalgic memory for others.

PETS MUST BE KEPT ON LEADS AND OFF TRAIN SEATS

Open: Steam trains operate every Sunday, Easter to October, plus Bank Holidays and Christmas.

Directions: on the A431 midway between Bristol and Bath at Bitton.

Set in 400 acres of unspoilt Kent countryside, this once working hop farm is one of Kent's most popular attractions. The spectacular oast village is home to an indoor and outdoor play area, interactive museum, shire horses and an animal farm, as well as hosting special events throughout the year.

Open: 10am-5pm daily (last admission 4pm).

Directions: A228 Paddock Wood

Kent's award-winning open air museum is home to a collection of historic buildings which house interactive exhibitions on life over the last 150 years.

Open: seven days a week from February to start November, 10am to 5pm.

Directions: Junction 6 off M20, follow signs to Aylesford.

We are a working farm, with lots of animals to see and touch. Enjoy a walk round the Nature Trail or refreshments in the tearoom. Lots of activities during school holidays.

Open: Summer: daily 10.30am- 5pm. Winter: weekends only 10.30am-4pm.

Directions: Junction 35 off M6, take B6254 towards Kirkby Lonsdale, then follow the brown signs.

FHG **·K·U·P·E·R·A·R·D·** READERS' OFFER 2008

SKEGNESS NATURELAND SEAL SANCTUARY
North Parade, Skegness,
Lincolnshire PE25 1DB
Tel: 01754 764345
e-mail: natureland@fsbdial.co.uk
www.skegnessnatureland.co.uk

Natureland
Seal Sanctuary

Free entry for one child when accompanied by
full-paying adult. Valid during 2008.

NOT TO BE USED IN CONJUNCTION WITH ANY OTHER OFFER

FHG **·K·U·P·E·R·A·R·D·** READERS' OFFER 2008

NEWARK AIR MUSEUM
The Airfield, Winthorpe, Newark,
Nottinghamshire NG24 2NY
Tel: 01636 707170
e-mail: newarkair@onetel.com
www.newarkairmuseum.org

Party rate discount for every voucher (50p per person
off normal admission). Valid during 2008.

NOT TO BE USED IN CONJUNCTION WITH ANY OTHER OFFER

FHG **·K·U·P·E·R·A·R·D·** READERS' OFFER 2008

THE TALES OF ROBIN HOOD
30 - 38 Maid Marian Way,
Nottingham NG1 6GF
Tel: 0115 9483284 • Fax: 0115 9501536
e-mail: robinhoodcentre@mail.com
www.robinhood.uk.com

One FREE child with full paying adult per voucher
Valid from January to December 2008

NOT TO BE USED IN CONJUNCTION WITH ANY OTHER OFFER

FHG **·K·U·P·E·R·A·R·D·** READERS' OFFER 2008

DIDCOT RAILWAY CENTRE
Didcot,
Oxfordshire OX11 7NJ
Tel: 01235 817200 • Fax: 01235 510621
e-mail: info@didcotrailwaycentre.org.uk
www.didcotrailwaycentre.org.uk

One child FREE when accompanied by full-paying adult
Valid until end 2008 except during Day Out With Thomas events

NOT TO BE USED IN CONJUNCTION WITH ANY OTHER OFFER

Well known for rescuing and rehabilitating orphaned and injured seal pups found washed ashore on Lincolnshire beaches. Also: penguins, aquarium, pets' corner, reptiles, Floral Palace (tropical birds and butterflies etc).

Open: daily from 10am. Closed Christmas/Boxing/New Year's Days.

Directions: at the north end of Skegness seafront.

A collection of 70 aircraft and cockpit sections from across the history of aviation. Extensive aero engine and artefact displays.

Open: daily from 10am (closed Christmas period and New Year's Day).

Directions: follow brown and white signs from A1, A46, A17 and A1133.

Travel back in time with Robin Hood and his merry men on an adventure-packed theme tour, exploring the intriguing and mysterious story of their legendary tales of Medieval England. Enjoy film shows, live performances, adventure rides and even try archery! Are you brave enough to join Robin on his quest for good against evil?

Open: 10am-5.30pm, last admission 4.30pm.

Directions: follow the brown and white tourist information signs whilst heading towards the city centre.

See the steam trains from the golden age of the Great Western Railway. Steam locomotives in the original engine shed, a reconstructed country branch line, and a re-creation of Brunel's original broad gauge railway. On Steam Days there are rides in the 1930s carriages.

Open: Sat/Sun all year; daily 21 June to 31 August + school holidays. 10am-5pm weekends and Steam Days, 10am-4pm other days and in winter.

Directions: at Didcot Parkway rail station; on A4130, signposted from M4 (Junction 13) and A34

FHG ·K·U·P·E·R·A·R·D· READERS' OFFER 2008

THE HELICOPTER MUSEUM
The Heliport, Locking Moor Road,
Weston-Super-Mare BS24 8PP
Tel: 01934 635227• Fax: 01934 645230
e-mail: helimuseum@btconnect.com
www.helicoptermuseum.co.uk

One child FREE with two full-paying adults
Valid from April to October 2008

NOT TO BE USED IN CONJUNCTION WITH ANY OTHER OFFER

FHG ·K·U·P·E·R·A·R·D· READERS' OFFER 2008

WILDERNESS WOOD
Hadlow Down, Near Uckfield,
East Sussex TN22 4HJ
Tel: 01825 830509• Fax: 01825 830977
e-mail: enquiries@wildernesswood.co.uk
www.wildernesswood.co.uk

one FREE admission with a full-paying adult
Valid during 2008 (not for Special Events/Bank Holidays)

NOT TO BE USED IN CONJUNCTION WITH ANY OTHER OFFER

FHG ·K·U·P·E·R·A·R·D· READERS' OFFER 2008

EARNLEY BUTTERFLIES & GARDENS
133 Almodington Lane, Earnley, Chichester,
West Sussex PO20 7JR
Tel: 01243 512637
e-mail: earnleygardens@msn.com
www.earnleybutterfliesandgardens.co.uk

£2 per person offer normal entry prices.
Valid late March to end October 2008.

NOT TO BE USED IN CONJUNCTION WITH ANY OTHER OFFER

FHG ·K·U·P·E·R·A·R·D· READERS' OFFER 2008

AVONCROFT MUSEUM
Stoke Heath,
Bromsgrove,
Worcestershire B60 4JR
Tel: 01527 831363 • Fax: 01527 876934
www.avoncroft.org.uk

AVONCROFT
MUSEUM OF HISTORIC BUILDINGS

One FREE child with one full-paying adult
Valid from March to November 2008

NOT TO BE USED IN CONJUNCTION WITH ANY OTHER OFFER

The world's largest helicopter collection - over 70 exhibits, includes two royal helicopters, Russian Gunship and Vietnam veterans plus many award-winning exhibits. Cafe, shop. Flights.

PETS MUST BE KEPT UNDER CONTROL

Open: Wednesday to Sunday 10am to 5.30pm. Daily during school Easter and Summer holidays and Bank Holiday Mondays. November to March: 10am to 4.30pm

Directions: Junction 21 off M5 then follow the propellor signs.

FHG GUIDES, ABBEY MILL BUSINESS CENTRE, PAISLEY PA1 1TJ • www.holidayguides.com

---

Wilderness Wood is a unique family-run working woodland park in the Sussex High Weald. Explore trails and footpaths, enjoy local cakes and ices, try the adventure playground. Many special events and activities. Parties catered for. Green Tourism Gold Award.

Open: daily 10am to 5.30pm or dusk if earlier.

Directions: on the south side of the A272 in the village of Hadlow Down. Signposted with a brown tourist sign.

FHG GUIDES, ABBEY MILL BUSINESS CENTRE, PAISLEY PA1 1TJ • www.holidayguides.com

---

3 attractions in 1. Tropical butterflies, exotic animals of many types in our Noah's Ark Rescue Centre. Theme gardens with a free competition for kids. Rejectamenta - the nostalgia museum.

Open: 10am - 6pm daily late March to end October.

Directions: signposted from A27/A286 junction at Chichester.

FHG GUIDES, ABBEY MILL BUSINESS CENTRE, PAISLEY PA1 1TJ • www.holidayguides.com

---

A fascinating world of historic buildings covering 7 centuries, rescued and rebuilt on an open-air site in the heart of the Worcestershire countryside.

PETS ON LEADS ONLY

Open: July and August all week. March to November varying times, please telephone for details.

Directions: A38 south of Bromsgrove, near Junction 1 of M42, Junction 5 of M5.

FHG GUIDES, ABBEY MILL BUSINESS CENTRE, PAISLEY PA1 1TJ • www.holidayguides.com

Visit the FHG website
www.holidayguides.com
for details of the wide choice of accommodation
featured in the full range of FHG titles

Steam trains operate over a 4½ mile line from Bolton Abbey Station to Embsay Station. Many family events including Thomas the Tank Engine take place during major Bank Holidays.

Open: steam trains run every Sunday throughout the year and up to 7 days a week in summer. 10.30am to 4.30pm

Directions: Embsay Station signposted from the A59 Skipton by-pass; Bolton Abbey Station signposted from the A59 at Bolton Abbey.

FHG GUIDES, ABBEY MILL BUSINESS CENTRE, PAISLEY PA1 1TJ • www.holidayguides.com

Visit James Herriot's original house recreated as it was in the 1940s. Television sets used in the series 'All Creatures Great and Small'. There is a children's interactive gallery with life-size model farm animals and three rooms dedicated to the history of veterinary medicine.

Open: daily. Easter-Oct 10am-5pm; Nov-Easter 11am to 4pm

Directions: follow signs off A1 or A19 to Thirsk, then A168, off Thirsk market place

FHG GUIDES, ABBEY MILL BUSINESS CENTRE, PAISLEY PA1 1TJ • www.holidayguides.com

A fascinating display of railway carriages and a wide range of railway items telling the story of rail travel over the years.

ALL PETS MUST BE KEPT ON LEADS

Open: daily 11am to 4.30pm

Directions: approximately one mile from Keighley on A629 Halifax road. Follow brown tourist signs

FHG GUIDES, ABBEY MILL BUSINESS CENTRE, PAISLEY PA1 1TJ • www.holidayguides.com

Please mention **Pets Welcome!**
when making enquiries about accommodation featured in these pages

Please note

All the information in this book is given in good faith in the belief that it is correct. However, the publishers cannot guarantee the facts given in these pages, neither are they responsible for changes in policy, ownership or terms that may take place after the date of going to press. Readers should always satisfy themselves that the facilities they require are available and that the terms, if quoted, still apply.

THE GRASSIC GIBBON CENTRE
Arbuthnott, Laurencekirk,
Aberdeenshire AB30 1PB
Tel: 01561 361668
e-mail: lgginfo@grassicgibbon.com
www.grassicgibbon.com

READERS' OFFER 2008

TWO for the price of ONE entry to exhibition (based on full adult rate only). Valid during 2008 (not groups)

NOT TO BE USED IN CONJUNCTION WITH ANY OTHER OFFER

INVERARAY JAIL
Church Square, Inveraray,
Argyll PA32 8TX
Tel: 01499 302381• Fax: 01499 302195
e-mail: info@inverarayjail.co.uk
www.inverarayjail.co.uk

READERS' OFFER 2008

*One child FREE with one full-paying adult
Valid until end 2008*

NOT TO BE USED IN CONJUNCTION WITH ANY OTHER OFFER

SCOTTISH MARITIME MUSEUM
Harbourside, Irvine,
Ayrshire KA12 8QE
Tel: 01294 278283
Fax: 01294 313211
www.scottishmaritimemuseum.org

READERS' OFFER 2008

*TWO for the price of ONE
Valid from April to October 2008*

NOT TO BE USED IN CONJUNCTION WITH ANY OTHER OFFER

GALLOWAY WILDLIFE CONSERVATION PARK
Lochfergus Plantation, Kirkcudbright,
Dumfries & Galloway DG6 4XX
Tel & Fax: 01557 331645
e-mail: info@gallowaywildlife.co.uk
www.gallowaywildlife.co.uk

READERS' OFFER 2008

*One FREE child or Senior Citizen with two full paying adults.
Valid Feb - Nov 2008 (not Easter weekend and Bank Holidays)*

NOT TO BE USED IN CONJUNCTION WITH ANY OTHER OFFER

Visitor Centre dedicated to the much-loved Scottish writer Lewis Grassic Gibbon. Exhibition, cafe, gift shop. Outdoor children's play area. Disabled access throughout.

Open: daily April to October 10am to 4.30pm. Groups by appointment including evenings.

Directions: on the B967, accessible and signposted from both A90 and A92.

19th century prison with fully restored 1820 courtroom and two prisons. Guides in uniform as warders, prisoners and matron. Remember your camera!

Open: April to October 9.30am-6pm (last admission 5pm); November to March 10am-5pm (last admission 4pm)

Directions: A83 to Campbeltown

Scotland's seafaring heritage is among the world's richest and you can relive the heyday of Scottish shipping at the Maritime Museum.

Open: 1st April to 31st October - 10am-5pm

Directions: situated on Irvine harbourside and only a 10 minute walk from Irvine train station.

The wild animal conservation centre of Southern Scotland. A varied collection of over 150 animals from all over the world can be seen within natural woodland settings. Picnic areas, cafe/gift shop, outdoor play area, woodland walks, close animal encounters.

Open: 10am to dusk 1st February to 30 November.

Directions: follow brown tourist signs from A75; one mile from Kirkcudbright on the B727.

Visitors can experience the thrill of a guided tour into an 18thC lead mine, explore the two period cottages, visit the second oldest subscription library and investigate the Visitor & Exhibition Centre. Taster sessions of gold panning available July and August.

Open: 1 April - 30 June: 11am-4.30pm July, August and Bank Holidays: 10am -5pm.

Directions: off M74. J14 if travelling north, J13 if travelling south.

Steam and heritage diesel passenger trains from Bo'ness to Birkhill for guided tours of Birkhill fireclay mines. Explore the history of Scotland's railways in the Scottish Railway Exhibition. Coffee shop and souvenir shop.

Open: weekends Easter to October, daily July and August.

Directions: in the town of Bo'ness. Leave M9 at Junction 3 or 5, then follow brown tourist signs.

On show is a large collection, from 1899, of cars, bicycles, motor cycles and commercials. There is also a large collection of period advertising, posters and enamel signs.

Open: March-November - open daily 11am to 4pm. December-February - weekends 11am to 3pm or by special appointment.

Directions: off A198 near Aberlady. Two miles from A1.

Award-winning attraction with unique 'Heather Story' exhibition, gallery, giftshop, large garden centre selling 300 different heathers, antique shop, children's play area and famous Clootie Dumpling restaurant.

Open: all year except Christmas Day.

Directions: just off A95 between Aviemore and Grantown-on-Spey.

FHG

K·U·P·E·R·A·R·D

READERS'
OFFER
2008

LLANBERIS LAKE RAILWAY
Gilfach Ddu, Llanberis,
Gwynedd LL55 4TY
Tel: 01286 870549
e-mail: info@lake-railway.co.uk
www.lake-railway.co.uk

One pet travels FREE with each full fare paying adult
Valid Easter to October 2008

NOT TO BE USED IN CONJUNCTION WITH ANY OTHER OFFER

FHG

K·U·P·E·R·A·R·D

READERS'
OFFER
2008

ANIMALARIUM
Borth,
Ceredigion
SY24 5NA
Tel: 01970 871224
www.animalarium.co.uk

FREE child with full paying adult.
Valid during 2008.

NOT TO BE USED IN CONJUNCTION WITH ANY OTHER OFFER

FHG

K·U·P·E·R·A·R·D

READERS'
OFFER
2008

FELINWYNT RAINFOREST CENTRE
Felinwynt, Cardigan,
Ceredigion SA43 1RT
Tel: 01239 810882/810250
e-mail: dandjdevereux@btinternet.com
www.butterflycentre.co.uk

TWO for the price of ONE (one voucher per party only)
Valid until end October 2008

NOT TO BE USED IN CONJUNCTION WITH ANY OTHER OFFER

FHG

K·U·P·E·R·A·R·D

READERS'
OFFER
2008

NATIONAL CYCLE COLLECTION
Automobile Palace, Temple Street,
Llandrindod Wells, Powys LD1 5DL
Tel: 01597 825531
e-mail: cycle.museum@powys.org.uk
www.cyclemuseum.org.uk

TWO for the price of ONE
Valid during 2008 except Special Event days

NOT TO BE USED IN CONJUNCTION WITH ANY OTHER OFFER

A 60-minute ride along the shores of beautiful Padarn Lake behind a quaint historic steam engine. Magnificent views of the mountains from lakeside picnic spots.

DOGS MUST BE KEPT ON LEAD AT ALL TIMES ON TRAIN

Open: most days Easter to October. Free timetable leaflet on request.

Directions: just off A4086 Caernarfon to Capel Curig road at Llanberis; follow 'Country Park' signs.

A collection of unusual and interesting animals, including breeding pairs and colonies of exotic and endangered species whose natural environment is under threat. Many were unwanted exotic pets or came from other zoos.

Open: 10am - 6pm April to October

Directions: only a short walk from the railway station and beach in Borth, which lies between Aberystwyth and Machynlleth.

Mini-rainforest full of tropical plants and exotic butterflies. Personal attention of the owner, Mr John Devereux. Gift shop, cafe, video room, exhibition. Suitable for disabled visitors. VisitWales Quality Assured Visitor Attraction.

PETS NOT ALLOWED IN TROPICAL HOUSE ONLY

Open: daily Easter to end October 10.30am to 5pm

Directions: West Wales, 7 miles north of Cardigan off Aberystwyth road. Follow brown tourist signs on A487.

Journey through the lanes of cycle history and see bicycles from Boneshakers and Penny Farthings up to modern Raleigh cycles. Over 250 machines on display

PETS MUST BE KEPT ON LEADS

Open: 1st March to 1st November daily 10am onwards.

Directions: brown signs to car park. Town centre attraction.

Index of Towns and Counties

FHG Guides

Visit the FHG website

www.holidayguides.com

for details of the wide choice of accommodation

featured in the full range of FHG titles

Please mention this FHG Guide when enquiring about accommodation featured in these pages

Note

All the information in this guide is given in good faith in the belief that it is correct. However, the publishers cannot guarantee the facts given in these pages, neither are they responsible for changes in ownership or facilities that may take place after the date of going to press. Readers should always satisfy themselves that the facilities they require are available and that the terms, if quoted, still apply.

www.holidayguides.com

Looking for Holiday Accommodation?

for details of hundreds of properties throughout the UK, visit our website

www.holidayguides.com

Visit the NEW
Winalot website today!

Winalot knows how important giving your dog a balanced diet and plenty of exercise is for their wellbeing, so we've totally re-designed our website to showcase our great balanced range of foods, and the best walks that Britain can offer for you and your furry friend.

www.winalot-dog.co.uk

FHG Guides Ltd have a large range of attractive
holiday accommodation guides for all kinds of holiday opportunities throughout Britain.
They also make useful gifts at any time of year.
Our guides are available in most bookshops and larger newsagents but we will be happy
to post you a copy direct if you have any difficulty. POST FREE for addresses in the UK.
We will also post abroad but have to charge separately for post or freight.

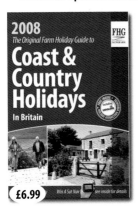

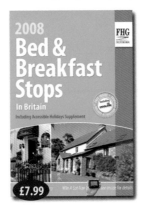

**The original
Farm Holiday Guide to
COAST & COUNTRY HOLIDAYS**
in England, Scotland, Wales and
Channel Islands. Board, Self-
catering, Caravans/Camping,
Activity Holidays.

BED AND BREAKFAST STOPS
Over 1000 friendly and
comfortable overnight stops.
Non-smoking, Disabled and
Special Diets Supplements.

**BRITAIN'S BEST LEISURE
& RELAXATION GUIDE**
A quick-reference general guide
for all kinds of holidays.

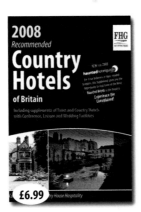

**Recommended
INNS & PUBS of Britain**
Pubs, Inns and small hotels.

**Recommended
COUNTRY HOTELS
of Britain**
Including Country Houses, for the
discriminating.

**SELF-CATERING HOLIDAYS
in Britain**
Over 1000 addresses throughout
for self-catering and caravans
in Britain.

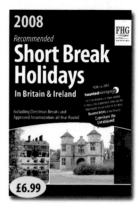

CHILDREN WELCOME!
Family Holidays and
Days Out guide.
Family holidays with details of
amenities for children and
babies.

The FHG Guide to
CARAVAN & CAMPING
HOLIDAYS
Caravans for hire, sites and
holiday parks and centres.

Recommended
SHORT BREAK HOLIDAYS
IN BRITAIN & IRELAND
"Approved" accommodation for
quality bargain breaks.

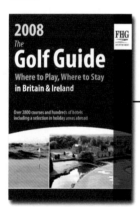

The GOLF GUIDE – Where to play Where to stay
In association with GOLF MONTHLY. Over 2800 golf
courses in Britain with convenient accommodation.
Holiday Golf in France, Portugal, Spain, USA and Thailand.

Tick your choice above and send your order and payment to

FHG Guides Ltd. Abbey Mill Business Centre
Seedhill, Paisley, Scotland PA1 1TJ
TEL: 0141- 887 0428 • FAX: 0141- 889 7204
e-mail: admin@fhguides.co.uk

FHG
KUPERARD

Deduct 10% for 2/3 titles or copies; 20% for 4 or more.

Send to: NAME...

             ADDRESS ....

             ....

             ....

             POST CODE ....

I enclose Cheque/Postal Order for £ ....

             SIGNATURE ....DATE ....

Please complete the following to help us improve the service we provide.

How did you find out about our guides?:

☐ Press   ☐ Magazines   ☐ TV/Radio   ☐ Family/Friend   ☐ Other